Oscar Wilde

Oscar Wilde

A Certain Genius

BARBARA BELFORD

BLOOMSBURY

First published in Great Britain 2000

Copyright © 2000 by Barbara Belford

The moral right of the author has been asserted

Bloomsbury Publishing Plc, 38 Soho Square, London, W1V 5DF

Grateful acknowledgment is made to the following for permission to reprint
previously published material:

Fourth Estate Ltd.: Excerpts from *The Letters of Oscar Wilde,* edited by
Merlin Holland and Sir Rupert Hart-Davis. Letters copyright © 1962, 1985,
2000 by The Estate of Oscar Wilde. Editorial matter copyright © 1962, 1985,
2000 by Sir Rupert Hart-Davis and Merlin Holland. Reprinted by permission
of Fourth Estate Ltd.

Henry Holt and Company LLC: Excerpts from *The Complete Letters of Oscar
Wilde,* edited by Merlin Holland and Sir Rupert Hart-Davis. Letters copyright
© 1962 by Vyvyan Holland. Copyright © 1990, 1997 by Merlin Holland.
Reprinted by permission of Henry Holt and Company, LLC.

A CIP catalogue record for this book
is available from the British Library

ISBN 0 7475 5027 1

10 9 8 7 6 5 4 3 2 1

Printed in Great Britain by Clays Limited, St Ives plc

To Deborah and Pino

C O N T E N T S

PART FOUR (1892–1895): FLAUNTING 185

PART FIVE (1895–1900): RECONCILING 245

INTRODUCTION

❧

OSCAR WILDE WAS a dazzling conversationalist: once heard never forgotten. His life was the triumph of flippancy over genius, and sometimes the triumph of genius over flippancy. He needed a paradoxical nature to create his brilliant antithetical views on the English and the Irish, male and female, truth and artifice, good and evil—and himself. By writing about serious issues that are still relevant—the corrosive effects of power, the quest for status, and class pretensions—he sums up what is past, embodies what is passing, and intimates what is to come. By flaunting the right to his own sexuality, Wilde catapulted Uranian passion out of adolescence and into maturity and gave birth to a homosexual consciousness. Anticipating modernism, he saw the value of interpreting and criticizing culture through one's personal visions. His life impinges on us still.

Wilde experimented with all literary forms: journalism, criticism, poetry, fiction, and biography; along the way he illuminated Aestheticism, Decadence, and Symbolism. He taught us that style not sincerity is what matters. As the author of *The Importance of Being Earnest,* the wittiest comedy of all time, rivaling even the works of Molière and Shakespeare, he changed the sound of laughter. His dramas taunted the English with the folly of their ideals and their hypocrisy. Once attacked as derivative, his words now make the unoriginal enlightened; present-day writers plunder his work searching for an epigram to say what they cannot about contemporary life. Noël Coward, Terence Rattigan, Ronald Firbank, P. G. Wodehouse, and Evelyn Waugh owe as much to Wilde as do the dramatists Joe Orton and Tom Stoppard, Paul Rudnick, Tony Kushner, Terrence

McNally, and Larry Kramer, who like Wilde attack the certainties and presumptions of the so-called normal life.

Any new biography brings Wilde, and his age, before another jury to be retried and judged. In his lifetime the end of "Victorianism" and all that it had come to represent was approaching, but nothing had evolved to take its place. It was Wilde who defined the conscience and the consciousness of the artist at a time when all other values were thrown into doubt. My aim has been to reclaim Wilde in all the brilliant details of his contradictions as he appeared to his contemporaries and to argue that his writing as well as his life has a certain genius.

HUNDREDS OF BOOKS have been written about Wilde. Most have stumbled when it came to humanizing the arrogant poseur. The first to succeed in capturing his extraordinary charisma and conversational abilities was *Oscar Wilde: His Life and Wit* (1946), written by Hesketh Pearson, a former actor who was ten years old when Wilde was released from prison. Early Wilde scholarship was dominated by H. Montgomery Hyde and Rupert Hart-Davis. A lawyer, Hyde edited *The Trials of Oscar Wilde* in 1948 from newspaper sources since there were no official transcripts and wrote a biography in 1975. Hart-Davis published a collection of Wilde's letters in 1962 and a supplement in 1985.

Modern Wilde scholarship begins with Richard Ellmann's *Oscar Wilde* (1987), the comprehensive biography against which all subsequent works will be judged. Recent books have tended to take specialist views. We have the Irish Wilde, the gay Wilde, and the Freudian Wilde. Ellmann's approach, in many ways critically astute, suffers from a reticence about discussing his subject's homosexuality as more than a private matter: it is divorced from contemporary politics and culture. Strong on the facts but weak on cultural context, particularly the conditions and personalities of the contemporary theatre that had so much of an impact on Wilde, it is not a dramatic biography or one that provides a sense of time and place. Ellmann wrote the tragedy of Wilde, not the life.

As much as I am indebted to Ellmann's scholarship, I must disagree with his thesis that Wilde contracted syphilis from a female prostitute at Oxford, that it influenced his work and hastened his early death. Those aspects of Wilde's life and personality that did not fit this argument were glossed over. One wonders whether Ellmann's insistence on syphilis was an effort to give Wilde some heterosexual patina to make him more sympathetic. Indeed, Wilde himself said that each biography is its own fiction because at best it takes a stance oblique to the truth. When one looks at the facts anew, Wilde's medical history makes syphilis difficult to substantiate.

The problem in writing any new biography of Wilde is that he comes to us with his life already written, so much of his anecdotal history precedes specific knowledge of any actual details of it. The first mythologizing and fictionalizing was by Wilde himself. So why another book about him? And why now? Because his life is a continual allegory and his social, political, and artistic views, which went right to the heart of Victorian society, are no less threatening today. Because his obsessive love for Lord Alfred Douglas is one of the nineteenth century's extraordinary love stories. He is a major figure in world culture and needs a fresh look. What better time to publish a new life than the centenary of his death, November 30, 2000?

I CAME TO KNOW Wilde through the women he loved. My first biography was of Violet Hunt, who claimed that she nearly became his wife in the 1880s. Her life introduced me to the Pre-Raphaelites, who inspired Wilde's own brand of Aestheticism. My next biography was of Bram Stoker, who brought me to Dublin and Trinity College, where he and Wilde were born and studied. Stoker ended up marrying Wilde's college sweetheart, Florence Balcombe. Best known as the author of *Dracula,* Stoker was business manager for Henry Irving and the Lyceum Theatre for three decades. His life initiated me into the West End, its theatres, clubs, and restaurants. Finally, "The Happy Prince," a childhood story that awed me with its themes of love, hope, and death, pulled me into five years of getting to know the inner Wilde. I discovered that his childlike nature extended to all his works—from *The Picture of Dorian Gray* to *The Importance of Being Earnest.*

What I want to show is how different stories can be embedded in the same factual material, depending on the perspective of the biographer's approach. I cannot boast of being the first to consult unsealed caches of letters or of discovering a lost diary. But everything is freshly culled, because everything that Wilde wrote bears the closest psychological inspection. If I manage to recapture his ebbs and flows, his duplicity, loyalty, and mendacity, to penetrate the magic of his conversation—for his authentic voice was never recorded—then the reader will have entered into the 1890s and I will have written a good book.

My research took me to Ireland, England, France, and Italy to see Wilde's homes and experience his favorite restaurants and cafés. I felt closest to him when I entered the atmosphere of the places where he wrote. Wilde was a reluctant writer and a great procrastinator when it came to carving out the solitary hours needed to compose. He suffered from writer's block and bouts of depression. But when he put pen to paper, he wrote quickly because the story was already in his head. Wilde started with an idea, an epigram or a paradox, which he told as a story or a parable, polishing it in the retelling and committing it to memory. His intellectual work done, he needed only an interlude in the pursuit of pleasure to put words on paper. But was he a genius? This question was persistently asked. How could he be considered a genius when he wrote the first draft of his masterpiece, *The Importance of Being Earnest,* in three weeks? To be a genius, the reasoning goes, a writer must suffer, each word written in torment; a writer must take years, not a matter of days, to produce innovative ideas. But Wilde's work habits defined a different kind of genius.

His last years are too often told as a dark tragedy, piled on top of the infamy of two years in prison. I found a brighter story to tell. Wilde lived as he wanted, old age was never for him; he had had a wonderful life and he was content to leave it on his own terms. In following his dictum that the "one duty we owe to history is to rewrite it," I hope this biography revokes the myth of Wilde as a tragic figure.

PART ONE

(1854–1878)

Becoming

*I made art a philosophy, and philosophy an art: I altered
the minds of men and the colours of things: there was
nothing I said or did that did not make people wonder. . . .
I awoke the imagination of my century so that I created
myth and legend around me. I summed up all systems in a
phrase, and all existence in an epigram. . . . I became the
spendthrift of my own genius, and to waste an eternal youth
gave me a curious joy.*

—*De Profundis*

CHAPTER ONE

Lord of Life

There is nothing like youth. The middle-aged are mortgaged to Life.
The old are in Life's lumber-room. But youth is the Lord of Life.
Youth has a kingdom waiting for it.

—*A Woman of No Importance*

Oscar Wilde's first public performance was in the drawing room of his Dublin home on Merrion Square, where the two-year-old entertained guests by reciting his name—Oscar Fingal O'Flahertie Wills Wilde—over and over. Savoring the vowels, trilling the fricatives, he gulped for air, chanting away, faster and faster like an intelligent windup toy, precocious, brazen, and insecure, until applause quieted him. Wilde was later to assert: "Everyone is good until they learn to talk." His mother called him a genius, and he agreed but others misunderstood. "The public is wonderfully tolerant," Wilde said. "It forgives everything except genius."

He mocked himself and society and made the world laugh at destiny. "My name has two O's, two F's and two W's," he later observed. "A name which is destined to be in everybody's mouth must not be too long; besides it becomes so expensive in the advertisement." Following his birth, Wilde's mother wrote a friend: "He is to be called Oscar Fingal Wilde. Is not that grand, misty and Ossianic?" "Names are everything," says Lord Henry Wotton in *The Picture of Dorian Gray*, and Oscar, who believed that his cradle was rocked by fate, had more than his share.

"I envy those men who become mythological while still living," W. B. Yeats once remarked to Wilde, who replied, "I think a man should invent his own myth." That he did. The name Oscar was an auspicious beginning, for it honored the son of Osín of the Gaelic epics, who was born in the Land of Eternal Youth.★ Like his namesake, Wilde loved youth, even more than art. "The soul is born old but grows young," he wrote. "That is the comedy of life. And the body is born young and grows old. That is life's tragedy." Fingal, Gaelic for "fair-haired stranger," goes back to Viking times and identifies a coastal region between the Liffey and Boyne Rivers.

With the addition of O'Flahertie, recalling the Galway heritage of his father, whose ancestors had married into the clan of the pre-Norman kings of West Connacht, Oscar was linked to an ancient Celtic family. His father had been given the name Wills as a tribute to a leading Roscommon family that included the playwright William Gorman Wills. In fact, Wilde's father dedicated his first book, *Madeira,* to Wills, a notable eccentric who filled his room with abandoned animals he rescued. The name was passed on to Oscar, who used it when it suited his fancy.

His mother called him "Oscàr," with an imperious accented *a;* his relatives preferred "Ossie." At public school he was "Grey-Crow," and at Oxford "Hosky" or occasionally "O'Flighty." In London, the American artist James Abbott McNeill Whistler dubbed him "Oscarino." Henry James referred to him as "Hoscar." Identity begins—and sometimes ends—with nicknames.

"How ridiculous of you to suppose that anyone, least of all my dear mother, would christen me 'plain Oscar,' " Wilde later said. "When one is unknown, a number of Christian names are useful, perhaps needful. As one becomes famous, one sheds some of them. . . . I started as Oscar Fingal O'Flahertie Wills Wilde. All but two of the five names have already

---

★Osín, a favorite of the Irish *seanchaí* or storyteller, rode off with Niamh Cinn óOir, daughter of the king of Tír na nóg, to an enchanted land of emerald fields and silver streams, where no one worked and no one grew old and time was endless. The mythical Oscar was born into this paradise. One night Osín dreamed of his father, Fionn MacCumhaill, leader of the Fianna, and decided to return to Ireland. Niamh warned him not to step on Irish soil. Three centuries had passed, and while he rode along comprehending this truth, he saw men trying to move a boulder with crowbars. He leaned down and shoved it on its way. His saddle strap broke and he fell to the ground. Like Dorian Gray, Osín turned into a wrinkled old man.

been thrown overboard. Soon I shall discard another and be known simply as 'The Wilde' or 'The Oscar.' "

Brilliance and daring created "The Oscar," which led to C.3.3., his prison cell number, and finally to Sebastian Melmoth, his nom de plume in exile, when, without an identity, Wilde was deprived of his currency in everyday life. Before his death, he decided that he wanted to be known as "the infamous St. Oscar of Oxford, Poet and Martyr." How far had he traveled from those jovial evenings when grown-ups applauded his recitations!

HIS PARENTS WERE brilliant and eccentric—bohemian characters often manipulated by biographers into the cause of Wilde's errant sexuality. Far more than the sum of their excesses, they lived in the next century while other mid-Victorians still grappled with industrialism. William Wilde became a notable eye-and-ear surgeon with a still-resonating legacy of scientific and folkloric research. He fathered at least three illegitimate children before marriage and was accused of rape after marriage. His wife, an inflammatory poet of nationalism and an innovative translator, became Dublin's most gossiped about hostess—known for her bizarre dresses and bawdy talk.

"Man is least himself when he talks in his own person," Wilde wrote in "The Critic as Artist." "Give him a mask, and he will tell you the truth." In the art of masks, Wilde's mother was a skillful teacher. Jane Francesca Elgee was born on December 21, 1821. Births were not registered then, but she gave this date in 1888, when she applied for financial aid from the Royal Literary Fund and it was in her interest to be older. At other times she was five years younger. In *A Woman of No Importance,* Lord Illingworth speaks for her when he says, "One should never trust a woman who tells one her real age. A woman who would tell one that would tell one anything." Oscar started to grow backward before he reached twenty-four, and by the time of his trials, when he was forty-one, he admitted to thirty-nine.

As a young woman, Oscar's mother was slender and stately, with glistening black hair, a perfect model for a statue of civic virtue. Although she ballooned into an ungainly, large-boned woman in her later years, she never lost the ability to enter a room with a savoir faire that silenced conversation. Outfitted in multilayered skirts over numerous petticoats, her face masked by a black-lace mantilla, she looked every inch a *donna* of the aristocracy, which she claimed as a putative descendant of Dante. To enhance this subterfuge, she may have Italianized her middle name from Frances to Francesca. Oscar learned that reality can be improved and that life should be a series of beautiful lies—maternal verities that he turned into a philosophy of life.

Her Irish background was Protestant and, on her mother's side, prosperous; all in all respectable, but Jane would have preferred Dante. Her father, Charles, an attorney, descended from a bricklayer with roots in the Northumberland area of Durham; her mother, Sarah Kingsbury, was the daughter of the vicar of Kildare and the granddaughter of the archdeacon of Wexford. Her maternal great-grandfather, Dr. Thomas Kingsbury, a friend of Jonathan Swift, was president of the Royal College of Physicians.

By far the most impressive relative was a maternal uncle by marriage, an eccentric, melancholy character who died before Oscar was born. His name was Charles Maturin, and he was a clergyman and the author of *Melmoth the Wanderer,* a classic gothic tale of sin and redemption that was published in 1820, two years after Mary Shelley's *Frankenstein*. Maturin was a dandy whom Oscar would have adored. A contemporary recalled how he "was the first in the quadrille—the last to depart. The ballroom was his temple of inspiration and worship." When he entertained, the shutters were closed and candles lighted even on sunny days, an atmospheric touch Oscar's mother imitated. Maturin liked to write surrounded by people and placed a red wafer on his forehead to indicate he was working; if a conversation intrigued him, he sealed his mouth shut with a homemade paste. It impressed Wilde that his great-uncle was respected by Baudelaire and that Balzac included Maturin with Goethe, Molière, and Byron as a genius of European letters, even writing a sequel to his novel called *Melmoth Réconcilié*.

Jane Elgee's father died when she was three. Within six years, her older sister and brother made advantageous marriages and left home. She lived with her mother and came of age at 34 Leeson Street, in a middle-class neighborhood located south of Dublin's Grand Canal. A lonely girl, she found solace in reading and teaching herself foreign languages. Fortunately, her widowed mother had family money to provide home tutoring.

In her twenties, she was drawn into politics through the Young Irelander poets, who had aligned themselves with Charles Gavan Duffy's *Nation*. Between 1846 and 1848, she published poetry there, under the nom de plume of John Fanshawe Ellis, later signing herself "Speranza," Italian for hope. (Her notepaper bore the motto *Fidanza, Speranza, Costanza*.) Speranza saw herself as "the acknowledged voice in poetry of all the people of Ireland."

In 1849, while Duffy was arrested for sedition and awaiting trial, she wrote two editorials ("The Hour of Destiny" and "Jacta Alea Est," or "The Die Is Cast"), which declared—a bit prematurely—that Ireland was at war with England. She admitted authorship of "Jacta Alea Est," but Duffy was tried anyway. In court she may—or may not—have stood up in the gallery and proclaimed: "I, and I alone, am the culprit, if culprit there be." Four juries failed to convict Duffy. *The Nation* was suppressed, and the wounded Young Irelanders dispersed. Speranza's fleeting arc from unknown poet to political celebrity ended, but she retained her pseudonym.

UNMARRIED AT TWENTY-EIGHT—and with no burning desire to find a husband—Speranza decided to translate books and poetry. Some accounts claim she mastered twelve languages, but the record shows fluency in Italian, French, and German; her translations of Russian, Turkish, Spanish, and Portuguese poetry for *The Nation* demonstrated an ability to look words up in a dictionary. Her first major translation (she would do six from 1849 to 1863) was Johannes Wilhelm Meinhold's sadomasochistic seventeenth-century fantasy, *Sidonia the Sorceress*. The poet Edmund Gosse observed how "this German romance did not begin to exist until an Irishwoman revealed it to a select English circle."

The novel's heroine, Sidonia von Bork, Abbess of the Convent of Marienfliess, tortures geese, whips young men, and dances on coffins. She fascinated Dante Gabriel Rossetti as well as his Pre-Raphaelite colleague Edward Burne-Jones, who painted her portrait in 1860. Speranza said she did the translation only for money and refused to have her name on the title page. Even so, *Sidonia* established her reputation, and her next project was Alphonse de Lamartine's *Pictures of the First French Revolution.*

Wilde said that Lady Duff-Gordon's translation of Meinhold's *The Amber Witch* and his mother's *Sidonia* were his "favourite romantic reading when a boy." Certainly *Sidonia* and *Melmoth* were literary legacies worthy of emulation. In both novels, paintings compete as characters, not an original concept but one Wilde used ingeniously in *The Portrait of Mr. W.H.* and ominously in *The Picture of Dorian Gray.* In *Melmoth,* the portrait of the ancestor who bargained with the devil to live 150 years without aging is hidden in an old lumber room, similar to the nursery where Dorian Gray conceals his picture when it becomes grotesquely disfigured.

SPERANZA LIVED THE intellectual and unromantic life of a spinster; she translated French and German books, wrote poetry, attended lectures and concerts, and cared for her ailing mother. She would have been a commonplace figure had she not embarked on a secret correspondence with a young man met during a trip to Scotland in 1847. They wrote to each other for fifteen years. Only fifty of her letters survive, and his identity remains a mystery. She was clearly infatuated with this Scotsman—her letters are candid about love and marriage but lacking the intimacy of the postal flirtations between Ellen Terry and George Bernard Shaw or George Sand and Gustave Flaubert.

In one letter she describes her ideal mate as "a Baronet of £5,000 a year with the Athenian's soul and your good heart." She flirts a bit: "I don't care for a friendship unless fringed with—not quite love perhaps—but something that is always on the point of becoming so," and shares her fantasies: "In love I like to feel myself a slave—the difficulty is to find anyone capable of ruling me. I love them when I feel their power." Lord Henry similarly observes in *Dorian Gray:* "I am afraid that women appreciate cruelty, downright cruelty, more than anything else. . . . We have emancipated them, but they remain slaves looking for their masters all the same. They love being dominated."

Jane shocked guests at her salons with offhand comments about sin being the only thing worth living for, but such talk was a mask, a calculated performance. Her recent biographer Joy Melville maintains that her "sense of morality was strong, and not being a woman with a strong sexual nature she was not tempted to stray." Except in letters. After corresponding for three years, her Scotsman wrote that he planned to marry. "Do forgive me if I am not very enthusiastic," she wrote him in 1850. "I shall have to wait ten years now I suppose before your ardour is sufficiently cooled down to find a rational opinion on any point literary or psychological." And she bitterly noted, "I hate men in love, the heart holds but one at a time."

The following year, her mother died. She could live either alone, which would be considered improper, or with relatives. Instead she married, but not with the thought of being a traditional wife. Her brother observed that "Jane has some heart, she has good impulses, but the love of self is the prominent feature of her character." When Oscar inherited this love of self, he transformed it into the first celebrity art form.

BLESSED WITH A tenacious nature, William Robert Wills Wilde could find scientific wisdom in a nursing porpoise or a mummified dwarf. The plaque at One Merrion Square in Dublin distinguishes him as an "aural and ophthalmic surgeon, archaeologist, ethnologist, antiquarian, biographer, statistician, naturalist, topographer, historian, folklorist." On another level, he was an unabashed sentimentalist who played Pygmalion to young Galateas, enjoying (like his son) being the older, cultured man who tutors the unsophisticated.

Oscar's father was born in March 1815 in the village of Kilkeevin near Castlerea, in the western county of Roscommon; his Irish ancestors were merchants, farmers, and clerics. His father, Thomas Wilde, was a kindly man, a physician who treated the poor and billed the gentry. Trained in his image, young William learned to dress head wounds after blackthorn fights and to set broken arms, and, as he matured, he developed that rare talent of being able to put patients at ease. When it was time for formal schooling, he put on his one good suit, hefted a suitcase weighted with books, and made his way to Dublin.

The physicians there were among the best in Europe and included William Stokes, often credited with the creation of the first stethoscope: a rolled-up sheet of paper. This technique allowed doctors to listen to the heartbeat without getting too close to the stench. Medical students had a steady supply of cadavers stolen from paupers' graves. Any prick with a dissecting knife led to infection, sometimes amputation of fingers. Bleeding, blistering, and purgation were used to treat most diseases. There were no anesthetics except hot baths and tobacco-smoke enemas (surgical anesthesia was introduced in 1846 at Boston's Massachusetts General Hospital); if patients did not faint, they were strapped down, and the surgeon who cut the fastest was considered the best. A bloodstained coat was a badge of honor.

IN THE MIDST of his studies, William Wilde was asked to accompany a recovering patient on an eight-month cruise to the Holy Land. He was only twenty-two when he boarded the 130-ton topsail schooner yacht *Crusader* on September 24, 1837, and sailed to Madeira, Algiers, Sicily, Egypt, Rhodes, Cyprus, Syria, Palestine, and Greece—a voyage that led to an international reputation outside medicine. The winter seas were rough, and he was frequently seasick, but not too indisposed to dissect porpoises flung onboard. He published his findings on how these mammals nurse their young and turned his diary into a two-volume book.

Most compelling was Egypt.* Few Europeans had traveled there since Napoléon occupied the country from 1798 to 1801. Following withdrawal of the French Army, ancient Egyptian sites were unprotected and easily plundered. Like many who came after him, Wilde found the thrill of illicit acquisition irresistible. During a tour of Sakara, he discovered a looted tomb with the mummified remains of a young male dwarf scattered on the sand. He salvaged the torso to bring back to Dublin, then wanted to add some embalmed ibises, the sacred, long-legged, white wading birds. When the guide led him to the tomb with urns of desiccated ibises, Wilde had forgotten the lantern. They decided to go on in the dark, crawling through the blackness. "I do not think in all my travels," he wrote, "I ever felt the same strong sensation of being in an enchanted place so much as

---

*Unlike his father, Oscar never saw Egypt but was fascinated by its art (particularly the Sphinx) and symbolism. He wore an emerald scarab ring on the little finger of each hand; he said the ring on his left hand was the cause of all his happiness and the one on the right all his unhappiness. When a friend suggested he remove the right-hand ring, he replied, "To live in happiness, you must know some unhappiness in life."

when led by this sinewy child of the desert through the dark winding passages." Together they dragged six urns into the light.

A fearless risk taker, Wilde was determined to scale the pyramid of Chephren at Giza, second in size to the Great Pyramid of Cheops. This meant a 707-foot ascent up the side over a forbidding slippery face, a climb that discouraged all but a handful of travelers. Two guides pushed and pulled until Wilde made it to the six-foot-square peak. As he looked down from 471 feet at his friends waving their hats and cheering, he was overcome with euphoria. "I began to think something wonderful had been achieved," he wrote in *Madeira,* "and some idea of my perilous situation broke upon me."

Returning to Ireland, Wilde published an article in the *Dublin University Magazine* advocating removal of Cleopatra's Needle to England.★ Founded independently of Trinity College in 1833, and affectionately called *DUM,* the publication attracted the important Irish writers of the early and middle Victorian periods. The editor was Isaac Butt, a champion of Home Rule and future chief prosecutor for the Mary Travers libel trial that would tarnish Wilde's reputation.

WILLIAM WILDE'S APPEARANCE was undistinguished. To many he looked ordinary, like most of the men seen walking along Sackville Street every day. But women observed the short, scruffy figure with pale mischievous eyes and a mustacheless beard emphasizing a wide, sensuous mouth differently. He had charisma, charm, and a gift for storytelling in a land with a proud oral tradition. Seventy-year-old Maria Edgeworth, who first used social realism in her novel *The Absentee* to expose English land-lords, became his patron. She encouraged Wilde to study abroad, to take a physician's Grand Tour, and provided letters of introduction, and probably some financing. Wilde went to Moorfields Hospital in London—then as now a center for ophthalmology—spent six months in Vienna, visited Munich, Prague, and Dresden, studied at Heidelberg, and in Berlin

---

★Wilde had seen the two red granite Cleopatra's Needles lying as they had for centuries at Heliopolis. His campaign was successful two years after his death: in 1878 the obelisk was transported—not without great difficulty—and erected on its present site, the Thames Embankment. And two years later the other needle was raised in New York's Central Park.

worked with Johann Friedrich Dieffenbach, one of the pioneers of plastic surgery.

He returned a trained specialist burnished with continental patina, a notebook filled with medical hypotheses, and useful ideas such as writing the patient's temperature and pulse rate on a slate, using flour and water, the early form of chalk. Wilde opened a surgery at 15 Westland Row, at the back of Trinity College; his mother and sister, Margaret, kept house for him. He started writing what became a guide to Austria's literary, scientific, and medical institutions, still a valuable reference work. *DUM* praised it as "another of the many instances of how agreeable a book can be made on apparently the least amusing topics, by a clever man, particularly when that clever man is a clever physician." With his appointment as editor of the *Dublin Quarterly Journal of Medical Science*, a publication with the contemporary prestige of *The Lancet* in England or the *Journal of the American Medical Association* in the United States, Wilde moved from son of a rural doctor to prominence in Dublin's medical and intellectual circles. What he lacked was an income to match this position.

THIS WOULD HAVE been the appropriate time for William Wilde to marry and prosper as a private physician to the rising middle class, but he could not ignore those Dubliners who slept on St. Stephen's Green or begged outside the Shelbourne Hotel. Following his father's charitable example, he founded a hospital for the destitute. Once Oscar proudly told a friend how his father had built St. Mark's "when he was only twenty-nine and not a rich man."

As an eligible bachelor, the young doctor should have been attending balls and parties, but that would have taken time away from his patients and his writing—and he wrote every day, often into the evening. His one indulgence was the theatre, where he became infatuated with Helen Faucit, Ireland's leading actress, known for her *Antigone* at the old Theatre Royal. But he had little patience for the courting process demanded by beautiful and famous women and probably concealed his admiration. That there were intimacies was known only by his acknowledgment of three illegitimate children.

A son, christened Henry Wilson, was born in 1838, at the time Wilde was exploring Egyptian tombs. Wilde educated him, took him into his surgery, and made him an heir to his estate. Two daughters, Emily and Mary, born in 1847 and 1849, were adopted by his eldest brother, the Reverend Ralph Wilde, and grew up as Wildes. By taking responsibility for his out-of-wedlock children, Wilde was being a proper Victorian, and in no way was his situation unusual or shocking. It did seem, however, that he wanted to avoid the responsibilities of marriage. Repeatedly, Oscar used the caprices of birth in his plays. "A family is a terrible encumbrance, especially when one is not married" appears in *Vera,* his first.

SPERANZA AND WILDE could not have known each other very long before they wed. They may have met when she reviewed his book *The Beauties of the Boyne and Blackwater* in *The Nation.* In *The Importance of Being Earnest,* Lady Bracknell says that she does not favor long engagements. "They give people the opportunity of finding out each other's character before marriage, which I think is never advisable." Speranza was thirty and Wilde was thirty-six. She needed a home and respectability after her mother's death. And it would have been reckless for Wilde to conceive more children outside marriage. She accepted the existence of his thirteen-year-old son and two young daughters. At their age, it mattered less whether the proposal was motivated by passion, intellectual kinship, or resignation. Speranza might have broached the question. Lord Henry tells Dorian that "it is always the woman who proposes to us, and not we who propose to women."

The wedding ceremony on November 14, 1851, in St. Peter's Church, Dublin, was attended by a small gathering, as the bride was still in mourning and, to judge from the dispatch to Scotland, more submissive than aroused. "For myself I died long ago—the old original Ego that you used to know," she wrote. "I love and suffer—this is all I am conscious of now and thus at last my great soul is prisoned within a *woman's destiny*—nothing interests me beyond the desire to make *him* happy—for this I could kill myself."

Speranza brought to the union not only Kingsbury money but influential friends such as William Rowan-Hamilton, the astronomer and mathematician, and the poet Aubrey De Vere. The couple moved up the street to 21 Westland Row, a Georgian terrace house with a fanlight and wrought-iron balconies. Wilde's mother and sister stayed on as part of the household. The front room on the ground floor was the surgery; the first-floor drawing room had the usual clutter of overstuffed chairs with anti-macassars, flickering gas lamps, and heavy mahogany furniture.

The year of his marriage, Wilde was appointed census commissioner, with the arduous task of compiling the first statistics on the incidence of deafness, blindness, and eye and ear diseases. He traveled throughout Ireland, accumulating medical histories as well as regional tales of super-stitions, legends, and charms. *Irish Popular Superstitions* was published in 1852 and expanded thirty-five years later by Speranza in *Ancient Legends, Mystic Charms, and Superstitions of Ireland*. Without Wilde's ability to tease the past from his patients, a bygone oral history would have vanished.

The Wildes were members of the generation for whom the discovery of Irish history and its literature came as a revelation. "If ever there was a nation that clung to the soil, and earned patriotism by the love of the very ground they walk on," Oscar's father wrote, "it is (or we may now write was) the Irish peasantry." Like other scholars who worked to preserve the old traditions, he believed that the Irish language should be cultivated by the upper classes. In his book on Lough Corrib, he warned that "spoken Gaelic is hourly dying out" and predicted that in twenty years it would cease to be used. But Gaelic survived and still is heard in parts of the west of Ireland.

Speranza held that the "Saxon basis is the rough block of the nation, but it is the Celtic influence that gives it all its artistic value and finish." But Oscar grew up seeing only creativity suffocated. During his Ameri-can tour he told an audience: "With the coming of the English, art in Ireland came to an end, and it has had no existence for seven hundred years. I am glad it has not, for art could not live and flourish under a tyrant." He concluded, "I am Irish by race, but the English have condemned me to speak the language of Shakespeare."

Dublin was changing. Since the union of 1801, when the aristocrats departed for London, the middle class, particularly physicians, lawyers, scientists, and academics, had forged new alliances, taking up residence around the Georgian squares. But Westland Row, where the Wildes started their family, was outside this orbit. Impatient and ambitious, they planned to improve their rank and address.

CHAPTER TWO

Merrion Square

❧

Children begin by loving their parents; after a time
they judge them. Rarely, if ever, do they forgive them.

—A WOMAN OF NO IMPORTANCE

Two sons were born at 21 Westland Row: William Charles Kingsbury, called Willie, on September 26, 1852, and Oscar, with his
carefully selected mantra of names, on October 16, 1854. Isola
Francesca Emily Wilde had her beginnings on April 2, 1857, at Merrion
Square, an address Wilde later appropriated for himself as a more elegant
birthplace.

Few books about Wilde omit the photo of him at the age of two
posing in a dress of cobalt blue velvet trimmed with lace; he wears white
stockings with bowed shoes on his small feet; his hair is rolled into sausage
curls, swept off a high forehead with a ribbon, revealing the heavy-lidded
eyes.

Early biographers seeking to explain Wilde's homosexuality decided
that his mother, disappointed that her second child was not a daughter,
dressed Oscar in frills, which aroused his interest in men. Present-day
wisdom discards such notions, but in the Ireland of the mid-eighties there
was a reason: dresses protected little boys from the *dreg due,* or blood fairy,
who, according to myth, ignored little girls but abducted little boys.

Speranza delighted in Oscar, but like so many mothers favored her firstborn, as Oscar would favor Cyril over Vyvyan. Physically, Oscar and Willie resembled the large-boned Elgees: tall and lanky when young, towering and overweight when older. They had their father's sentimentality and mystical blue eyes, their mother's narcissism and alabaster skin. A letter to Scotland described Oscar as "a great stout creature who minds nothing but growing fat," while Willie "was slight, tall and spirituelle [*sic*] looking, with large beautiful eyes full of expression. He is twined round all the fibres of my heart." There would always be money and sympathy for Willie, the lovable but undisciplined prodigal. Both sons competed for their mother's love; neither won, and childhood conflicts followed. "At every single moment of one's life," Wilde wrote in *De Profundis,* "one is what one is going to be no less than what one has been."

William Wilde's voluntary hospital, St. Mark's, flourished, as well it should have: it was the only hospital in Ireland or England offering instruction on diseases of the ear. Wilde published *Practical Observations in Aural Surgery and the Nature and Treatment of Diseases of the Ear,* the first textbook on the subject in English, in 1853★ and completed a six-hundred-page history of Irish medicine collected during the census of 1851.

Speranza realized that her husband was special but found the reality of living with a genius on a day-to-day basis uninspiring. Physically and intellectually, he was not the dominating man of her fantasies. Marriage and motherhood distracted her from writing and translating. Often she seemed to be competing with her husband to publish frequently and first. An impatient woman at best, Speranza found life at Westland Row inadequate to her ambitions.

THE FAMILY MOVED in 1855 to One Merrion Square, a large Georgian house on the sunny north-side corner (or, as Lady Bracknell might say, the fashionable side). There were few better addresses. Not the oldest but the largest and the most elegant, Merrion Square was built in 1762, twenty-two years after Mountjoy and Rutland Squares. The peers and

---

★This book describes surgical experiments for a mastoid or middle-ear abscess. Ironically, it was this condition, which may have originated from a fall in prison, that led to meningitis, the cause of Wilde's death in Paris at the age of forty-six.

members of Parliament who had lived there when the British ruled at Dublin Castle were now replaced by doctors and lawyers in frock coats and peg-top trousers and their wives in poke bonnets and crinolines.

Number One was the only house on the square with three steps—rather than one—leading up to the entrance, a glassed-in conservatory, and a wrought-iron balcony overlooking Merrion Street, where the family viewed parades and processions. Wilde saw most of his patients at St. Mark's but also had a small surgery at the back of the house with a separate entrance for private consultations. Speranza held her salons in the first-floor drawing room overlooking the square's private garden.

Used during the famine as a soup kitchen, the garden was locked during Wilde's childhood to exclude outsiders, much like the garden in his fairy tale "The Selfish Giant." Speranza's fondness for Neoclassical sculpture survives in stucco bas-reliefs in the foyer, where a bust of Maturin once had the place of honor. (It was in front of Number One in 1904 that James Joyce vainly waited for his first date with Nora Barnacle.)★

Employing her various languages, Oscar's mother ran an efficient international household that included a staff of six servants and a series of German, Swiss, and French governesses. In the fourth-floor nursery Willie and Oscar took the measure of each other—and declared war. Dark furies bred in the hothouse atmosphere of the nursery were later recalled in *The Importance of Being Earnest*. One day Oscar tried to appease Willie and gave him his stuffed bear. Unimpressed, Willie continued to tease him until Oscar shouted, "You don't deserve my bear. You must give me back my bear." But when poetic letters and engraved silver cigarette cases replaced toy bears to fetter love, he never asked for their return. Another time, the brothers were bathing in front of the fire when a nightshirt burst into flames. Oscar clapped his hands with delight while Willie shouted for the governess to extinguish the blaze. Afterward Oscar cried with rage that tragedy was averted. "I don't care for brothers," Basil Hallward says in *Dorian Gray*. "My elder brother won't die, and my younger brothers seem never to do anything else."

★One Merrion Square has been restored by the American College, Dublin, following nearly a quarter century of neglect. William Wilde's built-in mahogany bookcases survive in the ground-floor study and plaques honor Oscar and his father. At darkness a stained-glass window illuminates the Happy Prince, with Wilde's face. The garden, now open to the public, remains as overgrown and lush as Wilde portrayed it.

RISING AT DAWN, William Wilde walked to St. Mark's, made his rounds, and consulted or operated at other hospitals. In the evening, he was often invited to present antiquarian papers at the Royal Irish Academy or the Royal Dublin Society. If he dined out, it was usually with colleagues from the Medico-Philosophical Society or the Mystics, an eating club where food, drink, and laughter were more valued than lofty philosophical talk.

Despite a work-centered life, he spent more time with his sons than many Victorian fathers. Important events—birthdays, high marks, awards—were recognized by the Wildes' friends with evening celebrations for which Willie and Oscar were awakened and brought downstairs for a brief appearance. Children's parties seemed absent from Merrion Square. Both parents used their sons as extensions of themselves.

Oscar fondly remembered his father's deep voice doing justice to the cadences of Walt Whitman and his mother's whispers and squeals when she told the old stories of witches and blood fairies. His father retold the folktales collected from patients during the medical census and sang the Irish lullaby "Athá mé in mu codladh, agus ná dúishe mé" (I am asleep, and do not wake me), which he taught his sons.

Oscar's fairy tales have rather friendly antagonists, considering the many macabre ones that marched over his bedcovers. Before they went to sleep, the boys were taught to revere their mother's poems and the poetry of the Young Irelanders "as a Catholic child [does] the saints of the calendar." If Wilde had not been Irish and raised in such a fertile storytelling atmosphere, he might have become a writer who used pen and paper more and conversation less.

Speranza was overly ambitious for her boys. "Willie is my kingdom," she wrote to Scotland a month after Oscar's birth. "I will rear him a Hero perhaps and President of the future Irish Republic. *Chi sa?* I have not fulfilled my destiny yet." She envisaged Willie "ready to spring forth like another Perseus to combat evil." She had the leisure for such daydreams: eating breakfast in bed, reading or napping until noon; by two she was at her desk to sort through the morning mail, accept invitations, and receive visitors.

From the nursery window on the fourth floor, Oscar and Willie watched the horse-drawn carriages circling the square. It was at this time that Oscar embraced superstitions, which he later called "opponents of common sense." Like his mother, he believed in the evil eye, and he never hailed a hansom with a white horse, which he believed unlucky. (His mythical father, Osín, left the Land of Eternal Youth on a white stallion.)

SELDOM DID THE Wildes dine at home alone. Fathers of future famous sons, John Butler Yeats and George Henry Moore, known for their wit and erudition, were frequent guests. Willie and Oscar ate with their governess in the nursery and then joined the adults. Since bedtimes were not rigorously enforced, it was routine for the boys to fall asleep at their father's feet. On the drawing-room carpet, Oscar learned important lessons about the art of charming society, breeding in him a disdain for ordinary talk; he would suffer fools sooner than bores.

When Oscar was almost three, his sister, Isola (Gaelic for Iseult) Francesca Emily, was born, and her brothers were led into the nursery to greet her. Like siblings everywhere, Willie and Oscar were astonished that Isola was so small and were skeptical when told they were once the same size and in the same cradle.

Speranza had borne three children in five years and was impatient to return to a life of the mind. She began translating the German romantic novel *The First Temptation* by Wilhelmine Canz, whose plot involves the tragic death of an aesthete. At the same time, her husband published the first of three volumes cataloging antiquities in the Museum of the Royal Irish Academy. Even with a grand home and rewarding work, Oscar's mother was nostalgic for the bygone days of turmoil, when she had lived on the edge, when she was Speranza, the voice of freedom.

She wondered to her Scottish confidant: "I look back at my own self that then was. Now I have gone forth into another life with nothing but memory to make me aware of the identity, for all true identity has vanished." She complained as much as any latter-day feminist: "Alas! the Fates are cruel / Behold Speranza making gruel!" Being married to a genius meant keeping out of the way. "The best chance, perhaps, of domestic felicity," she wrote in the essay "Genius and Marriage," "is when all the family are Bohemians, and all clever, and all enjoy thoroughly the erratic, impulsive, reckless life of work and glory, indifferent to everything save the intense moments of popular applause."

Eventually, Speranza took up the mantle of martyrdom. "A Joan of Arc was never meant for marriage," she complained. "Life has such infinite possibilities of woe" was another favorite expression. Oscar would also agree that life is "a very terrible thing" and "the tragedy in one's soul." In "The Remarkable Rocket," a tale of how vanity distorts reality, he observes: "As for domesticity, it ages one rapidly, and distracts one's mind from higher things." Speranza consistently passed discontent on to her sons. She manipulated Oscar by signing letters as La Madre Devotissima, La Madre Dolorosa, or La Madre Povera. Never was she devoted, sad, and poor at the same time. Her favorite salutation was Caro Oscuro, Figlio Mio Caressimo, or Mio Caro Figlio (my dear son).

Despite anti-British sentiments, she attended balls and levees at the Viceregal Court; her entrance curbed all trivial gossip. What was she wearing this time? She often designed her costumes by assembling this and that from her closet. There was always a political message for Dublin Castle pinned on her skirt or bodice: bits of Limerick lace and Irish poplin or brooches copied from the ornaments of Ireland's early queens. La Madre makes a brief appearance in *Dorian Gray* as Lord Henry's wife, "a curious woman, whose dresses always looked as if they had been designed in a rage and put on in a tempest."

On St. Patrick's Day, 1859, the British ladies inhaled when she curtsied to the lord lieutenant wearing three skirts of white silk ruched with white satin ribbons looped with bouquets of gold flowers—and one large green shamrock. A plumed-feather wreath with a white tulle veil bordered in gold encircled her black hair. In the gentle blush of gaslight, Speranza looked like a bride; more unkindly she was seen as a wedding cake. "Am I not fallen to a mere woman?" she teased her Scotsman. "How marriage changes one. . . . We no longer live in glorious ideas and majestic abstractions."

William Wilde may have suffered manic-depressive episodes. Speranza described cycles of agitated work followed by "strange" and "hypochondriacal" periods when he wrapped himself "in a black pall" and was "stern, mournful and silent as the grave itself." Neither partner was easy to live with. Both needed mutual understanding beyond sexual intimacy but were not modern enough to discuss their marriage; in this respect they were conventional Victorians. Speranza had her unburdening letters to Scotland; her husband had his illegitimate son, Henry Wilson, now working for him, as trusted confidant.

In 1862, Wilde received the Swedish order of the Polar Star, and the following year Queen Victoria appointed him surgeon oculist to the queen in Ireland, not a demanding responsibility considering her dislike of visiting Ireland. In 1864, Wilde was knighted, not in recognition of his professional reputation, which was European, but for his work on the Irish Census, which annoyed Speranza, who saw the census as the least of his accomplishments. But she willingly retired Speranza for the title of Lady Wilde. The rank did not indicate that the Wildes had reached the upper classes; a peerage might have been different but an unlikely honor for a doctor.

At the investiture, *The Irish Times* reported, Lady Wilde's dress and train were of the "richest white satin, trimmed handsomely in scarlet velvet and gold cord, with bouillonnes of tulle, satin ruches and a magnificent tunic of real Brussels lace lappets." Regarding fashion, Lady Wilde wrote that a woman should match her personality and decide to be "either a superb Juno, or a seductive Aphrodite, or a Hebe, blooming and coquette, or a Pallas Athena, grand, majestic and awe inspiring." Lady Wilde preferred the last: goddess of wisdom, peace, and war.

"IN THIS WORLD there are only two tragedies," Oscar wrote in *Lady Windermere's Fan*. "One is not getting what one wants, and the other is getting it. The last is much the worst, the last is a real tragedy!" Perhaps he was remembering what happened to his father shortly after the announcement of the knighthood, when he was accused of alleged sexual advances—rape was hinted—with a young patient, Mary Travers. This convoluted story proves the wisdom of the line from *Earnest* that "the truth is never pure and seldom simple."

The daughter of a law professor at Trinity, Travers was impressionable, highly strung, and, as she demonstrated, obsessive. She was eighteen when she became Wilde's patient in 1854. Welcomed at Merrion Square, she took Willie and Oscar on outings. Sir William escorted her to lectures, bought her books and clothes, and, as a gifted cicerone, introduced her to a more cultured world. Eight years after they met, he tried to sever the association, offering to send her to Australia, where she had relatives.

First hysterical and then vindictive, Travers was not about to be dismissed and went public with her version of the relationship. One evening as Wilde lectured at the Metropolitan Hall, a pamphlet entitled *Florence Boyle Price: or a Warning by Speranza* was sold outside for a penny. Newsboys hawked it, shouting it contained letters written by Sir William. Travers told a parable about a woman called Florence (her alter ego), who is chloroformed and seduced by a Dr. Quilp (Sir William), who had "a decidedly animal and sinister expression about his mouth, which was coarse and vulgar in the extreme."

Drawing on the fanaticism that made Speranza's notoriety at the Duffy sedition trial, Lady Wilde reacted quickly and defensively. She attempted to buy up all the pamphlets and when that failed wrote to Mary Travers's father. His daughter was using unfounded threats to extort money from the Wildes and furthermore, she informed him, "consorts with low newspaper boys," which implied prostitution. The letter provided sufficient reason for Travers to sue for libel. Sir William was also charged because a husband was considered responsible for his wife's civil offenses.

Forgotten stories of past liaisons were repeated in pubs and drawing rooms so that all Dublin soon knew of the *other* children; with each retelling the number grew until Wilde had populated whole villages. Isaac Butt, his former editor at *DUM* and leader of the Irish Parliamentary Party at Westminster, was on the prosecution team. The court heard testimony that Sir William had sexually violated the plaintiff in 1862, but after a two-year interval such an accusation could not be taken seriously.

Lady Wilde took the stand and played to the gallery. When the prosecution inquired: "When Miss Travers complained to you of your husband's attempt upon her virtue, why did you not answer her letter?"

"Because I was not interested," she replied.

Butt emphasized Lady Wilde's apparent indifference to the allegations. As the loyal wife, she made a dignified witness, answering questions without a trace of malice toward either party. After all, she was a lady and no longer the Speranza who had disturbed the court in the Duffy trial. Since Sir William was not the defendant, he refused to take the stand and confront embarrassing questions. The court upheld the libel charge on the basis of incriminating letters (one inquired whether Travers needed underclothing or pajamas) but ignored the plaintiff's pleas of outraged innocence.

Travers was awarded a farthing (a quarter of a penny) in damages. Wilde had to pay more than two thousand pounds in costs. An expensive escapade, to be sure, but Lady Wilde was energized by the attention and publicity. She kept the occasion freshly minted by sending off letters reiterating that no one in Dublin took the charges seriously, explaining that Travers was "mad" and the "sneering" English newspapers inaccurate.

Of course this was untrue. Among the detractors was Sir William's medical rival, Dr. Arthur Jacob, who was envious of his colleague's self-advertising ways and seized the opportunity to denounce him in the *Medical Press* for not testifying and clearing his name—a reasonable criticism. *The Medical Times and Gazette* was supportive, even printing an aphorism—"Genius has its penalties as well as its privileges"—with which Oscar would concur. The trial did not significantly jeopardize Wilde's professional reputation, but the stress damaged his health. He had a chronic cough and appeared much older than his fifty years.

As Oscar would say, "All trials are trials for one's life." His father spent more time away from Dublin, indulging his mania for acquiring property and building houses. He already had four rental houses facing the sea at Bray, a resort south of Dublin. In 1853, he leased a fishing lodge on a wooded peninsula called Illaunroe (Irish for "little red island") on Lough Fee in Connemara and in 1865 acquired fifteen acres from the estate of his maternal ancestors, the Fynnes of Ballymagibbon. The land, located near Cong in County Mayo, was on an elevation overlooking Lough Corrib, with a distant silhouette of the Moycullen Hills. There were magnificent views of the lake and its numerous islands, some 365, one for each day of the year; on leap year an additional one was said to appear. It was an area rich with antiquities, particularly Cong Abbey, which Wilde helped to restore.

Within the property's boundaries was the location of the mythological battle of Magh-Tura, where Babor of the Evil Eye was slain. As near as possible, Wilde located the cairn-studded site of the battle and built a two-story peaked-roof house, which he called Moytura. When it was completed in 1866, he affixed a stucco medallion over the doorway with entwined *W*'s and the date. Traveling to Moytura was not difficult, even in the 1860s. A train left Dublin at 8:30 A.M. and pulled into Galway station at 1:45 P.M. There was time for lunch at the Great Southern Hotel before boarding the three o'clock steamer to Cong. Thirty-one miles separated Moytura from Illaunroe, an arduous journey along a winding dirt road if made by cart or on horseback.

Thereafter the family spent their holidays in the west rather than Bray. Oscar preferred the seclusion and sport of Illaunroe, then—as now—a place of mists and purple shadows, of clouds and sudden rains. There, as at other water-fringed sites, he could "hear things that the ear cannot hear and see invisible things." Like a Wildean paradox, Connemara is a dreamscape where light and shade and color and shape are never the same. Oscar found it magical, a place of renewal, which made him "years younger than actual history records." Yeats, whose mother's family was from nearby Sligo, recognized in Wilde the same "half-civilized blood," which comes from areas rich in heroic and supernatural lore.

OSCAR WOULD RIDICULE upper-class country life in England, where there were no Connemaras. The bons mots in *A Woman of No Importance* were easily struck: "I feel sure that if I lived in the country for six months, I should become so unsophisticated that no one would take the slightest notice of me" or "The English country gentleman galloping after a fox— the unspeakable in full pursuit of the uneatable." It was true: Oscar did not sit a horse well, but he thoroughly enjoyed fishing and shooting. At Illaunroe he rose at 5:00 A.M., anticipating dawn over the Atlantic, the air filled with millions of minute prisms and shattered into rainbow colors over Lough Fee. His enthusiasm for the outdoors spills over in the letters he wrote to Oxford classmates during the long vacations. It was the duty of the individual, especially the artist, to develop his personality to the fullest, and Oscar made baiting a hook a sublime act. He passed fishing lore on to his children, telling them stories about the "great melancholy carp" that had to be called from the bottom of the lake with Irish songs.

Willie and Oscar accompanied their father during his explorations of ancient sites when he gathered material for a historical guide. Written with an explorer's enthusiasm, *Lough Corrib: Its Shore and Islands* urges readers: "Westward, ho! Let us rise with the sun and be off to the land of the West—to the lakes and streams, the grassy glens and fern-clad gorges—the bluff hills and rugged mountains—now cloud-capped, then revealed in azure, or bronzed by evening's tints."

Oscar enjoyed excavating enough to apply for an archaeological studentship—which he did not receive—after Oxford. In the application, he explained that from his boyhood he had "been accustomed, through my Father, to visiting and reporting on ancient sites, taking rubbings and measurements and all the technique of *open air* archaeologica—it is of course a subject of intense interest to me." The family's outdoor classroom stretched from Lough Corrib to the Atlantic. Willie and Oscar sketched caves, cairns, monoliths, stone circles, and holy wells. Willie recorded Oscar and his father exploring Hag's Castle on the island of Inishmaan in Lough Mask.

One day they came upon an unmortared building containing two arched crypts; it measured five feet by three feet wide and resembled a lime kiln but was of the wrong construction. Sir William, who had never seen anything like it, was fascinated; he made several visits to Inishmaan and spent considerable time studying the structure. When he determined that conversations could be heard between the two crypts, he speculated that the ruin was an ancient prison or sweathouse once used by the nearby abbey. At the age of thirteen, Oscar had his first look at how a person was confined in a small space. That the experience could ever become personal would have surprised him.

CHAPTER THREE

Away from Home

✌

The only thing that sustains one through life is the consciousness of the
immense inferiority of everybody else.

—"THE REMARKABLE ROCKET"

Oscar and Willie were enrolled at the Portora Royal School near Enniskillen in February 1864. Oscar was young for boarding school, not yet ten, and Willie was twelve. They were a hundred miles from Dublin in the county of Fermanagh, now part of Northern Ireland. Situated above the juncture of upper and lower Lough Erne, the school provided a peaceful country atmosphere with nearby monastic ruins to explore. Portora saw itself as the Irish Eton; the school song was "Floreat Portora," sung to the same tune as "Floreat Etona." Like their English cousins, the Irish Protestant boarding schools educated the sons of the middle class, valued athletic rather than academic achievement, and believed that cold baths built character.

Portora was less stuffy and class-conscious than Eton, and unlike other Irish public schools admitted Catholics. For Oscar's seven years, it was a nurturing rather than a threatening institution. He discovered the classics, greedily read poetry, sharpened his wit, and, for the first time, socialized with boys his own age. Portora not Trinity grounded him in Greek scholarship. His contemporaries suggest he was popular (an important label at boarding school), recalling that he entertained rather than annoyed, avoided music and mathematics, and loathed games.

Portora classmates included Louis Claude Purser, a constant rival in classics, and Edward Sullivan, who noted Oscar's "romantic imagination." Both went on to Trinity, where Purser remained as Latin professor and Sullivan's scholarship concentrated on the *Book of Kells*. Recorded decades later, their memories are vague, indicating only that Wilde was just another student, wittier than some and brighter than most. He enjoyed his solitude and was often seen rowing on the river Erne but was not a good enough oar to compete, setting him apart from his classmates, who excelled in rugby, cricket, and rowing. He did not shirk controversy and was one of six students to sign a protest about the severity of punishment for a missed scripture lesson.

Although contemptuous of the playing fields, Oscar gained respect by his wit and skill in manipulating teachers. In class he asked questions like "What is a Realist?" to turn the discussion toward what interested him. "I have forgotten my schooldays," says Mrs. Cheveley in *An Ideal Husband*. "I have a vague impression that they were detestable." By all accounts, Wilde enjoyed Portora, for the simple reason that it permitted him to mature on his own terms.

He had a handsome, boyish face with hooded eyes turned down at the corners and the large, sensual lips of his father. This was Wilde before vanity, before masks camouflaged his original self. "To the world I seem, by intention on my part, a dilettante and dandy merely," he later wrote. "It is not wise to show one's heart to the world. . . . In so vulgar an age as this we all need masks."

BEING AT THE same school was irksome for Willie and Oscar; they walked the same corridors, ate in the same dining hall, and competed for best marks. At first, the headmaster thought Willie the better all-round student. Known as "Blue Blood," Willie was seen as "clever, erratic and full of vitality." He was a good enough pianist to attract a crowd in the common room, which must have annoyed Oscar, who lacked musical talent and never appreciated music, even during his Aesthetic period. If it served his purpose, he echoed Walter Pater's dictum that music is the artistic ideal to which all the other arts should aspire, but like Tolstoy he thought music a dangerous force that irritates rather than elevates the soul. In "The Critic as Artist," Wilde observed that music can create in the listener the illusion of "terrible experiences," of "fearful joys, or wild romantic loves," even if the person has led "a perfectly commonplace life." To Dorian, "music was not articulate. It was not a new world, but rather another chaos." But words were different. Lord Henry's musical words awaken erotic feelings in him because they evade explicit meaning.

Portora gave its students a heavy dose of the cheerless Protestantism of the Church of Ireland, which Oscar could have done without. There were morning and evening prayer assemblies, and daily scripture classes until the fifth form. On Sunday mornings the students paraded to St. McCartan's Cathedral in Enniskillen, where Oscar meditated on the stained-glass windows; in the evening they attended services at the parish church. During frosty winter days, students huddled around a stove in the school's flagstone entrance, known as Stone Hall, where Oscar imitated the medieval poses seen in the cathedral windows.

Ignorant of this schoolboy lark, W. S. Gilbert wrote the following lines for the posing aesthete Bunthorne, when he satirized Wilde and the Aesthetic movement in *Patience* in 1881:

> *I am not fond of uttering platitudes*
> *In stained-glass attitudes.*
> *In short, my mediaevalism's affectation,*
> *Born of a morbid love of admiration!*

Oscar excelled in discussions about God, politics, and literature, late-night rites at any school, which separated the dolts from the knowing. "In examinations the foolish ask questions that the wise cannot answer" was one of Wilde's phrases for the young. He had one feat that never failed to astonish. With his back to the stove in Stone Hall, he faced his classmates with a sizable book in his left hand and skimmed two facing pages at a time, flipping through in a blink. Afterward he recited an accurate synopsis of the material, for, like his father, he had an encyclopedic mind and a photographic memory.

The boys were at Portora when the Mary Travers libel trial against Lady Wilde began on December 12 and continued for five days. Newspaper headlines chronicled Sir William's relationship with the young woman who had taken them for walks around Dublin, and they returned for their Christmas holidays to a chaotic Merrion Square, then came back to snickering classmates when classes began in the new term. One day a group was discussing a recent heresy trial in England, involving a vicar who insisted that Christ was physically present in Holy Communion, another instance of the Anglicans wanting to adopt Roman Catholic beliefs. Oscar found the lawsuit fascinating and said he would like nothing better than "to go down to posterity as the defendant in such a case as 'Regina versus Wilde.' " He should have wished for something else—getting what one wants is life's greatest tragedy.

HOMOSEXUALITY WAS AN accepted part of life at English public schools, as would be seen when explicit coming-of-age novels were published in the twentieth century. From the beginning, these schools were pivotal in the development of a homosexual identity. But Portora's reputation differed from that of Eton and Harrow, Rugby or Winchester. Samuel Beckett's recent biographer portrays the Portora of the 1920s, when Beckett was a student, as a place where homosexuality did not seem to have been a part of life, although "sentimental friendships between older and younger boys, in which there was a greater or lesser element of chivalrous romanticism, were not uncommon and seem not to have been discouraged, either by officialdom or by public opinion."

The platonic relationship that Wilde believed to be the spiritual ideal between men was a comfortable part of student life. About intimate attachments at Portora, Wilde later told Lord Alfred Douglas, the significant love of his life, "There was nothing more than sentimental friendships." Wilde's adult behavior, Douglas said, could be described as "the usual public schoolboy business." Sentimental or spoony friendships started with looks, furtive glances at choristers and cricketers, or a walk along cloistered paths with an arm over another boy's shoulder.

The gaze as the shock of silent recognition dominates *Dorian Gray*. "When our eyes met," Basil Hallward says of Dorian, "I felt that I was growing pale. A curious sensation of terror came over me. I knew that I had come face to face with someone whose mere personality was so fascinating that, if I allowed it to do so, it would absorb my whole nature, my whole soul, my very art itself." Dorian becomes aware of his beauty only when he stares at his portrait, making him an eroticized subject to be worshiped at a distance.

A young boy might easily become seduced into being a connoisseur of male bodies if he read classics. Intense scrutiny of textbook pictures brought statues to life, for Greece glorified the nude male form over the female and idealized the intimate relationship between males as more spiritual than marriage. The bible of classicism at Portora was the *History of Ancient Art,* published in 1764 by the first of the modern Hellenists, Johann Joachim Winckelmann (1717–68), who never visited Greece and never saw the statues he so sensitively described. Oscar saw his first classical art at the age of ten, when the National Gallery of Ireland opened to the public. Located diagonally across from his home, it made a perfect Sunday outing for the family. In the sculpture gallery, casts of Greek and Roman originals were displayed between marble Corinthian columns.

PORTORA WAS VERITABLY monastic compared with Harrow, where John Addington Symonds was a student in the mid-1850s. Author of *Studies of the Greek Poets* and a leading theorist in the development of English homosexuality, Symonds recalled in his memoirs how "the talk in the dormitories and the studies was incredibly obscene. Here and there one could not avoid seeing acts of onanism, mutual masturbation, the sports of naked boys in bed together. There was no refinement, no sentiment, no passion; nothing but animal lust in these occurrences. They filled me with disgust and loathing."

In the *Phaedrus* and *Symposium,*★ Symonds discovered that "the voice of my own soul spoke to me through Plato, as though in some antenatal experience I had lived the life of philosophical Greek lover." Lytton Strachey said he read the *Symposium* at sixteen "with a rush of mingled pleasure and pain," as well as "surprise, relief, and fear to know that what I feel now was felt 2,000 years ago in glorious Greece." Convinced that

---

★Plato's most extended discussion of love between men is found in the *Symposium,* particularly the speech by Pausanias on the varieties of *eros,* and by Aristophanes on the origin of love. It is an anthology of views on love, offering no answers, existing to stimulate dialogue.

the study of Plato was injurious to some young men, Symonds wrote to Benjamin Jowett, whose English translations had sanitized Greek love. "Greek love for modern students of Plato is no 'figure of speech' and no anachronism," he said, "but a present poignant reality. . . . It is indeed impossible to exaggerate the anomaly of making Plato a textbook for students, and a household book for readers, in a nation which repudiates Greek love." But the master of Balliol had no intention of joining any anti-Plato campaign.★

Reading Plato stirred Oscar to esteem same-sex passion, but he was far more interested in ancient Greek as a spoken language and was infatuated with its musical cadences. Portora's headmaster changed his opinion of the brothers when Oscar in his third year finished fourth and Willie only thirteenth in classics. There were few with Oscar's brilliance for euphonious oral translations from Thucydides, Plato, and Euripides. His spontaneous empathy with Greek consistently demonstrated the inferiority of literal translation. One memorable example was using "the unvintageable sea" to translate Homer's phrase "the sea from which one gathers no grapes."

STUDENTS ARRIVED AT Portora with wicker laundry hampers that were sent home and returned full of clean clothes folded over biscuits, cakes, candy, or anything sweet or sausagelike to enliven the monotony of tasteless food. One's popularity at school could hinge on how generous parents were in sending food and how willingly it was shared. Oscar's earliest surviving letter, written in 1868, when he was thirteen, acknowledges the hamper:

> Darling Mama, The hamper came today, and I never got such a jolly surprise, many thanks for it, it was more than kind of you to think of it. Don't forget to send me the *National Review*. . . . The flannel shirts you sent in the hamper are both Willie's, mine are

---

★Symonds lamented the "inadequacy of language to represent states of thought." In *A Problem in Greek Ethics,* he wrote that all the languages of Europe "supply no term for this persistent feature of human psychology, without importing some implication of disgust, disgrace, vituperation." Plato as well found no exact word to fit his distinctions between "friendship, desire and mixed species."

one quite scarlet and the other lilac but it is too hot to wear them yet. You never told me anything about the publisher in Glasgow, what does he say? And have you written to Aunt Warren on the green note paper?

Said to accompany the letter was a sketch of Willie and Oscar with the caption "ye delight of ye boys at ye hamper and ye sorrow of ye hamperless boy." Oscar does not identify the "jolly surprise," although it was certainly food. The *National Review* contained his mother's new poem of rebellion, "To Ireland." Aunt Warren, Lady Wilde's sister, did not share her politics; writing her on green notepaper was a family joke. Was Lady Wilde responsible for color-coding her sons? Or did Oscar select the scarlet and lilac material that was sewn into nightshirts? And what were Willie's colors? Gray and beige?

Back at Merrion Square, Lady Wilde watched nine-year-old Isola grow up, read her sons' letters, and wrote as much as possible. She had recently published a second volume of poetry translations and had a new confidante, the Swedish writer Lotten von Kraemer, whom she met shortly after Isola's birth when von Kraemer visited Ireland during a state trip with her father, the governor of Uppsala.

There are no surviving photographs of Isola; as a presence she is more shadow than substance. She was alone in the nursery now that her brothers were away at school, perhaps sitting on the window seat overlooking the park. At a younger age, she may have worn the same velvet and lace dress in which Oscar was photographed. She is mentioned once in her mother's letters. When her daughter was a year old, Lady Wilde wrote von Kraemer "that little Isola is rapidly taking her place as pet of the house."

In the winter of 1867, Isola developed one of the swift nineteenth-century fevers. She was recuperating in the country with Sir William's sister, wife of the rector at Edgeworthstown, when she had a relapse and died on February 23. Sir William said the tragedy made him "a mourner for life." Lady Wilde's loss of her "radiant angel" was no less tragic. She wrote her Swedish friend that they "never dreamed that the word *death* was meant for her. Yet I had an unaccountable sadness over me all last winter, a foreboding of evil."

Although grief stricken, Sir William finished his book on Lough

Corrib, one of his favorite projects. "Daily work must be done," his wife wrote to Sweden, "and the world will not stop in its career even tho' a fair child's grave lies in its path." More resilient than realistic, Lady Wilde hoped that by writing the same platitudes frequently enough she might come to believe her own words.

Willie's reaction to his sister's death was not recorded, but Oscar was devastated. The physician who cared for Isola recalled the twelve-year-old as "an affectionate, gentle, retiring, dreamy boy" whose "lonely and inconsolable grief" sought vent "in long and frequent visits to his sister's grave in the village cemetery." Wilde always kept a lock of her hair with him and later wrote of his loss in "Requiescat":

> Tread lightly, she is near
> Under the snow,
> Speak gently, she can hear
> The daisies grow.

> All her bright golden hair
> Tarnished with rust,
> She that was young and fair
> Fallen to dust.

> Lily-like, white as snow,
> She hardly knew
> She was a woman, so
> Sweetly she grew. . . .

Experiencing death for the first time changed him; he felt more grown-up, more poetic because he had endured loss. In other poems, such as "Panthea" and "Charmides," he continued to explore this theme of unfulfilled womanhood and the sadness of death before maturity. In "Charmides," a dryad makes love to a dead man, while in the parable "The Fisherman and His Soul," it is the reverse: a young man makes love to a dead mermaid. After writing a letter to Sibyl, Dorian learns of her suicide and wonders: "Strange, that my first passionate love-letter should have been addressed to a dead girl. Can they feel, I wonder, those white silent people we call dead?" Morbidity often obsesses sensitive children on the threshold of adolescence, and it is hard to evaluate Oscar's feelings, but, like most siblings in this situation, he probably felt guilty that he was alive, even responsible for his sister's death, and confused about whether he could have saved her.

His reflection in *The Ballad of Reading Gaol* that "each man kills the thing he loves" casts a shadow over many facets of his life. If his sister could die suddenly, so could his mother or father. Throughout his life, Wilde feared abandonment. In his plays, he repeatedly returns to the theme of a mother not loving a child or of losing a child with disastrous consequences and in *Dorian Gray* darkly exploits death as the punishment for sexuality.

Isola's death made Lady Wilde a recluse, and she mourned her daughter for three years. She wrote to her Swedish friend that she would never again appear in public, not even at Dublin Castle. She told her Scottish friend that writing was her only pleasure because at her desk "the world does not meet one with cold unfeeling eyes." Nothing seemed real to her except "a dull resignation to the prospect of coming death." She was forty-six.

When eighteen-year-old Willie entered Trinity College in 1870, he took up residence in his old room, clearing away the cobwebs and his mother's moroseness. Dining with Willie—always entertaining after a few drinks—made her realize how isolation had drained her of wit and spontaneity. She decided to return to society as hostess of a weekly salon, going in one leap from depression to excess—a durable family trait. Her invitations read: "At Home, Saturday, 4 P.M. to 7 P.M." The wording was the accepted form, except she had added the word *Conversazione*.

An atmosphere of personal anarchy mixing with unorthodox guests made her salon different from that of any other Dublin matron. Within weeks, she was hailed as the Madame Récamier of Merrion Square.* Guests wandered through rooms lit by lamps and candles in homage to

---

*In 1876 such was the Wildes' reputation that they were mentioned in a Dublin guidebook: "The corner house, No. 1 Merrion Square, north, is the residence of the eminent antiquarian, Sir William Wilde, and his gifted wife, the well known Irish poetess 'Speranza.' "

the salons of Maturin; windows were shuttered and closely curtained even on sunny afternoons. No one came to eat or drink; it was too crowded for that. Coffee, wine, and biscuits were served in the foyer. The attraction was watching Lady Wilde stir up irreverent conversation.

One guest recalled that Merrion Square "was a rallying place for all who were eminent in science, art, or literature. Dr. Shaw, the versatile sarcastic Fellow of Trinity and a brilliant writer, was frequently seen. H. J. Fitzpatrick, the well-known biographer, seldom failed to show his melancholy aristocratic face. Dr. Tisdall gave some of his delightful and mirth-inspiring recitations." Lady Wilde introduced each guest many times over, gushing about their recent accomplishments. It was what she called a talent for affinities, for putting people together, although with Lady Wilde it was often a collision.

In the original version of *Dorian Gray,* which appeared in *Lippincott's Monthly Magazine,* Wilde portrays his mother as Lady Brandon, who "treats her guests exactly as an auctioneer treats his goods." In one scene she introduces a man, in a loud tragic whisper, with the words: "Sir Humpty Dumpty—you know—Afghan frontier—Russian intrigue: very successful man—wife killed by an elephant—quite inconsolable—wants to marry a beautiful American widow—everybody does nowadays—hates Mr. Gladstone—but very much interested in beetles: ask him what he thinks of Schouvaloff." Oscar toned down this satire when the novel came out in book form in 1891.

Sir William played his role as brilliant husband and engaging host, but when it became too crowded and noisy, he retreated downstairs to his study to hold court surrounded by medical colleagues. At such times husband and wife communicated by note. Listening to his stories of Egypt was a Trinity student named Bram Stoker, who would write the classic vampire tale, *Dracula.* The plot of Stoker's 1903 novel, *The Jewel of Seven Stars,* was suggested by Sir William's discovery of the mummified dwarf outside a tomb.

Lady Wilde's outrageous comments circulated from hostess to hostess, growing more ridiculous with each retelling. When Stoker introduced her to a young woman whom he described as "half English and half Irish," she replied: "Glad to meet you, my dear. Your English half is as welcome as your Irish bottom." Someone asked how she managed to gather such interesting people and she snapped: "By interesting them. It's quite simple.

All one has to do is to get all sorts of people—but no dull specimens—and take care to mix them. Don't trouble about their morals. It doesn't matter if they haven't any."

Once a visitor asked permission to invite a famous London newspaper correspondent. Lady Wilde replied: "By all means. But a correspondent would be a bigger draw. See if you can't get one." She greeted the daughter of a third-rate novelist with: "Welcome, my dear. You resemble your intellectual father, but you do not have his noble brow. Still, I see from the form of your eyelids that you have marked artistic qualities. . . . I hear you have a lover. This is a pity, since love puts an end to ambition. But don't on any account bind yourself until you have seen more of men."

Lady Wilde's costumes were endlessly amusing. "Round what had once been her waist, an Oriental scarf, embroidered with gold, was twisted," one guest noted. "Her long, massive handsome face was plastered with white powder; and over her blue-black glossy hair was a crown of laurels. On her broad chest were fastened a series of large brooches, evidently family portraits, which came down almost as low as the gastronomical region, and gave her the appearance of a perambulating family mausoleum." The towering, overweight hostess created a spectacle, but that was the intention. Comtesse Anna de Brémont, an American who knew Wilde and his mother for many years, saw "faded splendour," which "was more striking than the most fashionable attire, for she wore that ancient finery with a grace and dignity that robbed it of its grotesqueness."

"All women become like their mothers. That is their tragedy. No man does. That is his." Wilde grew up to contradict this paradox from *Earnest:* he not only became like his mother but surpassed her in his talent—and genius—for soliciting public attention.

CHAPTER FOUR

Budding Aesthete

❧

*There are moments when one has to choose between
living one's own life, fully, entirely, completely—or dragging out some
false, shallow, degrading existence that the world
in its hypocrisy demands.*

—*LADY WINDERMERE'S FAN*

O scar Fingal O'Flahertie Wills Wilde entered Trinity College on
October 10, 1871, six days shy of being seventeen, emotionally
and sexually immature but intellectually precocious. He signed
the rule book as simply Oscar Wilde. At Portora he had won the Carpenter
Prize for Greek Testament and received one of three Royal School
scholarships to Trinity. When he walked through the arched gateway of
the university of Swift, Congreve, Goldsmith, and Farquhar, and entered
the cobbled square with its great oak, under which Walt Whitman's "Calamus" poems had recently been shared by Bram Stoker and the Whitmanites, he felt trapped. It was all too familiar.

Most public school boys leave the best years of their lives behind
when they enter university; not so with Wilde. He had only come home
and like many other Dubliners lived under the parental roof for his first
year, then took rooms in a building called Botany Bay in the second quadrangle, for a time sharing them with his brother. As to a future career, he
gave it little consideration; he did what he found pleasurable if he awak-

ened in the morning or the afternoon. To excel in classics and win Trinity's awards was not an obstacle, although some late-night studying would be required. At this time, Wilde needed inspiration outside of academic achievement; he was searching for a spiritual awakening: a passionate idea, belief, or someone to stir his soul.

He looked around Trinity's baronial Long Room Library and saw familiar faces—Louis Purser and Edward Sullivan from Portora, and Edward Carson, with whom he had built sand castles as a child, destined to be the chief prosecutor at his trial. Disappointed if a don failed to challenge him, Wilde cut lectures, including those of Edward Dowden, the first professor of English literature. An outspoken advocate of Whitman's poetry, Dowden was competing with the entrenched classicists to secure prominence for English and American literature in Trinity's curriculum. Wilde, whose cavalier attitude won him no friends at the college, perhaps alienated Dowden, who refused to sign a petition for his release from prison.

Willie had been at Trinity for two years before Oscar arrived and, in his own way, had distinguished himself. He won a gold medal in ethics and was an officer of the Philosophical Society, where he gave papers with titles such as "Painting and National Morality." When his father was guest chairman, he delivered a defense of prostitution. He was also prominent in the Historical Society, the parliamentary debating society, founded by the statesman Edmund Burke in 1770. Oscar joined these two prestigious student organizations; in fact, Bram Stoker seconded him for the Phil, but he was known only by his absence.

Physically Willie also had changed. He grew a full beard to distinguish himself from the perpetually clean-shaven Oscar. It was said that Willie's talk was as memorable as that of his younger brother, but it "did not astonish as much as it charmed." Their rivalry was more distant now, except when they took up dueling pens in *Kottabos,* the college magazine.* This publication solicited a miscellany of Greek and Latin verse, translations, and original poetry of a playful or humorous nature. Both

---

Kottabos was started in 1869 by Robert Yelverton Tyrrell, professor of Latin, a rival eminence to John Pentland Mahaffy, professor of ancient history, considered one of the greatest classical scholars of his time. Mentioned by Aristophanes, *kottabos* was the name of a drinking game played by young men in ancient Greece, which consisted of throwing a portion of wine into a vessel in a special manner.

Wildes were poets in training, so their verse was derivative, or, as Oscar might have put it: Willie borrowed but he stole. Willie is remembered for a slight poem entitled "Salome," published in 1878. Oscar used the biblical story in 1892 for a controversial play of the same name, which Richard Strauss turned into an acclaimed opera.

A MONTH AFTER classes began, their illegitimate half sisters, Emily and Mary, died. They were twenty-four and twenty-two, accepted as the children of the Reverend Ralph Wilde, Sir William's eldest brother. They had attended the local balls in County Monaghan, where they lived, and at one Emily danced too close to the fire. Her dress burst into flames, and Mary was severely burned trying to save her. Both died within moments. In only four years, Sir William had lost three daughters, and he withdrew more and more by himself to Moytura.★

Wilde's preoccupation with death and destiny deepened. Late-night reading followed by late-afternoon sleeping was his remedy. He took solace in Swinburne and Keats, returned to the poetry of Whitman, which his father had recited, and enjoyed Edmund Burke's *A Philosophical Inquiry into the Origin of Our Ideas on the Sublime and Beautiful,* the required text for his aesthetics course. But the literature and style he preferred came from Baudelaire, Pater, and Mallarmé, sometimes Ruskin, but not Newman or Arnold. In Keats, who valued the imagination over the intellect, Wilde found an ally for his aesthetics of intensity and artifice. Visiting Keats's grave in 1877, he wrote a poem comparing the poet—dead of tuberculosis at twenty-five—with the martyred Saint Sebastian.

He felt a kinship with the Pre-Raphaelite Brotherhood, the most avant-garde artistic and literary movement of its time, founded in 1848 by seven artists and writers, including Dante Gabriel Rossetti, John Everett Millais, and William Holman Hunt. Wilde admired Rossetti's Decadent portraits of statuesque models clad in flowing gowns with somnambulistic expressions bordering on sexual ecstasy, as seen in *Beata Beatrix* and

★The girls were buried in Drumsnatt. The headstone bears a quotation from the Book of Samuel: "They were lovely and pleasant in their lives and in their death they were not divided." Every year for twenty years an anonymous veiled woman in black visited the grave.

Astarte Syriaca. Aesthetics and its significance occupied his thoughts. The word was coined in 1750 by the philosopher Alexander Baumgarten, but the concept goes back to Plato. Wilde was unsure about his personal aestheticism. Did it mean risk taking? Triviality? Exquisiteness? Solipsism? He adopted the idea of art for art's sake, meaning that art should be concerned only with itself. Although he made the axiom a rallying call, he did not originate the phrase, which was first used in 1804. On occasion he gave credit to the French writer Théophile Gautier, who popularized the doctrine.

In advocating that art exists for its beauty alone, Wilde rejected Ruskin's view that art should be informed by a moral purpose. When he came to America to lecture on the English Renaissance, he urged audiences to "love art for its own sake, and then all things that you need will be added to you." He observed: "We spend our days, each of us, in looking for the secret of life. Well, the secret of life is in art." If only a few attempted to experience art differently—and only for selfish reasons: who would not want to find the secret of life?—then Wilde had made his point. An important authority on his aesthetic theories was Walter Pater, whose *Studies in the History of the Renaissance*—"that book which has had such strange influence over my life"—was published in 1873. In the famously notorious conclusion, Pater advocates a life of passionate moments, of success through ecstasy:

> Not the fruit of experience, but experience itself, is the end. A counted number of pulses only is given to us of a variegated, dramatic life. How may we see in them all that is to be seen in them by the finest senses? How shall we pass most swiftly from point to point, and be present always at the focus where the greatest number of vital forces unite in their purest energy? To burn always with this hard, gem-like flame, to maintain this ecstasy is success in life.

Wilde had an affinity for epigrams, aphorisms, and paradoxes—never inferior anecdotes—as the centerpieces of conversation. Merrion Square's Saturday salons provided a stage and a captive audience for his mezzo-voiced dictums. Arrogantly, he started to transform himself into an objet d'art, eventually becoming a narcissistic artist who lived by his own laws. "Life imitates art far more than Art imitates life," he said. Even when Wilde babbled nonsense, he commanded attention. Lady Wilde admired her son's emerging personality and told George Moore's father that Willie had a first-class brain but Oscar would turn out to be "something wonderful."

His hair was long and parted in the middle. He kept an unfinished landscape—probably a view from Moytura—on an easel in his college room at Number 18 Botany Bay and told visitors he "just put in a butterfly," an allusion to Whistler's signature. Later Wilde recast the phrase to describe his writing day: "In the morning, after hard work, I took a comma out of one sentence. . . . In the afternoon, I put it back again."

Undergraduate life bored him; he complained that his classmates' "highest idea of humour was an obscene story." The "coarse *amours* among barmaids and women of the streets" disgusted him; he avoided pubs, the pulse of student life, and seldom entertained in his rooms. He was frequently at Merrion Square because Willie was away in London studying law at the Middle Temple. In fact, there were few surprises at Trinity for someone who had grown up just outside its gates and met professors at his parents' gatherings. "Come home with me," he is said to have said to a college friend. "My mother and I have formed a society for the suppression of virtue." Nothing so radical was going on at Merrion Square. Whatever erotic fantasies aroused Wilde, they were of an idealized or solipsistic nature.

DURING HIS THREE years at Trinity, Wilde's critical relationship was with his tutor John Pentland Mahaffy, who was fifteen years older, a ratio Wilde preferred when selecting young male companions. Mahaffy had entered Trinity at sixteen and remained there until 1914, when he was made provost at the age of seventy-five. No public school traditions clung to him. He had been educated abroad by tutors, lived in Greece, was a marksman and captain of the Trinity cricket eleven. A dedicated social climber, Mahaffy was the perfect mentor for a snob in training. Although married he lived a bachelor's life, but he had no interest in same-sex relationships despite being the first classicist to publish details on Greek love.

Intellectually, tutor and student were well-matched, and a still-growing Wilde soon stood eye to eye with the six-foot-three Mahaffy. It was Mahaffy who propelled Wilde from Dublin to Oxford and then on to London, who dragooned him to Greece and converted him to Hellenism, postponing his fascination with Roman Catholicism. Wilde called Mahaffy his "first and best teacher . . . the scholar who showed me how to love Greek things." Mahaffy authenticated Wilde's abilities when he needed approval, but it was an edgy relationship, and the two turned on each other when Wilde as a literary critic felt intellectually superior and Mahaffy as a moralist took Wilde's disgrace as a personal affront.

Mahaffy's brilliance as a classicist was surpassed only by his gifts as a conversationalist. "There can be no doubt," he wrote in *The Principles of the Art of Conversation,* "that of all the accomplishments prized in modern society that of being agreeable in conversation is the very first." Wilde never disagreed on this point. "Until you heard Mahaffy talk," one contemporary said, "you hadn't realized how language could be used to charm and hypnotize." Mahaffy was surely a model for Lord Henry, who mesmerizes Dorian Gray with his musical voice.

When Mahaffy published *Principles* in 1887, many of his rules sounded like Wilde talking: avoid pedantry, know nothing accurately, conversation is not contradiction. "One should absorb the colour of life," Lord Henry advises, "but one should never remember its details. Details are always vulgar." To Arthur Conan Doyle, Wilde said, "Between me and life there is a mist of words always. I throw probability out of the window for the sake of a phrase and the chance of an epigram makes me desert truth." Credited to Mahaffy are statements like "poets are born, not paid," and "it is the spectator and not life that art mirrors," which lacked Wilde's talent for paradox and did not turn reality on end.

Wilde believed there was no morality or immorality in lying. When he reviewed Mahaffy's book for the *Pall Mall Gazette,* he praised the principle that a liar makes a better conversationalist than "the scrupulously truthful man, who weighs every statement, questions every fact, and corrects every inaccuracy." The truth of lies was integral to Wilde's philosophy of individualism, which he later wrote about in "The Decay of Lying," where he proclaims that the "telling of beautiful untrue things is the proper aim of Art." His wit developed as a defense against his own fears and what he—rightly or wrongly—perceived as the negative opinions of others. When he said that all people are good until they learn to talk, he implied that to talk is to lie. Onstage Wilde's characters tell lies and exchange bored trivialities, revealing the beginnings of the modernist distrust of language.

Such distrust was intrinsic to the Irish literary tradition. *The Importance of Being Earnest* and later John Millington Synge's *Playboy of the Western World* are about the grand art of lying. One exposes a society that requires lying to function, and the other demonstrates how the power of a lie makes the man. The English were always "degrading the truth into facts," and the Americans, Wilde said, referring to the myth of George Washington cutting down the cherry tree, have as a "national hero a man who, according to his own confession, was incapable of telling a lie." Wilde frequently lied about himself. To advance his mythmaking, he encouraged his friends to lie also. As a result his life became a tangle of beautiful lies: it was exactly what he wanted—to be a mystery in plain sight.

AS A DISCIPLE, Wilde proofread Mahaffy's *Social Life in Greece from Homer to Menander* and probably had more influence on the content than ever will be known. In the 1874 first edition, Mahaffy describes same-sex love as "that strange and to us revolting perversion, which reached its climax in later times, and actually centered upon beautiful boys all the romantic affections which we naturally feel between opposite sexes, and opposite sexes alone." Such a description made clear what Plato's *Symposium,* even in the ancient Greek, had not and what Benjamin Jowett had veiled in his translation of 1871.

Mahaffy argued that same-sex love existed in early Greek society because men were more cultured than women, and as a consequence men could not find intellectual fulfillment in relationships with unsophisticated women. "We have as yet no Asphasia to advocate the higher education of women," he wrote. "We have in many cities a tendency to seclude women, and prevent them from being companions to their lovers. Thus their natural place was invaded by those fair and stately youths, with their virgin looks, and maiden modesty, who fired Solon and Theognis, and Socrates and Epaminondas—in fact, almost every great Greek in their greatest days."

His reasoning was an excuse more than an explanation, and Mahaffy shied away from discussing homosexuality in terms of desire and need. He wanted not to incite but to correct an oversight and was surprised when so much negative reaction followed his publication. Out of cowardice and political exigency, he capitulated and dropped the unspeakable from the second edition, but he should have stood his ground. The acknowledgment to Wilde for "having made improvements and corrections all through the book" disappeared as well.

As Wilde discovered when he electrified the Old Bailey with his powerful definition of the "love that dare not speak its name," the sentimental side to Greek love was often misunderstood. Such a love, he said then, was the basis of Plato's philosophy. "It is beautiful, it is fine, it is the noblest form of affection. There is nothing unnatural about it. It is intellectual, and it repeatedly exists between an elder and younger man, where the elder has intellect and the younger man has all the joy, hope, and glamour of life before him. That it should be so, the world does not understand. The world mocks at it and sometimes puts one in the pillory for it." Despite his affinity for sentimental Greek love, and even though he may have experienced some schoolboy groping, Wilde was not yet committed to same-sex passion. He planned to marry and was enough of an Aesthete to want purity for himself as well as his wife.

CHRIST WAS WILDE'S ideal: a romantic artist and poet, a sexually ambiguous individualist and Aesthete much like himself. "Christ's place is indeed with the poets," he wrote in *De Profundis.* The Crucifixion, as an image and as subject matter of art, had "fascinated and dominated Art as no Greek god ever succeeded in doing." The nearly nude Christ on the cross, often with an erection of the sinless generative organ, said by art historians to symbolize the Redemption, was for some the homoerotic icon of Catholicism. Anyone interested in Catholicism at this time read John Henry Newman's powerful autobiography, *Apologia pro Vita Sua,* about his conversion in 1845. Newman's life, the journey of one man searching for integrity and meaning, paralleled that of Wilde. Both approached Catholicism with great doubts.★

To Wilde, Catholicism was a paradox: homophobic and homo-erotic; medieval and modern; spiritual and sensual. It excited and exploited desire—then condemned it. Decadents and Uranians rushed into the Church of Rome. In France they included Joris-Karl Huysmans, author of *À rebours* (which Wilde would read on his honeymoon), Barbey d'Aurevilly, author of *Les Diaboliques,* and the poet Paul Verlaine, who underwent a conversion while in prison for shooting his lover, Arthur Rimbaud. In London, before they converted, Wilde met Lionel Johnson, John Gray, Aubrey Beardsley, and Marc-André Raffalovich. Catholicism was fashionable—particularly among homosexuals.† Wilde observed: "It is so easy to convert others. It is so difficult to convert oneself. To arrive at what one really believes, one must speak through lips different from one's own. To know the truth one must imagine myriads of falsehoods."

Wilde struggled with his need for the Church of Rome but always avoided commitment at the critical moment. At times of emotional weakness, the urge was harder to renounce. His interest in changing faiths was no longer a secret at home when he casually mentioned that he met a priest and attended Mass. If he brought up the recent doctrine of papal infallibility at the dinner table, an argument followed. The issue agitated his parents, but it was time for adolescent rebellion and estrangement. Excelling in tautological debate, Wilde easily vanquished his father. Lady Wilde was more reticent, and with good reason.

★An Anglican vicar, Newman (1801–90) was an Oxford scholar and theologian who spent half his life as an Anglican and half as a Roman Catholic. He was the leading Anglican clergyman of his day, founder of the Oxford Movement, a program of renewal for the Church of England, and vicar of St. Mary's Oxford. Following his conversion, he was ordained a priest and died a cardinal. Envious of his influence, one college dean changed the Sunday dinner hour to discourage undergraduate attendance at evensong.

†The term *uranism,* or *Uranismus* in German, originated in the 1860s with a Hanoverian lawyer named Karl Heinrich Ulrichs. He believed that uranism was a congenital abnormality in which a female soul was encased in a male body, which he called an *Urning.* In England, poets who wrote about same-sex passion called themselves Uranians. Names such as *invert, bugger,* or *sodomite* referred to the act, but no name existed for the person, except *Uranian.* The word *homosexual* made its first significant appearance in the English language in the 1892 translation of Krafft-Ebing's *Psychopathia Sexualis.*

TO UNDERSTAND THE role Catholicism played in Wilde's life, it is necessary to go back five years after Isola's birth to a time of friction—judging from his mother's letters to Scotland—in his parents' marriage. As a physician to the poor, Sir William saw mostly Catholic patients at St. Mark's, and he was far from being prejudiced, but his two brothers were Church of Ireland ministers; he attended Sunday services and felt comfortable with his inherited religion. Caught up by the vogue in Catholicism and influenced by recent converts, the more contrary Lady Wilde talked about going over herself. Instead she had her sons privately baptized.

The Reverend L. C. Prideaux Fox, chaplain of the Glencree Reformatory, located near a farmhouse the Wildes rented in Wicklow in 1862, when Oscar was eight, performed the baptisms; being private they were never registered. (Oscar's baptism into the Church of Ireland at St. Mark's Church, Pearse Street, Dublin, was registered on April 26, 1855.) That was the story Father Fox published in 1905, when he was eighty-five. Following the ceremony, he said Lady Wilde asked him to inform her husband. When he did, Sir William replied, "I don't care what the boys are so long as they become as good as their mother." A gentlemanly reaction but not the truth, as Oscar later discovered when his father steadfastly blocked his conversion, even controlling his choice beyond the grave.

There remains a touch of myth about this story. But why would a priest fabricate details at such a late date? Was Lady Wilde indulging one of her whims? Or did she hatch a scheme to irritate her husband? The latter seems plausible, given the scenario of Father Fox being the messenger of bad news. Oscar was said to have a vague recollection of this second baptism, enough perhaps to make a point of it in *Earnest*.

WILDE HAD LITTLE difficulty excelling at Trinity. He won the Berkeley Gold Medal for Greek,★ the highest award for classics given that year, for

---

★This medal became Wilde's collateral, and he would pawn it on numerous occasions. A pawn ticket was found among his possessions after his death, but the medal was never retrieved and its whereabouts are unknown.

a competitive exam on the Greek comic poets. His uncle Ralph had won the same medal a century earlier. He had two firsts: a composition prize for Greek verse and a Foundation Scholarship in classics. Lady Wilde sat down and invited the Merrion Square crowd "to cheer dear old Oscar on." He needed motivation to endure one more year when he wished to be elsewhere. Sensing his disquiet, Mahaffy is said to have mockingly urged: "Run over to Oxford, my dear Oscar: you are not clever enough for us in Dublin." He was more than ready to leave home, but he could not go without a scholarship and handily won one of two demyships in classics at Magdalen College, which paid ninety-five pounds annually for five years.

The euphoria that follows a child's intellectual achievement wafted through Merrion Square for months. Lady Wilde bragged how her genius Oscar would excel at Oxford as he had at Trinity. In her dreams, Willie was ready to launch a brilliant parliamentary career. Happily waving to Oscar as he departed on the Kingstown packet boat, Sir William was naively confident that all thoughts of Catholicism were left behind. But Oxford was a hazardous destination for anyone warned against Catholicism. There was Newman's influence as well as that of other persuasive converts, such as Henry Edward Manning and Gerard Manley Hopkins.

Wilde never looked back; it did not occur to him that this was his leave-taking from Ireland, although such a realization would not have disturbed him. Joyce made a myth out of his departure. Beckett made exile a necessity for his work. Wilde had an expatriate's life thrust on him, and he rushed toward it.

The "two great turning-points" of his life, he later said, occurred when his father sent him to Oxford and when society sent him to prison. It was a tidy way to package his survival as an outsider. Oxford was where he wrote the script for Oscar Wilde posing as an Englishman, where he became a stereotype inside a real person. Once in prison he discarded the masks and realized how he had become "the spendthrift" of his own genius, only to find himself trapped inside another stereotype with a new name: homosexual.

WHEN WILDE ENTERED Magdalen College in 1874, the day after his twentieth birthday, he was no longer the youngest boy but a youth. "We never get back our youth," he said, that "pulse of joy that beats in us at twenty." By the time he completed his education, he admitted, "It is a sad thing to think of, but there is no doubt that Genius lasts longer than Beauty. That accounts for the fact that we all take such pains to over-educate ourselves." Strikingly tall but still socially awkward, Wilde had a nervous habit of rattling on about undigested theories on art and life. "I was the happiest man in the world when I entered Magdalen for the first time," he said. "Oxford was paradise to me." It was also a larger universe than Trinity.

His pedigree, a "distinguished name" and "high social position," meant less at Oxford than it had at Trinity. In *De Profundis,* Wilde even clutches at the aristocracy by referring to his lover Lord Alfred Douglas as "a young man of my own social rank and position." Wilde tried to inflate his family background, but Sir William's honorary title paled beside the hereditary titles of his classmates; his mother may have ranked "intellectually," as he put it, "with Elizabeth Barrett Browning, and historically with Madame Roland," but her poetic howls for freedom had not crossed the Irish Sea. An Irishman with an English surname born to deflate the English ego—that was his legacy. He signed the blue form required of all entering students as Oscar O'Fflahertie Wilde (with the affectation of the double-*f* Norman spelling) and became known for a while as Oscar O. Wilde.

The first months were awkward, as they would be for any student transferring from Trinity. He had to prove himself all over again. Wilde was a person whose authority depended on the adoption of a manner or a mask; sometimes multiple personae were needed. The actor in him composed the drama day by day, and before he even realized it, he had invented a new Oscar. The secret was insincerity. "Is insincerity such a terrible thing?" Dorian asks. "I think not. It is merely a method by which we can multiply our personalities." In the twenty-six years ahead, Wilde reinvented himself many times. Influenced by Pater, inspired by imagination and driven by braggadocio, he selected an aesthetic nature for Oxford.

CHAPTER FIVE

Magdalen Manners

✺

I remember bright young faces, and grey misty quadrangles,
Greek forms passing through Gothic cloisters, life playing
among ruins, and, what I love best in the world,
Poetry and Paradox dancing together!

—OSCAR WILDE TO HENRY MARILLIER

In Wilde's Oxford rooms, Catholicism eclipsed Hellenism: there were pictures of Pope Pius IX, Manning and Newman, a bust of the Madonna, and a photograph of Burne-Jones's *Christ and Magdalene*. Two Sèvres vases, the inspiration for his comment "I find it harder and harder every day to live up to my blue china," overflowed with lilies. From the pulpit of St. Mary's, the vicar warned his congregation: "These are the days, dear friends, when a young man says not in polished banter, but in sober earnest, that he finds it difficult to live up to his blue china, then there has crept into these cloistered shades a form of heathenism which it is our bounden duty to fight against." The blue-china mot was launched and immortality assured when George Du Maurier used the sentiment underneath a *Punch* cartoon of October 30, 1880.★

★The blue-and-white china imported into England in the nineteenth century was known as "Old Nanking" and was usually from the Chinese Kang Hsi period (1662–1722), which refined cobalt blue to a brilliant and pure sapphire with no trace of purple or gray. Whistler started the blue-china mania in 1859 and soon he and Rossetti became rival collectors. Wilde came late to the craze, favoring French porcelain or Japanese imitations.

One of Wilde's first friends, J. E. Courtenay Bodley, was a wealthy Balliol student who remembered Wilde's lisp and Irish lilt. The accent went first, replaced by what Max Beerbohm called "a mezzo voice, uttering itself in leisurely fashion," and what Lillie Langtry found "one of the most alluring voices that I have ever listened to." Bodley introduced Wilde to Queen Victoria's youngest son, Prince Leopold, a student at Christ Church, and facilitated his initiation into the university's Masonic lodge, the Apollo. A scholarship of ninety-five pounds a year did not cover membership fees and the formal dress required to join the Masons, but living beyond his means bothered Wilde less and less, and being in debt became a lifelong addiction.

Lean and lanky, he wore his brown hair shorter than at Trinity; when he looked in the mirror, his wide-open, ardent eyes delighted him; a large mouth and heavy jaw did not. He knew his face was not that of a genius, but a colorful tie or a curly-brimmed hat drew the eye away from irregular features. In the ubiquitous checked suits then in style he looked like any other intense undergraduate. No longer openly scorning athletics, he was seen rowing on the river and loudly cheering at cricket and boxing matches. Over his four years at Oxford, Wilde occupied three different rooms: the most splendid, called Kitchen Stairs, overlooked the river Cherwell; there he scratched his initials (O.F.O'F.W.W.) into the glass window. His close friends all lived near him at Magdalen and were known by their nicknames: Dunskie, Kitten, and Bouncer. He was called "Hosky." Destined for clerical and professional careers, they were likable fellows who posed no threat to Wilde's intellect or sexuality.

David Hunter Blair (Dunskie), the son of a Scottish baronet, praised Wilde's "extra-ordinary conversational abilities." Blair was on the brink of going over to Catholicism and wanted to take Wilde along. Wilde called Richard Reginald Harding (Kitten, after the song "Beg your parding, Mrs. Harding, Is my kitting in your garding?") "my greatest chum." William Welsford Ward (Bouncer), a bellicose anti-Catholic, said Wilde's sociability counted for more than athleticism at Magdalen: "His qualities were not ordinary, and we, his intimate friends, did not judge him by the ordinary standards."

Ward and Wilde were both reading Greats, the student term for Honour School of Literae Humaniores, the most elite school at Oxford; it demanded intensive study of the classics—ancient history, philosophy, and philology—and rigorous skepticism. Wilde described Greats as the only curriculum where one could be simultaneously "brilliant and unreasonable, speculative and well-informed, creative as well as critical, and write with all the passion of youth about the truths which belong to the august serenity of old age."

On Sunday evenings Wilde entertained lavishly, emulating his mother's Irish hospitality. There were no tiny glasses of sherry accompanied by one plate of biscuits, the typical frugal English fare. In *Earnest,* Wilde satirizes the British obsession with tea to the extent that Act One seems to be all about cucumber sandwiches. Blair recalled "brimming bowls of gin-and-whisky punch and long churchwarden pipes, with a brand of choice tobacco." There was always someone at the piano pounding out music. When the crowd drifted off, the foursome lounged around the fire and talked as "boys will," he said, about "everything and other things as well." Wilde dispensed epigrams and poetry—his own and others'.

Flushed with punch and warmed by the coals, they hypothesized about the future. Ward knew he was expected to join the family law firm in Bristol; Harding would have a career with the London Stock Exchange, and Blair startled everyone by becoming a monk. Ward asked Wilde what he wanted to do. "God knows?" he replied. "I won't be a dried-up Oxford don, anyhow. I'll be a poet, a writer, a dramatist. Somehow or other I'll be famous, and if not famous, I'll be notorious." He said he might lead a life of pleasure and then "rest and do nothing." And it all came true just as Wilde predicted. Because he believed in fate and accepted that man cannot control his destiny, Wilde saw existence in brighter colors than most of his friends, and every day had possibilities.

WHEN WILDE RETURNED to Ireland, his letters to Ward and Harding began: "My dear Bouncer," "My dear Kitten," or "My dear boy." Using "boy" or "dear boy" was Wilde's way of maintaining juvenescence. Sometimes he teases Ward with images of same-sex attraction, reporting that a classmate had "been out every night to see a Brasenose man, but I have just found out that *all* the men there have gone down, so I suppose he mistook the Lane for the College." Another time, he admits to reading Catullus while lying in bed "with Swinburne (a copy of)," later gossiping about a student and a choirboy seen together in a private box at the theatre. Wilde reports that the student "is extremely moral and only mentally spoons the boy."

A Romantic, Wilde saw himself as being given great gifts; he disarmed friends and earned enemies by appearing brilliant without effort, for he was seldom seen studying or reading at the library, although he consistently had his name posted in the column for highest honors. Wilde's secret was the power of sustained intellectual concentration; like Samuel Johnson he was an eye reader and had a genius for total recall. Blair compared him with the scholar in *Tom Brown at Oxford,* "who after an evening of dissipation would bind a wet cloth round his throbbing brow, drink buckets of strong black coffee, and read Pindar until the chapel bells began to ring for morning prayer."

OXFORD'S LUMINARIES INCLUDED John Ruskin, then fifty-five, who held the coveted post of Slade Professor of Fine Art. Despite his learning and influence, the forever melancholy Ruskin failed to reconcile life's realities with his artistic philosophy. An irrational desire for very young girls clouded his thinking. Euphemia (Effie) Gray was twelve when he saw her, nineteen when they wed, and twenty-five when she left him for the painter John Millais, the marriage annulled for reasons of "incurable impotency."

After Wilde attended Ruskin's lectures on Florentine art, he longed to visit Italy. To meet the grand old man, he joined his Hinksey Road project of 1875, initiated with volunteer undergraduates to celebrate the dignity of labor. Wilde arose at dawn—a major sacrifice for a night person—and traveled to the village of Ferry Hinksey, where he pushed wheelbarrows filled with paving material. He succeeded in attracting Ruskin's attention, and a friendship ensued. The road, though, was abandoned and disappeared.

Ruskin was greedy for attention, and Wilde could be a consummate flatterer. The relationship continued once Wilde moved to London, abetted by obsequious letters: "There is in you something of prophet, of priest, and of poet, and to you the gods gave eloquence," Wilde wrote, "so that your message might come to us with the fire of passion, and the marvel of music, making the deaf to hear, and the blind to see." But Ruskin saw aesthetics differently from the way Wilde did. He found the term a degrading word that made art an amusement, when it should be form and texture, perspective and angles, medieval and Gothic, and he had muted enthusiasm for the Renaissance, which Pater declared the inspiration and the spiritual mother of Decadence.

Wilde had to wait until his third year to meet Pater. The thirty-eight-year-old reclusive agnostic scholar was the sort of cerebral oddity only a university like Oxford could accommodate. He had studied at Queen's, taken a fellowship at Brasenose, and remained there—his ecstatic moments limited to gazing at frozen marble youths—until his death in 1894 at the age of fifty-four. Pater may not have lived with as much abandon as he wrote, but his *Studies in the History of the Renaissance* was already the bible of a whole generation of English intellectuals. More than Arnold, Tennyson, or Ruskin, Pater became the voice of nascent modernism. Wilde told Yeats that *Studies* was "my golden book; I never travel anywhere without it; but it is the very flower of decadence: the last trumpet should have sounded the moment it was written."

WHEN THE MAGDALEN group finished discussing themselves, their classmates, aesthetics, and Greats, the topic often came around to Catholicism. Wilde told Blair about his father's attitude toward the church when he was at Trinity. "I am sure," he said, "that if I had become a Catholic at that time he would have cast me off altogether, and that he would do the same to-day." Fathers did this sort of thing, as Wilde observes in an early draft of *Earnest:* "Mothers, of course, are all right. They pay a chap's bills and don't bother him. But fathers bother a chap and never pay his bills." In 1875 Blair traveled to Rome and returned a Catholic, which startled Wilde, but he was not ready to give up his two gods: money and ambition. Blair persevered by arranging for a priest to give him instruction, but Wilde was not receptive. He did, though, enjoy the company of priests, seeing them as a third sex: homosexual but chaste in a sublimated way like Cardinal Newman, who was celibate but androgynous and perceived as a dandy.

That summer Wilde planned his first visit to Rome with Mahaffy and a Dublin friend, William Goulding. There was no talk of conversion in this staunchly Protestant group. During the trip, Wilde expressed his religious longings through poetry. These first poems, spiritual but tempered by pagan images, were published in the *Dublin University Magazine;* the *Irish Monthly;* the *Illustrated Monitor,* another Dublin Catholic magazine; and Trinity's *Kottabos.* He toured Florence, Bologna, Venice, and Verona, posting enthusiastic letters to Merrion Square, some with sketches of the antiquities, which he knew would please his father. When he ran out of money, he wrote the aptly titled "Rome Unvisited," lamenting that he did not see "the only God-anointed King, / And hear the silver trumpets ring."

His mother's letters inevitably reported on his brother's lack of ambition. Willie had returned to Merrion Square and had been called to the Irish bar in 1875, but instead of securing briefs, he preferred drinking in the pubs or ice skating at the new rink. He had failed in that most crucial area of life, the intellect, or, as Lady Wilde wrote in *Social Studies:* "The intellect is a delicate-stringed instrument that rusts if not played on, and it is by the collision of mind with mind that we learn our own value." Since her dreams of Willie leading Ireland to independence were not to be, she decided to find him a wealthy wife.

Oscar had minimal interest in Willie's courtships but found his mother's breathless descriptions of his sallies into society useful when he became a playwright: "Willie got introduced to Lady Westmeath, young, Greek head, ivy wreath—he *devoted* himself entirely to her and ignored all his nearest and dearest friends of the Corporation lot [meaning lawyers]. 'Who are all these people?' asked Lady W. 'Really I don't know,' said Willie. 'Never saw them before. . . .' 'Oh, of course,' said Lady W. 'They're not in my lot, but one *must* come to these places sometimes.' 'Quite so,' said Willie, 'let us sit down in a corner and look on.' "

On a more somber note, his mother told Oscar that his father's health was deteriorating. Sir William suffered from a variety of complaints, including asthma, gout, bronchitis, and a weak heart. His condition became critical during the spring of 1876. Oscar was at Oxford studying Greek and Latin for Honour Moderations (Mods) and arrived home just in time to be at his father's bedside before he died on April 19. During the deathwatch Wilde observed a veiled woman, probably the mother of Sir William's recently deceased daughters, sitting silently by his bed. Her presence demonstrated how much Lady Wilde loved her husband, Wilde told his first biographer, Robert Sherard.

NOW TWENTY-ONE, Wilde felt alone, with only fond recollections of the hours spent with his father exploring for antiquities in Cong and Connemara. Returning to Oxford, he apathetically sat for his Mods exam and feigned curiosity about the results. Waiting until *The Times* was out, he casually picked it up at the Mitre and read about his First. His father's death had robbed him, he wrote Kitten, of "any real pleasure" in the honor; he told Bouncer he dreaded returning to Merrion Square, "with everything filled with memories."

When Sir William's estate was settled, it was near bankruptcy. Merrion Square and Moytura House were heavily mortgaged, and there was insufficient income from the other properties to maintain Number One. "I am sorry to say the family affairs grow more dilapidated every day," Lady Wilde wrote Oscar. "Were I young like you I would take a pupil to read with. Youth can earn, age cannot. But I suppose the consolations of religion and philosophy will be sufficient—at least they cost nothing." His mother looked for guidance, but Oscar shifted the responsibility to Willie, who, after all, was the favorite and living at home.

IT WAS THE right psychological moment for a romantic distraction. Wilde was vulnerable and needy of admiration. Other attractive girls had caught his eye, but none so stunning as Florence Anne Lemon Balcombe. The third of five daughters in a family of seven, she lived in Clontarf outside Dublin; her father, Lieutenant-Colonel James Balcombe, had served in the Crimea and named her after Florence Nightingale. Harding was the first to share Wilde's happiness: "I am just going out to bring an *exquisitely pretty girl* to afternoon service in the Cathedral. She is just seventeen with the *most perfectly beautiful face I ever saw and not a sixpence of money.*" Wilde noticed women's faces but seldom described their bodies. Not that he was ill at ease or passive with women, quite the opposite; he was stimulated by their company and like most young people thought that falling in love would transform his life.

Florence had challenging gray-blue eyes and a crown of brown hair that wound around her head like the finest silk. At five feet eight, she was tall for a woman of her time but just the right height for walking down

Grafton Street with the six-foot-three Oxonian. That summer of 1876, Wilde did a charming pencil sketch of her wearing a wistful, ethereal look, and they "walked out" together until he left for his annual fishing holiday in Connemara.

Failing to entice Ward and Harding to join him for poteen, trout, and partridge, he invited another Oxford friend, Frank Miles, son of the rector of Bingham in Nottinghamshire, who wanted to be an artist. Miles was also a keen gardener who introduced Wilde to the *Lilium auratum,* or golden-rayed lily, long before Gilbert and Sullivan's *Patience* linked the flower with the Aesthetes. (The lily was also the Magdalen College emblem.) At Illaunroe they awakened at dawn, pulled on their Wellingtons, and did not return until they had caught or bagged the evening meal. Wilde wrote Bouncer that he was "too much *occupied with rod and gun for the handling of the quill.* I have only got one salmon as yet but had heaps of sea-trout which give great play. I have not had a blank day yet. Grouse are few but I have got a lot of hares so have had a capital time of it."

He dabbed a purplish blue watercolor of the view from Moytura and inscribed it "for Florrie." Miles painted a fresco (still visible) over the arch in the front hall at Illaunroe of two cherubs (resembling artist and host) fishing; it is called *Tight Lines,* an angler's good-luck wish. After a week, Willie joined them. Writing to his latest girlfriend, Margaret Campbell, he referred to Illaunroe as his "*real* Irish home." He would paint a sunset for her, he said, and went on to describe how the mail was delivered ten miles by "a pretty little bare-footed girl—brown & picturesque," whom he also meant to paint. Tactless Willie had a way of making women feel inconsequential.

RETURNING TO OXFORD, Wilde was understandably depressed over his father's death and the financial muddle at home. He had difficulty studying for the annual Ireland Scholarship, a test of classical knowledge, which demanded concentrated preparation. When he failed to apply himself, he was even more despondent. "I look back on weeks and months of extravagance, trivial talk, and utter vacancy of employment," he wrote Ward, "*with feelings so bitter that I have lost faith in myself.*" He did not win the scholarship.

To console himself, he arranged to travel with Mahaffy during the spring vacation of 1877, but only as far as Genoa. Then he would go to Rome. Wilde saw this delayed visit as a turning point in his feelings about the church. "This is an era in my life, a crisis," he wrote Kitten. "I wish I could look into the seeds of time and see what is coming." At Genoa, the wily Mahaffy lured him to Greece by way of Ravenna and Brindisi. Again Rome went unvisited. They saw Olympia and Mycenae, crossed the Peloponnese on horseback, visited Argos and Nauplia, sailed to the island of Aegina, and on to the port of Athens. Mahaffy's gusto over everything Greek—including food and wine—was infectious. Rome, as well as Oxford, was forgotten.

Playing one of his preferred roles, that of ingenuous boy, Wilde informed his Oxford tutor that he would be ten days late for term. "Seeing Greece is really a great education for anyone," he wrote, "and will I think benefit me greatly, and Mr. Mahaffy is such a clever man that it is quite as good as going to lectures to be in his society." The dons were unimpressed. Oxford had produced classical scholars for generations without their seeing the Parthenon or the ancient site of the Olympic games. When ten days stretched to twenty-two and Wilde had not returned, he was rusticated, or sent down for the rest of term, and fined half his scholarship for the year.

"I was sent down from Oxford for being the first undergraduate to visit Olympia," he complained. Secretly delighted, he met Blair and Ward in Rome. Before he could unpack, Blair had him kneeling before Pius IX for a private audience. The Pope encouraged Wilde to follow Blair into the church; afterward the two friends left St. Peter's in silence. When Wilde locked himself in his hotel room to write the sonnet "Urbs Sacra Aeterna," Blair thought it was a sign that his friend was ready to convert but soon realized that Greece had changed him—he "had become Hellenized, somewhat Paganized."

IN LONDON, WILDE spent whatever money he had, saving only enough to reach Dublin, and prepared for his first public appearance. He had the right invitation: the opening of the Grosvenor Gallery on May 1, 1877. The *Dublin University Magazine* asked him to write a review of this landmark event, which broke the hegemony held by the Royal Academy for more than a century by providing a space for contemporary French paintings and the avant-garde as exemplified by James Whistler. The review was Wilde's first published prose and his debut as an art critic. He wrote an ambitious essay that attempted to link painting with the writings of Pater, Ruskin, Morris, Swinburne, and Symonds.

Socially, it was a glamorous evening with men in top hats and ladies in ostrich feathers. Inspired by a dream—or so he told his tailor—Wilde wore a bronze-colored coat with the back shaped like a cello. In an exhibition where the familiar children and scenes from *The Vicar of Wakefield* were absent, Wilde created as much comment as Whistler's expressionistic paintings. "One should either be a work of art, or wear a work of art" was one of his "Phrases and Philosophies for the Use of the Young." But after one becomes a work of art, lies and masks are necessary.

Lacking funds to stay in London, when he wanted to enjoy his instantaneous fame, Wilde reluctantly returned home for the remainder of his rustication. Willie greeted him and made a scene, insisting he reveal the *real reason* he was sent down. Lady Wilde dismissed the Oxford incident as "wretched stupidity." Florrie was waiting for him, as he told Kitten, "more lovely than ever." He read *Aurora Leigh,* gave lectures on Greece to college girls, and when the shooting season opened in September went to Clonfin House in County Longford.

One of the American visitors at the country house had brought over a blank album published in New York in 1870 called *Mental Photographs, an Album for Confessions of Tastes, Habits and Convictions.* Wilde filled in thirty-nine of the forty questions with uncanny foresight as to his character and interests. Already in place is the Wildean mockery of his own qualities and faults. The sweetest words in the world: "Well Done!"; the saddest: "Failure!" His favorite occupation: "Reading my own sonnets." Character traits he detested: "Vanity, self-esteem, conceit," and admired: "Power of attracting friends." His most distinguishing characteristic: "Inordinate self-esteem." If he could not be himself, he wanted to be a "cardinal of the Catholic Church." His idea of happiness: "Absolute power over men's minds, even if accompanied by toothache." His aim in life: to achieve "Success, fame or even notoriety." Florence (for Florrie) was his favorite girl's name, and when married he said that "devotion to her husband" should be the distinguishing characteristic of his wife. Curiously, "What is your motto?" was left blank.

WILDE'S TALENT FOR self-advertisement was instinctive. It began in a modulated tone with letters and grew into a verbal brilliance epitomized by his successful plays of the 1890s. During rustication he spent more time than usual with the newspapers. An article in *The Times* about the massacres of Christians in Bulgaria caught his imagination: he composed a sonnet on the subject and sent it to William Ewart Gladstone, then between terms as prime minister.

"I am little more than a boy," he explained as a way of seeking help to publish his poetry. Wilde correctly assumed that an Oxford man would not be ignored, and Gladstone's reply arrived suggesting he submit his work to *The Spectator.* He did and was rejected. Next he took issue with a proposed Keats memorial and sent a monograph to the Keats scholar William Michael Rossetti, Dante's brother. It was, he abjectly noted, "little more than a stray sheet from a boy's diary." Luckily his correspondents were unaware that the boy was twenty-three.

Obsequiousness came easily with the eminent, but arrogance ruled with editors. Wilde's inexperience as a writer called for a bit more humility than he demonstrated when he returned the proofs of his Grosvenor Gallery review. He stipulated: "I always say I and not 'we.' We belongs to the days of anonymous articles, not to signed articles like mine." Furthermore, he added: "To say 'perhaps' spoils the remark," and "my sonnet must be printed in *full large type:* it looks and reads *bad* as it stands." Wilde was known as a bully before he was acknowledged as a writer.

Passing himself off again as a mere boy, Wilde sent a copy of his *DUM* review to the unmet Walter Pater, who replied: "You possess some beautiful, and for your age, quite exceptionally cultivated tastes: and a considerable knowledge too of many beautiful things." Pater invited him to visit when he returned to Oxford. Later he would ask, "Why do you always write poetry? Why do you not write prose? Prose is so much more difficult." Wilde took the challenge and set out to surpass Pater's prose, eventually dismissing him and his style. (When told that Pater had died, Wilde reportedly inquired, "Was he ever alive?" But ridicule of the living was atypical for Wilde.)

That summer, Henry Wilson, Wilde's illegitimate half brother, died of pneumonia at the age of thirty-nine. Wilde told Harding he was a cousin "to whom we were all very much attached." Wilson had never married, so Oscar and Willie expected to be his sole heirs. But Sir William had used his son to keep Oscar in the Church of Ireland. The bulk of the estate went to St. Mark's Hospital; Willie received two thousand pounds, Wilde only one hundred, on condition that he remain a Protestant. Even Oscar's beloved Illaunroe was not free and clear; if he converted within five years, he forfeited the property. "It is a terrible disappointment to me," he complained to Ward. "I suffer a good deal from my Romish leanings, in pocket and mind."

IN HIS ACADEMIC pursuits, Wilde loved to predict failure and be jubilant when proved wrong. He wrote Kitten and Bouncer that a First in Greats was impossible and he had steeled himself to settle for a Fourth. He stayed at Magdalen to study during Easter break, regretting, as he wrote Florrie, that he could not make it to Ireland. Taking a few days in Bournemouth, he wrote again, reminding her that the previous Easter she had sent him a card in Athens "over so many miles of land and sea—to show you had not forgotten me." At the end of term, he had a First in Greats.

With a First in Mods, he had earned a double First, astonishing the dons, his classmates, and—for once—even himself. His scholarship was extended for a fifth year because he still had to pass the divinity exam failed two years earlier. No classics fellowships were available at Magdalen; he took the examination at Trinity, but not even Mahaffy's support got him an appointment. Although teaching was an obvious choice for Wilde, he was too independent and brilliant for doctrinaire dons to want at their table.

When he thought there was nothing more to swagger about, he won the Newdigate Prize for his poem *Ravenna*. His mother trilled like an archangel: "Oh Gloria, Gloria! . . . It is the first pleasant throb of joy I have had this year. . . . Well, after all, we have Genius." Lady Wilde understood the importance of the award: "This gives you a certainty of success in the future—You can now trust your own intellect, and know what it can do."

To be a winner of the Newdigate Prize, first given in 1806, was to be a member of a select club, which included Arnold, Ruskin, Symonds, and others who smoothed Wilde's entrance into London society. When the perennial curmudgeon W. S. Gilbert, soon to satirize Wilde in *Patience,* heard about the honor, he snapped, "I understand that some young man wins this prize every year." Wilde enjoyed the irony of it all. Had he not visited Ravenna on the way to Greece and been rusticated, he might not have won the Newdigate. Ravenna was the assigned topic that year, and being there had given him an atmospheric advantage. At the June Encaenia of 1878, in accordance with tradition, he walked in the academic procession with the vice-chancellor, heads of college, and other dignitaries to the Sheldonian Theatre, where he nervously began his poem:

> *A year ago I breathed the Italian air—*
> *And yet, methinks this northern Spring is fair,—*
> *These fields made golden with the flower of March,*
> *The throstle singing on the feathered larch,*
> *The cawing rooks, the wood-doves fluttering by,*
> *The little clouds that race across the sky;*
> *And fair the violet's gentle drooping head,*
> *The primrose, pale for love uncomforted,*
> *The rose that burgeons on the climbing briar, . . .*

A beaming Mahaffy and a somber, if not sober, Willie Wilde sat in front; apparently absent was Lady Wilde. Afterward Wilde and some friends were photographed with a marble bust of the young Augustus, Wilde's trophy for being the first Magdalen undergraduate to receive the Newdigate since 1825.

He was not pleased, however, with his annual two hundred pounds from his father's estate, a decent income for anyone except Wilde. Then he learned that Florrie was to wed Bram Stoker, his Trinity classmate, whom Henry Irving had offered the position of acting manager at the Lyceum Theatre in London. Irritated that Florrie had not told him herself but far from heartbroken, he gravely asked for the return of a Christmas gift, a gold cross inscribed with his name.

"Worthless though the trinket be," he wrote, "to me it serves as a memory of two sweet years—the sweetest of all the years of my youth—

and I should like to have it always with me. . . . whatever happens I at least cannot be indifferent to your welfare; the currents of our lives flowed too long beside one another for that." That Florence Balcombe attracted both men reveals more about their attitudes toward women than it does about her character. Both were obsessed with the notion of chaste womanhood (as Stoker demonstrates in *Dracula*), and Florrie posed no threat to the idealized mother figure they sought.

THE OXFORD UNIVERSITY GAZETTE announced that Oscar Fingal O'Flahertie Wills Wilde—with all his names in place—received his bachelor of arts degree on November 28, 1878. Halfhearted attempts to obtain an archaeological studentship or to follow in Matthew Arnold's footsteps as an inspector of schools failed. Wilde loved Oxford but wanted, he said, "to eat of the fruit of all the trees in the garden of the world." Strolling along Magdalen's "bird-haunted walks" on one of his last days there, he pledged to throw "the pearl" of his "soul into a cup of wine," to go "down the primrose path to the sound of flutes," to live "on honeycomb."

Richard Ellmann contends that around 1878, while at Oxford, Wilde contracted syphilis from a female prostitute. Such women were available in and around the High Street or at the more elegant houses that catered to randy young lords. There is no evidence, however, that Wilde was ever tempted to join other students in lustful merrymaking even after a night of drinking whiskeys and soda. Bragging about visiting a brothel is the kind of outrageous fabrication that Wilde would use to interrupt a conversation during his period of self-mythologizing.

By the time Ellmann wrote his biography, talk of Wilde's syphilis had been around for many years. In Arthur Ransome's biography of 1912, the author clearly states that Wilde's death was "directly due to meningitis, the legacy of an attack of tertiary syphilis." The book was dedicated to Robbie Ross, who, along with Reggie Turner, was present at Wilde's death. Subsequent biographers such as Frank Harris, Hesketh Pearson, and H. Montgomery Hyde perpetuated the story, perhaps assuming that Ross would have objected to Ransome's statement about syphilis if he had believed it untrue. Perhaps Ross did, for the second edition in 1913 omits any mention of syphilis. At first Turner supported the syphilis theory, but he later retracted his statements. As for Ransome, he never gave a source for his diagnosis.

Lacking medical records or a cause of death on the death certificate (the doctors who attended Wilde during his final illness treated him for cerebral meningitis, a complication arising from an inflammation of the middle ear), or any reference by Wilde in his letters to having Baudelaire's disease, where is the evidence beyond hearsay? Where were the classic symptoms? The primary stage of the disease exhibits painless sores or ulcers that feel like a button buried beneath the skin. In the secondary stage, which starts six to eight weeks later, a rash appears, the glands swell, and there is a loss of appetite and weight. While at Oxford, Wilde was healthy and fit, although he was prone to colds and suffered, along with everyone else, during influenza season. Later he complained of gout, a condition physicians often predicted for their gourmand patients.

Wilde's teeth, already protruding and irregular and sometimes described as stained, signified the disease for Ellmann. Since Wilde had a habit of talking with his hand covering his mouth, Ellmann assumed he did so to conceal his blackened teeth, a symptom that he was undergoing mercury treatment.* Wilde "adopted mercury rather than religion as the specific for his dreadful disease," Ellmann writes. "Perhaps now the parable of Dorian Gray's secret decay began to form in his mind, as the spirochete began its journey up his spine towards the meninges." Ellmann never cites a source for Wilde's mercury treatments, only his blackened teeth. (Actually, mercury leaves a dark line on the gums but does not darken the teeth.) Any discoloration of his teeth came from Wilde's heavy smoking and from nicotine eating into the enamel. When he arrived in America in 1882, the *New York Tribune* reported on "a shining row of upper teeth which are superlatively white." Lillie Langtry once referred to them as green. The color of Wilde's teeth was in the eye of the beholder.

Evidence does not exist—and probably never will—to justify Ell-

---

*Rubdowns of mercury were the only treatment available in the 1870s. Dr. Paul Ehrlich did not discover his "magic bullet," the arsenic-based drug Salvarsan, until 1910. When Sir Alexander Fleming discovered penicillin in 1928, he found a remedy that killed the germ but not the patient.

mann's conviction that Wilde died of neurosyphilis, that the disease influenced his early poetry, and that it ultimately led to his conversion to Catholicism. But believe it Ellmann did. This belief, Ellmann said, was central to his "conception of Wilde's character" and his "interpretation of many things in his later life." In fact, his biography is interwoven with the idea.

PART TWO

(1879–1883)

Reinventing

HÉLAS!

To drift with every passion till my soul
Is a stringed lute on which all winds can play,
Is it for this that I have given away
Mine ancient wisdom and austere control?
Methinks my life is a twice-written scroll
Scrawled over on some boyish holiday
With idle songs for pipe and virelay,
Which do but mar the secret of the whole.
Surely there was a time I might have trod
The sunlit heights, and from life's dissonance
Struck one clear chord to reach the ears of God:
Is that time dead? lo! with a little rod
I did but touch the honey of romance—
And must I lose a soul's inheritance?

—Oscar Wilde

CHAPTER SIX

Artists and Beauties

❧

To get into the best society, nowadays, one has either to feed people,
amuse people, or shock people—that is all!

—*A WOMAN OF NO IMPORTANCE*

At the opening of the Grosvenor Gallery, Wilde had become a work of art when he wore a shimmering bronze cutaway coat shaped like a cello, a brocade waistcoat, and a blue satin ascot tie. As he entered the crush, his voice fluttered and purred. "Ah! Yes. Indeed! Good evening," he said, extending a white-gloved hand like a fat alabaster star. That the pleasure produced by his cello coat needed no justification was a rebellious theory. "Individualism is a disturbing and disintegrating force," Wilde wrote. "Therein lies its immense value. For what it seeks to disturb is monotony of type, slavery of custom, tyranny of habit and the reduction of man to the level of a machine." The defense of pleasure was added to Wilde's principles that made art an end in itself and put the needs of the individual above society.

In his review of the Grosvenor opening, Wilde praised Whistler's traditional portrait of Carlyle but snubbed his *Nocturne in Black and Gold: The Falling Rocket,* which depicted fireworks over Cremorne, a popular amusement park on the north bank of the Thames. Wilde wrote that it was "worth looking at for about as long as one looks at a real rocket, that is, for somewhat less than a quarter of a minute." John Ruskin gave it less than a second, writing in *Fors Clavigera* that he had "seen and heard much of Cockney impudence before now, but never expected to hear a coxcomb ask two hundred guineas for flinging a pot of paint in the public's face."[*]

This insult led to the libel action *Whistler v. Ruskin,* heard on November 25, 1878, in Westminster Hall. By taking the acknowledged arbiter of British taste to court, Whistler sought to determine the nature of art and individual aesthetics. Ruskin claimed he wrote the truth, putting the onus on Whistler to prove that this truth was also a lie. Wilde, like anybody else who bothered to open a newspaper, read about the confrontation and was pleased to see his philosophy of the truth in lies argued before the Court of Exchequer.

Whistler and Wilde were yet to meet, but Wilde knew a bit about the dandy artist who would befriend him and then attack him, claiming that Wilde had borrowed artistic theories for his own use. He knew that Whistler had spent his childhood in St. Petersburg and, following expulsion from West Point, had lived as a bohemian in Paris. Whistler arrived in London in 1859 at age twenty-five to blitz the Royal Academy and by 1872 had painted the famous portraits of the little white girl and his mother.

RESPLENDENT IN A double-breasted suit of navy blue serge, Whistler jousted with the attorney general, finally admitting that his painting had taken but two days to complete. "The labor of two days, then," he was asked, "is that for which you ask two hundred guineas?" "No," Whistler triumphantly replied, "I ask it for the knowledge of a lifetime." The jury found that, although there was a technical libel, Ruskin had published fair criticism. Whistler received a farthing in damages, giving him the same symbolic victory as Mary Travers's in Lady Wilde's libel trial.

Whistler was wearing the farthing on his watch chain when he and Wilde formally met in 1879. The meeting took place at Frank Miles's stu-

---

[*]From 1871 to 1884, Ruskin published monthly booklets under the title *Fors Clavigera: Letters to the Workmen and Labourers of Great Britain,* which were intended to provide cultural sustenance for British workers. He tried to put himself on the workers' level by using terms like "Cockney impudence." He asked why a man's hard-earned wages should pay for art that does not reflect reality.

dio, on the top floor of a dark, haunting three-story building at 13 Salisbury Street, off the Strand. One poseur greeted the other, and the competition began. When Wilde came down from Oxford and took the floor below the studio, he appraised his new address and christened it Thames House for its best feature: a river view. A penchant for naming friends now extended to homes.

The first artist known for being known, Whistler was an outsider who became a celebrity without reinventing himself—as Wilde did—as an Englishman. Wilde discarded his Irish brogue, but Whistler amplified his brusque Yankee accent. Whistler entertained with American breakfasts of pancakes and maple syrup; Wilde preferred the egg-and-sausage-laden buffets of Oxford. In his white suits and lavender hat, Whistler had a sense of style as pretentious as anything Wilde ever fabricated. In an age of mass journalism, he realized as Wilde would that there was no bad publicity. Ellen Terry called them the most remarkable men she had ever known. "There was something about both of them," she said, "more instantaneously individual and audacious than it is possible to describe."

Wilde admitted to being an artist and, if pressed on what he did, then a poet. When Oxford's Aestheticism became too transparent, he withdrew into his mythic self, a Celtic phenomenon known as a shape-shifter, one with the ability to become anything: a wave, an animal, another person. His favorite legendary warrior was Cuchulain, who inflated himself to gigantic proportions and turned different colors to frighten the enemy. In the process of swelling himself up, Wilde did not set boundaries, finding it impossible to embrace egotism and ambition at the same time. The instinct to see life as a humorous tragedy was too strong and the addiction to his own conversation too irresistible. "I hate people who talk about themselves, as you do, when one wants to talk about oneself, as I do," complains the rocket in Wilde's fable on vanity, "The Remarkable Rocket." After nearly a year in London, Wilde was disappointed with his progress; he wrote Harding that he had not "set the world quite on fire as yet."

Neither had he published any poetry since Oxford. The paper on his writing table went dusty from disuse; he thought and talked more than he wrote and was easily distracted by the stairs creaking as visitors climbed past his sitting room to the studio. Miles's reputation as a quick-sketch artist drew an eclectic audience, including Prince Leopold, Walter Sickert and Whistler, Ellen Terry and Sarah Bernhardt. Opening the door was Sally, a violet seller and occasional model rescued from the streets to serve tea and entertain with her Cockney accent (a calculated ambience that blurred class differences). No matter that the furniture was rickety, the cutlery mismatched, the wine cheap, and the sausage dry, the visitors were the atmosphere. Lord Henry's wife tells Dorian: "You must come. I can't afford orchids, but I spare no expense in foreigners. They make one's rooms look so picturesque."

THE COMÉDIE-FRANÇAISE seldom left Paris, but the theatre had to close for repairs and a six-week London season was scheduled at the Gaiety Theatre in the summer of 1879. Wilde and the actor Norman Forbes-Robertson planned a welcome at Folkstone when Sarah Bernhardt—not yet an international star but an actress with a shameless reputation—arrived on the Le Havre ferry. Wilde threw an armful of lilies at her feet, shouting: "Hip, hip, hurrah! and a cheer for Sarah Bernhardt!"

Bernhardt feared the British as an "alien public," but when they applauded her entrance in *Phèdre,* she said to herself: "Yes, yes—you'll see—I shall give you my blood, my life, my soul." For the first time, Wilde said, he "realised the sweetness of the music of Racine." He christened her "the Divine Sarah." Enthusiasm bubbled over into a sonnet that concluded:

> *For thou wert weary of the sunless day,*
> *The heavy fields of scentless asphodel,*
> *The loveless lips with which men kiss in Hell.*

Wilde asked his brother to intercede and have the sonnet printed in *The World,* and nine days later Wilde read his first published work since arriving in London.

Wilde installed himself as the actress's unofficial secretary, arriving backstage with flowers and a subdued fondness. "Most men who are civil to actresses and render them services have an ulterior motive," Bernhardt said. "It is not so with Oscar Wilde. He was a devoted attendant, and did much to make things pleasant and easy for me in London, but he never appeared to pay court." Bernhardt thought men wanted her only as a woman; Wilde wanted her as the star of his first but yet unwritten play and dreamed of casting her as Queen Elizabeth I, wearing "monstrous dresses covered with peacocks and pearls!"

LILLIE LANGTRY WAS twenty-three when Wilde met her in 1877 at Miles's studio. A Pre-Raphaelite beauty with a graceful neck, straight nose, pale skin, full breasts, broad hips, and golden brown hair loosely knotted at the nape of her neck, she was, Wilde thought, "the loveliest woman in Europe." There was an immediate rapport between them. Langtry recalled his "great eager eyes" and a face "so colourless that a few pale freckles of good size were oddly conspicuous," and she remarked on "a well-shaped mouth, with somewhat coarse lips and greenish-hued teeth."

Physically, there was little except Wilde's eyes and voice to delight her. What she admired most was his showmanship, which she adapted to serve her own needs. "She is more than a mystery—she is a mood" was an apt description, which he used in *A Woman of No Importance*. Langtry was the first woman to arouse Wilde's passionate nature, and he was constantly at her side: they attended lectures on Greek art; he taught her Latin; they fussed over her limited wardrobe.

Emilie Charlotte Le Breton was the only daughter of the dean of Jersey, who (in common with Wilde's father) was answerable for more than one illegitimate child. At twenty-one she married the thirty-year-old Irish widower Edward Langtry, a yachtsman with shipping interests in Belfast, who soon was bankrupt. In mourning for her brother until she could afford a new gown, Mrs. Langtry, as she was called in society, made herself the center of any group in a severe black dress brightened only by lace collar and cuffs.

Artists noticed her at one of Lady Sebright's parties in the spring of 1876. Millais painted her as an ingenuous country girl in a portrait called the *Jersey Lily*. Whistler and Frederick Leighton had her sit for them. "Lillie Langtry happens to be, quite simply," said Millais, "the most beautiful woman on earth." Edward John Poynter posed her in a Grecian-style yellow gown, and when Wilde admired the portrait, she insisted he keep it to replace the unfinished landscape on the ubiquitous easel. Frank Miles made hundreds of India-ink sketches that he sold as originals or reproduced as postcards. The camera and printing press had created a new audience for cheap reproductions, and Langtry's picture sold everywhere.

Wilde christened her "the Lily," and she scrawled her name on the white wall in his sitting room when she was known only for being beautiful. The Salisbury Street coterie delighted in descriptions of parties she attended where there were "striped awnings, linkmen with flaring torches; powdered footmen; soaring marble staircases; tiaras, smiling hostesses; azaleas in gilt baskets; white waistcoats, violins, elbows sawing the air, names on pasteboard cards, quails in aspic, macédoine, strawberries and cream."

When she became the favorite of the Prince of Wales, the future Edward VII, Wilde saw less of his Lily. She moved with her husband to 17 Norfolk Street, off Park Lane, where Whistler painted a baroque sky on the drawing-room ceiling and gilded palm-leaf fans on the plum-colored walls and put floating water lilies in flat blue-glass bowls. During a country house weekend with the prince, she wrote to ask Wilde's advice on what to wear to the fancy-dress ball. After she failed to reach him, she told him she had designed "a soft black Greek Dress with a fringe of silver crescents and stars and diamond ones in my hair and on my neck and called it Queen of the Night." Wilde thought the jewels detracted from the dress's classical lines.

WILDE PLEDGED TO dedicate a sonnet to the Lily. According to his mythologizing, he slept in her doorway for inspiration—a cold, uncomfortable, and undignified night. Hardly a poet's place. Still, he convinced others he did and made the point that "there is only one thing in the world worse than being talked about, and that is not being talked about." "The New Helen," published in *The World* shortly after the sonnet to Bernhardt, was inscribed "To Helen, formerly of Troy, now of London." One verse recalls unrequited love:

> *The lotus-leaves which heal the wounds of Death*
> *Lie in thy hand: O, be thou kind to me,*
> *While yet I know the summer of my days;*

For hardly can my tremulous lips draw breath
To fill the silver trumpet with thy praise,
So bowed am I before thy mystery;
So bowed and broken on Love's terrible wheel,
That I have lost all hope and heart to sing,
Yet care I not what ruin time may bring
If in thy temple thou wilt let me kneel.

"Roses and Rue," written after Wilde's marriage, was dedicated "To L.L.":

"You have only wasted your life"—
(Ah! there was the knife!)
Those were the words you said,
As you turned your head.

I had wasted my boyhood, true,
But it was for you.
You had poets enough on the shelf,
I gave you myself!

Another actress he hoped would star in his unwritten play was Helen Modjeska, who made her London debut in 1880 at the advanced age of thirty-six. She thought it improper to go to tea with such a youth, so they met in her dressing room at the Royal Court Theatre. "What has he done, this young man," Modjeska finally asked a colleague in her Polish accent, "that one meets him everywhere? Oh yes he talks well, but what has he done? He has written nothing, he does not sing or paint or act—he does nothing but talk. I do not understand."

Wilde answers similar criticism of his alter ego Lord Goring in *An Ideal Husband*. "How can you say such a thing?" asks Mabel Chiltern. "Why, he rides in the Row at ten o'clock in the morning, goes to the Opera three times a week, changes his clothes at least five times a day, and dines out every night of the season. You don't call that leading an idle life, do you?"

Modjeska had left Warsaw and a promising career in 1876 to learn English and perform in America, working toward her goal of acting

Shakespeare in London, an ambition she fulfilled as Juliet to Forbes-Robertson's Romeo. During her run at the Royal Court, Wilde saw her open in *La Dame aux camélias* and then in *Adrienne Lecouvreur* and *Maria Stuart,* a success that prompted Henry James to say that the principal ornament of the English stage was a Polish actress in a German play.

To give the restless young man with the armfuls of flowers a meaningful task, Modjeska asked him to translate a poem she had written called "Sen Artysty." Polish was not one of Wilde's languages, although he may have told Madame differently, but a dictionary and a sense of style were all he needed to ready "The Artist's Dream" for publication in *The Green Room,* a theatre magazine. A translation credit impressed him but provided no money for his creditors. His career as a poet was too needful of muses to prosper.

MERRION SQUARE WAS sold in 1879 to pay Sir William's debts, and with it went any likelihood that Lady Wilde and Willie would remain in Dublin. Willie had failed to establish a reputation as a barrister or to attract a wealthy wife; he also failed, before his brother, as a playwright with two dramas—*French Polish* and *Evening Stream*—published but never performed. Bored with Ireland and the Irish, he told Margaret Campbell: "They are all so alike over here—same set, same talk, same ideas, same shallowness. . . . Society's almost as deep—well—as a frozen rink—i.e., six inches."

He earned drinking money by filing social briefs to *The World,* the London weekly that published his brother's sonnets. A typical entry described what Campbell wore to a soiree at the Royal Irish Academy: "a charming 'dull gold' dress (combined with a coiffure peculiarly artistic and aesthetic) that many heads turned round to look at. I am afraid I cannot quite describe the colour; but I fancy (it is a pretty antiquarian council) that it must resemble the sheen of some gold vase or bracelet just flashed into the sunlight by Dr. Schliemann from the darkness of one of his Mycenae tombs."

Reluctant to sever ties with Ireland, Wilde ignored his mother's letter asking him to find a suite of rooms in Salisbury Street, near Number 13, if possible. Willie finally found lodgings at One Ovington Square in Kensington, off the Brompton Road, a suitable distance away. The bailiffs arrived at Merrion Square and took possession. Lady Wilde sat in the foyer and watched the commotion as if in a trance. On May 7 she left Ireland forever. Wilde returned only twice, and then only to lecture.

At fifty-eight, Lady Wilde was still a fighter, impatient to publish and compete with her sons as she had with her husband. By any measure she was the most prolific and wrote for a range of specialized publications: the estimable *Pall Mall Gazette,* known for its serious literary and political coverage; the *Queen,* a weekly for women; and the *Burlington Magazine,* which appealed to the upper classes; as well as the *St. James Magazine, Tinsley's,* and *Lady's Pictorial.* By 1881 she could afford a move to 116 Park Street off Grosvenor Square, where she reestablished her salon. Willie still lived under the maternal roof.

In Dublin she had no rival as a hostess, as she boasted to her Scottish friend: "Beauty is the grand characteristic of the Dublin Belles, so in that department I leave them undisturbed in possession of their domain and am content with undisputed sovereignty in mine." In London it was a crowded field, with many elegant ladies vying for important names. Known as a welcoming stop for arriving Irish artists, including Shaw and Yeats, Park Street was always crowded on Saturdays, airless and dark. Enthroned behind the tea table, Lady Wilde resembled a female Buddha. Eventually, her son Oscar was the major attraction.

A MEMBER OF St. Stephen's Club on the Victoria Embankment, Wilde knew London's West End haunts from his Oxford days. A perfect evening— if he had enough shillings or if someone else was paying—was a stall seat at the theatre and supper afterward at the Café Royal. As a theatregoer, he planted himself firmly in the front of the house: boxes, stalls, and dress circle—in that order. While growing up in Dublin, Wilde had received his theatrical education in the pit at the Theatre Royal or the Queen's, venues that attracted touring stars such as Barry Sullivan, Dion Boucicault, and Geneviève Ward. As an aspiring playwright, he saw the audience as an extension of the play—an inspired audience made a successful play.

Wilde's favorite actor was Henry Irving, who ruled the Lyceum Theatre in the Strand along with his former Trinity classmate Bram Stoker, who as manager greeted first-night patrons at the top of the gilded double staircase. Irving had played Dublin many times before he became Britain's leading actor in 1878, revealing a power to make the viewer see the character, not the actor. Irving's receptive temperament, Wilde said in "The Soul of Man Under Socialism," came from achieving "his own perfection as an artist" and from refusing to give the public what it wanted.

Destined to be the first actor knighted, Irving was, in Wilde's words, a "vivid personality." It was said that only William Gladstone and Cardinal Manning attracted as much attention in public. Caricaturists ridiculed the actor's walk, drawing him with bent knees and back or a dragging leg like that of the Aesthete in *Iolanthe*. Irving was always self-conscious about his walk; onstage he moved with a springing motion almost like dancing. Playing with the vocabulary of Aestheticism, Wilde described Irving's legs as "limpid and utter. Both are delicately intellectual, but his left leg is a poem." A sonnet lauding his classical roles has this memorable last line: "Thou trumpet set for Shakespeare's lips to blow!"

Irving was touched by Wilde's "childish love of the romantic candlelit theatre" that he had created. When Oxford inaugurated its first drama society in 1885 with a performance of *Henry IV*, Wilde noted in the *Dramatic Review* what Irving had always wanted for the acting community: academic recognition. "Why should not degrees be granted for good acting?" he asked. "Are they not given to those who misunderstand Plato and who mistranslate Aristotle? And should the artist be passed over? No." On his way to a knighthood, Irving entertained on a lavish scale. Wilde was often present at the intimate (usually men only) dinners in the Beefsteak Room, tucked away backstage. On the occasion of the hundredth night of *The Merchant of Venice,* the Lyceum stage was struck and transformed into a flowering pavilion of scarlet and white. Wilde was there and read a sonnet to Ellen Terry as Portia.

Always finding opportunities to explore the artist's complex relationship to art and reality, Wilde introduced in *Dorian Gray* the actress Sibyl Vane, who loses her power to imagine when she falls in love with Dorian. "As a rule, people who act lead the most commonplace lives," Dorian tells Basil after he learns of Sibyl's suicide. "They are good husbands, or faithful wives, or something tedious. How different Sibyl was. She lived her finest tragedy. She was always a heroine." Dorian justifies his shabby treatment of her by saying, "It is not good for one's morals to see bad acting."

Sharing a box on November 28, 1879, for *The Merchant of Venice,* John Ruskin and Wilde watched Irving's controversial Shylock. The actor did not wear the red cap required for Jews by Venetian law, and he portrayed Shylock as an intellectual, with gray hair and a pale countenance, replacing the shuffling usurer with a heroic saint. After the performance, Wilde and Ruskin parted, for Wilde was invited to a ball celebrating the wedding of Millais's daughter. "How odd it is," Wilde remarked of the evening: he had attended a play set in Venice with the author of *Stones of Venice* and a gala where the bride was the daughter of Ruskin's former wife. There was also Ruskin's resignation, almost to the day, as Slade Professor at Oxford. "I cannot hold a Chair from which I have no power of expressing judgment without being taxed for it by British law," he had said, referring to his humiliation at Whistler's libel trial.

ONE DAY IN 1879, at the home of the artist William Bell Scott, Wilde met a seventeen-year-old Pre-Raphaelite beauty maturely dressed in a plain terra-cotta dress with a black fichu flung around her neck. Her name was Violet Hunt, and she was the daughter of Alfred William Hunt, a respected watercolorist, and Margaret Raine Hunt, a successful novelist of the three-decker period, whose best-known book, *Thornicroft's Model,* is about a Rossetti-type aesthetic painter. Hunt chattered on about her mother, telling Wilde that Swinburne's favorite book was Lady Wilde's translation of *Sidonia the Sorceress.* Margaret Hunt was also a translator: her 1884 version of *Grimm's Household Tales* was the edition on which the later *Grimm's Fairy Tales* was based. "Do you know, I am almost beginning to be afraid of your mother," Wilde said. "I shall not dare to ask her to let me call," he went on, boldly adding, "Beautiful women like you hold the fortunes of the world in your hands to make or mar. We will rule the world—you and I—you with your looks and I with my wits." Hunt recalled how Wilde "always talked less in italics than in Capitals."

A flirtatious Hunt ("out of Botticelli by Burne-Jones" was Ellen Terry's description) told her diary she had fallen "a little in love" when she and Wilde sat and talked on the window seat, where "there was hardly room for the slip of a girl that I was and the lusty big fellow with the wide, white face, the shapely red mouth and the long lock of straight peasant-like black hair that fell across his fine forehead." Descriptions of Wilde as a romantic youth do not get any better.

As dowryless as Florence Balcombe but more seductive, Hunt made any man she was with the center of attention and gloriously vain. Her father, a Newdigate winner from Corpus Christi College, was on the fringes of the Pre-Raphaelites. Ruskin thought him the most promising landscape painter exhibiting, even though he had failed—not for lack of talent but for want of political maneuvering—to be elected to the Royal Academy. Jealous that Ruskin was godfather to her eldest sister, Venice, Hunt waited for a felicitous time to offer herself as his bride.

That time arrived following the annulment of Ruskin's marriage, when he fell in love with ten-year-old Rose La Touche but promised to wait until she was eighteen (and he was forty-seven) to propose. Her parents refused this offer, but Ruskin continued to press his suit. When Rose died at the age of twenty-seven, he sank into prolonged melancholia; then thirteen-year-old Violet impetuously announced she would marry him. Margaret Hunt should have discouraged such folly, but she was too ambitious for her husband not to tell Ruskin of the offer, which included another waiting period.

But Ruskin was fatigued with forbearance. "I really think Violets must be nicer than roses after all—Another three years to wait—though! What a weary life I have of it." He said he did not like grand faces in women, "but infinitely delicate & soft ones—for instance, Violet and Venice as I can fancy them at eighteen—And the older I grow—the younger I like faces to be—so foolish am I. I don't think I can possibly care for anybody more than eighteen—unless I've known them before."

LATER HUNT WAS prepared to marry Wilde. She was enchanted when he called her "the sweetest Violet in England." Until his American lecture tour, he visited Tor Villa on Sundays to see her and talk with her father, whom he teased about his "wonderful radicalism." These visits, she said, procured her "an enviable notoriety." Her memoirs claim that she "as nearly as possible escaped the honour of being Mrs. Wilde." Her diary records, "I believe that Oscar was really in love with me—for the moment and perhaps more than a moment."

In an unpublished version of "My Oscar (a Germ of a Book)," she gives a more accurate story, noting that "all the proposal that got through to me was a single white Eucharist lily without a stalk, reposing on cotton wool in a box, ridiculed by my younger sisters." In her autobiographical novel, *Their Lives* (1916), Philip Wynyard (Wilde) wants to marry Christina (Violet) but hesitates because her parents have no money. Finally Christina's father settles the problem by announcing that he "would never give [his] daughter to him."

Although there were opportunities to wed, Hunt preferred a capricious life as the mistress of married literary men such as H. G. Wells and Ford Madox Hueffer (later Ford). Long after her beauty faded and deep wrinkles lined the once stunning eyes, she still talked about Wilde's proposal. Wilde's women remembered him fondly in their old age. Florence Stoker kept his view from Moytura on her wall until she died at seventy-eight, a lonely widow nearly blind. "Oscar's little water-colour creates much envy in the breasts of the Oscar cult," she told visitors.

CHAPTER SEVEN

Aesthetes and Dandies

❧

A man who can dominate a London dinner-table can
dominate the world. The future belongs to the dandy. It is the
exquisites who are going to rule.

—*A Woman of No Importance*

I t took planning, not to mention funds, to become known in London. Wilde spread his credit around West End restaurants but found that the theatre provided the best visibility, with whispers of "There goes Oscar Wilde!" echoing through the stalls. Seen at the Lyceum's *Othello,* the ubiquitous Oscar amused everyone, leaning languidly from one box, greeting friends in the stalls, and reappearing in yet another box. During the interval, he was seen with his arm around Bram Stoker's shoulder. Later he kissed Florence Stoker's hand on the staircase. It gave him great pleasure to see Florrie in the audience.

Wilde knew nothing about writing a play except that he wanted to say something rather than sell anything. In the eighties, serious theatre was controlled by the actor-manager Henry Irving, whose parts—other than Shakespearean—were written for him. William Gorman Wills wrote *Vanderdecken* to satisfy his whim to be the Flying Dutchman but received no royalties. Beyond commissions were the imported Parisian boulevard dramas, plays such as *Frou-Frou, La Dame aux camélias,* and *Le Demi-Monde,* and British-produced woman–with–a–past melodramas, which tended to be more sympathetic than their French counterparts. Piles of unsolicited plays gathered dust in the offices of every actor-manager. Few were ever produced.

A new playwright often began by adapting the plays of Alexandre Dumas fils or Victorien Sardou, authors of the so-called well-made play, which depended on intrigue and contrived devices to create suspense. With his disdain for artifice, Shaw dubbed Sardou's work "Sardoodle-dom." Wilde skipped over such apprenticeships and went directly to borrowing techniques, including the famous handbag device in *Earnest,* to drive his plots.

It was an unexciting time for new plays, a transition period before Ibsen's dramas of social realism and Shaw's social criticism. Arthur Wing Pinero and Henry Arthur Jones were the prominent dramatists. Outspoken but not didactic, Pinero was more interested in motive and psychology than in ideas. *The Second Mrs. Tanqueray* (1893) and *The Notorious Mrs. Ebbsmith* (1895) depict women battling with the stricter moral code, while Shaw's *Mrs. Warren's Profession* takes on the evils of prostitution, and Wilde's *A Woman of No Importance* turns issues of illegitimacy into a social comedy.

Born into an affluent family of Portuguese Jewish descent, Pinero had to wait nine years until his father, an Islington solicitor, died to become an actor in the Lyceum company. Irving singled him out to play Claudius in a provincial tour of *Hamlet* and produced some of his early one-act plays. In 1881, with the success of *The Money Spinner* at the St. James's Theatre, he gave up acting and for fifty-seven years averaged a play a year. Unlike Wilde, Pinero disliked self-publicity and seldom took a curtain call on first nights.

Diligent but uninspired, Jones lacked the style of Pinero, the dialogue of Wilde, and the satiric edge of Shaw, but he loved the drama. He grew up a farmer's son in Wales and at eighteen saw his first play, an evergreen melodrama called *Leah,* which was so affecting that he decided to write imitations of other plays.★ To that end, he worked by day in a draper's shop

---

★An example of how adapting foreign dramas led to theatrical careers: Augustin Daly (1838–99) was a New York newspaper drama critic for ten years before he adapted *Leah* in 1862 from Salomon Hermann von Mosenthal's *Deborah,* a German melodrama written in 1850.

and in the evening saw the same plays over and over. His first production in 1879, *A Clerical Error,* was followed three years later with the success of *The Silver King* (written with Henry Herman), but it was a decade until he had a hit with *The Middleman.*

Wilde called Pinero "a stage carpenter" with the writing style of "a grocer's assistant" who produced characters made of dough; he also said he had three rules for writing plays: the first was not to write like Jones and the second and third rules were the same. Even so, Pinero and Jones were the popular dramatists whose plays Wilde saw, so it was inevitable that he borrowed here and there.

THROUGH HIS FAMILY Wilde was known to the Irish playwrights Dion Boucicault and W. G. Wills. The author of *The Corsican Brothers* and *The Colleen Bawn,* Boucicault worked primarily in America. In 1860 he returned to Dublin a national hero and was entertained at Merrion Square when Wilde was six years old. Boucicault's caricature of the horsey outdoorswoman Lady Gay Spanker in *London Assurance* appealed to Wilde, as did *Forbidden Fruit,* whose dual-identity plot resembles that of *Earnest.* Boucicault wrote good-humored badinage ("Love ends in matrimony, wine in soda water"), but it was thin banter compared with Wilde's.

Although he and his father shared Wills's family name, Wilde did not pursue the connection with the aging dramatist.* He probably thought him pathetic: a playwright who wanted to be a painter, supporting himself by writing showcases for Irving. When Ellen Terry appeared as Queen Henrietta Maria in Wills's play *Charles I* in June 1879, Wilde dashed off a sonnet during the third act. Terry said the lines "In the lone tent, waiting for victory, / She stands with eyes marred by the mists of pain, / Like some wan lily overdrenched with rain" conveyed exactly what she tried to portray in the second act. Wilde christened her "Our Lady of the Lyceum," giving her a Madonna's halo.

There was another epiphany for Wilde when Irving opened Alfred,

---

*There is no evidence that the two families were related. The first Wilde (Ralph), Oscar's great-grandfather, came to Castlerea as an agent for the Wills family, owners of Willsgrove near Castlerea in County Roscommon.

Lord Tennyson's new play, *The Cup*, on January 3, 1881. To conceal a thin plot, Irving ordered spectacular sets, including a full-scale Temple of Artemis and a crowd scene with one hundred vestal virgins. One of them was Florence Stoker. Beside himself at the coincidence of Terry and his Florrie sharing the same stage, Wilde sent Terry two crowns of flowers. "Will you accept one of them," he wrote, "whichever you think will suit you best. The other—don't think me treacherous, Nellie—but the other please give to Florrie *from yourself.*" Romantically he added, "I should like to think that she was wearing something of mine the first night she comes on the stage, that anything of mine should touch her. Of course if you think—but you won't think she will suspect. How could she? She thinks I never loved her, thinks I forget. My God how could I!" Terry went along with the subterfuge. She knew that the Stokers entertained Wilde and that his huffing and puffing was only a love of secrecy and intrigue.

WILDE SAT DOWN and wrote his first play, *Vera; or, The Nihilists.* Chekhov's first play, *Ivanov,* written when he was twenty-seven, had the voice that would write *The Seagull* and subsequent plays. But the voice that would write *The Importance of Being Earnest* needed more training. An anachronistic political drama set in Moscow in the late eighteenth century, when there were no nihilists, *Vera* had a plot based on an incident in 1878, when Vera Zasoulich attempted to assassinate the St. Petersburg police chief for imprisoning her nihilist lover. Championing individualism and sexual freedom, the Nihilists were exotic news in the 1880s. A play about the Irish troubles would not have been wise, but republican feelings could be served with a play about a similar political movement.

Wilde changed the locale to Moscow, called his heroine Sabouroff, and made the old czar the target. The revolutionary Vera is torn by loyalty to the cause and her love for the czarevich, who promises constitutional reform. There is a bizarre moment when Vera arrives at a secret meeting of revolutionaries wearing a vermilion ball gown underneath a black cloak. It was Lady Wilde center stage. When Vera's lover becomes the new czar and the next victim, she kills herself, pretending that her bloody dagger was used on her lover. "I have saved Russia," she exclaims and dies—for love. Wilde said he wanted to express "that Titan cry of the peoples for liberty," but it was passion, not politics, that interested him. Nihilist Russia was merely the fervent background for a romantic drama. The play suggested support for the monarchy, but the theme favored revolutionary ideas. It was a risky venture to get produced.

Royally dressed in dark red leather with gold-embossed lettering, *Vera* was presented to Wilde's favorite actresses, who he hoped would beg for the leading role. A copyright performance was set for the morning of December 17, 1881, at the Adelphi Theatre with Mrs. Bernard Beere. She was not a Bernhardt, a Terry, or a Modjeska, but Wilde was optimistic; he was convinced that he had written something wonderful.

Unfortunately, there was another Russian revolutionary named Vera, the leader of the terrorist organization People's Will. Vera Figner had overseen seven failed attempts to assassinate Czar Alexander II. The eighth succeeded when he died of injuries after a bomb hidden in an Easter cake was tossed into his sleigh as it headed for the Winter Palace on March 13, 1881. The Russian incident—although eight months old—together with the fact that the Prince of Wales, Lillie Langtry's lover, was married to the sister of the new czarina, made the political content a convenient excuse for Wilde when he postponed the performance; a more probable cause was his inability to raise enough money for the reading.

WILDE NEEDED RECOGNITION, and, like so many poets of his generation, he decided to self-publish a volume of sixty-one poems (mostly sonnets)—thirty of which had previously appeared in magazines. He proposed a skillful marketing strategy: there would be five editions of 250 copies each, issued within a year, with the fifth appearing in 1882. Three American editions were similarly issued in 1881. What a popular poet, he hoped people would say. And only twenty-six years old!

An epigraph planned—but later discarded—for the title page announced in French what Wilde was too embarrassed to say in English: *Mes premiers vers sont d'un enfant, mes seconds d'un adolescent* ("My first verses are those of a child, my second those of an adolescent"). An accurate assessment. Once Wilde entered Oxford, classical, pagan, and religious themes supplanted the sensual and flowery.

As always, he sent copies to Gladstone, Swinburne, Symonds, Arnold, and Robert Browning. He wrote Arnold that he had "only now, too late perhaps, found out how all art requires solitude as its companion." Of course, Wilde loathed solitude, but he hoped an image of himself as St. Jerome writing in a cell might impress the virtuoso prophet. Arnold replied that he had not read the poems but on the basis of the titles assumed that Wilde had "found out the force of what Byron so insisted on that one must shake off London life before one can do one's best work." Arnold was misled by the Hellenic references; still, if Wilde had returned to Greece, he might have, like Byron, entered a new phase as a poet. Instead, in the drawing rooms of America, London, and Paris, he invented a man who became famous for just being himself.

The critics savaged *Poems*. *Punch* called it "Swinburne and water." His work labeled unoriginal and immoral, Wilde's only maneuver—popular at the time—was to ask a friend for a laudatory review. Oscar Browning at Cambridge rose to the occasion, writing in the *Academy* that "England is enriched with a new poet," noting Wilde's "fresh, vigorous mind" and his "command of varied and musical language." It was praise worthy of Wilde himself.

What hurt most were accusations of insincerity; insincerity was essential to Wilde's art of multiple masks. And how unfair of the critics to accuse him of unoriginality. They obviously did not understand that if he sounded like Swinburne, he had only improved on one work of art to create a new one. Had not Swinburne stolen from Keats? Did not Brahms use a theme from Beethoven's Ninth for his first symphony? "I live in terror of not being misunderstood," he said. The British were indeed Philistines. "I am but too conscious of the fact that we are born in an age when only the dull are treated seriously," he would complain in "The Critic as Artist."

Ingenuously, Wilde thought the negative reviews were a reaction to his immaturity as a poet. But the critics had a secret agenda. Wilde had trumpeted his greatness all over London, and his slim volume—no matter how beautiful the white parchment binding and the handmade Dutch paper—was an inadequate debut. Wilde's posturing was beginning to rankle the littérateurs he most wanted to impress.

Close friends were supportive: Violet Hunt loved the poems. Wilde's effusive response to her praise shows that the naysayers were getting to him. "In an age like this when Slander, and Ridicule and Envy walk quite unashamed among us," he wrote, "and when any attempt to produce serious beautiful work is greeted with a very tornado of lies and evil-speaking, it is a wonderful joy, a wonderful spur for ambition and work, to receive any such encouragement and appreciation as your letter brought me." Later, when prose rather than poetry compelled him, he told Yeats: "We Irish are too poetical to be poets; we are a nation of brilliant failures, but we are the greatest talkers since the Greeks."

THE OXFORD UNION solicited a copy, which Wilde inscribed: "To the Library of the Oxford Union, my first volume of poems, Oscar Wilde Oct 27 '81." The request was pro forma for alumni; libraries filled shelves with such requests. When the acquisition was announced, a minority cried plagiarism, citing borrowings from Shakespeare, Byron, and Swinburne, and convinced the majority to return the book. It was a "coarse impertinence," Wilde said, but he did not toss his blue china vase into the fireplace: he was an artist, on occasion a work of art, but never a temperamental artist. "It is only the unimaginative who never invents," he maintained. "The true artist is known by the use he makes of what he annexes, and he annexes everything."

In acknowledging that artists plagiarize from others as well as themselves, Wilde told a well-known truth. In "The Critic as Artist," he observes that all "artistic creation is absolutely subjective. The very landscape that Corot looked at was, as he said himself, but a mood of his own mind." In "The Decay of Lying," Vivian explains, "Art takes life as part of her rough material, recreates it, refashions it in fresh forms," and, as Wilde did in his poetry and prose, "is absolutely indifferent to fact, invents, imagines, dreams." Of course, Wilde was equally at home with the opposite view, although fatuous in an interview after the success of *An Ideal Husband:* "Nobody else's work gives me any suggestion. It is only by entire isolation from everything that one can do any work. Idleness gives one the mood in which to write, isolation the conditions."

Lord Henry speaks for Wilde when he tells Dorian: "Good artists exist simply in what they make, and consequently are perfectly uninteresting in what they are. A great poet, a really great poet, is the most unpoetical of all creatures. But inferior poets are absolutely fascinating. . . . The mere fact of having published a book of second-rate sonnets makes a man quite irresistible. He lives the poetry that he cannot write." That irresistible man, of course, was Oscar Wilde.

As for indecency, Wilde was in his infancy, growing toward *Dorian Gray*. Still, "Charmides," about a lover caressing a marble statue, is carnal, with lines such as

> *The grand cool flanks, the crescent thighs, the bossy hills of snow.* . . .
>   *And then his lips in hungering delight*
> *Fed on her lips, and round the towered neck*
> *He flung his arms, nor cared at all his passion's will to check.*

Frank Miles's religious father was shocked. He warned that his room-mate's poetry was "licentious and may do a great harm to any soul that reads it." In the summer of 1880, Miles and Wilde had left Thames House for One Tite Street in Chelsea, a three-story, red-and-yellow-brick house with a green-slate roof and balconies. Wilde called it Keats House because the previous owners were the Skeates. Now Canon Miles, who had paid for the renovations done by Edward William Godwin, Ellen Terry's former lover, decided that Wilde was a bad influence and should live elsewhere. His son did not protest.★

A rite of passage in every life, betrayal invariably pained Wilde and became a brooding point in his work. Frank Harris's biography claims he was furious when Miles told him he had to leave, and there was a scene with much yelling and throwing about of clothes. Wilde vowed never to speak to Miles again. He moved to furnished rooms at 9 Charles Street (now Carlos Place), off Grosvenor Square and across from the Coburg (Connaught) Hotel.

AT TWENTY-SIX, Wilde was an Oxford gentleman who lived on his own and on credit, unlike his brother, who lived with, and off, their mother. He had an unproduced play and a batch of bad reviews for a book of poems he'd had to publish on his own. But he still had his reputation as a dandy and a brilliant conversationalist. He continued to burnish the image of the

---

★Miles spent a great deal of time with Lord Ronald Sutherland-Gower, seven years his senior and a known homosexual, and feared that his father might discover his ambiguous sexuality. His father died shortly after Wilde departed, and six years later Miles was taken to an insane asylum near Bristol. He died there in 1891, when Wilde was on the threshold of fame.

apostle of aesthetics, a poet with a lily in his hand. His mannered attitudes and epicene posturing were never viewed as signs of an invert nature. From the time of the Regency, a same-sex subculture of which others were unaware had gathered around aristocrats. Dressed in satin and lace, colored stockings and powdered wigs, the court fops were effeminate but manly. Sexuality was never an issue; ambiguity made the dandy interesting. Beau Brummell, who symbolized for Regency London overrefinement, leisure, and a preoccupation with fashion, became a despot of wit and taste, a position he invented rather than inherited. That wit could be valued over being well-born was not lost on Wilde.

In the eighties, the satirical magazine *Punch* reflected the opinions and prejudices of the British upper-middle classes. Its leading cartoonist, George Du Maurier, had lived with Whistler in the bohemian Paris of the 1850s; when he lost the use of his left eye at age twenty-three, he abandoned painting for a less demanding medium. He had satirized the Aesthetes since 1873, at first by theme, such as the mania for blue-and-white china. In one drawing, an aesthetic bridegroom presents a teapot to his wife, remarking, "It is quite consummate, is it not?" "It is, indeed! Oh, Algernon, Let us live up to it!" The worship of blue china was not confined to Wilde; in fact, Whistler and Rossetti collected blue china long before Wilde worried about living up to it at Oxford.

Du Maurier's captions invented the language of aesthetics, with words like "utterly utter," "quite," "exquisite," "beautiful," and "divine." The Aesthetes' floral preferences were noted, particularly the lily, an image revered by Rossetti. In 1880 Du Maurier introduced the painter Maudle and the poet Jellaby Postlethwaite, whose aesthetic murmurings impress society. Postlethwaite, who speaks like Wilde but looks unlike him as an emaciated poet with prominent cheekbones, sees his success in floral terms: "The Lily had carried me through my first season, the Primrose through my second. The question arose: what Flower of Flowers is to carry me through my next?" On February 12, 1881, Wilde's face appears on Maudle, who lounges on a settee talking to Mrs. Cimabue Brown, identified as a Philistine from the country. Her son wants to be an artist, and Maudle (sounding like Wilde) advises: "Why should he Be anything? Why not let him remain for ever content to Exist Beautifully?"

Punch featured Wilde as its thirty-seventh "Fancy Portrait," following the publication of *Poems*. His face is in the center of a sunflower accompanied by this critical ditty:

Aesthete of Aesthetes!
What's in a name?
The poet is WILDE,
But his poetry's tame.

Other *Punch* cartoonists had fun with his name, too, and Wilde appears variously as Oscuro Wildegoose, Drawit, the Wilde-eyed poet, and Ossian Wilderness. When Du Maurier's caricatures were discussed at Burne-Jones's studio, Violet Hunt recalled, "Burne Jones suddenly hissed out, as he could hiss when roused: 'Say what you like, there is more wit in that man's little finger than in du Maurier's whole body.' "

BY SATIRIZING AESTHETIC affectations on stage, W. S. Gilbert provided the turning point Wilde's life needed. In his Savoy opera *Patience*, Gilbert introduces two poets: Reginald Bunthorne, the fleshly, and Archibald Grosvenor, the spiritual. As role models, Rossetti, Swinburne, and Whistler were uppermost in Gilbert's mind, but the public saw only Wilde on the program cover: an Aesthete in knee breeches and black stockings, floppy tie and wideawake hat, a modification of the French artist costume of 1830. Wilde did not invent the so-called aesthetic dress. Inspired by a similar costume worn at his Oxford Masonic lodge, he borrowed the look for his American tour and made it his own work of art. As early as September 1876, when Wilde was an Oxford undergraduate, Du Maurier dressed Boniface Brasenose in knee breeches and a smoking jacket with quilted lapels.

In addition to the librettos written with Arthur Sullivan, Gilbert excelled at those dramatic forms—burlesque, fairy play, pantomime—that characterized the nineteenth century. For Gilbert, laughs were always at the expense of some person or institution. His verbal dexterity (rhyming *aesthetical, heretical,* and *emetical*) was gimmicky, but he created hummable tunes. Before Wilde or Shaw, Gilbert satirized human vanity, hypocrisy, and stupidity but directed the sting at the bourgeois, not at Wilde's preferred target—the upper classes.

Patience opened at the Opera Comique on April 23, 1881, and transferred in October to inaugurate the new Savoy Theatre, the first theatre in the world to use electric lights, generated by an engine chugging away in a nearby shed. The plot revolves around some lovesick maidens who are more attracted to the poets who pose and gaze at lilies (modeled on Du Maurier's cartoons) than to the blue-and-gold-uniformed dragoons. Bunthorne assumes an aesthetic attitude to attract Patience, the village milkmaid, who sings of her longing to discover the meaning of love, then meets a stranger, Grosvenor, who immediately proposes. The affections of Patience for the two poets and those of the maidens for the dragoons combine to complicate the plot.

Generations of actors playing Bunthorne have attempted to translate Wilde's *quasi niente* of tone and gesture into a studied emphasis on what today would be called camping or queening. Wilde called it "swaggering," a word suggesting arrogance of movement, a nineteenth-century strut done with supreme self-confidence. Wilde swaggered when his vanity bubbled over, but the language was mostly verbal. He denied that he bought a lily daily and walked it through town to Lillie Langtry's home. "To have done it was nothing, but to make people think one had done it was a triumph," he said. The anecdote inspired Gilbert to write:

> *Though the Philistines may jostle,*
> *You will rank as an apostle*
> *In the high aesthetic band,*
> *If you walk down Piccadilly*
> *With a poppy or a lily*
> *In your mediaeval hand.*

Gilbert did not have the Aesthetes all to himself. Dramatists found Wilde an irresistible subject. There were even parodies of parodies. Sometimes Wilde refused to see himself onstage.* Being lampooned was

---

*Before *Patience* there was *The Grasshopper* (1877), a burlesque of the opening of the Grosvenor Gallery; *Where's the Cat?* (1880), with Herbert Beerbohm Tree in the Wilde part, and *The Colonel* (1881), by F. C. Burnand, editor of *Punch*.

only another kind of self-promotion, but to be taken seriously, Wilde needed to discourage any more buffoonery.

Then, at the perfect time, a dignified offer arrived to tour America as the apostle of Aestheticism or, as Wilde put it, "to show the rich what beautiful things they might enjoy and the poor what beautiful things they might create." *Patience* had opened in New York, and the plan called for Wilde—a real Bunthorne—to promote the operetta. The coast-to-coast tour was suggested to Richard D'Oyly Carte's business manager by Mrs. Frank Leslie, director of the publishing company founded by her late English-born husband and editor of *Frank Leslie's Lady's Magazine*— destined to become Wilde's sister-in-law.

Extravagantly described as a visiting artist whose recent volume of poems had made "a profound sensation" in England, Wilde was to celebrate poetry and art and be entertained by America's cultural elite. And, if he proved popular with audiences, there was money to be made. All traveling expenses and a half share of the profits tempted him to accept. There was no reason to remain in London in two furnished rooms with his social life dislocated by the break with Frank Miles. He began thinking about what he should wear and what he would say.

CHAPTER EIGHT

A Second Self

❧

Nothing should be able to harm a man except himself.
Nothing should be able to rob a man at all. What a man really has, is
what is in him. What is outside of him should be
a matter of no importance.

—"THE SOUL OF MAN UNDER SOCIALISM"

Wilde imagined America with chilly scenes of snowcapped mountains and frozen streets with arctic winds snapping at his legs, a climate worse than England's. Obviously he needed new clothes and warm ones. Along with several velvet aesthetic costumes to wear while lecturing, he asked his tailor to make an ankle-length, Lincoln green, otter-lined, seal-trimmed overcoat with frogged closures. Oversized, with extrawide cuffs and a deep-notched collar, this coat became Wilde's favorite item of clothing; it had an aura that possessed him, and when it was sold while he was in prison, he mourned it as one does a lost friend. It "knows me perfectly," he said.

After settling on the contents of his steamer trunks, Wilde solicited letters of introduction. The American ambassador, James Russell Lowell, who had favorably reviewed his *Poems* in the *Atlantic Monthly*, wrote Oliver Wendell Holmes that "a clever and accomplished man should no more need an introduction than a fine day." (In Boston, Wilde dined with "the Autocrat of the Breakfast Table" and afterward sent Holmes an edition of his poems.) Burne-Jones wrote appreciatively to the scholar Charles Eliot Norton. "The gentleman who brings this little note to you is my friend Mr. Oscar Wilde, who has much brightened this last of my declining years. . . . he really loves the men and things you and I love." To feed his fantasy that he would visit Japan—and in case he did—Wilde asked the Japanese vice president of foreign affairs in London for introductions to cultural organizations.

Any British traveler found it difficult to learn about America in 1882, ten years before a Baedeker on the country was published. Current facts were available only in select newspapers. But Wilde never craved facts and statistics: they intruded on expectations. In "The Decay of Lying," Vivian complains about the invasion of facts: "Their chilling touch is over everything. They are vulgarizing mankind."

Wilde planned to complete his first lecture on the English Renaissance during the eight-day voyage from Liverpool; he boarded on Christmas Eve and celebrated until the SS *Arizona* steamed into New York harbor on January 2, 1882. Wilde was at the railing in his new coat and a broad-brimmed black hat. His lecture was incomplete, but he had good quotes for the press. If Wilde said something clever, he never thought, "That's brilliant. I'll write it down." His epigrams went through a lapidary stage: presented, polished, then committed to paper. Performances took place during the drawn-out seven-course meals that helped to pass time on transatlantic crossings.

Before Wilde cleared customs, he was famous for his alleged quote "I have nothing to declare except my genius." Another bon mot, delivered secondhand, noted that "the Atlantic is a disappointment. It did not roar." His comment had delighted passengers, and one repeated it when a journalist asked how Mr. Wilde had enjoyed the voyage. After sailing through a Mediterranean cyclone between Athens and Naples, Wilde expected more from an ocean.

As promised, the Grand Hotel at Thirty-first Street and Broadway was first-class; his two-room suite had a view of the new Wallack's Theatre in the heart of a developing theatre district. Previously theatres had clustered downtown at Union Square, an area no longer fashionable. When the upper classes began to move uptown, the theatres followed, to Madison Square and Long Acre Square, which became Times Square in 1904. Ten blocks from Wallack's was the Metropolitan Concert Hall, later the city's first opera house. As soon as Wilde left the hotel, reporters were after him seeking quotes, demanding to hear his impressions of America.

Somewhat sarcastically, he observed that American men "seem to get a hold on life much earlier than we do." And the women were superior. "On the whole, the great success of marriage is due partly to the fact that no American man is ever idle, and . . . no American wife is considered responsible for the quality of her husband's dinners . . . the horrors of domesticity are almost entirely unknown." The United States is the only country where Don Juan is not appreciated, he said, "and the men— docile and unromantic—have made it such a paradise that this is perhaps why, like Eve, the women are always so anxious to get out of it." Divorce was a positive family value. "When people are tied together for life they too often regard manners as a mere superfluity, and courtesy as a thing of no moment," he said, rehearsing an insight repeated in his social come- dies, "but where the bond can easily be broken, its very fragility makes its strength, and reminds the husband that he should always try to please, and the wife that she should never cease to be charming."

IN ADDITION TO Colonel W. F. Morse, who managed tours for Carte, Wilde had two secretaries, a Negro valet who was told to say, "Massa Wilde is too busy to recept today," and a carriage with a Negro groom in livery. "In a free country one cannot live without a slave," he wrote Norman Forbes-Robertson, describing his valet as "rather like a Christy minstrel, except that he knows no riddles." One secretary answered letters, and the other sent off snippets of his brown hair to avid young ladies. Wilde said that this secretary "is rapidly becoming bald"; as for himself, he was behaving "as I always have behaved— 'dreadfully.' "

Wilde's plays employ valets and butlers as pivotal dandified characters to negotiate hapless men and women in and out of social crises. Earnest's opening lines between Lane and Algernon are a paradigm of class satire: "Did you hear what I was playing, Lane?" asks Algy. "I didn't think it was polite to listen, sir," he replies. In An Ideal Husband, Lord Goring, described by Wilde as the "first well-dressed philosopher in the history of thought," has a trivial conversation with his servant about his buttonhole that ends not in interior smirks but in loud laughter when Lord Goring remarks: "Extraordinary thing about the lower class in England—they are always losing their relations." "Yes, my lord!" Phipps replies. "They are extremely fortunate in that respect."

Invitations to luncheons, dinners, and receptions arrived daily. His valet held calling cards on a silver salver while Wilde separated sycophants from deserving disciples. He told Betty Lewis, wife of his solicitor George Lewis, that he felt like the Prince of Wales. "I now understand why the Royal Boy is in good humour always; it is delightful to be *petit roi*." Such euphoria may have masked a fear that his first lecture, still needing work, would go over badly.

NAPOLEON SARONY PHOTOGRAPHED Wilde in twenty-seven different poses, with changes of clothes, hairstyle, and aesthetic attitude. These publicity photos, however, were not processed in time for the first lecture. (Wilde had the local artist James Edward Kelly sketch and then etch his portrait for use in advertising circulars.) In the history of nineteenth-century photography, Sarony was as famous as Mathew Brady was for Civil War coverage. Both competed as portraitists. Brady's portraits of Abraham Lincoln, Walt Whitman, and Ulysses S. Grant sent a moral message, while Sarony preferred to be entertaining.

By using a "posing machine," Sarony manipulated and then immobilized the subject's head, arms, and torso into the desired pose for the duration of the exposure. Some subjects viewed this as an instrument of torture, but without it Sarony could not have made dramatic poses appear natural. He inspired the look and left technicalities to an assistant, usually looking out the window while the pictures were taken. He paid celebrities to be photographed but recouped expenses by selling collectible postcards. Sarah Bernhardt received fifteen hundred dollars for the famous series of her on a "fainting couch." Morse wanted Sarony's prestige, so the fee was waived for Wilde.

Like his namesake the Emperor Napoléon Bonaparte, Sarony was diminutive—only five feet tall; he sported a flamboyant handlebar mustache and wore a red fez to add inches to his height. His Union Square studio was as eccentric as its occupant, filled with Egyptian mummies, Japanese and medieval armor, Russian sleighs, bizarre idols, and, hanging from the ceiling, a stuffed crocodile. At sixty-one, he was, like Wilde, a shameless self-promoter.

Sarony produced an impressive series revealing how "the lord of language," as Wilde called himself, commanded many moods. In black cape and broad-brimmed hat tilted to one side, Wilde is seductive, vampiric even. In aesthetic dress, he is poetic but manly: legs encased in black stockings, his small feet in patent-leather slippers with bows—all in perfect proportion to his height. The face is a beautiful, contemplative oval. The lens registers the lustrous, wavy hair parted in the middle and curling behind the ears, and the heavy-lidded eyes that turn down at the corners, and how sometimes the right eye appears smaller than the left. But the star of the shoot was the massive overcoat. Enveloped in fur, Wilde resembles a Nordic deity in a carved armchair frozen in the thinking position, elbow on knee and hand on cheek. A favorite with collectors, this pose was the focus of a copyright action when a lithographic company made 85,000 prints of it. Sarony proved his case that photography was art.

ALL TWELVE HUNDRED seats at Chickering Hall were sold out at a dollar each, and standing room was full when Wilde arrived backstage on a cold, windy January 9 for his first lecture. He strode onstage with a circular black cloak thrown over one shoulder, walking slowly to model the knee breeches and black stockings worn with a lace-trimmed shirt under a dark purple coat lined in lavender satin. "Since you have heard *Patience,* which has been given for so many nights," Wilde said, "you might listen to me for at least one evening." That pragmatic opening brought a few laughs, and he reached for loftiness: "You must not judge our aestheticism by the satire of Mr. Gilbert any more than you can judge of the strength and splendor of the sun or sea by the dust that dances in the beam or the bubble that breaks upon the wave." The audience understood a remark that the Pre-Raphaelites had three things on their side the "English public never forgives: Youth, power and enthusiasm."

But the themes of "the English Renaissance" were complicated by cultural references, and the talk lacked anecdote or wit. Wilde performed as a polymath, leaving people either baffled or bored. Applause was spontaneous and loud; at least he had dazzled with personality. *The New York Times* said he spoke in a "sepulchral voice"; subsequent lectures were deemed boring, monotonous, wearisome, toneless, and, on one evening, "a rhythmic chant in which every fourth syllable is accentuated." Wilde never considered himself anything but a novice when it came to confronting row upon row of upturned faces.

On arrival he outlined his priorities, putting playwright and poet ahead of lecturer. He said his play *Vera* was not performed in London because he could not cast it—a slight lie but an easier explanation than the relevant political and financial problems. "It must be produced with able actors. If a satisfactory cast can be obtained here it may be produced," he told journalists, throwing down the gauntlet for an American actress to pick up.

THE ORIGINAL FOUR-MONTH tour expanded to ten months, ending after 140 lectures in 260 days in a hundred cities and towns coast to coast and into Canada. Audiences were mostly women and ranged from scattered heads to auditoriums of fifteen hundred. Wilde never gave Mark Twain much podium competition, but anyone who saw him recalled the experience as special. Back in London, America's reception of the apostle of Aestheticism was closely followed. "Nobody is sanguine about his success," *The Times* reported, "but nobody knows what he can do beyond writing poetry and posing as a leading figure in a limited circle."

So important was Wilde's aesthetic dress that audiences complained if he wore evening clothes. His appearance changed from place to place. When he arrived on the *Arizona,* his face was "utterly devoid of color—like putty—eyes bright and quick—face oval, long chin—doesn't look like a Du Maurier model—more like an athlete—instead of having a small, delicate hand to only caress a lily, his fingers are long and when doubled up would form a fist that would hit a hard knock."

In the *New York World,* his teeth were described as "large and regular, disproving a pleasing story which has gone the rounds of the English press that he has three tusks or protuberants far from agreeable to look at." *The Washington Post* observed how the "upper half of his person resembled an English curate—his lower extremities an Italian brigand, his legs a general and remote resemblance to two sticks of licorice."

In Buffalo, New York, he wore "a short after-dinner jacket of fawn-colored velvet trimmed with silk braid of a shade lighter, and a vest of the same material." And he proffered fashion hints. "The essence of good dressing is perfect congruity," he said. "One must be careful not to be too premature, but I feel that at present velvet is the most beautiful dress for a man. As a rule I wear gray or brown velvet myself."

Admired but too often criticized, Wilde dreaded getting the morning papers. "I have been quite amused at the struggle each of the gentlemen has had to write what I did not say," he said at one press conference. "If you survive yellow journalism, you need not be afraid of yellow fever." A young reporter from the *St. Louis Post-Dispatch* learned that Wilde's "reading of a good vigorous attack acts like a dish of caviar." When asked about his private life, he replied, "I wished that I had one."

Then he so charmed a reporter from the *Sacramento Daily Record-Union* that he was hailed as "the poor man's friend" and "the most misrepresented foreigner that ever visited our shores." As a poor man's friend he was indeed misrepresented; poverty, as Wilde points out in "The Soul of Man Under Socialism," disturbed him only if he was forced to look at it. If he had been universally praised, he would have doubted himself. "I know that I am right, that I have a mission to perform," he told a New York journalist. "I am indestructible!" In "The Critic as Artist," Gilbert says, "Ah! Don't say that you agree with me. When people agree with me I always feel that I must be wrong."

PRESENTING UP TO six lectures a week, Wilde was a goodwill ambassador for England as well as for himself. He visited museums and schools; he amusingly advised the elders of Griggsville, Kansas, to change the name of their town if they wanted him to lecture on aesthetics. He recast the first convoluted lecture into "The Decorative Arts" and for towns where he appeared twice added "The House Beautiful." He advised the ladies to put down rush matting if they could not afford Persian rugs. Certain aspects of American decor, like secondhand furniture and "dreadful monstrosities called cast-iron stoves," infuriated him. Pictures hung in hallways were atrocious, he said; "hang them where time can be had to look at them."

Halfway across the continent, he learned to personalize lectures. In Chicago he praised the aid given after the 1871 Great Fire, saying it "was noble and beautiful as the work of any troops of angels who ever clothed the naked." Then he described the city's first water tower as a "castellated monstrosity with pepper-boxes stuck all over it." There were unappreciative murmurs; Wilde had insulted Chicago's beloved landmark, built in 1867. Ignoring the restlessness, he forged on, "I am amazed that any people could so abuse Gothic art, and make a structure look, not like a water-tower, but like the tower of a medieval castle."

Wilde's aesthetic theories were frustrating. Did he really prefer an ugly round tower to a decorative castle? That was a contradiction of Gautier's axiom that if a thing becomes useful it ceases to be beautiful. As part of his aesthetic canon, Baudelaire believed in artifice, which improved on nature. The castle's design was only a fanciful intrusion on the landscape; it made no moral, political, or social statement. The audience exited grumbling. "I didn't expect to learn anything, and I haven't!" said one. It was rough going making Aestheticism "the basis for a new civilization," as Wilde wanted.

IN PHILADELPHIA, THE publisher J. M. Stoddart, who first published *Dorian Gray,* arranged a visit to Camden, New Jersey, to meet Walt Whitman, "the Good Gray Poet," whose image appeared on cigar boxes. Wilde first heard Whitman's poetry of camaraderie and democracy read aloud by his parents. Years before there was a concept of sexual identity (according to the *Oxford English Dictionary,* the term *homosexuality* entered the language in 1892), he was in accord with those poems in *Leaves of Grass* exalting grand affections for other men. Wilde greeted Whitman with the words "I have come to you as to one with whom I have been acquainted almost from the cradle."

They talked about Swinburne and Tennyson and the Aesthetic movement. "I can only say that you are young and ardent," Whitman said of Wilde's mission, "and the field is wide, and if you want my advice, go ahead." Wilde said he preferred poets with "a charming style," or "beauty of theme." Whitman perceived him with wiser eyes. "Why, Oscar, it always seems to me that the fellow who makes a dead set at beauty by itself is in a bad way," he said. "My idea is that beauty is a result, not an abstraction." Wilde expanded on the comment. "Yes, I remember you have said, 'All beauty comes from beautiful blood and a beautiful brain,' and after all, I think so too."

They spoke for two hours. Wilde put his hand on the poet's knee, and they drank homemade elderberry wine. Before departing, Wilde had to drink a large glass of milk punch (milk and whiskey), a mixture he never wanted to taste again. Whitman waved farewell from the porch. "Good-by, Oscar; God bless you." Wilde boasted to journalists: "I admire him intensely—Dante Rossetti, Swinburne, William Morris and I often discuss him. There is something so Greek and sane about his poetry; it is so universal, so comprehensive. It has all the pantheism of Goethe and Schiller." That Wilde had never discussed Whitman with these poets was superfluous to the image he wanted to project.

Years later Whitman would recall Wilde as "a great big, splendid boy . . . so frank, and outspoken, and manly . . . a fine handsome young-ster." But he puzzled over his reputation: "I don't see why such mocking things are written of him. He has the English society drawl, but his enun-ciation is better than I ever heard in a young Englishman or Irishman before."

ON ST. PATRICK'S DAY, the Irish Americans in St. Paul, Minnesota, welcomed Wilde as the son "of one of Ireland's noblest daughters—of a daughter who in the troublous times of 1848 by the works of her pen and her noble example did much to keep the fire of patriotism burning brightly." In a brief talk, Wilde predicted an artistic revival for an inde-pendent Ireland. The next month he told an audience in San Francisco: "I do not know anything more wonderful or more characteristic of the Celtic genius, than the quick artistic spirit in which we adapted ourselves to the English tongue," he said. "The Saxon took our lands from us and left them desolate—we took their language and added new beauties to it." Lady Wilde believed the Irish "gift of natural eloquence" to be a major factor in the success of Irish Americans, while her son saw the country as a place where deviancy could resolve its differences with society. Thoreau made a virtue of civil disobedience, and Whitman's homosexuality was no obstacle to his success as a poet.

Being a professional Irishman was a different—liberating and enjoyable—experience. As a reviewer of others' opinions, Wilde had opposed the British occupation of Ireland, calling it "one of the great tragedies of modern Europe," and had praised the Irish American. "To learn the secret of its own strength and of England's weakness, the Celtic intellect has had to cross the Atlantic. . . . What captivity was to the Jews, exile has been to the Irish." Speaking in an unguarded, patriotic voice in public was something he had thus far avoided as he chiseled an English profile. It was, however, the Irish Catholics, those outside the Protestant Ascendancy, who welcomed him here; he had grown up surrounded by the native Irish but never had reason to appreciate their accomplishments. A fourth lecture, "The Irish Poets of 1848," saluted Charles Gavan Duffy, Thomas Davis, and, of course, his mother.

WHEN THE TOUR reached Boston, the actor-playwright Dion Boucicault dropped by Wilde's hotel. At breakfast, Wilde asked him to read *Vera,* but Boucicault was more concerned with the sideshow following Wilde around America. Boucicault had told the *Boston Transcript* that Wilde was "the easy victim of those who expose him to ridicule and to the censure of the thoughtful. Those who have known him as I have since he was a child at my knee know that beneath the fantastic envelope in which his managers are circulating him there is a noble, earnest, kind and lovable man." Although shrewd in promoting himself, Wilde was not a man of business. "I do wish we could make him less Sybarite—less Epicurean," Boucicault wrote to Mrs. George Lewis. He offered a loan of two thousand dollars for Wilde to continue the tour on his own. At sixty-one, Boucicault was a relic from a former theatrical age and a bit of an eccentric, but out of respect Wilde listened to his arguments, knowing he would make a greater muddle of the tour than Morse.

At their next meeting, Boucicault read *Vera* but was not complimentary: it needed major rewriting. The narrative spine, he told Wilde, was "good and dramatic," but the "ribs and the limbs" did not proceed from the spinal column. The "action stops for dialogue," he said, when the dialogue should be "the necessary outcome of the action exerting its influence on the characters." Wilde bristled. Dialogue was his specialty, destined to be dominant in his plays. He nodded politely and forgot everything Boucicault said.

On January 31, at the Boston Music Hall, Wilde took command of the tour. Sixty Harvard students booked seats and marched into the auditorium wearing knee breeches and black stockings, each waving a lily or a sunflower. Wilde knew in advance about the demonstration and entered not in knee breeches but in evening dress. "As I look about me," he said with amusement, stressing each word, "I am impelled for the first time to breathe a fervent prayer, 'Save me from my disciples.' "He raised his hands in a Christlike gesture that produced wild clapping and cheering.

To engage the students, Wilde told them about the Ruskin road-building project and made his participation sound most industrious. He described Oxonians discarding their oars and cricket bats for picks, shovels, and wheelbarrows. It was inconsequential that the road sank into the marsh after two months. If these young men had the spirit to work for the sake of a noble ideal of life, Wilde said, then with them he could "create an artistic movement that might change, as it has changed, the face of England. So I sought them out—leader they would call me, but there was no leader, we were all searchers only." Such sincerity—which he never cared for—and spontaneity made Wilde an instant celebrity. The *Boston Transcript*, which had ridiculed his costume and called him "the $-sthete," now said he had "achieved a real triumph, and it was by right of conquest, for force of being a gentleman, in the truest sense of the word."

LIKE HENRY IRVING, Ellen Terry, and Bram Stoker, who would tour America a year after him, Wilde detested the long train trips between lectures. Crisscrossing the country with cities and plains flashing by outside was, well, boring. "I hate to fly through the country at this rate," Wilde told reporters. "The only true way, you know, to see a country is to ride on horseback. I long to ride through New Mexico and Colorado and California." Wilde was not being fatuous; he had traversed on horseback the rugged terrain of the Peloponnese, riding to Olympia with Mahaffy. In his mind, and in his prizewinning poem, *Ravenna,* Wilde "galloped, racing with the setting sun, / And ere the crimson after-glow was passed, / I stood within Ravenna's walls at last!"

Of all the regions of America, he preferred the West, "with its grizzly bears and its untamed cow-boys, its free, open-air life and its free open-air manners, its boundless prairie and its boundless mendacity!" He visited Leadville, the silver capital of Colorado, situated high in the Rocky Mountains, where he heard every man carried a gun. "I was told that if I went there they would be sure to shoot me or my travelling manager," he said. "I wrote and told them that nothing that they could do to my travelling manager would intimidate me."

Dressed in baggy trousers underneath his favorite overcoat, his long hair tucked into a black miner's slouch hat, Wilde was lowered by bucket into the Matchless Mine. He opened a new shaft, named "the Oscar," with a silver drill and had supper with the miners at the bottom. A table was set with small glasses and opened bottles, and everyone sat on stools. "The first course was whiskey, the second whiskey, the third whiskey, all the courses were whiskey, but still they called it supper," Wilde wrote Nellie Sickert. "The amazement of the miners when they saw that art and appetite could go hand in hand knew no bounds; when I lit a long cigar they cheered till the silver fell in dust from the roof." Wilde held his own with the two-fisted drinkers and tossed off a shot "without flinching." He said that "they unanimously pronounced me in their grand simple way 'a bully boy with no glass eye.'" At the casino the drinking continued. Wilde noticed a sign on the piano: "Please do not shoot the pianist. He is doing his best." This remark, Wilde said, was the "only rational method of art criticism I have ever come across." (The saying "Don't shoot the piano player" is often attributed to Wilde.)

During the silver boom, the Matchless had made a fortune for Horace Tabor, and in 1879 he built a three-story, brick-and-stone opera house with a Victorian interior of red plush and gilt that seated 880.★ Lillian Russell and Harry Houdini had been there before Wilde walked onstage to read from the wrathful autobiography of Benvenuto Cellini, the Renaissance goldsmith who created for Francis I a renowned saltcellar. The miners did not know Cellini from Bellini, but Wilde sagely made the cultural experiment work. He explained how Cellini worked, in particular, how he cast his Perseus. "I was reproved by my hearers for not having brought him with me," he reported. "I explained that he had been dead for some little time which elicited the inquiry, 'Who shot him?'"

The freedom seekers of the new American West were his kind of people, for they knew how to celebrate life. One evening during his exile, Wilde was drinking at a Paris café when he turned to his companion and

★The 1893 silver crash closed most of the mines. By 1899 Tabor was bankrupt and dying, but he still believed that silver would rebound. He whispered to his wife, Baby Doe, "Hang on to the Matchless," a deathbed request she honored. For thirty-five years she lived alone, penniless and confused, writing her dreams and hallucinations on scraps of paper. She was discovered in her one-room cabin in 1935, frozen to death. The Ballad of Baby Doe immortalizes her life.

said he was thinking of living in America, in the West. It was a place, he said, that "a man is a man to-day, and yesterdays don't count—that a desperado can make a reputation for piety on his current performances. What a country to live in!"

EVER SINCE TOURS began, there have been scenes, arguments, and stormy confrontations. It was inevitable that Wilde finally lost his temper with his business manager Colonel Morse. "It is very annoying to me to find that my Southern tour extends far beyond the three weeks you spoke of," he wrote Morse. "It is now three weeks since I left New York, and I am informed that I have two weeks more. Five weeks for sixteen lectures—nothing could be worse in every way. It is quite stupid and gross and will do me great harm." He also had a head of steam up about a newspaper comment Morse placed about a cartoon depicting Wilde as the Wild Man of Borneo. "No mention should have been made of the cartoon at Washington," he admonished. "I regard all caricature and satire as absolutely beneath notice. . . . The matter was mine and should have been left for me to decide on."

Wilde always had a love-hate relationship with the press. He admitted to Nellie Sickert that "even the papers though venal and vile, and merely the mouthpieces of the slanderer, often repeat and write sensibly about me. . . . I feel I am doing real good work here, and of course the artists have received me with enthusiasm everywhere." One was Joaquin Miller, a self-invented character with many a dubious tale, including the story that he lost a finger in a fight with wolves while a driver for Wells Fargo. Following publication of *Songs of the Sierras* in 1871, Miller styled himself as a civilized Buffalo Bill, sporting a sombrero, pointed gray mustache, and long curls. Storming London, he arrived at the Savage Club with great Indian whoops ready to sell poems to the duchesses.

When students at the University of Rochester mimicked the Harvard demonstration, Miller complained about the mockery, urging Wilde not to "lose heart or come to dislike America. For whatever is said or done the real heart of this strong young world demands, and will have, fair play for all." Quick to exploit a publicity opportunity, Morse advised Wilde to reply with a letter to the *New York World*. Pompous and grandiose, perhaps because it was written for publication, the letter shows how Wilde prattled on when inflated with his own importance: "Who are these scribes who, passing with purposeless alacrity from the police news to the Parthenon, and from crime to criticism, sway with such serene incapacity the office which they so late swept?" he asked. " 'Narcissuses of imbecility' . . . let them peer at us through their telescopes and report what they like of us. But, my dear Joaquin, should we put them under the microscope there would be really nothing to be seen."

Even so, Wilde created some memorable, albeit stereotypical, American characters and dialogue. "Perhaps after all, America never has been discovered," Lord Henry says. "I myself would say that it had merely been detected." Hester Worsley in *A Woman of No Importance* is an example of the wealthy young American who comes to England to marry a title. "American women are wonderfully clever in concealing their parents," Lord Illingworth says, only to be told that Hester's father made his fortune in American dry goods. "What are American dry goods?" asks Lady Hunstanton. "American novels," replies Lord Illingworth.

In "The Canterville Ghost," a California family leases a country house equipped with an apparition. "I come from a modern country, where we have everything that money can buy," says Hiram B. Otis, the American politician, who is writing a history of the Democratic party. "I recken [*sic*] that if there were such a thing as a ghost in Europe, we'd have it at home in a very short time in one of our public museums, or on the road as a show." His wife, Wilde observes, never adopted ill health as a form of European refinement and was quite English—"an excellent example of the fact that we have really everything in common with America nowadays, except, of course, language."

Wilde had shown America that an Irishman could talk like an Englishman and be well-educated and well-dressed. He had earned his celebrity, but being an aesthetic curiosity had wearied him. The new Oscar would be a dandy, not a direct descendant of Brummell or Disraeli but more of an aristocrat of the dinner table, like Baudelaire. It was inevitable that Wilde would link Aestheticism with Decadence.

CHAPTER NINE

New Scenarios

✢

Experience is the name every one gives to their mistakes.

—*LADY WINDERMERE'S FAN*

After the rigors of descending mine shafts and the frustrations of defining Aestheticism, Wilde needed the diversions only a city like New York offered and decided not to return to London when the lecture tour ended in mid-October. Only his mother wanted him home. When she wrote, "I thought you had sailed away to Japan," he appeased her with some of his American earnings. Lady Wilde expected a celebratory welcome for her famous son: "You are still the talk of London—the cabmen ask me if I am anything to Oscar Wilde—the milkman has bought your picture!" Although his mother predicted that he would be "mobbed" on his return and forced to seek shelter in cabs, Wilde was not that convinced about his reception: he feared that the English press would recall only the myopic tabloid satires rather than his innovative ideas about decorative art.

New York welcomed the exhausted lecturer while he examined his options. He stayed for two and a half months, restlessly moving from hotel to hotel until he found rooms at 61 Irving Place, at the corner of Seventeenth Street in what was then the theatre district, and finally at 48 West Eleventh Street in Greenwich Village. Hostesses fought over occasions to entertain him. One awed young woman recalled how Wilde "burst like a resplendent meteor" into her charmed circle; he sat next to her at a luncheon and opened the conversation by saying: "The great crises of our lives are never events but always passions." The two stared at each other silently, then simultaneously broke into laughter. On a more serious note, Wilde predicted, not for the first time, that he would leave an indelible mark upon his generation.

At the home of a Dublin friend, Professor John Doremus, Wilde met Elisabeth Marbury, who at twenty-six had been evading marriage since she came out in society according to the protocol of an Edith Wharton novel. She was old New York, and despite a Quaker-Presbyterian background, her parents considered the theatre educational. Every Friday evening the family attended performances at one of New York's fifteen theatres, where they chose among the classics and drama (she saw John Gilbert in Sheridan's *The School for Scandal* in 1870), musicals and burlesques, French opéra bouffe and variety shows.

Already a grandmotherly looking figure with a masculine bearing, Marbury was destined to be the preeminent American theatrical agent of the nineties. Initially Wilde delighted her. "Like many others I fell under the thrall of his gifts as a conversationalist and could listen with delight to the brilliancy of his talk," she recalled. As Wilde's agent, she later took a more critical view when he flaunted his homosexuality even as she lived in a lesbian relationship. Wilde never understood how his behavior spread fear throughout homosexual circles in England and America.

At this time Wilde acted as his own agent. With characteristic savoir faire, he brought actresses the script of an unproven playwright in a country where he was known more as an objet d'art than as a talented writer. He learned through trial and error the difficulties of negotiating a contract. That *Vera* needed revisions, as Boucicault had suggested, never motivated him to make changes before seeking a lead. He had verbalized the scenes long ago and could not rewrite without the inspired urgency of conversation.

UPON LILLIE LANGTRY'S arrival in New York with her touring company, Wilde put aside the frustrations of selling his play. On the morning of October 23, he arose at the unheard-of hour of three, dressed in a black velvet jacket, and put on his beloved overcoat. He took a hansom to the pier for the 4:30 A.M. launch that chugged out to the SS *Arizona,* the same ship on which he had had his disappointing encounter with the Atlantic. He boarded carrying an abundance of white lilies and presented them one by one, to the actress's amusement.

The New York Times reported his tie "was gaudy and his shirtfront very open, displaying a large expanse of manly chest"—surely a fabrication, for Wilde would never publicly expose his body. A Canadian reporter asked him if he had "discovered" Mrs. Langtry. "I would rather have discovered Mrs. Langtry than have discovered America," he replied. In many ways he had discovered her back at Salisbury Street, when he introduced her to poetry, advised her to wear yellow, and encouraged her dramatic ambitions. She was never a talented actress, but she had presence, remembered her lines, and filled seats by wearing fabulous jewels so that the ladies in the audience could debate which ones were gifts of the Prince of Wales.

Wilde's adoration did not go unnoticed. "As for the love-smitten Oscar Wilde, he is head over heels in love," reported one journalist. The proclaimed couple fell into their familiar roles as fashion consultants. Wilde told the Lily not to wear long boots for her part of Rosalind in *As You Like It;* she fussed with his unmanageable hair and tugged on his tie. Wilde insisted on posing her for Sarony, who had paid five thousand dollars for the privilege; she laughed and talked through the sitting and rejected the first set of proofs. "You have made me pretty; I am beautiful," she told Sarony, who responded with one of his impish shrugs. Americans were paying five dollars for her portrait, and the French wanted five hundred copies.

Wilde explained that Americans were not uncivilized, only decivilized. He assumed himself to be the favored protector for dinners at Delmonico's and other celebrations. But he was upstaged by a playboy called Freddy Gebhardt, who used Langtry's greed for expensive gifts to his advantage. They were often a threesome at dinner. On the morning of her debut as Hester Grazebrook in *An Unequal Match,* Wilde introduced her to a remarkable man called Steele MacKaye, whose innovations—the movable stage and the tip-up seat—were precursors of modern theatre-craft.

His father, Colonel James MacKaye, had spied for President Lincoln and founded the American Telegraph Company, but the son—impractical and extravagant—epitomized the American dreamer. At sixteen he left school to study painting in Paris, then switched to acting, spending unlimited family funds in a quest for fulfillment. He trained with François Delsarte, an actor who claimed he had discovered "the natural and infallible laws of human expression." Delsarte urged students to watch children at play and to study the human body in hospitals, morgues, asylums, and art galleries. Despite travel and education, MacKaye never achieved maturity, perhaps because he had the wealth to be reckless.

Lanky and darkly sinister at forty, with long, black, curly hair, he was a magnetic individualist whose personality-driven ideas overwhelmed Wilde. The latest was a movable stage: one stage on top of the other, installed inside an elevator shaft, which shifted up or down to different levels by pulleys and counterweights. MacKaye explained to his visitors how a set was changed while another scene was in progress at stage level. Holding a pocket watch, he demonstrated that it took only forty seconds to switch sets.* Anything mechanical was mysterious to Wilde, but he could visualize how such a mechanism could benefit a dramatist, and he showed his interest by asking questions.

Langtry wandered over to a window overlooking the Park Theatre, where her play was to open that evening—and gasped. It was on fire, a common enough occurrence in the gaslight era. Since Wallack's Theatre was unoccupied, the play opened there a week later. Wilde attended with MacKaye and afterward, at the invitation of W. H. Hurlbert, editor of the *New York World,* went to the paper's composing room, where he wrote his review seated amidst the ink-smudged typesetters. Avoiding any opinion of the overall production (which he disliked), Wilde praised Langtry's beauty (it had launched a new movement in English art) and her costumes (they surpassed the scenery). He even mentioned the safety curtain at the Madison Square Theatre, another of MacKaye's devices.

MacKaye wanted to build the first million-dollar theatre and asked

---

*There was a drawback: the two stages went in only one direction. MacKaye then designed another stage to move in any direction; also to his credit were an adjustable proscenium to control the size of the stage opening, a system for projecting moving clouds, and, his most bizarre project, a "spectatorium" with twenty-five stages, on which he planned to perform Columbus's voyage to America.

Wilde for *The Duchess of Padua* and *Vera* to open his extravaganza at Broadway and Thirty-third Street. Investors were harder to sign up. Wilde ingenuously assured his partner that the influential people he had met in America would open their checkbooks. Only youthful enthusiasm, gilded charm, and foolish optimism kept the fantasy in motion. "Do not yet despair," Wilde told MacKaye when things were bleak on all sides, "you and I together should conquer the world."

MacKaye chased the money and Wilde pursued the actresses. The script for *Vera* was making the rounds, but there were only working notes for *The Duchess of Padua*. The inspirational rush that had produced sonnets to Bernhardt and Terry was missing. Wilde went to plays to evaluate actresses and decided that the right one could inspire a scenario for *The Duchess*. Mary Anderson, seen in a recent *Romeo and Juliet* that Wilde did not enjoy, was intrigued with the proposal. Confidence soaring, he promised his play would put her "with the great actresses of the earth." They started to work as a prelude to negotiating a contract.

Wilde wanted an advance of five thousand dollars to write the play and a royalty on each performance. Anderson's stepfather and business manager, Hamilton Griffin, whom Wilde called "the Griffin," was appalled at the terms. After prolonged discussion, they agreed that MacKaye would direct a production in late January 1883. Wilde would receive one thousand dollars on signing and an additional four thousand if Anderson accepted the play. "The world is at our feet," Wilde told MacKaye, and they celebrated. But two weeks later Anderson and the Griffin postponed production for a year to ensure a longer run. The script was due March 1. Without the urgency of a shorter deadline, Wilde disappeared into the New York social scene.

MacKaye urged him not to forget about *Vera*. Marie Prescott, another popular actress, read the play and liked the title role but wanted revisions. Wilde's reply to such requests was usually a good-natured "but who am I to tamper with a masterpiece?" Then he did the necessary alterations. After negotiating with Anderson, Wilde adopted a more uncompromising attitude and asked for permanent control of acting rights, one thousand dollars down, production in the fall of 1883, and a fifty-dollar royalty on each performance. An agreement was drafted. Now the world really was at their feet! Off they went to celebrate at Delmonico's. Wilde generously lent MacKaye two hundred dollars of his advance, which he tried to retrieve with unlikely success the next year. By the time *Vera* opened, however, MacKaye had embarked on a series of failed enterprises; he attempted to write a nine-volume work on Delsarte, sold real estate in Sioux City, South Dakota, and prospected for gold in North Carolina. The two dreamers never saw each other again.

On December 27, 1882, Wilde sailed for England on the SS *Bothnia*, taking with him $5,605.31, his profit from the tour, and the $800 remaining from his first advance. Revisiting the Atlantic, he brooded on the betrayal of Frank Miles, who had not championed artistic freedom and had not stood up to his father's criticism of Wilde's *Poems*. In addition there was the defection of his protégé James Rennell Rodd, considered heir to the title of Oxford Aesthete and a Newdigate winner in 1880 for a poem on Sir Walter Raleigh. When Rodd came down from Balliol, Wilde had encouraged him as a poet, introducing him to Burne-Jones and Whistler.

They had traveled together to Belgium in the summer of 1879, accompanied by Rodd's parents and sister. The following year they went along the Loire and stopped in Paris. Wilde playfully took the nom de plume Lord Robinson, and Rodd answered to Sir Smith, a portent of Wilde as Sebastian Melmoth in the same city. But Rodd was wary of Wilde's need for control and companionship. When he published his first book of poems, *Songs in the South,* in 1881, Rodd refused to change passages that Wilde considered artificial.

If there was one thing Wilde could not tolerate, it was rebellion from disciples; hence, he moved to regain control. Leaving for his lecture tour, he had promised Rodd that he would find an American publisher for *Songs,* now called *Rose Leaf and Apple Leaf.* During his absence, Rodd transferred his allegiance to Whistler, who had returned from Venice with a brilliant series of etchings. Rodd had good reason to distance himself from Wilde as his mentor's flamboyant image drew more attention. Prudence was demanded at the beginning of his diplomatic career, which culminated as ambassador to Italy from 1908 to 1919.

In Philadelphia, Wilde convinced J. M. Stoddart to publish *Rose Leaf.* Wilde wrote the preface and decreed the design: parchment covers, verses printed in brown ink on only one side of the paper, and interleaved blank apple green pages. The cover and title page bore the seal of Wilde's favorite signet ring: the profile of a young boy in ringlets. The choice was obviously a courting gesture. The volume was "a *chef d'oeuvre* of typography," the beginning of "an era in American printing," he told Stoddart by way of congratulating himself.

A thirty-five-hundred-word "L'Envoi" to launch the young poet was primarily devoted to Wilde's aesthetic philosophy, which was not always Rodd's. More disturbing was Wilde's discussion of their travels together in terms that could be misconstrued by the Foreign Office. There was also an inappropriate dedication. The British edition was dedicated to Rodd's father and inscribed "To Oscar Wilde—'Heart's Brother'—These few songs and many songs to come." Without consulting Rodd, Wilde used the same words to dedicate the American edition to himself. Rodd tried to have the page removed, but the 175 copies were already off to bookstores.★

Wilde's generosity toward young poets earned him many protégés and disciples; most were strictly platonic relationships exemplifying the ideal of the older man teaching the younger, but some were intimate, in varying degrees. Wilde needed the illusion of friendship and demanded unconditional love and loyalty. Ingratitude made him want to found only schools without disciples. Deemed a "false friend," Rodd complained of Wilde's "Olympian attitude" but later called him a "daring and gifted personality" who had brought him "nearer to emancipation from convention."

Wilde shed some of his bitterness over betrayal when he wrote "The Devoted Friend," published in *The Happy Prince and Other Tales* in 1888. Selfish and mean-spirited, Hugh, the so-called devoted friend, exploits Hans, an agreeable young man who does chores for him in exchange for a broken wheelbarrow. When Hans drowns as a result of Hugh's demands, Hugh declares, "I will certainly take care not to give away anything again. One always suffers for being generous." At the same time Wilde introduces his contrary notions about pain and sympathy. Hugh maintains that unhappy people "should be left alone and not bothered," but "a true friend always says unpleasant things, and does not mind giving pain." With few exceptions, Wilde's affection and loyalty

★The phrase "heart's brother" comes from Rodd's poem "By the South Sea," included in *Rose Leaf*: "Shall we get hence? O fair heart's brother! / You are weary at heart with me, / We two alone in the world, no other: / Shall we go to our wide kind sea?"

existed without malice, without giving pain, a rare trait in so brilliant a conversationalist.

WILDE RETURNED TO a London without Rossetti, who had died on Easter Sunday, April 9, 1882, while Wilde was on a train from Sacramento, California, to Salt Lake City, Utah. He had spoken so often of Rossetti that he came to believe in their phantom friendship and never knew that the Pre-Raphaelite had disliked his *Poems*. "I saw the wretched Oscar Wilde book," Rossetti wrote Jane Morris, "and glanced at it enough to see clearly what trash it is. Did Georgie [Burne-Jones] say that Ned [her husband] really admired it? If so, he must be gone drivelling." Rossetti never aligned himself with the Aesthetes, but he was their mythmaker, "a subconscious influence," Yeats said, "and perhaps the most powerful of all." For some years he had fought an addiction to chloral hydrate as well as suffering mood swings from depression to paranoia.

Violet Hunt told Wilde she had visited Tudor House, where Rossetti lived on the Chelsea Embankment, and saw all his possessions, including *The Ladies' Lament,* painted by his wife, Lizzie Siddal, tagged for auction in the "dreary studio." Years later, when Hunt wrote *The Wife of Rossetti,* she claimed that Lizzie poisoned herself because of her husband's infidelities with his models. In Wilde's absence, Hunt had matured into a liberated New Woman; she had visited Paris, learned German, read George Sand's biography, and decided that romantic adventures were better than marriage.

Visiting Tor Villa, Wilde placed himself in the big armchair so he could slouch and lounge with his feet resting on the red-velvet stool encircling the fireplace fender. Hunt showed him the scrapbook with clippings from his tour, and they laughed at the headline "Mr. Wilde Disappointed with the Atlantic." Hunt found him "not nearly so nice." One evening, as they talked about maps of the ancients, he teased her: "Oh, Miss Violet, think of a map drawn of a whole continent, and beside the names of an insignificant city or two a blank and Hic sunt leones! Miss Violet, let you and me go there."

"And get eaten by lions?" she replied.

In Hunt's autobiographical novel, *Their Lives,* Philip Wynyard (Wilde) has "full pouting pale lips" that remind Christina (Hunt) of the "debased

Roman Emperors whose busts stand in one of the corridors of the British Museum" and whose "habit of drawing in his breath in a susurrant,
self-satisfied manner at the end of a would-be poignant sentence" disgusts
the heroine. Christina "could not imagine his kissing her—or herself
wanting him to do it."

WILDE TOOK BACK his old rooms at Charles Street and visited his
mother and brother, who still lived nearby on Park Street. Lady Wilde had
given up on Willie's marriage, but when Oscar's arrival revived her match-
making mood, he quickly bolted to Paris to write his play. His first trip to
Paris had been with his mother and brother in 1867, after Isola's death.
Paris would become his second city now that Dublin was in the past.
Wilde revered Balzac, Flaubert, and Baudelaire; his spoken French was
excellent, his written prose less so, and opinions varied about the purity
of his accent. When he wrote *Salomé,* he said that he wanted to command
another language and make something beautiful out of it.

Anticipating a welcome as leader of the British Aesthetic movement,
he settled into a first-floor suite overlooking the Seine at the Hôtel du
Quai Voltaire, on the booksellers' quay. Baudelaire had taken a room in
this establishment in the artists' quarter in 1856 and stayed for two years
while writing *Les Fleurs du mal;* Wagner's stay in 1867 had produced *Die
Meistersinger von Nürnberg.* Wilde worshiped Baudelaire but thought
Wagner too belligerent. In *Dorian Gray,* Lord Henry's wife remarks, "I like
Wagner's music better than anybody's. It is so loud that one can talk the
whole time without other people hearing what one says." At least *Die
Meistersinger*—if its aura lingered—did not have boisterous gods and
goddesses. All muses were welcome if they kept Wilde at his writing desk.

With less than two months to complete *The Duchess of Padua,* he set
about arranging his apartment. A copy of Baudelaire's poems went on the
nightstand; on the writing desk were his calling cards—volumes of *Poems*
in gold-embossed vellum covers—scenario notes, and a packet of handmade paper from De La Rue in London. Putting black words on white,
silky-textured, hallmarked sheets was an artistic act on which Wilde
splurged as he would on champagne. He envisioned himself an ancient
calligrapher bent over snowy scrolls of Japanese *washi,* a paper as smooth
as skin.

In imitation of Balzac—who marked the transition from reality to fiction by putting on a white cashmere monk's cowl tied with a belt of Venetian gold from which hung a paper knife, a pair of scissors, and a penknife—Wilde wore a white wool dressing gown when at his writing table. To be more Balzacian, he ordered a copy of the novelist's famous ivory walking stick with a lapis lazuli pommel. The author of *La Comédie humaine* daily stoked the muse with two dozen cups of coffee, his slow path to caffeine poisoning, but Wilde preferred nicotine, buying cigarettes by the thousands to keep up with his chain smoking. He kept a large blue porcelain bowl on the writing table as an ashtray, and next to that a vase of flowers to neutralize the smell. Wilde cherished everything about the smoking ritual: the light, the first puffs, the stamping out, and the starting over. He agreed with Pierre Louÿs, the French poet and novelist to whom he would dedicate *Salomé,* that cigarettes were the only new pleasure invented by man in eighteen hundred years; a cigarette was Wilde's closest friend, without which he could not write.

While visiting a school in America, Wilde was shocked by a No Smoking sign. "Great Heaven!" he exclaimed. "They speak of smoking as if it were a crime. I wonder they don't caution the students not to murder each other on the landings." During Lady Bracknell's interrogation in *Earnest,* Jack admits that he smokes. "I am glad to hear it," she says. "A man should always have an occupation of some kind." In *A Woman of No Importance,* Lord Alfred observes that gold-tipped cigarettes "are awfully expensive, I can only afford them when I am in debt." In *Dorian Gray,* Lord Henry speaks for Wilde when he says: "A cigarette is the perfect type of a perfect pleasure. It is exquisite and it leaves one unsatisfied."

AT HIS WRITING desk, his gaze fixed on the Louvre's blue-gray roof studded with eye windows, Wilde went to work with uncharacteristic discipline. Since invitations were not a distraction, he worked without too many interruptions, putting "black upon white" as he liked to say, in his fluid, musical handwriting, in which an *of* suggested two clasped circles. *The Duchess of Padua,* a Renaissance revenge tragedy written in blank verse, was the least favorite of his dramas; in 1898 he said it was "unfit for publication—the only one of my works that comes under that category. But there are some good lines in it." He returned to *The Sphinx,* a poem begun at Oxford that would bewitch him until 1894. In the morning, when he lit his first aromatic cigarette, convoluted words formed couplets in his head: words like *Lupanar* to rhyme with *nénuphar,* and *catafalque* to go with *Amenalk.*

The ambiguous, silent sphinx, with its whorish eroticism and ancient secret (Wilde called women sphinxes without secrets), had long fascinated him. There were endless echoes he wanted to reinvent, from Flaubert's *La Chimère* to Alfred Hunt's Newdigate poem "Nineveh." In a feverish outpouring, he completed the first draft, eighty-seven couplets in the meter of Tennyson's *In Memoriam.* It was a poem that became a game, and by the time it was published a decade later, it was an eclectic extravaganza, owing as much to Paterian Aestheticism as to French Symbolism, and even to nursery rhymes with lines such as

> *But you can read the hieroglyphs*
> *on the great sandstone obelisks,*
> *And you have talked with Basilisks,*
> *and you have looked on Hippogriffs.*

When Paris did not court him, Wilde went into the cafés and restaurants to make his presence known. He was in the mood for spending money. When a Left Bank habitué wanted to return to Brittany and join the Navy, Wilde provided a new suit and the train fare. Not one to let a bank invest his money, Wilde kept it with him, ready for any spontaneous wasteful moment. His attitude toward money never varied: "The only thing that can console one for having no money is extravagance," he said, and this was a lifetime philosophy, even in the dark days. "I don't want money," Lord Henry says in *Dorian Gray.* "It is only people who pay their bills who want that, and I never pay mine."

Wilde found companionship not with a French poet but with the impressionable Robert Harborough Sherard, a twenty-one-year-old aspiring writer, eight years Wilde's junior and a great-grandson of Wordsworth. Sherard looked the part of a disciple: honey-colored hair, handsome, and plausibly heterosexual. Sent down from New College, Oxford, he told Wilde of his studies and adventures, including a year at the University of Bonn studying law and, curiously, Sanskrit; he boasted of surviving a duel in Naples over a beautiful girl. During Wilde's three months in Paris, they were constantly together. Sherard's growing devotion through the balance of Wilde's lifetime bordered on idolatry. Although Sherard wrote five books about Wilde, he failed to accept his homosexuality and never understood the man who found him so attractive.

Entertained at Foyot's, an expensive restaurant on the rue de Tournon, Sherard won Wilde's admiration by pointing out that wine was not white but yellow; thereafter Wilde ordered wine by that color. Sherard's family had shared a house with Victor Hugo in Guernsey; he arranged for Wilde to meet Hugo at a reception, but the old man was asleep in his chair and could not be roused for an introduction. They visited Sarah Bernhardt, appearing then in Sardou's *Fédora,* at her home on the avenue de Villiers. Wilde brought her wallflowers. They had lunch at the fashionable Café de Paris (Bignon's) on the avenue de l'Opéra, where Wilde overspent, maintaining that it was his duty to show the bourgeois that there were artists who did not starve in garrets.

SHERARD WAS THERE to record Wilde's childishness when he put on his favorite overcoat, hugged himself in its ample folds, and said, "So nice and warm." He was there to see a new butterfly emerge: "All *that* belonged to the Oscar of the first period," Wilde said. "We are now concerned with the Oscar Wilde of the second period, who has nothing whatever in common with the gentleman who wore long hair and carried a sunflower [or a lily] down Piccadilly." The Oscar of the second period dressed like a Frenchman, had his hair bobbed and curled after a bust of the young Nero in the Louvre. He was reclaiming his youth. Visits to the barbershop to have his locks done with a curling iron pleased him so much that he convinced Sherard to do the same. Together they slummed around Paris. But the story that one night Wilde went with a well-known prostitute from the Eden Music Hall remains hearsay.★

★In the 1930s, when A. J. A. Symons considered doing a biography of Wilde, Sherard wrote him: "The only reflection I made to myself on the morning when I heard of the Eden episode was to wonder how a well-fed, well-wined, full-blooded man as Oscar was at 29 could so control himself as to restrict his sexual contacts to once in 42 days." It is clear that Sherard was not with Wilde that evening, but it is unclear whether he heard the story from Wilde or from someone else.

As he was being introduced around Paris, Wilde thought he was garnering friends, but it takes more than speaking the language to impress the French. A meeting with Edgar Degas was disappointing. The artist told Walter Sickert that Wilde had "the look of someone playing Lor' Byron in a suburban theatre." Wilde wanted to meet the French Symbolist poet Paul Verlaine ("the one Christian poet since Dante"), who was now a poet of sexual inversion and decadence. He saw Verlaine in an absinthe stupor at the Café Vachette, looking seedy and depressed over the death of his lover Lucien Létinois. Once Verlaine had impressed Wilde with the religious fervor of his poems, but seeing him destitute and ugly, with the face of a satyr, Wilde turned away in disgust. "Verlaine is in the gutter, but he writes poetry on the pavement," he later remarked.

The novelist and memoirist Edmond de Goncourt, who was more welcoming, met Wilde several times. Goncourt's novel *La Faustin* examines the conflicts between life and art through the title character, an actress who needs love to perform. Excited by this theme, Wilde made up a sketch about an actress with the opposite problem: love divests her talent. This became the story of Sibyl Vane in *Dorian Gray*. A decade later, when Wilde was on the threshold of theatrical success, Goncourt published entries from his journal in *L'Écho de Paris,* referring to Wilde as *"au sexe douteux"* (of doubtful sex) and quoting his description of Swinburne as "a flaunter of vice."

Wilde saw Swinburne only once, at a reception in the 1880s. He sent him an account of his visit with Whitman, hoping to establish a friendship when he returned from America, but that failed, partly because Wilde's preface to *Rose Leaf and Apple Leaf* upset Swinburne, who described Rodd as "Oscar Wilde's young man—the Hephaestion of that all-conquering Alexander." Ignoring the reference to himself, Wilde told Goncourt that he had misunderstood their conversation. The "English public, as usual hypocritical, prudish, and philistine, has not known how to find the art in the work of art: it has searched for the man in it," he wrote. "Since it always confuses the man and his creations, it thinks that to create Hamlet you must be a little melancholy, to imagine Lear completely mad. So it has built around M. Swinburne a legend of an ogre and a devourer of children. M. Swinburne, an aristocrat by birth and an artist by temperament, has merely laughed at these absurdities."

Wilde was to use the same defense four months later with *Dorian Gray*. (When Goncourt published his journal as a book, he omitted both references.)

WILDE COMPLETED *The Duchess*, calling it the *"chef d'oeuvre* of my youth." He sent Mary Anderson the script and anxiously awaited her approval; he had spent most of the initial thousand-dollar advance and anticipated the remaining four thousand on his contract—if she accepted. When the telegram arrived six weeks later, Sherard was with him and watched while he read it—without expression. "Robert," he finally said, "this is very tedious. We shan't be able to dine with the Duchess tonight." But celebrate they did. Sherard took Wilde to the Café de Paris, where they drank yellow wine to forget. Thereafter they dined at the Hôtel Voltaire, where Wilde could sign and accumulate debt. Anderson explained that a play in blank verse would not be commercial. (Did Wilde not say he was using blank verse when they met in New York?) "The play in its present form, I fear would no more please the public of today than would 'Venice Preserved,' or 'Lucretia Borgia,' " she wrote. But the play had its good points. Wilde told the French actor Coquelin that the ending "is quite tragic; my hero, at his moment of triumph, makes an epigram which falls flat."

Wilde handled rejection by involving himself in other work. The New York premiere of *Vera* was scheduled for late August, four months away. Wilde wrote Marie Prescott detailed letters. "Never be afraid that by raising a laugh you destroy tragedy," he said. "On the contrary, you intensify it." This was his theory of opposites as applied to the theatre. "One of the facts of physiology," he explained, "is the desire of any very intensified emotion to be relieved by some emotion that is its opposite."

On August 2, 1883, Wilde boarded the SS *Britannia* for the nine-day voyage to New York. On his arrival, *The New York Times* noted his new look: long trousers, cutaway velvet coat, patent-leather boots, and a Byronic collar with a scarf and diamond pin. Opening night, August 20, was, as feared, hot and humid. The program called *Vera* Oscar Wilde's "new play," making him sound like a prolific dramatist. By the fourth act, critics were squirming in their seats. "It was not an intellectual audience,"

Comtesse Anna de Brémont recalled, "and what capacity it possessed for enjoyment melted under the stress of the heat."

James Kelly, the artist who had first sketched Wilde, recalled there were cries to bring down the curtain. "It comes as near failure as an ingenious and able writer can bring it," the *Times's* critic wrote, hurtfully adding that "Wilde was very much of a charlatan and wholly an amateur." Even Prescott's acting was compared to scolding, even her vermilion dress as designed by Wilde was berated. The play closed after seven performances, and Prescott took it on tour to recoup her losses.

The next morning, Kelly called at the Brunswick Hotel and found a chastened Wilde at breakfast. "Kelly, Kelly, my first play!" Wilde cried out when he saw him. Kelly suggested he forget the other night and take a walk with him to meet the young Thomas Edison, who worked at 65 Fifth Avenue. Defensive about the play's failure, Wilde said to Edison: "Dion Boucicault told me, 'Oscar, from the way you have written your play, it would take Edwin Booth, Henry Irving, Sarah Bernhardt, Ellen Terry and Ada Rehan to render it; you depend too much on the actors. Now when I write a play, if the leading man gets sick, or in any way fails me, I call up one of the ushers—and if he repeats my lines, the play will be a success.' " Edison laughed heartily at this, glanced at Kelly, and jerked his head toward Wilde: "He's laarning—he's laarnin'—he's learnin'!"

Mary Anderson, who was making her London debut at the Lyceum as Parthenia in *Ingomar,* wrote to William Winter, critic for the *New York Tribune,* "They say here [*Vera*] is the worst failure ever in America. . . . Willie Wilde said last night he was so sorry I had opened in such a *bad play* as *Ingomar.* . . . I should like Oscar to write as good a one." For *The Entr'acte,* Alfred Bryan drew a cartoon of Willie and Oscar tearfully embracing after *Vera* closed.

WILDE DID NOT rush back to London; he accepted invitations to be entertained in Newport and Saratoga. He had Sarony photograph him with curly hair; he posed for a life-size oil portrait by Harper Pennington that must have pleased him, for he looked successful and Balzacian, right down to the ivory walking stick. A month later he was back at Charles Street with a roommate. Sherard had abandoned plans to take a job in the East in order to stay with Wilde. They had a fine address, but the beds were hard and the bathroom outside. They entertained with Oxford-style breakfasts, smoked Parascho cigarettes, and drank liqueurs into the afternoon.

Reluctantly, Wilde returned to lecturing. A regional tour was planned to present "The House Beautiful" and the newly written "Impressions of America." For a temperament that thrived on change, to be a lecturer was traveling backward, particularly when his commitment to Aestheticism was wavering. Wilde took a greater interest in his mother's desire that he marry.

PART THREE

(1884–1891)

Rebelling

Our most fiery moments of ecstasy are merely shadows of
what somewhere else we have felt, or of what we long some
day to feel. . . . I myself would sacrifice everything for a
new experience, and I know there is no such thing as a new
experience at all. I think I would more readily die for what I
do not believe in than for what I hold to be true. I would go
to the stake for a sensation and be a skeptic to the last!
Only one thing remains infinitely fascinating to me, the
mystery of moods. To be master of these moods is exquisite,
to be mastered by them more exquisite still. Sometimes I
think that the artistic life is a long and lovely suicide, and
am not sorry that it is so.

—Oscar Wilde to Henry Marillier

CHAPTER TEN

Mrs. Oscar Wilde

❧

*The real drawback to marriage is that it makes one unselfish. And
unselfish people are colourless. They lack individuality. Still, there
are certain temperaments that marriage makes more complex.
They retain their egotism, and add to it many other egos.
They are forced to have more than one life.*

—THE PICTURE OF DORIAN GRAY

An exceptional woman by all accounts, Constance Mary Lloyd met
her future husband in the spring of 1881, when Wilde and his
mother paid a social call on Dublin friends living in London. He
saw a tall, slender woman with chestnut-colored hair coiled at the back of
her neck. She was Irish on her mother's side and made known to him her
love for Keats. "By the by, Mama," Wilde said suddenly on the way home,
"I think of marrying that girl." He had found an ideal wife. Lady Wilde
immediately put the courtship protocols in motion, inviting Constance
to her Saturday salon. The following week Wilde was asked to tea at
Constance's house; afterward she wrote her brother, "I can't help
liking him, because when he's talking to me alone he's never a bit affected,
and speaks naturally, excepting that he uses better language than most
people."

Otho Lloyd observed the couple closely; he recalled how Wilde's eyes
followed his sister around the room whenever they were separated. There

was much to admire. Refined and highly intelligent, Constance Lloyd was twenty-three, had studied painting and music, had read Dante in the original. She was not a worldly woman, like Violet Hunt or Lillie Langtry; her sympathies were not with fashionable society but with social reform. An empathy with the less fortunate connected her to her own forlorn childhood, a time she wanted to share with Wilde. But he was indifferent to misfortune. Otho Lloyd said Wilde could not be bothered with people "who relived their tragedies." In *Dorian Gray,* Lord Henry remarks after learning of Dorian's traumatic childhood, "I can sympathize with everything, except suffering. . . . The less said about life's sores the better."

Sympathy with pain was not the highest form of sympathy or intrinsic to Wilde's philosophy of individualism as expressed in "The Soul of Man Under Socialism." "Anybody can sympathize with the sufferings of a friend," he wrote, "but it requires a very fine nature—it requires, in fact the nature of a true Individualist—to sympathize with a friend's success." Although he hints that one should sympathize with both, Wilde clearly sees pleasure as better because it "intensifies the sum of joy in the world." He uses extreme examples—citing saints and martyrs—for this argument, when all his future wife wanted was to share her joylessness as a child; they even had family secrets in common: their fathers had publicly disgraced themselves.

To be sure, Ada and Horace Lloyd lacked certain nurturing instincts, but they were not Dickensian monsters. Constance's grandfather John Horatio Lloyd, a queen's counsel, was a successful barrister who handled legal matters for many of the British railway companies. Two sons followed him into the law, but the third, Constance's father, bypassed the family firm to set up a practice specializing in arbitration.

At twenty-seven he married Ada Atkinson, who came from a respectable Dublin family. The couple lived at Harewood Square in London, where Constance and Otho were born within two years of each other, Constance on January 2, 1858. Horace Lloyd was an absentee father, most often at his club or following the Prince of Wales to European playgrounds and spas, particularly Baden-Baden. There were signs of philandering, and Horace had been arrested for exposing himself to nursemaids in the garden in an inn of court. An embittered Ada turned away from her children. They turned to each other for emotional support.

Constance was four when her maternal grandfather died and her grandmother became the family matriarch in Dublin. Constance grew up with an Irish sensibility and a love for the country, which she shared with Wilde. When she was sixteen, her father died of an undisclosed ailment at the age of forty-six. Ada found herself well-off and remarried four years later, but she made her life separate from that of her children. Otho was at Oxford, and Constance, then twenty, went to live with Grandfather Lloyd at 100 Lancaster Gate, a household sternly managed by his unmarried niece, Constance's Aunt Emily.

Just as Constance and Wilde were feeling comfortable together, Wilde left for America. He returned only to leave for Paris, then New York for the ill-fated opening of *Vera*. After a brief time back in London, he went to lecture in the provinces. Their courtship lasted three years. When Lillie Langtry was touring with her theatre company in America, Wilde wrote her that he was in love with "a grave, slight, violet-eyed little Artemis, with great coils of heavy brown hair which make her flower-like head droop like a blossom, and wonderful ivory hands which draw music from the piano so sweet that the birds stop singing to listen to her." (Whenever Wilde described beauty, he used images devoid of warmth; *ivory* was a favorite word.) "I am so anxious for you to know and to like her," he continued, "it is horrid being so much away from her, but we telegraph to each other twice a day, and I rush back suddenly from the uttermost parts of the earth to see her for an hour, and do all the foolish things that wise lovers do."★

While Wilde converted provincial audiences to art and beauty, Constance was lovesick and lonely. She told her brother, "I am with Oscar when he is in town, and I am too miserable to do anything while he is away." She thought him the greatest poet, the greatest conversationalist, and believed he would become the greatest playwright. As Wilde ob-

---

★Langtry was not in England for the wedding, and it is unclear when Wilde introduced his Artemis (protector of the young and virgin goddess of the hunt) to the actress. She sent them tickets to *Peril* in April 1885, but Constance was pregnant and Wilde returned them, suggesting she come to tea; they both attended a matinee of *The Lady of Lyons* on March 23, 1886.

served, "No man has any real success in this world unless he has women to back him." Marriage would give him that. More than anything, Constance needed love, and Wilde—when so inclined—could be loving and attentive.

CONSTANCE WAS FLATTERED when Wilde asked her opinion of *Vera*. She knew the play had failed and wondered whether he was testing her critical abilities. She postponed a judgment until she reached Dublin, a visit coinciding with two of Wilde's lectures. What she wrote balanced diplomacy with integrity, revealing a woman of insight and independence. She called *Vera* "a very good acting play" with "good dramatic situations" and praised "the passages on liberty and the impassioned parts," but she found some of the minor dialogue "slightly halting or strained."

Violating Wilde's edict about discussing pain, she continued: "The world surely is unjust and bitter to most of us. I am afraid you and I disagree in our opinions on art, for I hold that there is no perfect art without perfect morality, whilst you say that they are distinct and separable things, and of course you have your knowledge to combat my ignorance with. Truly I am no judge that you should appeal to me for opinions, and even if I were, I know that I should judge you rather by your *aims* than by your work, and you would say I was wrong." Constance was spirited. At the outset Wilde felt she could challenge him.

On his return to Dublin in November, the first since his father's death in 1876, Wilde stayed at the elegant Shelbourne Hotel, which was more costly than the usual touring stopovers: he obviously wanted to make an impression on the Atkinson relatives. During the visit, Constance found him "decidedly extra affected" but realized he was nervous. Wilde was being scrutinized as a serious suitor and was lecturing for the first time in his hometown—enough to make anyone insecure.

He proposed on November 25 while in Ireland, in what was apparently a spontaneous desire to wed. But did he prepare a speech? Was it like the scene in *Earnest* when Jack asks Gwendolen, "Well . . . may I propose to you now?" And she replies, "I think it would be an admirable opportunity. And to spare you any possible disappointment, Mr. Worthing, I think it only fair to tell you quite frankly beforehand that I am fully determined to accept you."

All Constance told her brother was "Prepare yourself for an astounding piece of news! I am engaged to Oscar Wilde and am perfectly and insanely happy!" Otho welcomed Wilde as a new brother, telling him that "if Constance makes as good a wife as she has been a good sister to me your happiness is certain; she is staunch and true." A curiously worded, though prescient, congratulation. But Constance warned her fiancé: "I am so cold and undemonstrative outwardly: you must read my heart and not my outward semblance if you wish to know how passionately I worship and love you." In *The Duchess of Padua*, Wilde has the duchess tell her lover: "Do you not remember your own words: woman's love makes angels of us men? / Well, men's love makes women sufferers, who for their sakes bear all things."

BETWEEN CONSTANCE AND Wilde there followed the wonder of passionate beginnings. "We are, of course, desperate in love," Wilde wrote a friend. "I have been obliged to be away nearly all the time since our engagement, civilising the provinces by my remarkable lectures, but we telegraph to each other twice a day, and the telegraph clerks have become quite romantic in consequence. I hand in my messages, however, very sternly, and try to look as if 'love' was a cryptogram for 'buy Grand Trunks' and 'darling' a cypher for 'sell at par.' "

Constance's replies were overly needy, expressing a vulnerability Wilde could not understand until he found himself reacting in a similar manner with Lord Alfred Douglas. "Do you believe that I do love you most passionately with all the strength of my heart and mind?" she wrote. "When I have you for my husband, I will hold you fast with chains of love and devotion so that you shall never leave me, or love anyone as long as I can love and comfort you." Innocent, loyal, and romantic, Constance believed that if she loved Wilde to the depth of her being, she could save him from temptation. It was an attractive loyalty that made Wilde even more guilty when he betrayed her.

At some point, judging from Constance's few surviving letters, the engaged couple exchanged confidences about past relationships. She had surely heard about his friendship with Lillie Langtry. Since women with pasts fascinated Wilde, he made them central to his comedies, but their pasts were a bit more wicked than Constance's admission that a previous engagement had been broken off by her fiancé. "I don't think I shall ever be jealous," she decided. "Certainly I am not jealous now of anyone: I trust in you for the present: I am content to let the past be buried, it does not belong to me." Constance was a mystery and a mood. "She scarcely ever speaks," Wilde remarked. "I am always wondering what her thoughts are like."

"IT'S A RIDICULOUS attachment," twittered the Swallows about the Reed in "The Happy Prince"; "she has no money, and far too many relations." Disapproving of the betrothal, Aunt Emily lapsed into dour silences whenever Wilde visited. They had a "cold and practical" family, Constance complained to Otho, adding, "I won't stand opposition, so I hope they won't try it." When Violet Hunt heard the news, she told her diary, "I hear that Oscar's fiancée only has £400 a year instead of £800. I expect to hear of that engagement being broken off." Actually, Constance had £250 a year, which would increase to £900 at her grandfather's death. But Grandfather Lloyd was not ready to give his blessing to a young man without solid prospects. Like Lady Bracknell, he asked about Wilde's income and debts. Wilde admitted to owing £1,000. Lloyd wanted him to pay off £300 before setting a wedding date; then he would give them £5,000 against Constance's inheritance to lease and furnish a home.

Wilde's family had no reservations. Willie began a letter to Constance "My Dear Little Sister," referring to the fact that she was only nine months older than Isola would have been, if she were alive. "My dear old Boy," he wrote his brother. "This is indeed good news, brave news, wise news, and altogether charming and amazing in the highest and most artistic sense." Lady Wilde was practical: "What will you do in life? Where live?" she asked. "Meantime you must go on with your work. I enclose another offer for lectures. I would like you to have a small house in London and live the literary life and teach Constance to correct proofs and eventually go into Parliament." Such a domestic scene was not what she had settled for with Sir William. She demanded a separate identity. Her feminist values, however, were abandoned when it came to her son, who needed a full-time wife to rise in politics.

THE COUPLE LEASED a four-story house at 16 (now 34) Tite Street, at the opposite end from where Wilde and Frank Miles had lived. Chelsea had become a popular area with the building of the Embankment in 1771—sewage no longer washed up to the doorways. Carlyle, Rossetti, and Whistler made Chelsea their home. Bram and Florence Stoker lived close by, at 17 St. Leonard's Terrace. John Singer Sargent was a future neighbor. Edward William Godwin, who renovated Chelsea houses for Miles and Whistler, was hired to refurbish the interior; the Victorian row-house exterior remained as monotonous as its neighbors'.

The wedding was a private ceremony, held on May 29, 1884, in St. James's Church, Sussex Gardens. Constance's wedding dress, designed by Wilde in the Pre-Raphaelite tradition, was cowslip yellow satin with a high neck and puff sleeves; around her waist was a silver girdle, a gift from the groom, who also fashioned the interlocking wedding rings. A veil of saffron-colored gauze, embroidered with pearls, was held by a crown of myrtle leaves, the sacred plant of Venus. She carried a bouquet of white lilies and ferns. The six bridesmaids, all Constance's cousins, wore tunic dresses in shades of blue, yellow, and green.

The Irish Times reported that the bridegroom with his curled hair "looked more like George IV than usual." Lady Wilde wore gray satin, with matching chenille-fringed trim, and a broad-brimmed hat accented by a long ostrich plume, tilted in the style of the Duchess of Devonshire. At the reception, the eighty-five-year-old Lloyd patriarch scrutinized the newest family member in his blue morning dress and gray trousers. Wilde looked prosperous and dignified, but he still wore his ornate rings.

Following a wedding breakfast the next day, the couple departed on the boat train for Paris. Wilde crossed to the Right Bank and the Hôtel Wagram on the rue de Rivoli for his honeymoon. The suite overlooking the Tuileries was filled with flowers for their arrival. One of the first to offer congratulations was Robert Sherard, who joined the bridegroom for a walk. An ebullient Wilde excitedly started to describe the wedding night. "It's so wonderful when a young virgin"—an embarrassed Sherard stopped him.

A few days later the *Morning News* interviewed Wilde as he lay stretched out on a sofa surrounded by books. He was reading Stendhal's *Le Rouge et le noir,* a book he often revisited. "For my part, I think the most exquisite thing in reading is the pleasure of forgetfulness," he said. "It is so nice to think there are some books you cared for so much at a certain epoch in your life and do not care for now. There is a positive delight in 'cutting' an author and feeling I have got beyond him." He went on to praise Sarah Bernhardt's *Macbeth,* which the Wildes had seen several times. "There is nothing like it on our stage, and it is her finest creation. I say her creation deliberately, because to my mind it is utterly impertinent to talk of Shakespeare's *Macbeth* or Shakespeare's *Othello.* Shakespeare is only one of the parties. The second is the artiste through whose mind it passes."

While Constance read Hugo's *Les Misérables,* Wilde picked up the recently published *À rebours,* by Joris-Karl Huysmans, which became his bible of Decadence. It arrived in stores two weeks before Wilde's honeymoon and was the talk of Paris. In its hero, Des Esseintes, whose passions exceed Paterian ecstasy, Wilde found a nascent Dorian Gray. Dorian reads a book assumed to be *À rebours,* amazed that the hero was "a kind of prefiguring type of himself. And indeed, the whole book seemed to him to contain the story of his own life, written before he had lived it." *Dorian Gray* did the same for Wilde.

The hotel catered the couple's first dinner party, much to Constance's relief. As she told Otho, "Everything is sure to go right in a hotel. I am rather looking forward to it." Guests included the artists John Singer Sargent and John Donoghue, the French critic Paul Bourget, and Henrietta Reubell, a wealthy American with a Parisian salon. After a quiet week in Dieppe, enjoying the sea air and walking along the promenade, the couple returned to London in late June to find Tite Street far from habitable. The five thousand pounds was gone, and Wilde increased his debt to seventeen hundred pounds. The newlyweds shuttled in and out of hotels and lodgings, a stressful beginning to married life. Not only was Godwin behind schedule but the contractors were overcharging, and litigation followed. On July 18, 1884, Grandfather Lloyd died, and Constance received her inheritance.

Wilde substituted as *Vanity Fair*'s drama critic when his brother went on holiday, and he began another lecture tour of the provinces. From Edinburgh, he lovingly wrote his wife: "Here am I, and you at the Antipodes. O execrable facts, that keep our lips from kissing, though our souls are one. . . . I feel your fingers in my hair, and your cheek brushing mine. The air is full of the music of your voice, my soul and body seem no longer mine, but mingled in some sweet ecstasy with yours. I feel incomplete without you." What more wonderful thought could a husband have than "I feel incomplete without you." Although some saw the marriage as artificial ("some deliberate artistic composition," said Yeats), they never looked closely enough to see the depth of Wilde's passion during those first years.

IN JANUARY 1885, what Wilde called "the House Beautiful" was finally ready, remarkable not for its exterior—largely unchanged today—but for its interior decoration, which Wilde said matched the pure color of his speech. No pictures survive, but the rooms are described in various memoirs. The dining room was painted in different shades of white, with white curtains embroidered in yellow silk. Wilde pronounced it "absolutely delightful." There were no Morris designs to be seen. A room with wallpaper makes the eye restless, Wilde said. In general all wallpaper offended him. "Modern wallpaper is so bad," he said in a lecture, "that a boy brought up under its influence could allege it as a justification for turning to a life of crime." One of his last comments was that he and his hotel wallpaper were "fighting a duel to the death. Decidedly one of us will have to go."

In the all-white drawing room, rare engravings and etchings, including a Venetian scene by Whistler, formed a deep frieze along the walls. The only touches of color were two Japanese feathers inserted into the plaster ceiling. Hanging over the carved mantelpiece, also painted white, was a gilt-copper bas-relief of a young girl by John Donoghue, which illustrated "Requiescat," Wilde's poem to his sister, Isola. The study was buttercup yellow with lacquered vermilion woodwork. A favorite piece was a satiny ivory table, so soft and beautiful that Wilde wanted to engrave his sonnets on it. "Quill pens and notepaper are only good enough for bills of lading. A sonnet should always *look well*," he said.

Wilde loved objects: classical statues, blue-and-white china, paintings, gilt-embossed books, but he lacked the obsession—not to mention the funds and discipline—for acquiring them, so he never became a true collector. Most often his mementos were also memories: a statue he bought in Greece during the trip with Mahaffy; a painting from Rome to remind him of David Hunter Blair, a Monticelli, a Japanese painting of children at play, a drawing of Eros by Simeon Solomon, and a reproduction of Praxiteles' bust of Hermes. His most prestigious item was Thomas Carlyle's writing table, which the historian's mother gave Carlyle for his rooms at Edinburgh University.

Yeats noticed a red lampshade positioned over a terra-cotta classical figure on the center of a red cloth covering a white table. Such minimalist accents blended into rooms that were comfortable and lacked clutter, that were light and airy rather than dark with Victorian velvet and fringe. Yeats said Wilde led an imaginary life and "perpetually performed a play which was in all things the opposite of all that he had known in childhood and youth. He never put off completely his wonder at opening his eyes every morning on his own beautiful house and to remember that he had dined yesterday with a Duchess." Merrion Square, with its curtained windows and dirty teacups, was the past.

OBSERVERS THOUGHT CONSTANCE a remarkably quiet and demure wife for an extrovert like Wilde, not understanding that he preferred a listener. She was a pleasant hostess when she felt confident that the evening was going well, but afterward worried that her guests did not enjoy themselves, displaying all the familiar entertaining anxieties. Wilde sparkled at dinner parties, went to the theatre several times a week, and thought his social life would remain the same after marriage. Evenings at home without guests began to bore him; a gregarious Irishman, he needed to be around more than one other person to enjoy himself. Constance, however, was happy to nest and enjoy their beautiful home.

When Mary Anderson came to town, Wilde wanted to see her *Romeo and Juliet*. He had not enjoyed it the first time in New York, even though William Winter, dean of American drama critics, called her Juliet "the most essentially womanlike and splendidly tragical." Wilde should have resented Anderson's rejection of *The Duchess,* but he seldom held grudges and never for long. Following the performance, he sent his congratulations—"What was a bud has grown to a blossom, and those who admired you as a woman must reverence you now as an artist"—but he did exaggerate when he compared her with Bernhardt. He had taken only a brief hiatus from playwriting and wanted all the actresses indebted to him when he returned.

Dressed in green, the Wildes were a striking couple at a Grosvenor Gallery private view. One of his favorite colors, along with yellow and vermilion (he hated mauve and magenta), green signaled an opportunity to wear the beloved fur-trimmed overcoat. Constance wore a velvet ensemble in the same Lincoln green under a shawl embroidered with iridescent beads. In "Pen, Pencil and Poison," Wilde's dandy poisoner has "that curious love of green, which in individuals is always the sign of a subtle artistic temperament, and in nations is said to denote a laxity, if not a decadence of morals." Whether consciously or unconsciously, Wilde made Constance an extension of himself, as he had with Lillie Langtry. As usual, his ideal woman was an illusion, an artifice, a costumed statue. "For his sake she posed in Grecian, early Venetian, Medieval, Caroline, Dutch, and *Directoire* and she did not like it a bit," wrote one biographer.

THEIR FIRST CHILD was born within a year of the wedding." 'My wife has a cold' but in about a month will be over it," Wilde wrote Godwin. "I hope it is a boy cold, but will love whatever the gods send." On June 5, 1885, Constance gave birth to a son, who was christened Cyril Wilde. There were no middle names, a change from his father's grandeur. The parents asked the polymath Edward Heron-Allen to cast Cyril's horoscope. What was read in the stars under his sign of Gemini is not known, but Wilde put great stock in omens. "I love superstitions, they are the colour element of thought and imagination," he said. "They are the opponents of common sense."

Wilde observed Cyril as every new father observes his child—with disbelief. He told Norman Forbes-Robertson, "The baby is wonderful: it has a bridge to its nose! which the nurse says is a proof of genius! It also has a superb voice, which it freely exercises: its style is essentially Wagnerian." Cyril was presented with a brother on November 5, 1886. He was baptized Vyvyan Oscar Beresford. His parents spelled it Vivian; the provenance of Beresford remains a mystery. Wilde once said, "Every one has some secret reason for christening a child."

Because both pregnancies were difficult, Constance was often confined to bed. Unprepared for the change in his wife's physical appearance, Wilde found her unattractive: the goddess had become too real. Along with Baudelaire, Wilde believed that a woman should appear magical, a golden idol ready to dazzle men, and to be worshiped. But ugliness was a malady. "Desire is killed by maternity," he said, "passion buried in conception." If this was the consequence of love, he reasoned that women were not made for passion, only for motherhood. He told Sherard that illness and suffering inspired him with repulsion. "A man with the toothache ought, I know, to have my sympathy, for it is a terrible pain. Well, he fills me with nothing but aversion."

For Constance, however, the discomfort and pain of pregnancy and childbirth were quickly forgotten. Cyril was the family favorite, who, she wrote a friend, "chatters all day long and amuses me so much." But he later developed what may have been rheumatic fever or an undiagnosed kind of nonparalytic polio. Constance said he was "growing crooked" and needed massage and exercise. As to temperament, Cyril was "very affectionate and tremendously self-willed, an exceedingly clever boy, but he does not give his mind to anything much yet." Vyvyan was "sharper and quicker." Constance accepted that her younger son was the clever one and that Cyril had inherited the "Irish gift of speaking well altho' he has not got the Irish facility of turning his hand to anything."

AT THE END of November 1885, when Cyril was five months old, Wilde received a letter from Henry (Harry) Currie Marillier. It was a pleasant surprise and an opportunity to recall the days at Salisbury Street, when Marillier, a student at Christ's Hospital, lived in the basement and brought Wilde his morning coffee to earn a few pence. Now a classics student at Cambridge, he invited Wilde to a production of *Eumenides*. Appreciating the diversion from domesticity, Wilde encouraged a friendship. Marillier visited Tite Street, and the two talked of Keats, Poe, and Baudelaire. "I have never learned anything except from people younger than myself," Wilde wrote him, "and you are infinitely young."

A few months later, when Wilde was in Glasgow for a lecture, he unburdened himself. The artistic life, he told Marillier, was "a long and lovely suicide." He observed that "our most fiery moments of ecstasy are merely shadows of what somewhere else we have felt, or of what we long some day to feel." A return to Oxford in February 1886, for the opening of the New Theatre, brought back memories. "Young Oxonians are very delightful, so Greek and graceful and uneducated," he solemnized, "they have profiles but no philosophy." The word *profile* was used by Wilde to identify any desirable youth.

Wilde was restless. "I myself would sacrifice everything for a new experience," he told Marillier, "and I know there is no such thing as a new experience." In *Dorian Gray,* he writes about having one great encounter to repeat over and over. Loving a woman was not that involvement. Constance no longer made him feel complete.

CHAPTER ELEVEN

Crossing Over

✣

"Know thyself!" was written over the portal of the antique world.
Over the portal of the new world "Be thyself" shall be written.
And the message of Christ to man was simply "Be thyself."
That is the secret of Christ.

—"THE SOUL OF MAN UNDER SOCIALISM"

Wilde loved Constance and had married her with the intention of spending a long and happy life with her; he never anticipated how her motherhood would disturb his aesthetic sensibilities or how domesticity could alter his formerly entertaining bachelor life. Lady Bracknell understood: "I have always been of opinion that a man who desires to get married should know either everything or nothing," she tells Jack. "Which do you know?" Jack hesitates before replying: "I know nothing, Lady Bracknell." "I am pleased to hear it," she responds. "I do not approve of anything that tampers with natural ignorance. Ignorance is like a delicate exotic fruit; touch it and the bloom is gone." Lady Bracknell was not speaking of sexual confusion or curiosity, but Wilde's ignorance was confounded and complicated by the presence of Robert "Robbie" Baldwin Ross.

Seventeen years old, fifteen years younger than Wilde, a Canadian by heritage, Ross was born in Tours, France, during a stay there for his father's health. John Ross was an attorney, active in Canadian politics as speaker of the Senate, and the son-in-law of Robert Baldwin, first prime minister of

Upper Canada. He died when Robbie was two, and the boy's mother moved the family to England to be educated. Within two years, she remarried a fellow Canadian and settled at 85 Onslow Square, London. Ross was spoiled by his two older sisters. It was a close and loving family until Ross admitted his same-sex preferences.

Through a combination of tutors, schools, travel, and nurture, Ross had come to look and act mature beyond his years, as if he had grown old in the womb. He was not one of Wilde's graceful profiles. Wilde said he had the face of Puck—but photographs show him looking more like a kindly ferret. Ultimately Ross became known as Wilde's "devoted friend" and was named his literary executor and editor of the fourteen-volume edition of Wilde's works published in 1908. He secured the copyrights for the estate and had immense power in molding Wilde's literary reputation. But he lacked emotional insight into Wilde and never understood his obsession for Douglas. Some of the more dubious stories about Wilde trace back to Ross: the prostitute visit at Oxford that resulted in syphilis and the ghastly description of Wilde's body exploding on his deathbed.

When Wilde and Ross first met is not known, but by 1887 Ross was friendly enough with the Wildes to stay at Tite Street as a paying guest while his mother went abroad. Constance liked him, and he was fond of Cyril and Vyvyan. With Wilde's help, Ross prepared for his Cambridge entrance examination; when Wilde was away lecturing, Ross dined with Constance. A practicing homosexual, Ross recognized Wilde's need to fulfill his nature. They became lovers.

Although the first time has been portrayed as a year earlier, no evidence documenting the date of the intimacy exists. A seduction in Wilde's vermilion-trimmed study surrounded by Hellenic mementos was convenient. Secondhand gossip about the encounter drifted down after Wilde's death, naming "little Robbie Ross" as the seducer. Wilde had long waited for such an embrace and did not resist. Only later would he understand that "a kiss may ruin a human life," a line he gives to Mrs. Arbuthnot in *A Woman of No Importance*. Ross probably introduced Wilde to fellatio and the classical intercrural modes of copulation.*

---

*Intercrural unions appear frequently on ancient painted Greek vases. Scenes often depict a bearded older man facing a shorter, clean-shaven youth. The older man has his hands around his partner's waist, his head below his shoulder, his knees bent, and is thrusting his penis between the youth's thighs. Sometimes the couple is wrapped in a single cloak, recalling Alcibiades' attempt to seduce Socrates by creeping under his blanket.

Now that he had accepted the same-sex desire that had followed him since youth, Wilde felt liberated, happy to be alive. He embarked on his most prolific period as a writer. From 1887 to 1891, he wrote reviews (sometimes weekly), worked two years as editor of a women's magazine, published fairy tales, essays and dialogues, a novel, and a third play, *Salomé*. Acceptance of his sexuality was a more compelling incentive to work than creditors' letters. He was also a criminal under British law, a status he had long fantasized about and would use in his fiction; hereafter, choosing among espousal, parental, and forbidden love would be complicated.

Perfection, for Wilde, was love, passion, and friendship contained in one beautiful personality. Between men and women, he wrote in *Lady Windermere's Fan,* "there is no friendship possible. There is passion, enmity, worship, love, but no friendship." But what of the emotional bond of affection and trust that can support a woman indefinitely and would have sustained Constance? Wilde never understood that a platonic ideal is possible between opposite sexes. By the time he wrote *An Ideal Husband,* he realized that the only thing worse than an absolutely loveless marriage was a marriage in which there is love on one side only.

"The one charm of marriage," Lord Henry tells Dorian, "is that it makes a life of deception absolutely necessary for both parties." For the three months that Ross lived with the Wildes, there was no need for such subterfuge; only discretion while at Tite Street was necessary. Ross went up to King's College in 1888, involved himself with radical journalism, and saw little of Wilde until 1891. "I hope you are enjoying yourself at Cambridge—whatever people may say against Cambridge it is certainly the best preparatory school for Oxford that I know," Wilde wrote. Ross sent Cyril and Vyvyan a white Persian kitten. "The children are enchanted with it," Wilde wrote Ross, "and sit, one on each side of its basket, worshipping—It seems pensive—perhaps it is thinking of some prim rose garden in Persia, and wondering why it is kept in this chill England." A white-on-white *objet,* the little kitten disappeared into the white carpet and the white Chippendale chairs.

WILLIE WILDE EXCELLED at granting favors and in the social aspects of journalism. It was big brother who had Wilde's sonnets to Sarah Bernhardt and Ellen Terry published in his paper, *The World*. Moving around Fleet Street from newspapers to magazines, Willie was lackadaisically employed by *The Daily Telegraph, Punch,* the *Gentlewoman,* and *Vanity Fair.* In 1880, he launched a satirical journal, *Pan,* which did not publish a second issue. Shaw, who never appreciated the power of popular journalism, said Willie "must be ruthlessly set aside by literary history as a vulgar journalist of no account." He was wrong. Willie and his kind are a vanished breed, but once they were the stuff of legends in newsrooms on both sides of the Atlantic.

No matter what the excesses of the night before, Willie performed well under deadline pressure, writing word after word, clearly and accurately, as quickly as he spoke. He was able, an admiring colleague said, "to sum up a situation, political or social, in a single moment" and then write a "clear, witty statement every time," with a "pulsing sense of intellect" and "lambent though cynical Irish wit" that "seemed to stand out from the printed page." His stories lacked epigrams, to avoid comparison with Oscar's.

Despite his talents, Willie played the self-deprecating stage Irishman. He once described his workday as beginning at noon, when he walks into the office and greets the editor: " 'Good morning, my dear Le Sage,' who replies: 'Good morning, my dear Wilde, have you an idea to-day?' 'Oh yes, Sir indeed I have. It is the anniversary of the penny postage stamp.' 'That is a delightful subject for a leader.' "

Assignment approved, Willie eats a few oysters and drinks half a bottle of Chablis at Sweeting's, strolls toward the park, considers going to the British Museum to grub up a lot of musty facts, but decides doing so "would be unworthy of a great leader writer." By late afternoon he retires to his club, where he writes "three great meaty, solid paragraphs" that a messenger delivers into the hands of his editor. Willie loved the gratification of reading his words in print only hours after he wrote them. He could leave an event before midnight, file his story in an hour, return to finish the evening, and on the drive home buy the paper and read the account of the party he had just left.

Being popular was an important quality on Fleet Street. A contemporary recalled how Willie entered the Café Royal to "peer round short-sightedly till he found a genial coterie." Arthur M. Binstead, a journalist from the *Pink 'Un,* the racing paper, found him the "personification of good nature and irresponsibility," observing that the "bother of earning a living proved highly repugnant to his really frank and sunny disposition." Max Beerbohm, however, was repulsed by Willie's appearance: "Quel monstre! Dark, oily, suspecte [*sic*] yet awfully like Oscar: he has Oscar's coy, carnal smile & fatuous giggle & not a little of Oscar's esprit. But he is awful—a veritable tragedy of family-likeness."

Sitting with his rowdy group of journalists, Willie was often embarrassed when his brother cut him on the way to his group in the Domino Room. The brothers were friendly when they met at Lady Wilde's, where Willie lived, enjoying maternal approval, but Willie expected his brother to acknowledge him by inviting him into his social circle. "My Darling Boz. Forgive me," he wrote after an argument. "We have hot tempers *all* of us, but we love each other. . . . I am much more lonely in the world than you are Oscar, & I feel things—that's all." Willie mobilized his mother to make Oscar respect him. In a letter she pointedly asked: "Did you read Willie on soda water—it is so brilliant?" With the best intentions, Lady Wilde tried but failed to stimulate in Oscar appreciation for Willie as a writer; thus the dream of her sons conquering the literary world hand in hand—like so many of her dreams—died.

SHAW THOUGHT JOURNALISM vulgar, and Wilde agreed. In "The Critic as Artist," Gilbert observes: "As for modern journalism, it is not my business to defend it. It justifies its own existence by the great Darwinian principle of the survival of the vulgarest." After all, "journalism is unreadable, and literature is not read." In "The Soul of Man Under Socialism," Wilde again attacks: "In the old days men had the rack, now they have the Press." And in "Pen, Pencil and Poison," perhaps apropos of Willie: "To have a style so gorgeous that it conceals the subject is one of the highest achievements of an important and much admired school of Fleet Street leader-writers."

Mostly Wilde attacked journalism as the adversary of the artist. In "The Soul of Man," he compliments France as a country where "they limit the journalist, and allow the artist almost perfect freedom. Here we allow absolute freedom to the journalist, and entirely limit the artist." Still, as an artist, Wilde had benefited from the press's scrutiny; in fact, publicity (satirical or not) was largely responsible for his success. From the time he put on his cello coat and cultivated his aesthetic pose, he was caricatured in art and words. By creating his aesthetic persona, *Punch* made him visible and secured his American tour. Wilde did not like to admit it, but publicity motivated him to live up to his reputation—or change it.

AT TITE STREET, Wilde balanced his contrary needs with a family life that he truly enjoyed. He was a delighted—and devoted—father who liked nothing better than to become a child again and play in the nursery with his sons. Lecturing, however, was repetitive. How much longer could he inspire beauty in the provinces? As long as there was no other work, he continued to travel and return home to greet Constance and the children, meet his friends at the Café Royal, write some reviews, then go off to King's Cross and the north. His fee was five pounds a lecture, decent money (if not spent at restaurants), but it was Constance's income that ran the household.

Eventually, Wilde, like every other man before and after him, discovered that there is an inevitable—and unenviable—sameness to marriage. Every morning he awoke to a day pretty much like the day before. His favorite ritual was bathing. In "Lord Arthur Savile's Crime," the title character prepares for his bath: "The light stole softly from above, through thick slabs of transparent onyx, and the water in the marble tank glimmered like a moonstone. He plunged hastily in, till the cool ripples touched throat and hair, and then dipped his head right under, as though he would have wiped away the stain of some shameful memory. When he stepped out he felt almost at peace."

Wilde's rites were less aristocratic but nonetheless satisfying. A small table next to the tub was set with a box of cigarettes and a large bowl for an ashtray. Lighting a cigarette, he inhaled once or twice, extinguished it, and lit another. Smoke and steam enveloped him in a fog of tranquillity; he spent hours soaking, smoking, and silently writing in his head. Sometimes he so delighted himself that he laughed aloud when he mounted a bejeweled epigram in its setting. Thinking preceded speech, or, as he said, "talk itself is a sort of spiritualized action." Christ spoke in proverbs and parables; Wilde called them paradoxes or prose poems. Christ had his cult, and Wilde had his.

· · ·

IRONICALLY, VULGAR JOURNALISM was drawing Wilde deeper into its disreputable bowels; with lecture bookings declining, he depended on freelance income. From 1887 to 1891, he wrote nearly a hundred anonymous reviews for W. T. Stead's *Pall Mall Gazette* and was read less frequently in *Court and Society Review*. Stead, a sex-obsessed zealot who hounded adulterous politicians and believed that marital fidelity was the pinnacle of British life, became famous for a sensational series of articles on child prostitution. Entitled "The Maiden Tribute of Modern Babylon," the series influenced passage of the Criminal Law Amendment Act of 1885, which raised the age of consent to sixteen and proscribed all public and private homosexual acts—it was the law that sent Wilde to prison.

For the *Gazette*, Wilde reviewed books by unknown authors or literary figures, a former tutor or a false friend—everything from manuals and cookbooks to poetry and first novels. After anointing the author of a marriage guide "the Murray of matrimony and the Baedeker of bliss," Wilde said he should have received a royalty since the quotation was used so frequently in advertising. His former disciple James Rennell Rodd had his second volume of poetry dismissed as "healthy and harmless." Mahaffy's *Greek Life and Thought: From the Age of Alexander to the Roman Conquest* was roundly criticized. Wilde complained that his Trinity mentor "might have made his book a work of solid and enduring interest, but he has chosen to give it a merely ephemeral value, and to substitute for the scientific temper of the true historian the prejudice, the flippancy, and the violence of the platform partisan." Writing of Swinburne's *Poems and Ballads*, he reproached the author for being at the mercy of words and for lacking "any sense of limit. His song is nearly always too loud for his subject."

Although unsigned, Wilde's reviews have signature hallmarks of humor and erudition. He describes "The Chronicle of Mites" as "a mock-heroic poem about the inhabitants of a decaying cheese, who speculate about the origin of their species and hold learned discussions upon the meaning of Evolution and the Gospel according to Darwin. This cheese epic is a rather unsavoury production, and the style is, at times, so monstrous and so realistic that the author should be called the Gorgon-Zola of literature."

A cookery book gets an appetizing send-off: "A man can live for three days without bread, but no man can live for one day without poetry, was an aphorism of Baudelaire's: you can live without pictures and music, but you can't live without eating, says the author of 'Dinners and Dishes': and this latter view is no doubt the more popular. Who indeed, in these degenerate days, would hesitate between an ode and an omelette, a sonnet and a salmis?"

Central to Wilde's growth as a thinker, this freelance period helped to formulate his theories of literary criticism. He was moving away from Matthew Arnold's dictum that criticism should see the work as it is toward a personal approach that sees the work as it really is not. Wilde ranked the critic with the artist: it takes an artist to praise, he said, but anyone can pick something apart. Wilde was amused "by the silly vanity of those writers and artists of our day who seem to imagine that the primary function of the critic is to chatter about their second-rate work." The critic's duty is to educate the public and awaken the age to new ideas and desires. These themes would coalesce in a book of criticism, *Intentions,* published in 1891.

THROUGH HIS WORK for the *Gazette,* Wilde entered another house of journalism. In November 1887, the first issue of *The Woman's World* appeared with "Edited by Oscar Wilde" printed in large black letters on a pink cover. Wilde's lively articles had impressed Thomas Wemyss Reid, new general manager of Cassell & Company publishers, who asked him to look over back issues and send him ideas on how to revitalize Cassell's new publication *The Lady's World: A Magazine of Fashion and Society.*

Ahead of his time, Wilde rejected the stale formula of fashion, food, and decoration. The magazine was "too feminine, and not sufficiently womanly," he wrote Reid, too similar to *Queen* and *Lady's Pictorial;* it had a "taint of vulgarity"; it was not a magazine that "aims at being the organ of women of intellect, culture, and position." Reid knew the magazine had problems, and Wilde found as many as possible, suggesting articles dealing with what women think and feel written by notable personalities.

Wilde instinctively knew that celebrities sell magazines. He presented Reid with a modern manifesto and earned his first—and only—full-time job, which he held from May 1887 to October 1889. His salary was six pounds a week, but Wilde saw benefits beyond a steady income.

An astute Shaw impudently observed that Wilde was a "snob to the marrow of his being." Everything Wilde did was calculated to enhance his comfort or prestige. As editor of a woman's magazine, he could meet the aristocracy, flattering the countesses and ladies with promises of bylines and full-page illustrations. An editor molds a publication in his own image and that of his friends; since Wilde was partial to the peerage, he wrote down a list of potential contributors, including Lady Archibald Campbell, Lady Dorothy Nevill, the queen of Rumania (Carmen Sylva), Violet Fane, Mrs. Comyns Carr, Olive Schreiner, Mrs. William Bell Scott, Marie Corelli, Lucy Garnett, Mrs. Alfred Hunt and her daughter Violet, his mother, and his wife.★

"Tomorrow I start for Oxford to arrange about Lady Margaret's article, and to meet some women of ability. We must have the Universities on our side," Wilde wrote Reid. "On Monday I have a meeting at Mrs. Jeune's. . . . I hope that Lady Salisbury will be there. . . . I have already engaged Lady Greville . . . and will go to Cambridge before the end of the month. . . . I also wish to go to Paris to see Madame Adam about a letter every two months. I find personal interviews necessary." To potential contributors, he stressed that his magazine would be quite different from *The Lady's World*—which, he said, seemed "to have been a very vulgar, trivial, and stupid production, with its silly gossip about silly people, and its social inanities."

The Woman's World was different in appearance and content; it reflected Wilde's aesthetic interests, but its intellectual thrust could be ponderous. Some articles ran to four thousand words. The old gossip column was replaced with Wilde's compendium of literary notes on recent books. He designed a new cover, discarding the green wrapper and statuary art for pink paper, red ink, and a sensuous William Morris–style design of undulating vine leaves supported by serpentine caryatids.

★Constance appropriately contributed articles titled "Children's Dress in This Century" and "Muffs"; his mother contributed the poem "Historic Women"; neither of the Hunts published in the magazine.

Finding writers gave him the pleasant opportunity of getting back in touch with old friends such as Nellie Sickert, sister of the painter, whom Wilde met when she was only a girl and susceptible to his malarkey. She recalled how he talked nonsense until he saw a skeptical frown on her face and with mock sadness said, "Well, it's as good as true." He knew her well enough to admit his insecurity. "I hope I will be able to make it a success," he wrote, "but I am not allowed as free a hand as I would like." Still at university, Sickert wrote an education article and Wilde paid her a guinea—a shilling more than the standard pound—a page because the piece was her first paid journalism. Wilde believed that artists should be paid and paid well. In "The Happy Prince," the Swallow delivers one of the statue's sapphire-jeweled eyes to a poor playwright, who delightedly cries: "I am beginning to be appreciated."

WILDE'S LETTERS TO contributors were patient, cajoling, and encouraging—sometimes all three. "I do not propose at present to have any notices of current theatrical events. We have to go to press six weeks before issue, on account of the illustrations," he replied to a query. Instead he asked the author to write three thousand words on any subject and let him know what she was doing, "as I should not like it to clash with any other article." He wrote asking that Queen Victoria send her early verses. An amused queen replied, "Really what will people not say and invent. Never cd [could] the Queen in her whole life write *one line* of *poetry* serious or comic or make a *Rhyme* even. This is therefore all *invention* & a *myth*."

Wilde was an excellent editor. He knew that even the most confident author needed praise and encouragement—and frequently. He advised Violet Fane: "I think the sonnet is quite clear as it stands. No *lover* could possibly miss the allusion to the old proverb about the gorse and kissing time, and it is only for lovers that poets write. Anything approaching an explanation is always derogatory to a work of art. If the *public* cannot understand the line, well—they cannot understand it."★ He praised Harriet Hamilton King: "I have just been reading again your poem about

★Wilde refers to this line in "Hazely Heath": "The yellow gorse, like kissing-time—or death," which refers to the proverb "When gorse is out of bloom, kissing is out of favour."

Nicotera—what a wonderful picture of the sea it holds! Keats even would have envied you your 'purple barge, in purple shadow on the seas.' Such colour and music together are rare."

THRICE WEEKLY HE rode the underground from Chelsea's Sloane Square to Charing Cross; from there he walked up the Strand and Fleet Street to Ludgate Circus, passing on the left the street of the Old Bailey, where he would be tried in 1895, and up to Ludgate Hill. The process of getting to his office—arising early and moving among jostling crowds— was initially appealing. "Work never seems to me a reality, but a way of getting rid of reality," he said. Arriving at the civilized hour of eleven, he greeted Arthur Fish, his assistant editor and a career journalist at Cassell's.

That Wilde was not allowed to smoke in the office made each hour torture; he was not one to take a quick puff at the pub downstairs; in fact, he abhorred pubs and bars and all places where people drank standing up instead of sitting comfortably at a café table. Forbidden cigarettes in prison, he philosophically said in a moment of untruth: "You make up your mind that you cannot smoke, and you resign yourself to the inevitable with ease." But anyone who knew Wilde knew the difficulties he had with self-discipline.

He left the office earlier and earlier to spend the remainder of the day pretending to be an editor at the Café Royal. Younger by six years and in awe of Wilde, Fish made excuses for his boss's absences. By the sound of Wilde's step, Fish determined whether he would get to work or postpone everything. On a bad day, Wilde sighed heavily and asked, "Is it necessary to settle anything today?" If not, he put on his hat and left. In the spring, Fish found him more cheerful, entering the office "with epigrammatic brightness" to illuminate a dull room.

Eventually he just dropped in. His column "Literary and Other Notes" was neglected (he wrote only eleven during his editorship). Exaggerating, of course, Wilde told W. E. Henley, another Cassell editor, that he had stopped answering letters. "I have known men come to London full of bright prospects," he explained, "and seen them complete wrecks in a few months through a habit of answering letters." Wilde kept the contributors happy, but after a year his letters lost their personal touch. One

Cassell editor called him "so indolent but such a genius." Wilde's major regret in life was always his indolence.

Inevitably, there were complaints about missed columns and lower circulation. Wilde worked harder for a while but soon slacked off; the consistency necessary for office work mystified—and eluded—him. As sales continued to slide, the publishers reverted to the old emphasis on fashion. In March 1889, Wilde received a six-month termination notice. One of his last contributions was a book review on the history of embroidery and lace. *The Woman's World* folded the following year.

Typifying Wilde's generosity to underlings, he wrote to Fish on his marriage that there are "only two things in the world of any importance, Love and Art; you have both; they must never leave you." On his departure, Wilde wrote to Reid, thanking him and his staff for their courtesy and expertise; he singled out Fish as "a most reliable and intelligent sub-editor." Reid was sorry to see Wilde leave: he was amusing to have around the office, when he was there.

BEYOND BEING A wife and mother, Constance published two children's books—*Grandma's Stories* and *A Long Time Ago*—and wrote unsigned theatre reviews and dramatic notes for such publications as *Lady's Pictorial,* where she reported on the Lyceum's end-of-season banquet onstage, which the Wildes attended. Determined to make her husband proud, Constance overcame her shyness and fear of public speaking. W. T. Stead predicted that she would soon be one of the popular "platform ladies." She advocated teaching children the evils of war at a conference sponsored by the Women's Committee of the International Arbitration and Peace Association in April 1888.

She joined the Rational Dress Society and edited its *Gazette,* a publication dedicated to eliminating tight-laced corsets, bustles, and high heels. In an article on the correct attire for women writers, she suggested "no false coils or frizzy fringe on the brow to heat the temples and mar the cool logic of thought." Opponents blamed breath-constricting corsets for everything from liver malfunctions and stomach ulcers to chronic constipation. An example of healthy dress was a loose-fitting cashmere tunic that Constance wore over matching trousers.

THE WILDES WERE fascinated with chiromancy (palm reading), spiritualism, mesmerism, and phrenology. Wilde believed in the evil eye and all the wondrous Irish superstitions that his parents had collected and published. He read books of magic and collected spells and potions, explaining to Yeats that the best way to eliminate an enemy is to "carve a Cerberus upon an emerald and put it in the oil of a lamp and carry it into a room where your enemy is, two new heads will come upon his shoulders and all three devour one another."

All over London groups met to explore the occult. Wilde preferred palmistry, which drives the plot of "Lord Arthur Savile's Crime." Listening to pontificators was not for him, but he encouraged Constance's interests. She attended meetings of the Theosophical Society, begun by Helena Petrovna Blavatsky, one of the great Victorian eccentrics, who is credited with bringing the word *occultism* into common use. The society encouraged unconventional living, including homosexual acts, and Madame Blavatsky set the tone with demonstrative affection for her chief disciple, Annie Besant, the socialist and free thinker. Perhaps in reaction to this atmosphere, Constance moved on to a more mystical group, called the Hermetic Order of the Golden Dawn, which practiced ritual magic.

Founded by a London coroner and prominent Rosicrucian Freemason named William Wynn Westcott, the Golden Dawn attracted magicians, charlatans, and eccentrics of all kinds, as well as W. B. Yeats and Annie Horniman, founder of Dublin's Abbey Theatre. Its enduring legacy was occult fiction, examinations of the dark side of life. At the initiation ceremony in 1888, Constance wore a black tunic with a cord wound three times around the waist and red shoes; she chose as a motto *Qui patitur vincit:* "He who suffers, conquers." A year later she reached the rank of Philosophus, the highest grade in the outer order, and was required to move up to the secretive second level, which ran the organization. By that time it was 1890; with the publication of *Dorian Gray,* she sadly told a friend, "No one will speak to us." She was learning the meaning of her intuitive motto.

NEVER IMPRISONED BY maturity, Wilde was a true *senachi,* the name given to legendary Irish storytellers. He loved the enchanted nonsense of *Alice's Adventures in Wonderland* as well as Andrew Lang's Fairy Books. Now he had two wide-awake sons to entertain with his tales, which he called "studies in prose," written "partly for children, and partly for those who have kept the childlike faculties of wonder and joy." Wilde was little more than an overgrown child himself. His younger son, Vyvyan, in his book *Son of Oscar Wilde,* recalled how his father would burst into the nursery and go down on all fours, "being in turn a lion, a wolf, a horse." Wilde mended the toys broken in such rambunctious play and, when he grew tired of playing, told fairy stories or tales of adventure, of which he had a never-ending supply. Cyril once asked why "The Selfish Giant" brought tears to his father's eyes; Wilde replied that "really beautiful things always made him cry."

Not all the sleepy-time stories were recorded, but Wilde did publish *The Happy Prince and Other Tales* in 1888. The volume excited the critics, and for the first time he was taken seriously as a writer. One reviewer favorably compared him with Hans Christian Andersen; another called the bitter satire different from Andersen; yet another said the stories revealed Wilde's genius "at its best." Ellen Terry told Wilde that she wanted to read one of his tales "some day to NICE people—or even NOT nice people, and MAKE 'em nice."

In 1887 *Court and Society Review* published "The Canterville Ghost" and "Lord Arthur Savile's Crime," both tales of redemption with happy endings. Virginia, the young American heroine of "The Canterville Ghost," learns from her experience with the ghost "what Life is, and what Death signifies, and why Love is stronger than both." In the second story, Wilde explores the notion of the artistic impulse seeking expression through the criminal, a theme he returned to in "Pen, Pencil and Poison."

"Lord Arthur Savile's Crime" combines Wilde's interest in aristocratic character, criminality, and chiromancy. Count Louis Hamon, known as Cheiro, was London's foremost palm reader; in addition to seeing clients privately, he entertained at fashionable parties like the one described in the story. The tale, like much of Wilde's fiction, started out with the dull working title "George Ellison and the Palmist"; as usual, Wilde told this story of destiny fulfilled to the artist W. Graham Robertson during a walk in the country. Robertson later complained that Wilde's tales "lost much of their charm" when written out. Yeats reviewed the story and called it "amusing enough."

Lord Arthur commits murder as an act of duty so that he can wed his fiancée without fear of scandal. At first he does not know what his fortune portends: "Could it be that written on his hand, in characters that he could not read himself, but that another could decipher, was some fearful secret of sin, some blood-red sign of crime?" According to Cheiro's palmistry textbook, the hand of such a murderer would have a short, thick thumb and a short, thick, and red headline on the palm. Realizing his destiny, Lord Arthur fears that he will "wake the slumbering city from its dreams." Wilde continues this ambiguous coding in a scene where Lord Arthur observes two men reading a billboard: "An odd feeling of curiosity stirred him, and he crossed over." Wilde too had "crossed over" into a new world, one quite different from the Hellenic ideal of his university days. Now he made each lingering gaze at a youth a dangerous adventure by which he awoke London and the world.

CHAPTER TWELVE

Enemies and Friends

❧

There are terrible temptations that it required strength,
strength and courage, to yield to. To stake all one's life on a
single moment, to risk everything on one throw, whether the stake be
power or pleasure, I care not—there is no weakness in that. There is a
horrible, a terrible courage.

—*An Ideal Husband*

I n a time of hirsute chins, a perpetually clean-shaven Wilde inspected his reflected profile every morning and asked whether it was the portrait of a "criminal." The mirror assured him it was the face of an artist-criminal with the mask of a genius. A satisfying answer. Masks tell more than faces. During the closing years of the eighties, driven by furtiveness, Wilde worked at literature with a vengeance, producing four notable essays published in *The Fortnightly Review* and *Nineteenth Century*, and later collected as *Intentions*.

The energy released by combining the artist with the criminal fascinated him. In "Pen, Pencil and Poison," ostensibly a biographical essay on the writer-painter Thomas Griffiths Wainewright (also a forger and serial killer), Wilde was less interested in retelling a well-known story than in promoting his views on crime and creativity. Of Wainewright he said that "his crimes seem to have had an important effect upon his art. They gave a strong personality to his style, a quality that his early work certainly lacked," a description that sounds autobiographical. "The fact of a man being a poisoner is nothing against his prose."

As Wilde variously demonstrated in his plays, interesting personalities are created out of sin, and wickedness exists so that good people can find others attractive. In "Shakespeare and Stage Costume" (retitled "The Truth of Masks"), Wilde starts out discussing the need for authentic costume design, but at issue is his theory that allows for contradictory principles. "A Truth in art," he writes, "is that whose contradictory is also true," and "The Truths of metaphysics are the truths of masks." Sin returns in "The Critic as Artist," a two-part dialogue between Gilbert and Ernest. "What is termed Sin is an essential element of progress," explains Gilbert. "Without it the world would stagnate, or grow old, or become colourless. By its curiosity Sin increases the experience of the race."

Discussing why the creative ranks over the critical, Ernest suggests abolishing critics and the magazines that publish "the industrious prattle of what they do not understand." Gilbert points out that the critical spirit is Greek and that "if the Greeks had criticised nothing but language, they would still have been the great art-critics of the world." Ernest sympathizes because "the creative faculty is higher than the critical." But without the critical, Gilbert rejoins, there is no artistic creation.

The highest criticism, Gilbert argues in Wilde's voice, is "the record of one's own soul. It is more fascinating than history, as it is concerned simply with oneself. . . . It is the only civilised form of autobiography, as it deals not with the events, but with the thoughts of one's life." To build a literary theory on personality was Wilde's aim: "It is only by intensifying his own personality that the critic can interpret the personality and work of others. . . . As art springs from personality, so it is only to personality that it can be revealed." In Pater's version, the preferred word was *temperament*—vague and nonjudgmental. Wilde's use of *personality* found its power in narcissism.

Through publishing "Critic" and "Lying" in *The Fortnightly Review,* Wilde became friendly with Frank Harris, one of the era's more controversial journalists and literary figures; in addition to being an influential London editor for two decades, he wrote short stories, plays, and biographies, including *Oscar Wilde: His Life and Confessions* (1916). Shaw, who was not a close friend of Wilde's, contributed his reminiscences of Wilde to the second edition of Harris's biography in 1918. Wilde and Shaw first met at Lady Wilde's salon in 1879 when Shaw recalled a palpable tension. "We put each other out frightfully; and this odd difficulty persisted between us to the very last, even when we were no longer mere boyish novices and had become men of the world with plenty of skill in social intercourse."

Two years younger than Wilde, Shaw grew up on Hatch Street in Dublin, where his mother supported the family by giving music lessons. Wilde's family secrets were insignificant compared with Shaw's: his father was a drunk, and his mother may have been involved with her resident singing teacher (rumored to be Shaw's biological father). While Wilde was at university, Shaw was a real-estate clerk collecting rents in the Dublin slums. Self-righteous and physically obsessive, Shaw was a perfect zealot for all the causes of the day, from vegetarianism to the healthy claims made for unbleached woolen clothing.

Skilled in musical appreciation and determined to be a writer, Shaw arrived in London in 1876, two years before Wilde; he wrote music reviews for the *Star* and unsuccessful novels with forgettable titles like *Immaturity,* and became a socialist. After attending a lecture at the Fabian Society, Wilde decided to write his own views in "The Soul of Man Under Socialism." Asked what he thought of the essay, Shaw replied that "it was very witty and entertaining, but had nothing whatever to do with socialism."

Not with socialism perhaps but certainly with individualism. Wilde's hymn to freedom demonstrated that he was more an anarchist than a socialist; his dogmas benefited the artist: "It is through disobedience that progress has been made, through disobedience and through rebellion," he states and then cautions that "the note of the perfect personality is not rebellion, but peace," and "the form of government that is most suitable to the artist is no government at all." Wilde wanted to convert the unconverted to his way of thinking: "Selfishness is not living as one wishes to live, it is asking others to live as one wishes to live. And unselfishness is letting other people's lives alone, not interfering with them." A world of unselfish people? No wonder Shaw had a few laughs.

Shaw recalled something between six and twelve meetings with Wilde, listing the fifth as an incongruous encounter at a naval exhibition in Chelsea. "It was my sole experience of Oscar's wonderful gift as a raconteur," said Shaw, who worked to retain his Irish accent and was unimpressed with Wilde's brand of Hibernian charm used to impress the English. Whenever Shaw wanted to reproach Wilde publicly, he criticized his "Merrion Square Protestant pretentiousness" but allowed him to be "a citizen of all civilised capitals," and "at root a *very Irish* Irishman, and as such a foreigner everywhere but in Ireland." More and more, Wilde suppressed his Irishness in favor of a persona that astonished.

With some truth, Shaw claimed that Wilde lacked close friends in society and failed to build a solid social foundation, which contributed to his downfall. He "was incapable of friendship, though not of the most touching kindness on occasion," Shaw wrote Harris in 1916. "The vulgar hated him for snubbing them; and the valiant men damned his impudence and cut him. Thus he was left with a band of devoted satellites . . . and a dining out connection . . . with here and there a man of talent and personality enough to command his respect." Years earlier, on the same subject, Wilde told Yeats that Shaw had "no enemies, and none of his friends like him." What Shaw ignored was Wilde's inclination to shun those who challenged his intellect. His Oxford connections allowed him to visit Pater and Ruskin or to ask Swinburne to write in favor of his mother's Civil List pension, but when it came to dining out, he wanted youthful profiles by his side.

As an Oxford graduate, Wilde arrived in London with an established group of friends—those from Magdalen and those from other colleges. Constance brought confidantes into the marriage, in particular Lady Mount-Temple, a distant cousin and surrogate mother, whose house in Torquay was a favorite writing place for Wilde. But there were no couples or families with children whom they saw regularly. On Fleet Street, Wilde came and went too quickly to form any ties, except with editors such as Harris and Henley.

There was Yeats, of course, and had not the young poet's nationalistic interests taken him elsewhere, the two writers might have become better friends, although Wilde tended to avoid friendships with those whose intellectual talents were equal to or greater than his. Between the two was an unspoken love of Ireland. Yeats spent his youth in Sligo, a market town on Ireland's western coast, set between ocean and mountains and as rich in heroic and supernatural lore as Connemara. The two men shared what Yeats called "half-civilized blood," and when Wilde spoke of hearing mystical, invisible voices at Illaunroe, Yeats understood. To please his father, who was a fashionable Dublin portrait painter, Yeats studied art, but he had abandoned it for poetry and was now on the verge of appreciation with the publication of *The Wanderings of Oisin*—his search for meaning through mythological figures. Wilde noted it in the *Pall Mall Gazette,* perhaps with the nostalgia that eight years earlier he would have welcomed similar words about *Poems.* "Books of poetry by young writers are usually promissory notes that are never met," he wrote. "Now and then, however, one comes across a volume that is so far above the average that one can hardly resist the fascinating temptation of recklessly prophesying a fine future for its author." Sincere or insincere (one never knew with Wilde), he was proven right.

Yeats attended Lady Wilde's salons when he arrived in London but met her son in 1888 at the home of the Cassell's editor W. E. Henley, where Wilde famously remarked that "the basis of literary friendship is mixing the poisoned bowl." Five years before, an eighteen-year-old Yeats heard Wilde lecture in Dublin on "The House Beautiful" and marveled at his perfect sentences, which seemed to have been written "overnight with labour and yet all spontaneous." Sensing Yeats's hero worship, Wilde invited him to Christmas dinner. Yeats had grown up surrounded by Dublin intellectuals and was hardly an ingenuous youth, even though he recalled himself as such that day at Tite Street, writing in his autobiography that he was "perplexed by my own shapelessness, my lack of self-possession and of easy courtesy . . . astonished by this scholar who as a man of the world was so perfect."

Youthful impressions can be misleading, but Yeats said he knew Wilde "at the happiest moment of his life. No scandal had touched his name, his fame as a talker was growing among his equals, and he seemed to live in the enjoyment of his own spontaneity." That changed when Wilde became the toast of the West End, a successful playwright and an absentee husband and father. Yeats said Wilde was a man who "could not endure the sedentary toil of creative art and so remained a man of action."

After dinner, when Constance excused herself to see to the children,

Wilde read parts of "The Decay of Lying" from the January 1889 issue of *Nineteenth Century*. In its unequivocal support of lying, Wilde's most modern essay became an enduring blueprint for the artistic imagination; it also explained his paradoxical nature: he advocated lying by being honest. The telling of beautiful lies was essential to Wilde's image of himself as a work of art; thus his tales of bisexual bravado or strenuous physical activity should be suspect, for they contradict his nature. Wilde was so convincing as his own mythologizer that the dubious stories endure: they are too good not to be true. The aim of the liar, he said, "is simply to charm, to delight, to give pleasure. He is the very basis of civilized society, and without him a dinner-party, even at the mansions of the great, is as dull as a lecture at the Royal Society."

BETTER THAN MOST of his contemporaries, Wilde understood that writing is only the beginning of a process, which involves design, printing, distribution, reviewing, and promotion—all the building blocks of twentieth-century book publishing. Wilde possessed a natural artistic eye refined through collaboration with Charles Ricketts, who designed and illustrated all of his books except *Salome,* which made Aubrey Beardsley, an artist of frightening originality, an icon of the 1890s. Ricketts excelled in many fields: illustrator, book designer, wood engraver, painter, sculptor, and set designer.★

Wilde's first editions were all printed on cotton-rag paper, which does not oxidize, rather than on paper made from tree fibers, which turns brown, then brittle, and crumbles like a dead leaf. He was a fortunate man of letters to be publishing when the heated press made it possible to stamp bindings in gold leaf before they were bound to the text. A book like *The Sphinx,* with its dramatic tableaux imprinted on continuous vellum covers, represented the quintessence of fin de siècle design, before a new century replaced opulence with the dust jacket. In *Dorian Gray,* Lord

---

★Ricketts designed the binding and/or the decoration for *The Picture of Dorian Gray* (1891), *Intentions* (1891), *Lord Arthur Savile's Crime and Other Stories* (1891), *Poems* (1892), and *The Sphinx* (1894); with Charles Shannon he designed *A House of Pomegranates* (1891). Shannon was responsible for the binding design of the plays. *The Happy Prince and Other Tales* was illustrated by Jacomb Hood and Walter Crane, who became a well-known illustrator of children's books.

Henry admires a Gautier edition printed on Japanese paper and bound in "citron green leather, with a design of gilt trellis-work and dotted pomegranates." (*Dorian* itself was bound in gray pastel paper and stamped with tiny gold marigolds.)

Ricketts had ended a five-year apprenticeship to the wood engravers' guild and was at the beginning of his career when he dropped off some sketches at *The Woman's World*. Wilde liked his work and assigned him articles to illustrate. During his guild studies, Ricketts met Charles Shannon, a boyish-looking aspiring painter with whom he lived for fifty years; they were self-sufficient bachelors and men of arts and letters who spent a lifetime becoming aristocrats of good taste. "Bending over their blocks they looked like figures from a missal," said the artist Will Rothenstein.

In the summer of 1889, Wilde knocked on the door of The Vale, a Regency House off the King's Road in Chelsea where the couple lived—quietly and discreetly. They had recently published *The Dial,* a collection of writings and illustrations from unknown contributors. Wilde had received a copy and, impressed with its aesthetic sensibilities, dropped by to offer congratulations. "What a charming old house you have, and what delightful Japanese prints," he said on entering the drawing room. "Yes the Japanese understand conciseness and compact design. And you have yellow walls, so have I. Yellow is the colour of joy." Wilde noticed what the couple called pretty things: Greek lecythi, Tanagra statuettes, Venetian glass, drawings by Hokusai, Persian miniatures.

Ricketts greeted a man of thirty-five who looked older. "His face had grown full about the mouth and chin," he later recalled, "the eyes were intelligent, below their heavy lids, and lit the face which, at times, during moments of suspicion or introspection, became mask-like." Ricketts said that Whistler, whom he described as "a Hungarian bandmaster, aping Mephistopheles," was more a dandy in dress than Wilde.

Small, wiry, intense, with a Vandyke beard and dark eyes, Ricketts was born in Geneva and reared in a cultured, musical home, the son of an English father and a French mother. Wilde noticed that he was the extrovert and Shannon the quiet one, or, as one visitor put it, "the reasonable wife." A contemporary observed that between the two existed "the most marvelous human relationship," a union "more bracing than comfortable." Wilde decided that "Marigold" was the perfect name for Shannon; Ricketts he called "Orchid." That evening marked the beginning of a seven-year partnership—Wilde writing and Ricketts building (his word) beautiful books.

Wilde found The Vale "the one house in London where you will never be bored, and where you are not asked to explain things." Any working relationship between writer and artist can be competitive, even uneasy. This one began cordially enough, with Ricketts wanting Wilde to drop by whenever he wished, but frequent visits made Wilde take his hosts for granted. Once he angered Ricketts with the abrupt comment that he made "beauty out of a little coloured paper smeared with gold," reducing his intricate art to nursery finger painting. Never revering artists as he did poets, Wilde also overstepped courtesy when he announced one evening: "Both you and Shannon are ascetics of art, you turn away from life and, like most painters, you lack curiosity." By the time they produced *The Sphinx* in 1894, there were serious artistic differences. Wilde saw the collaboration as a source of "advantage and resentment," Ricketts said.

But during 1891, Wilde was gracious to the Marigold and his Orchid—and their interesting friends. There were Friday evening dinners with artists such as Rothenstein, Sturge Moore, and Walter Sickert; Wilde looked forward to talking with the lesbian couple Katharine Bradley and her niece, Edith Cooper, who wrote verse and drama under the nom de plume Michael Field and lived nearby. He came, also, to appreciate Ricketts as a sophisticated raconteur, a worthy opponent. The fare was frugal but eaten off a tabletop of lapis lazuli. Everyone sat in white-scrubbed kitchen chairs. Shannon cooked up eggs with leftovers or served rolled tongue with bread and butter and quince jam. There was always inexpensive wine. Years later, when Wilde heard that Ricketts and Shannon were making a little money, he remarked: "Ah, I suppose when you go there to supper they give you *fresh* eggs now." The main attraction was always the swift parries and ripostes. All noticed how Ricketts and Shannon were obsessed with Wilde, how they copied his voice and speech. He became "everything to them," recalled Michael Field.

But Ricketts had an aggressive side beneath his charming manners. One evening he attacked Wilde for bringing an inferior guest to the artistic discussion. When the uninvited departed, Ricketts demanded: "Why did you bring this man here?" "An obscure worshipper who bowed in the outer court," Wilde loftily replied, wanting to dismiss the matter. "So I, the god, beckoned him in." There was another unpleasant evening when John Addington Symonds became obnoxious with his self-appointed mission to have Whitman and other prominent figures admit to same-sex passions. Asked to leave, Symonds looked up at Ricketts from the bottom of the stairs and persisted: "But you are, aren't you? You do, don't you?"

"THERE WERE TWO personalities in him," Ricketts said of Wilde: "the exhibitor of well-rehearsed impromptus, of which he had a stock, and the spontaneous and witty critic of Life." The process of invention varied: a plot or a situation would flash upon him, but more often he invented a story and told it, and, if he liked the sound of it, wrote it down. The sound of the words was as important in prose as in plays as he tried to recapture the musical cadences of the ancient Greek. Literature, Wilde said, was an elaborate design appealing more to the eye than to the ear; he missed the nuances of classical times, when the voice was the medium, and the ear the critic.

He swaggered a lot, acting like his character the Remarkable Rocket, who proclaims, "I like hearing myself talk. It is one of my greatest pleasures. I often have long conversations all by myself, and I am so clever that sometimes I don't understand a single word of what I am saying." It amused Ricketts how often Wilde merged ego and hero worship, giving the impression that he had known Rossetti, Baudelaire, and Gautier. "Flaubert had just told me," remarked Wilde one evening, that "he was lost in admiration when I recited to him these lines: 'The land was dry and burnt up with heat. The people went to and fro over the plain, like flies crawling upon a disk of polished copper!'" Of course, everyone knew he was joking.

One evening Wilde read to Ricketts and Shannon an expanded version of his short story "The Portrait of Mr. W. H.," published in *Black-wood's* in July 1889. In it he argues that Shakespeare's sonnets were inspired by same-sex love for an actor in his company named Willie Hughes or Hewes, who played the leading female roles, since women were barred from performing on the Elizabethan stage. Wilde read the sonnets—

making puns and faces at sexually suggestive lines—and outlined the story, which uses as proof a period portrait of Hughes later revealed to be a forgery. Wilde wanted readers to understand what Ricketts and Shannon already knew—that friendship can transcend sensuality.

The central paradox of "Mr. W. H." presumes that if you convince someone else of a belief, you lose the belief yourself; a thing is not necessarily true because a man dies for it. William Blackwood, publisher of the prestigious Edinburgh magazine, found the story powerful and was unconcerned by the homosexual allusions. "I propose publishing this work in a delicate slim volume powdered with gold," Wilde told Ricketts about the expanded version. "Already I have been warned that the subject is most dangerous," he boasted. "Our English homes will totter to their base when my book appears," he said, referring to the story's initial rejection by *The Fortnightly Review.*

Asked to create something mock-Clouet (Jean Clouet was a sixteenth-century Flemish painter of miniatures) for the frontispiece, Ricketts painted an imaginary portrait on a decayed piece of oak, which Shannon framed in a fragment of worm-eaten molding. "It is not a forgery at all, it is an authentic Clouet of the highest authentic order," Wilde wrote, to show he believed it an Elizabethan original rather than a forgery of a fictional forgery.* Wilde credited Robbie Ross for inspiring "The Portrait of Mr. W. H." "The story is," he told Ross, "half yours, and but for you it would not have been written."

After being tutored by Wilde during his stay at Tite Street, Ross went up to Cambridge, but he spent only a year there, leaving in 1889 after a ragging incident when he was dunked in the college fountain and caught pneumonia. He quarreled with his family about his homosexuality, left London for Edinburgh to work at the *Scots Observer,* but returned to edit the Society of Authors magazine. Ross made few demands on Wilde. He was content to dine with him outside the glare of the Café Royal at small

---

*Ricketts made Wilde a gift of the portrait, which disappeared from recorded history after it was knocked down for a guinea at the bankruptcy sale of his possessions in April 1895. It was purchased by a bookseller on the Brompton Road, who resold it for five pounds to an unidentified customer. Publication of the expanded version of *The Portrait of Mr. W. H.* was complicated by reorganization at the Bodley Head and by Wilde's trial, and the book did not appear until 1921 in America and 1958 in England.

cafés in Soho, where they ordered a three-shilling meal and Wilde tried out themes for "The Decay of Lying." An agreeable listener, Ross was never an intellectual force behind Wilde's creativity. Giving him credit for "Mr. W.H." and "Decay" was Wilde's way of making his disciple feel important. Ross took his muse status more seriously.

VISITS TO THE VALE were interrupted when Wilde met, through a letter of introduction from American friends, the fascinating personality Clyde Fitch. Fitch was eleven years younger (Wilde preferred an age difference of eleven to sixteen years), a playwright at the onset of a successful and prosperous career, and a dandy in the Whistler tradition. He wore a sky blue suit and painted a frieze of cherry blossoms around the walls of his room on his first day at Amherst College in Massachusetts. Later he adopted a black-and-white checked suit with purple cravat, white hat, and silver-mounted walking stick.

Fitch's frothy plays reflecting the passions of the smart set were of the moment (at one time he had four plays running simultaneously on Broadway) and are seldom revived.★ He worked hard to maintain an ostentatious standard of living (his Park Avenue home was a museum where guests drank Château d'Yquem from antique spiral Venetian glasses); he wrote or adapted fifty-five plays in twenty years. "Writing plays was like copying something you know by heart," he said. Fitch had collaborated on a play based on Beau Brummell, the English fop and friend of George IV when he was Prince of Wales; it opened in May 1890 at Madison Square Garden, and its success brought him into New York's artistic circle, including the salon of Elisabeth Marbury and her companion, Elsie de Wolfe, an actress who became a celebrated interior decorator.

Without a script to borrow from, Fitch put a Wildean gloss to his Brummell dialogue with lines such as: "Men shake hands much too often. A glance of the eye, Reginald—a glance of the eye," and "Observe

---

★Fitch's name is evoked and memorialized in the classic Hollywood theatre film *All About Eve* (1950). When the actress Margo Channing, played by Bette Davis, throws a tantrum, her director calls the melodramatic lines worthy of a Clyde Fitch play.

me, Mortimer, am I quite correct? Are there creases in my cravat! I would not wish to make creases the fashion." Wilde gave Fitch the copy of *Blackwood's* with "The Portrait of Mr. W. H." His response was everything that Wilde could have wished. "You precious maddening man," Fitch wrote.

> Your letters are more than you—because they come and you *don't*. Last night when I came home I flung myself in the best evening clothes and all with *my* Blackwood. "I will just look at it," I thought. But I could not leave it. I read, unconscious of the uncomfortability of my position and of the fact that one arm and two legs were asleep, fast.
>
> Oh! Oscar! The story is *great*—and fine!
>
> *I* believe in Willie Hughes: I don't care for the laughter, I only know I *am* convinced and I *will*. I will believe in Willie H. Sometime, if the Gods are kind I shall *send you* a picture of Mr. W. H., it may be another forgery—But that won't make any difference, will it?

They met at Fitch's hotel but not frequently enough. Fitch wrote: "It is 3 and you are not coming. I looked out of the window many, many times. . . . I have not slept. I have only dreamt, and thought. I don't know where I stand nor why. Passionately yours." Another letter addresses Wilde as "Oh! you adorable creature! You *are* a great genius. And oh! such a sweet one. Never was a genius so sweet so adorable. . . . You are my poetry—my painting—my music—you are my sight, and sound, and touch." Fitch returned to London the next year and sought to rekindle the relationship. "*Nobody* loves you as *I* do. When you are here I dream. When you are away I awake . . . we have our secrets," he wrote. In 1892 Fitch was again in town, staying at the Albany, Jack Worthing's address in *Earnest,* but by then Wilde had met John Gray and then Lord Alfred Douglas.

TENTATIVELY WILDE EXPLORED London's underground homosexual world, aware of the dangers. Like everyone else, he read about Lord

Arthur Somerset's plight in September 1889, when he had to leave England because of alleged offenses with telegraph boys at a homosexual brothel in Cleveland Street. Until Douglas insisted on more hazardous sexual venues, Wilde met young men through friends. He probably met John Gray at The Vale. Gray had written two pieces for the first edition of *The Dial.* Twelve years younger than Wilde, a working-class carpenter's son from Bethnal Green, Gray was being turned into an aristocratic dandy by his mentors Ricketts and Shannon.

It was Wilde, however, who created Gray's public image, by introducing him to the right people and giving him the right patina. In *Dorian Gray,* Lord Henry describes the satisfaction of such a relationship: "To project one's soul into some gracious form, and let it tarry there for a moment; to hear one's own intellectual views echoed back to one with all the added music of passion and youth; to convey one's temperament into another as though it were a subtle fluid or a strange perfume; there was a real joy in that—perhaps the most satisfying joy left to us in an age limited and vulgar."

Gray was overpowered by personality, for Wilde made his young men feel they were the center of his attention (and they were for that moment); he was interested in them, their views, their poetry—but not their problems. That Gray was a poet of startling originality made Wilde's excursion that much more exciting. The exact nature of the relationship is a matter for conjecture, but there is no reason to doubt that they were lovers. Wilde said in *De Profundis,* "My real life, my higher life" was with Gray and others like him, but then he said so much in anger in that letter to Douglas that this could mean only what he explained at his trial: love was a higher state than adoring someone madly.

During the day Gray supported himself with civil service jobs, working his way up to clerk in the Foreign Office Library. His evenings were spent at the Independent Theatre, which staged private club performances of Ibsen's *Ghosts* and other censored plays, and occasionally at the Rhymers' Club. Begun as a gathering of Irishmen living in London, the Rhymers gathered at The Crown and the Cheshire Cheese, a pub off Fleet Street associated with Samuel Johnson, the eighteenth century's foremost conversationalist. Through the club Gray met Yeats, Arthur Symons, and Ernest Dowson. Wilde made infrequent appearances because he scorned

CHAPTER THIRTEEN

The Dorian Prophecy

❧

*Every impulse that we strive to strangle broods in the mind and
poisons us. The body sins once, and has done with its sin, for action is a
mode of purification. . . . The only way to get rid of temptation is to
yield to it. Resist it, and your soul grows sick with longing
for the things it had forbidden to itself.*

—THE PICTURE OF DORIAN GRAY

More frequently now, Wilde traveled up to Oxford from
Paddington to attend an opening of the Dramatic Society or
to match wits with Pater. His double life drew him back: he
surrounded himself with undergraduate profiles, recalled how he forged
his aesthetic persona along Magdalen's tree-lined walks, and renewed his
pledge to feast on honeycomb. During a visit in February 1890, he sought
out Lionel Johnson, an aspiring poet. Wilde made himself at home in
Johnson's New College rooms, smoked his cigarettes, dissected Pater, and
noticed familiar signs of ambivalence: on a table was a bottle of Glengarry
Scotch and open volumes of *Les Fleurs du mal* and *Leaves of Grass;* on the
wall portraits of Cardinals Newman and Wiseman—reminders that Johnson
had pledged to convert to Catholicism when he graduated. A troubled
young man (whose alcoholism contributed to an early death at age thirty-
five), Johnson said his "sorrows never come from consciousness of wrong,
but from the vague shadow of unrest thrown over life by passing things."

In his best-known poem, "The Dark Angel," he wrestles with moments when "all the things of beauty burn with the flames of evil ecstasy."

Wilde mesmerized Johnson with flippant comments about everything and everyone, and the visit resonated beyond the immediate moment. Johnson told his friend Lord Alfred Douglas: "I am in love with him." The twenty-year-old youngest son of the ninth Marquess of Queensberry was intrigued.✶ Douglas had been a practicing homosexual since a schoolboy at Winchester, where he met Johnson; he was at Wilde's old college and recognized the name but, not being a reader or a scholar, knew little of Wilde's literary reputation. When *Dorian Gray* was published in 1890 in *Lippincott's,* Johnson gave Douglas his copy, insisting that he read it, which he did, "fourteen times running," fully recognizing himself in the story of a young man falling in love with his own beauty.

The following summer Johnson brought Douglas around to Tite Street, where—in the words of W. H. Auden—"the Overloved met the Underloved." Balzac's fictional meeting between Vautrin and Lucien de Rubempré at the coach house was one of Wilde's favorite erotic moments in literature—a *coup de foudre.* Basil Hallward's stroke of lightning on first seeing Dorian was the realization that "I had seen perfection face to face." Wilde observed Douglas's pallid beauty and thought of Hyacinth when Apollo loved him. The meeting was brief, with only time for tea and for Douglas to charm Constance and be amused (as Johnson had predicted) by Wilde's lively banter. "Laughter is not at all a bad beginning for a friendship," Lord Henry remarks, "and it is far the best for ending one." They talked of Magdalen and Greats, which Douglas was close to failing. Since Wilde had earned a First in this difficult course, he offered to coach the younger man and rewarded his enthusiasm for *Dorian Gray* with a signed deluxe copy.

Wilde was too sensitive to the temper of his life, one of foreshadowings and forebodings, not to marvel at another extraordinary example of life imitating art. If he had not invented Dorian, with "his finely-curved

---

✶John Sholto Douglas, in biographical accounts, is often referred to as either the eighth or the ninth Marquess of Queensberry. This confusion stems from a renumbering of the title following World War II. At this time, James, son of the second Duke of Queensberry (1672–1711), reputedly an idiot from birth who had in his lifetime been passed over for the title, was recognized. As a result, the then current Marquess, the tenth, became the eleventh Marquess, and Bosie's father, in his lifetime the eighth, the ninth.

scarlet lips, his frank blue eyes, his crisp gold hair," before he beheld Douglas with his blond hair and blanched skin blending into Tite Street's all-
white drawing room, he could have done so at that very moment. And had
not Wilde's attentions been elsewhere—writing a new play for George
Alexander—the relationship might have started immediately. Instead
Wilde went to the country near Lake Windermere, where Robbie Ross
later joined him, and he completed the first of his social comedies, *Lady
Windermere's Fan.*

LIKE ALL OF Wilde's prose pieces, *Dorian Gray* began as a story told to
friends. The derivative plot of a man and his portrait that does not grow
old had been in his subconscious since youthful readings of *Sidonia*
and *Melmoth,* embellished by borrowings from other authors. During a
gathering at The Vale, Wilde told a separate narrative about an actress who
loses her power to persuade when she falls in love. Combining
Dorian and Sibyl might never have happened had not J. M. Stoddart—
who introduced Wilde to Whitman and published Rodd's *Rose Leaf and
Apple Leaf*—journeyed to London in August 1889. As editor of *Lippincott's
Monthly Magazine,* he was commissioning short fiction and invited Wilde
and Arthur Conan Doyle to dinner to discuss their work in progress. Doyle
contributed his second Sherlock Holmes adventure, *The Sign of Four,* and
Wilde parried with his own mystery, describing *Dorian Gray* as an
unsolved murder story.

Wilde agreed to deliver a manuscript in two months but, true to
form, asked for more time: the October deadline stretched into the spring
of 1890. Stoddart asked for a hundred thousand words; Wilde replied that
the English language did not have that many beautiful words. Then Stoddart demanded the manuscript, which forced Wilde to finish it in three
weeks. As a fledgling novelist, he struggled with the same problems that
Dion Boucicault had criticized in his first play, *Vera:* too much dialogue
and too little action. Typically, the characters in Wilde's social comedies
sparkle only in drawing rooms, seldom moving outside to risk worldly
interaction. Despite a beginning, middle, and end, *Dorian Gray* is more a
meditation than a narrative. Like Huysmans's *À rebours,* it appears
randomly improvised, which Wilde knew or half-knew. Plot lacunae were
intensified by murder, suicide, or accidental death; Dorian, in essence,

executes himself when he attacks his portrait with a knife. At the end, only Lord Henry remains alive, and his wife has divorced him. It made sense to have Dorian remove obstacle after obstacle to keep his ghastly secret, but then Wilde decided—in response to hostile reviewers—to make Aestheticism rather than Decadence the moral focus for the novel; he added six new chapters and a preface, and made other revisions.

"EVERY PORTRAIT THAT is painted with feeling is a portrait of the artist, not of the sitter. The sitter is merely the accident, the occasion," says Basil Hallward about Dorian's picture. Despite Wilde's remark that "an artist should create beautiful things, but should put nothing of his own life into them," *Dorian Gray* is very much the author's autobiography. Dorian's beautiful face, a mask concealing an evil soul, is no different from its author's use of multiple masks to conceal his true sexuality. The plot reveals Wilde's talent as a writer of concealment—a power that came from not speaking directly about the subject most important to him. Whatever was private was coded in a style so witty and delightful that it made Wilde's return to playwriting imperative. The novel form helped Wilde to reveal himself, while the dramatic form allowed him to celebrate. "To reveal art and conceal the artist is art's aim," he said, a noble sentiment for everyone else, when for him it was the opposite.

With its multilayered symbolism and compulsive hedonism, *Dorian Gray* has never been out of fashion or absent from university reading lists. Successive generations have not heeded Wilde's warning that "All art is at once surface and symbol. Those who go beneath the surface do so at their peril. Those who read the symbol do so at their peril." The novel's excitement for the reader comes from interpreting a haunting, narcotic story of self-deceiving vanity and from experiencing the erotic transformation of a person into an objet d'art. On another level, *Dorian Gray* is a study of male homosexual panic within a love triangle of three men. Dorian laments that "each man lived his own life, and paid his own price for living it. The only pity was one had to pay so often for a single fault." Mrs. Erlynne in *Lady Windermere's Fan* sees retribution as endless: "One pays for one's sins, and then one pays again, and all one's life one pays."

An active participant in his own self-destruction, Dorian commits acts of inhumanity that are stamped on his portrait; by the end of the novel, confronting his hideously disfigured image, he realizes that he is beyond redemption and by attacking his conscience kills himself. "Yes; there is a terrible moral in *Dorian Gray*," Wilde said, "a moral which the prurient will not be able to find in it, but which will be revealed to all whose minds are healthy. Is this an artistic error? I fear it is. It is the only error in the book." Wilde wanted to tell a story of multiple personalities and succeeded in crafting a cautionary tale of his own many selves, making it easy for his enemies to remark behind his back: "Just like that Dorian Gray character."

Dorian was, Wilde said, "what I would like to be—in other ages, perhaps"; he was wistfully admitting his lack of beauty in the pursuit of decadence. Clearly Wilde saw a mirage of himself in Dorian's death scene, when the character is withered and wrinkled like the mummy his father discovered in Egypt (the rescuers even have to break through the windows of the attic as if it were a tomb). Dorian is identified only by his rings, a reminder of the scarab ring that Wilde never removed. Lord Henry is what the world thought Wilde to be: an acrobat of words who mesmerized with epigrams, who "played with the idea, grew wilful, tossed it into the air and transformed it; let it escape and recaptured it; made it iridescent with fancy, and winged it with paradox," a taunter who convinces Dorian that "nothing can cure the soul but the senses, just as nothing can cure the senses but the soul." Basil Hallward is "what I think I am," Wilde also said, and he might have added that these feelings were more accurate whenever he took off his mask and the mirror reflected the face of an unattractive and unloved genius.

By using Dorian as his hero's Christian name, Wilde advertised the book's homoerotic ambitions. He knew the history of the Dorian tribes from his classical education, but any educated person could identify the allusion—if they risked accepting the symbol. Of the three major tribes—Dorians, Ionians, and Aeolians—it is generally thought that Greek homosexuality originated in the military of the Dorian states (the "Sacred Band" of Thebes was composed only of pairs of homosexual lovers) and spread through Dorian influence. Combined with the last name of his disciple, the name Dorian Gray was a boldly coded declaration.

.　　.　　.

WHEN WILDE WAS tried on charges of gross indecency at the Old Bailey, the prosecution read passages from the *Lippincott's* version to support the claim that *Dorian Gray* was an immoral book. The fact that there were two versions seemed irrelevant to the court. The *Scots Observer* had condemned the magazine story in an unsigned review as dealing "with matters only fitted for the Criminal Investigations Department or a hearing *in camera.*" It was declared "false art—for its interest is medico-legal," underscoring the prevalent belief that inversion was a medical disease.

Edward Carson, the defense attorney, referred to the book version of 1891 as "purged." He then made personal Hallward's remark to Dorian that he adored him "madly, extravagantly, absurdly." Asked if he had ever "adored a young man madly," Wilde, in the dock, replied, "No, not madly. I prefer love—that is a higher form. . . . I have never given adoration to anybody except myself." In the book version, Hallward's words are changed from amorous to aesthetic: "You became to me the visible incarnation of that unseen ideal whose memory haunts us artists like an exquisite dream. I worshipped you."*

Other revisions wrapped Dorian's sins in ambiguity, diluted the all-male world with additions of Dorian talking to aristocratic ladies, and included background on Sibyl Vane and her family. Wilde made relations between the three characters—all representing his various sides—less erotic and deleted innocent physical contact between Basil and Dorian. In 1890, Basil is stirred by Dorian's "beauty," but in the second version the attraction is his "personality." Wilde added length by appending witticisms—pulled from lists he made of sayings that passed his aural test for sound and balance—to the ends of trivial conversations. In *Lippincott's*, Lord Henry apologizes to Dorian for being late: "I went to look after a piece of old brocade in Wardour Street, and had to bargain for hours for it." In 1891 he adds: "Nowadays people know the price of everything, and the value of nothing." Originally Lord Henry tells Basil, "If you want to make him [Dorian] marry this girl, tell him that, Basil. He is sure to do it, then." Later he also quips: "Whenever a man does a thoroughly stupid thing, it is always from the noblest motives."

---

*Wilde recycled the sentiments in *Lady Windermere's Fan,* when Lord Darlington tells the astonished Lady Windermere: "I love you—love you as I have never loved any living thing. From the moment I met you I loved you, loved you blindly, adoringly, madly!"

Fear of disclosure through implications of homosexual behavior drives the novel, often occurring when subterfuge involves some other guilt or crime. Dorian is at once "a man whom no pure-minded girl should be allowed to know" and one whose friendship "is so fatal to young men." One is never sure of the extent of Dorian's sins, but it is his disregard for humanity and lack of generosity rather than any sexual act that determine his destruction. "There is no such thing as a moral or animmoral book. Books are well written, or badly written. That is all, ilde announces in the preface, which was useful to have said five years before he had to defend *Dorian Gray's* morality in court, but it confounds the fascinating chain reaction of literary influences. Lord Henry quotes—and misquotes—Pater's *Studies in the History of the Renaissance* without ever mentioning the author, Wilde's first aesthetic authority. When Lord Henry wants to seduce Dorian into the hedonistic life, he supplies him with a "poisonous" book, assumed to be *À rebours,* Wilde's bible of Decadence. Ultimately Wilde creates in Dorian an authoritative guide for the next generation of pleasure seekers.

DRAWING ON HIS own experience during shooting seasons at Irish country houses, Wilde wrote authentically of the scene where Sibyl's brother is accidentally shot: "Suddenly from a lumpy tussock of old grass, some twenty yards in front of them, with black-tipped ears erect, and long hinder limbs throwing it forward, started a hare. It bolted for a thicket of alders. . . . and as the hare bounded into the thicket he fired. There were two cries heard, the cry of a hare in pain, which is dreadful, the cry of a man in agony, which is worse."

As for atmosphere, Wilde doubtless had secondhand knowledge of the sordid neighborhoods that Dorian explores, since Wilde's firsthand slumming was in the future. Everything he needed was within the covers of *The Sins of the Cities of the Plain or the Recollections of a Mary-Anne,* available in 1881, a vivid picture of the Victorian homosexual underworld. Richard Rowe's *Found in the Streets,* published in 1880, describes an opium den much like the one Dorian patronizes, with the Malays "crouching by a little charcoal stove playing with bone counters" and an old man trying to brush imaginary red ants off his sleeve. Wilde would not have been averse to using opium; he and Douglas would enjoy hashish during a trip to Algeria in 1895, when Wilde told André Gide, "I have a duty to myself to amuse myself frightfully." But Wilde preferred stimulants that allowed him to be genius, gourmand, and talker: opium's characteristic somnolence posed no threat of addiction.

Wilde explores the nature of love through the story of Sibyl Vane, whose love for Dorian inhibits her superb talent to suspend disbelief in her real self and perform Shakespeare in the squalid surroundings of an East End theatre. "You have killed my love," Dorian berates her. "You used to stir my imagination. Now you don't even stir my curiosity. You simply produce no effect. I loved you because you were marvelous, because you had genius and intellect, because you realized the dreams of great poets and gave shape and substance to shadows of art. You have thrown it all away. You are shallow and stupid." That love kills a woman's mystery was Wilde's recognition of his own failed marriage, expressed in Dorian's chilling observation "There is always something ridiculous about the emotions of people whom one has ceased to love."

THOSE IN THE Uranian community were more fearful than pleased when Wilde drew attention to their covert behavior. "If the British public will stand this they can stand anything," said J. A. Symonds, commenting on the magazine version of 1890. "I resent the unhealthy, scented, mystic congested touch which a man of this sort has on moral problems," added Symonds, himself a homosexual. He conceded that the story was "an odd and very audacious production, unwholesome in tone, but artistically and psychologically interesting." Still, he bristled at the homosexual nuances at the very time he was assisting Havelock Ellis with a study of homosexuality, which later became volume two of *Studies in the Psychology of Sex*.

About his sexual preferences, Wilde provided sufficient innuendo in "The Portrait of Mr. W. H.," but *Dorian Gray* was more daring and made him vulnerable to attack. Following its publication, Constance was aware that people treated her differently, but she gave no indication that she knew about the nature of her husband's relationships with young men. She trusted and loved him, perhaps realizing—as her mother-in-law had with Sir William—that allowances must be made for genius.

Reviewers in *The Daily Chronicle* and the *St. James's Gazette* attacked in force. The *Chronicle* criticized the story's "effeminate frivolity, its studied insincerity, its theatrical cynicism, its tawdry mysticism, its flippant philosophisings and the contaminating trail of garish vulgarity." Wilde defended his modern morality tale with letters to both publications. The *St. James's Gazette* had implied that the story should be suppressed by the government—and worse, called *Dorian Gray* "tedious and dull." Wilde abhorred any suggestion of censorship over imaginative literature as much as he did attribution of boring prose to himself. "All excess, as well as all renunciation, brings its own punishment," he told the *Gazette,* adding that there were two defects in the book: "it is far too crowded with sensational incident, and far too paradoxical in style." By expanding *Dorian Gray* and adding subplots, Wilde corrected the first error; by emphasizing the contradictions, he enhanced his style.

Ricketts designed the book with a vellum spine and half-parchment boards but positioned the author's name and title at the bottom of the spine instead of the traditional placement at the top. He later called it "a dreadful book . . . a poor, early, money-making effort." In a *Bookman* review, Pater praised Wilde's "skill" and "subtlety," noting that the tragic ending illustrated how "vice and crime make people coarse and ugly." Yeats designated it "a wonderful book." But overall the reviews were negative. The *Athenaeum* found the novel "unmanly sickening, vicious (though not exactly what is called 'improper'), and tedious." The author's mother offered the most encouragement: "It is the most wonderful piece of writing in all the fiction of the day. . . . I nearly fainted at the last scene."

PHOTOGRAPHS SHOW John Gray's profile as more perfect than Robbie Ross's, but Gray was darkly handsome whereas Dorian is a golden deity—Wilde's physical ideal. While Gray impressed Wilde with his incipient poetic talent, he was noticed by another poet, positioning Wilde at the apex of a homosexual triangle. The third man was Marc-André Raffalovich, son of wealthy Russian-Jewish émigrés, born in Paris and a student at Oxford before he left after a year to spend his way into smart society. Despite hosting lavish dinner parties, he was never accepted; it was a xenophobic time in England, and his Semitic appearance—a crown of black, tight curly hair and almond-shaped eyes—was more noticeable on a singularly unattractive person.

Violet Hunt wrote of him, "extremely ugly, knows it," but she appreciated his "confiding, ingenuous, apologetic manner." The story that his mother sent him to London to avoid embarrassment at her Parisian literary salon on the fashionable avenue Hoche owes its survival to Hunt's gossipy nature. To the list of those Hunt claimed wanted to marry her, his name should be added: he offered a marriage of convenience and suggested she use the epitaph "a woman made for irregular situations."

Wilde had favorably reviewed Raffalovich's second volume of poetry, *Tuberose and Meadowsweet,* in 1885, approving of its "heavy odours of the hothouse," but he provoked a pedantic squabble over the poet's three-syllable pronunciation of the first word of the title. Wilde perversely referred to him as Raffalovich when everyone else called him "Raff," and—in an unguarded malicious moment—reportedly said that he "came to London with the intention of opening a salon and succeeded in opening a saloon." This rare example of Wildean wit at someone else's expense resulted in enmity between the two.

Raffalovich could have been the role model for Isaacs in *Dorian Gray,* the "horrid old Jew" with "an oily, tremulous smile" and "jewelled hands," who manages the Holborn theatre where Sibyl Vane performs. Wilde turns up in Raffalovich's first novel, *A Willing Exile,* published the same year as *Dorian Gray,* as the dandy Cyprian Brome, who has a circle of friends interested only in beauty and fashion. One evening Constance surprised everyone by casually remarking to Raffalovich: "Oscar says he likes you so much—that you have such nice improper talks together." She was referring to a discussion they had had about Rachilde's *Monsieur Vénus.*★ Raffalovich used the innocent listener defense: there had been no discussion, only Wilde's views. He vowed, "Never again did I speak with him without witnesses."

AS RAFFALOVICH SAW it, there was no better revenge than splitting up Wilde and Gray. Gray was enjoying the reflected fame of sharing his

---

★Rachilde was the pseudonym of Marguérite Eymery, wife of Alfred Vallette, the founder of the review *Mercure de France* and the eponymous publishing company. Her novel on male homosexuality, published in 1889, caused her to be dubbed Mademoiselle Baudelaire and Queen of the Decadents.

name with the scandalous Dorian Gray; he even signed his fictional alter ego's name to a letter sent to Wilde in January. But when the amusement went beyond Wilde's circle, Gray was annoyed. He forced the *Star* to publish an apology for referring to him as the original for Dorian; Wilde also complained to *The Daily Telegraph* for similar comments. In a moment of untruth, he referred to Gray as "an extremely recent" acquaintance.

Perhaps the most tormented personality yet to be taken up by Wilde, Gray was also the most talented, earning a place—along with Thomas Hardy and A. E. Housman—in anthologies of Victorian verse as a significant poet of the 1890s. He was twenty-five, but Lionel Johnson said he had the face of a fifteen-year-old. Wilde recognized his startling talent but found Gray difficult to manipulate. Gray wanted to be a poet on his terms; at the same time, he was undergoing a spiritual revolt that would lead him to renounce his Decadent poetry. In 1889 he had gone over to Catholicism but quickly became a lapsed convert. Promoted to junior clerk at the Foreign Office Library, he had more time to write and lived frugally in shabby rooms in the Temple, several rambling old buildings (described by Dickens in *Great Expectations*) sloping from the south side of Fleet Street to the Thames Embankment. Symons, Yeats, and George Moore also lived in the artists' refuge.

During 1892, while preoccupied with rehearsals for *Lady Windermere's Fan* and the beginnings of a romance with Lord Alfred Douglas, Wilde continued to encourage Gray as a poet. He offered to underwrite the production costs of a first volume of poetry and signed a contract with the Bodley Head in June; the money would have to come from future play royalties. By the end of the year, Gray was in an extreme nervous state—ambivalent about Catholicism and worried about the sinful implications of being Dorian's namesake. What he resented most was Wilde's growing interest in Douglas: it was obvious that he was being pushed aside. Following his father's death, Gray suffered a breakdown and was found wandering about Piccadilly murmuring to himself: "I must change my life. I must change my life."

It was the perfect opportunity for Raffalovich to insinuate himself. He offered Gray financial protection and unconditional affection. But he demanded a public break with Wilde: "You cannot be Oscar's friend and mine." As a result, Wilde withdrew from the book contract; with a wealthy patron to back him, Gray easily negotiated his own agreement that gave him 20 percent. Then he systematically expunged any questionable passages to erase links between himself and Wilde.

Beautifully bound by Ricketts, *Silverpoints* appeared in 1893, a showcase for Decadent poetry, including Gray's best-known poems, "The Barber" and "Mishka," and "imitations" of Verlaine and Baudelaire. But the design overshadowed the poetry. The tall, narrow format (four inches by eight and a quarter) was based on the Persian saddle book, sized to be carried in the pocket of a jacket—for ease of reading. The deluxe edition had a vellum cover, embossed with flamelike leaves against a wavy, shimmering latticework. The work was precocious and anticipated the new French Symbolist poetry as exemplified by Verlaine. Gray later called the volume "the odious Silverpoints."

Spoken of as a young man with a promising career behind him, Gray became a translator, wrote poetry, collaborated with Raffalovich on plays, and lived out the platonic ideal. Together for forty-two years, they celebrated "sublime inversion, a sublimated form of homosexuality," which Raffalovich described as a chaste, ennobling relationship dedicated to spiritual ends. Believing that homosexuality was inherent rather than chosen and not a matter of moral responsibility, Raffalovich championed intellectual and spiritual friendships—which it seemed were harder to achieve without the strength of Catholicism.*

BY THE END of 1891, Wilde could look back at a year of successes and surprises. He had found Hyacinth in Lord Alfred Douglas, published his first novel, written a political treatise, and reincarnated *The Duchess*. Lawrence Barrett, the American actor-manager who had offered to produce the play in 1882, when it was optioned to Mary Anderson, was again interested in the blank verse drama. When Barrett wanted some revisions, Wilde visited him in Kreuznach in July 1889. ("The Rhine is of

---

*Raffalovich converted to Catholicism in 1896; two years later Gray went to Rome and entered a seminary; he was ordained a priest in 1901 and sent to Edinburgh as a curate. Raff followed him and lived nearby. He used his wealth to build St. Peter's Church in South Edinburgh and wrote scientific treatises on homosexuality, including *Uranisme et unisexualité*, published in France in 1896, which contained the first full account of Wilde's trials to appear in any language.

course tedious," Wilde wrote Ross, "the vineyards are formal and dull, and as far as I can judge the inhabitants of Germany are American.")

To clear the air after the *Vera* debacle, they changed the title to *Guido Ferranti* and withheld the name of the playwright. It opened at New York's Broadway Theatre on January 26, 1891, and closed on February 14. Even so, Wilde was thrilled. He wrote George Alexander that Barrett thought the run "a huge success" and that he was going to include the play in his season. It was not unusual to introduce a play for a short run and then put it into repertoire, but that did not happen; it closed. It was never much of a secret that Wilde was the author. The *Tribune*'s William Winter called him "a practiced writer and a good one."

In a swaggering mood, Wilde moved on to securing a London run. Henry Irving turned down the opportunity. But George Alexander, who had taken over the St. James's Theatre to showcase English dramatists, considered the possibilities, though he decided he preferred to risk time and money on something fresh. Offering Wilde fifty pounds, he asked him to try a modern subject, to write about what he knew. In this way Alexander became midwife to the social comedies. When he faced difficulties writing, Wilde offered to return the advance, but Alexander encouraged him to keep trying. "I am not satisfied with myself or my work," Wilde explained. "I can't get a grip of the play yet: I can't get my people real. The fact is I worked at it when I was not in the mood for work, and must first forget it, and then go back quite fresh to it. I am very sorry, but artistic work can't be done unless one is in the mood; certainly my work can't. Sometimes I spend months over a thing, and don't do any good; at other times I write a thing in a fortnight."

A summer visit to the Lake District near Lake Windermere helped Wilde break through. In October, Alexander's patience was rewarded when he listened to Wilde read *A Good Woman,* later titled *Lady Windermere's Fan.* Realizing that the play would be a hit, Alexander offered to buy it outright for a thousand pounds. In one of Wilde's more astute business negotiations, he refused and asked for a percentage, which brought him several thousand more.

The witticisms in *Lady Windermere's Fan* surpassed any comedy since Sheridan; Wilde's use of sparkling dialogue to uncover character and conflict set him apart from the probing conversations of Ibsen. It upstaged any previous well-made play in its use of dramatic convention, particularly in the scene where Mrs. Erlynne, the woman with a past, destroys her reputation anew by coming out from hiding in the lord's rooms, thus saving the honor of her long-lost daughter, who is hiding in another corner. Dialogue was everything, action incidental. After struggling with old forms in *Vera* and *The Duchess*—and breaking out with *Dorian Gray*—Wilde knew he had harnessed his genius. Nothing pleased him more than discovering a new self; at thirty-seven, his youth was past, but he had found his voice. And Paris would have the pleasure of his company.

He reminded Constance how productive he had been on his last visit, when he completed *The Duchess* and forged new stanzas for *The Sphinx*. A few months in Paris and he would produce something wonderful, he told his wife. What occupied his imagination was a work to impress the Symbolists: a version of the biblical tale of Salome, who danced for the head of John the Baptist, a subject previously immortalized by Flaubert in "Hérodias." By coincidence, Stéphane Mallarmé was struggling with a poem entitled "Hérodiade." Wilde considered poetic treatments but decided on a play written in French. His version would be named *Salomé*.

Earlier in 1891, when Wilde had been in Paris, he had presented a copy of *Dorian Gray* to Mallarmé, the acknowledged leader of Symbolism. They met at a *mardi,* one of the Tuesday evening salons held in Mallarmé's modest fourth-floor flat in the rue de Rome, near the St. Lazare railway station. Known for his innovative syntax and referents, often unintelligible or misunderstood, Mallarmé dominated a *cénacle* that included the last and most prestigious generation of *Mardistes,* led by Pierre Louÿs, who introduced Mallarmé to his young friends Gide, Paul Valéry, and Camille Mauclair. Twelve years Wilde's senior, the bearded Mallarmé looked older than forty-nine, a fact that his followers attributed to creative suffering. In his presence, Wilde endured unaccustomed silences, behaving like a disciple when the master spoke.

Mallarmé claimed his poetry attempted to paint not the thing but the effect it produced; to this end, he invented a singular vocabulary linking art and beauty to pleasure by texture, color, shape, touch, and smell. A similar language had stirred Wilde's imagination when he read *À rebours* on his honeymoon, a perfect opulent language for *Salomé*. And like Des

Sir William Wilde.

Lady Wilde in her late fifties.

Moytura House, overlooking
Lough Corrib, in County Mayo,
where the Wildes spent vacations.

Oscar in blue velvet and
lace at age two.

Wilde as an
undergraduate at
Magdalen College,
Oxford.

In 1878, his last year at
Oxford.

With his best friends,
Reginald "Kitten"
Harding, left, and William
"Bouncer" Ward.

Wilde did this pencil sketch of Florence Balcombe, his first love, in 1877. It is the most impressive example of his talents as an artist to survive.

Florence, or Florrie, around the age of seventeen, when she and Wilde first met. He said she had the "most perfectly beautiful face" he had ever seen.

Violet Hunt, left, followed Florence in Wilde's affections. She was also seventeen, and "the sweetest Violet in England," he said.

Lillie Langtry, the luminous beauty from the Isle of Jersey, was the mistress of the Prince of Wales before she became a famous actress. Wilde called her "the loveliest woman in Europe."

SARA BERNHARDT. No 10.

SARONY, COPYRIGHT, 1891, BY NAPOLEON SARONY 37 Union Sq. N. Y.

Sarah Bernhardt, Wilde said, was one of the three women he most wanted to marry. Langtry and Queen Victoria were the other two.

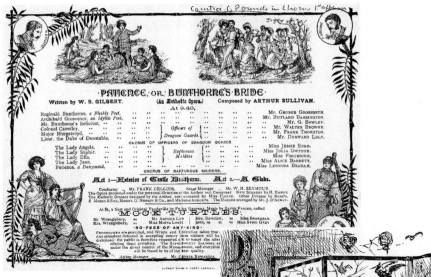

Program for *Patience* at the
Savoy Theatre.

The aesthetic craze inspired numerous *Punch*
cartoons by George Du Maurier. In this
scene, below, the character of Maudle
resembles Wilde.

THE SIX-MARK TEA-POT.

[*By Geo. du Maurier.*]

Æsthetic Bridegroom. "It is quite consummate, is it not?"
Intense Bride. "It is, indeed! Oh, Algernon, let us live up to it!"

MAUDLE ON THE CHOICE OF A PROFESSION.

Maudle. "How consummately lovely your Son is, Mrs. Brown!"
Mrs. Brown (a Philistine from the country). "What! He's a nice, manly Boy, if you mean that, Mr. Maudle. He has just left School, you know, and wishes to be an Artist."
Maudle. "Why should he be an Artist?"
Mrs. Brown. "Well, he must be something!"
Maudle. "Why should he Be anything? Why not let him remain for ever content to Exist Beautifully?"
[*Mrs. Brown determines that at all events her Son shall not study Art under Maudle.*]

While at Oxford, Wilde remarked that he
worried about living up to his blue china.
By the time he arrived in London, the
aspiration was a fashionable concern.

Napoleon Sarony photographed Wilde in twenty-seven poses before his American lecture tour in 1882. Wilde loved his oversize fur-trimmed coat.

Wilde often made a dramatic stage entrance by swirling his cape.

Sporting a short, curly hairstyle, Wilde was photographed in 1884 on the Isle of Wight, during a provincial lecture tour.

Wilde in 1889. The portrait is inscribed to Arthur Fish, his assistant editor at *The Woman's World*.

Robert Ross, or Robbie, below, as he looked in the early 1890s.

John Gray, whom Wilde honored by using his surname for *The Picture of Dorian Gray*.

The title page of volume two of *The Woman's World*, August 1888.

Constance Wilde with her firstborn, Cyril, in 1889, when he was five.

Wilde and Bosie photographed at Oxford in the spring of 1893.

Program for the Haymarket Theatre, where *A Woman of No Importance* and *An Ideal Husband* opened.

Babbacombe Cliff, above, in Torquay. The black studio, at right, was called Wonderland. There Wilde worked on *A Woman of No Importance* and *Salomé*.

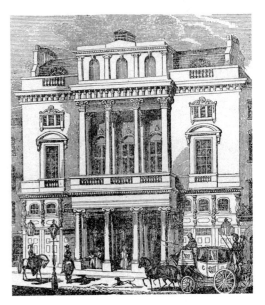

Façade of the St. James's Theatre in King Street, where *Lady Windermere's Fan* and *The Importance of Being Earnest* were first performed.

Following the failure in New York of Wilde's first play, *Vera*, *The Entr'acte* depicted brother Willie, the critic, consoling him.

BROTHER WILLIE.—"NEVER MIND, OSCAR; OTHER GREAT MEN HAVE HAD THEIR DRAMATIC FAILURES!"

FANCY PORTRAIT.

Following the success of *Lady Windermere's Fan*, *Punch* mocked Wilde for smoking onstage during his curtain speech.

QUITE TOO-TOO PUFFICKLY PRECIOUS!!

Being Lady Windy-mère's Fan-cy Portrait of the new dramatic author,
Shakspeare Sheridan Oscar Puff, Esq.

["He addressed from the stage a public audience, mostly composed of ladies,
pressing between his daintily-gloved fingers a still burning and half-smoked
cigarette."—*Daily Telegraph.*]

Wilde in 1892, when he made his name as a playwright.

Frontispiece, below, by Aubrey Beardsley for the English edition of *Salome*, with a caricature of Wilde's face and a carnation in the moon.

Bosie photographed in Cairo at the age of twenty-four.

Reginald "Reggie" Turner.

The front page of *The Illustrated Police News* for May 4, 1895, depicting the end of the libel trial brought by Wilde against the Marquess of Queensberry. In the bottom right corner is 16 Tite Street.

A nineteenth-century postcard of the Café des Tribunaux in Dieppe, where Wilde took his evening aperitif.

Ernest Dowson, poet and fellow absinthe lover, left, frequently saw Wilde in Dieppe.

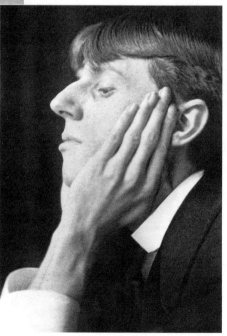

Aubrey Beardsley at first evaded Wilde in Dieppe, but then went shopping with him for a hat.

Wearing boaters,
Wilde and Bosie
pose together in
Naples during the
summer
of 1897.

The Hôtel d'Alsace on the rue des
Beaux-Arts in Paris, where Wilde lived
intermittently from 1898 until his
death on November 30, 1900.

When Wilde went to Rome in April
1900, above, he had seven
audiences with Pope Leo XIII.
He bought a camera and had his picture
taken at St. Peter's.

Wilde photographed on his deathbed
by Maurice Gilbert, one of his closest friends
during his last years in Paris. The flock
wallpaper that he hated so much is faintly
visible in the background.

Jacob Epstein's monument in Père Lachaise
Cemetery, Paris, where Wilde's remains
were transferred from Bagneux in 1909.

Oscar Wilde's first grave, at
Bagneux, left.

Esseintes, the hero of that novel, Wilde found Salomé a haunting goddess, a Helen of Troy who poisons all who see her.

ARRIVING IN LATE October, Wilde stayed at the Hôtel de l'Athénée in the rue Scribe on the Right Bank. One of his first visits was to the Louvre to view *The Apparition,* Gustave Moreau's 1876 visionary watercolor of Salomé, which Huysmans called "the symbolic incarnation of undying lust." Wilde sought to disprove Des Esseintes's claim that no writer had ever "succeeded in rendering the delirious frenzy of the wanton, the subtle grandeur of the murderess." Given Wilde's natural obsession with portraits, cast as characters in two of his works, he traced Salomé's iconographic history and its relationship to prose. The biblical princess had inspired Rubens, Leonardo, Dürer, Ghirlandaio, and Titian, but Moreau's two versions came closest to Wilde's concept of sexual abandon. In one, the seductress dances for Herod, her body shimmering in a silver aura; in the other, the severed head of the Baptist, surrounded by a halo, appears to her in a vision. Moreau's luminous images pursued Wilde through the boulevards and followed him into his own absinthe-induced hallucinations.

In the cafés, at dinners, wherever Wilde found receptive audiences, he told the story of Salomé. One evening, according to the biographer Vincent O'Sullivan, he returned to his hotel, saw a blank notebook on the table, and started to write. "If the book had not been there," Wilde said, "I should never have dreamed of doing it." If this confidence represents a creative truth, then Wilde produced a first draft while in Paris, polished it when he returned to London, and sent the script back to Paris for editing.

ON WILDE'S 1883 visit, when he wrote *The Duchess,* he had wanted to be noticed but lacked important literary credentials beyond his volume of poems. Now *Dorian Gray* had elevated his reputation. *L'Écho de Paris* labeled him "le 'great event' des salons littéraires" that season. Wilde went to Rachilde's salon planning to compliment the author on *Monsieur Vénus* and was shocked to be introduced to a young girl. Most important were his new friends: the disparate trio of Pierre Louÿs, Marcel Schwob, and

André Gide. Wilde assessed the twenty-two-year-old sexually repressed Gide and concluded that he needed a Lord Henry in his life. At one literary function, Wilde stared at his mouth and announced: "I don't like your lips. They are straight like those of someone who has never lied. I want to teach you how to lie, so your lips become beautiful and twisted like those of an antique mask."

During the next three weeks, the pair were inseparable. Gide's friends assumed that he had fallen in love with Wilde, but whatever his feelings, they were never revealed because Gide ripped out the relevant pages from his journal. As a taunter rather than a seducer, Wilde challenged Gide's addiction to the truth, his religious values, his conventional living. Eminent and powerful, Wilde had a profound effect on this immature and vulnerable only child of the Protestant bourgeois whose father died when he was ten. Gide complained to Paul Valéry that Wilde had done him "nothing but harm." He said Wilde "[is] piously setting about killing what remained of my soul," Gide wrote, "because he says that in order to know the essence of something, one has to suppress it."

A decade later, Gide recalled that Wilde had at this time "what Thackeray calls the 'chief gift of a great man': success. His gestures and his look triumphed. His success was so sure that it seemed as if it preceded Wilde and that he merely had to come forward after it. . . . Some compared him to an Asiatic Bacchus; others to some Roman emperor; others to Apollo himself—and the fact is that he was radiant."

Even so, Wilde was also perceived as cold and distant, particularly when he feared that he was not making a grandiose impression. "I choose my friends for their good looks, my acquaintances for their good characters, and my enemies for their good intellects," he said. "A man cannot be too careful in the choice of his enemies." On this latter advice, Wilde was a miserable failure. Friends admired him, but he was never feared. The statement "I trust him" was not easily used about Wilde.

A chain-smoker who lit up sixty cigarettes a day, Pierre Louÿs was sixteen years younger than Wilde; he was darkly fascinating and heterosexual, an inveterate practical joker who abandoned himself to life, convinced that he would succumb to tuberculosis like his mother and older brother. His habit of writing in purple ink on handmade paper in what was described as medieval script fascinated Wilde. Gide and Louÿs had been friends since 1888, when they attended the same gymnasium. Joining them at the cafés was Marcel Schwob, an authority on the fifteenth-century poet François Villon and coeditor with Louÿs of the Symbolist review *Mercure de France.*

Well-connected through his venerable Jewish family, which traced its lineage back to the Crusades, Schwob generously entertained Wilde at his home on the rue de l'Université, leaving a most unattractive description of his new friend, who, he said, had "a large pasty face, red cheeks, an ironic eye, bad and protrusive teeth, a vicious childlike mouth with lips soft with milk ready to suck some more."

Putting on record Wilde's growing love of the "green fairy," Schwob called him a "terrible absinthe drinker, through which he got his visions and his desires." Like smoking, absinthe had its rituals, making it more a drug than a drink. When absinthe arrived at the table, Wilde poured water over the sugar cubes balanced on a trapezoid-shaped slotted spoon; water cut the bitterness, and more water diluted the 70 percent alcohol content. In time the hallucinogenic effects activated the imagination.★ Wilde once remarked that "after the first glass, you see things as you wish they were. After the second, you see them as they are not. Finally you see things as they really are, and that is the most horrible thing in the world."

They were a quirky group. Gide was awkward as he pretended to be a Left Bank intellectual complete with cape and beard. Louÿs abhorred homosexuality but celebrated love between women in his writings, while Schwob reveled in unearthing macabre stories (Edmond de Goncourt called him "a hallucinatory resurrector of the past") peopled with such characters as a leprous king, an Indian raja, and a Roman noblewoman. Even though Schwob wanted to evoke the uniqueness of men, divinities, mediocrities, and criminals, he is remembered today as Daniel Defoe's translator. He did a French translation of "The Selfish Giant," which he

---

★The hallucinogen was oil of wormwood, which contains thujone, a relative of the active ingredient in cannabis. Absinthe was banned in Switzerland in 1908, in the United States in 1912, in France in 1915, but never in Britain. Because of this loophole, absinthe imported from the Czech Republic became available in London to celebrate the New Year in 1999.

published in *L'Écho de Paris,* where he worked, and dedicated his 1892 short story "Le Pays bleu" to Wilde, who reciprocated when "The Sphinx" appeared in 1894.

BY THE TIME Wilde crossed the channel, he had every right to be pleased with himself. He had completed his first work written in another language; he had talked with Proust about Ruskin; he had met Stuart Merrill, an American expatriate poet who saw Wilde as "gigantic, smooth-shaven and rosy, like a great priest of the moon in the time of Heliogabalus"; and he had befriended the minor poet Jean Moréas, known for his 1886 Symbolism manifesto published in *Le Figaro.* Wilde's personality had pierced the forbidding literary elite. He celebrated Christmas with his family and toasted the new year of 1892 with Perrier-Jouët '89. It would be a good year. Success in the theatre brought him fame and wealth, and he fell passionately in love.

PART FOUR

(1892–1895)

Flaunting

*Luxury—gold-tipped matches—hair curled—Assyrian—
wax statue—huge rings—fat white hands—not soigné—
feather bed—pointed fingers—ample scarf—Louis Quinze
cane—vast malmaison—cat-like tread—heavy shoulders—
enormous dowager—or schoolboy—way of laughing with
hand over mouth—stroking chin—looking up sideways—
jollity overdone—But real vitality—Effeminate, but vitality
of twenty men—magnetism—authority—Deeper than
repute or wit—Hypnotic.*

—Oscar Wilde as described by Max Beerbohm

CHAPTER FOURTEEN

More Than Laughter

*In the drama, there may occur in the first act of the play something
whose real artistic value may not be evident to the spectator till the
third or fourth act is reached. Is this silly fellow to get angry and call
out, and disturb the play, and annoy the artists? No. . . .
He is to go to the play to gain an artistic temperament. . . .
No spectator of art needs a more perfect mood of receptivity
than the spectator of a play.*

—"THE SOUL OF MAN UNDER SOCIALISM"

Wearing a coat with a black velvet collar, a white waistcoat
with a black moiré ribbon emblazoned with seals, and a
green carnation buttonhole, Wilde entered from stage left
and leaned insolently against the proscenium arch. A gold-tipped cigarette
smoldered in his white-gloved hand. That moment towered above all
Wilde's other public appearances—from childhood recitations at Merrion
Square and the reading of *Ravenna* at Oxford's Sheldonian Theatre to the
podiums of a hundred American cities. He inhaled and exhaled with satisfaction. "Ladies and Gentlemen: I have enjoyed this evening *immensely*,"
he told the opening-night audience at the St. James's Theatre. "The actors
have given us a *charming* rendering of a *delightful* play, and your appreciation has been *most* intelligent. I congratulate you on the *great* success of
your performance, which persuades me that you think *almost* as highly of

the play as I do myself." Caps waved down in the pit. There was applause followed by bewilderment from the stalls and rousing cheers from the steep gallery with its wooden seats.

Later the audience and critics thought the words rang of ridicule. Wilde saw his audience as characters whose world was reflected—not imitated—in his play. He knew just how far to go with social criticism; the audience should savor scandal without being offended. But he was not praising them as much as patting himself on the back for *Lady Windermere's Fan*. His curtain-call speech on February 20, 1892, went beyond the usual homilies of even an egoist like Henry Irving. Friends applauded sincerely. An Oxford colleague, Arthur Clifton, escorted Constance and her aunt, Mrs. William Napier. Wilde cautioned him that "she will be very nervous." Seated with Wilde's first lover, Robbie Ross, was Wilde's current infatuation, Edward Shelley, an office boy at the Bodley Head. Willie Wilde, estranged from his brother, was there as a critic with a negative disposition. A recluse who seldom left Oakley Street, Lady Wilde was at home for this and all her son's first nights. "You have had a brilliant success! and I am so happy," she wrote.

Many critics thought Wilde's insouciant appearance with a dangling cigarette arrogant and conceited. Conflicting versions of what was said made the rounds. Did Wilde say, "It's perhaps not very proper to smoke in front of you, but . . . it's not very proper to disturb me when I am smoking"? Did he purposely affront Victorian propriety? Or was he too nervous to discard his constant companion? *Punch* published a cartoon of him leaning against a pillar, three puffs of smoke circling his head, a toppled statue of Shakespeare and an open box of cigarettes at his feet. The caption: "Quite Too-Too Puffickly Precious!! Being Lady Windy-mere's Fan-cy Portrait of the new dramatic author, Shakespeare Sheridan Oscar Puff, Esq." Wilde labeled his impromptu talk "delightful and immortal." All the fuss was really about how he held his cigarette.

Henry James reported that the "unspeakable animal" had responded to curtain calls by appearing with a metallic blue carnation in his buttonhole and a cigarette in his fingers. Despite efforts to be aloof, James was resentful. "There is of course absolutely no characterization and all the people talk equally strained Oscar," he told a friend. The "impudent" speech was "simply inevitable mechanical Oscar—I mean the usual trick of saying the unusual—complimenting himself and his play. It was what he was there for and I can't conceive the density of those who seriously reprobate it."

THE GREEN CARNATION followed the lily and the sunflower of the aesthetic period as Wilde's signature flower. It was natural but looked artificial. Green, the color of absinthe, of gold-embossed bindings, symbolized Decadence, a new beautiful and interesting disease, as Arthur Symons put it. But perhaps the green carnation was only a green carnation. "What does it mean?" Graham Robertson had asked Wilde. "Nothing whatever," Wilde replied, "but that is just what nobody will guess."★

Wilde's success marked not only the debut of a new dramatic talent but also the beginning of change throughout the West End. Henry Irving's reign as actor-manager and the Lyceum's as leading venue for serious theatre were no longer unchallenged. In 1888 Irving staged a brilliant *Othello* with controversial interpretations. Ellen Terry's Lady Macbeth was scheming and fragile, unaware of the evil in her husband. Irving played the Thane of Cawdor as a black-hearted rogue, a traitor who displays courage only when at bay. But editing Shakespeare to fit his talents was as far as Irving wanted to go.

George Alexander, a former Lyceum apprentice, was more adventurous; he wanted choices beyond the classics, melodramas, and boulevard comedies. After leaving Irving in 1889, he spent a year as actor-manager at the Avenue Theatre before leasing the St. James's in 1891. His idea was to create a theatre for English dramatists, and he asked not only Wilde but also Arthur Conan Doyle and John Galsworthy to write plays. Alexander looked for comedies, but comedies with a social message. Another ambitious actor-manager, Herbert Beerbohm Tree, worked his own brand of magic at the Theatre Royal, Haymarket.

When it came to challenging Victorian domestic morality, Wilde could be as revolutionary and iconoclastic as Ibsen and later Shaw. Ibsen's influence in England was fresh and inspiring: *A Doll's House* opened in

---

★Wilde wore the Malmaison, or the breakfast-tray white carnation, which changed color when plunged into a water-based aniline dye called malachite green. An earlier method used the fumes of burning sulfur. The assumption that the green carnation was worn in France as a sign of homosexuality has never been documented.

1889, and two years later, Elizabeth Robins, an actress much admired by Wilde, appeared in *Hedda Gabler*. Although modern in outlook, Wilde's comedies still depended on the old forms of the "well-made" play, as well as melodrama and farce.

Alexander presided over the St. James's for twenty-seven years. He was shrewd and known for his furious energy. Unlike Irving, he was secure enough to have a company with actors more competent than he. He played the dandy, and that meant playing himself. Wilde said Alexander did not so much act as behave. To devotees the twelve-hundred-seat theatre was a cross between the Comédie-Française and a monastery. Located on King Street, Piccadilly (farther west than most theatres), it was built in 1835 on the site of Nevot's, a hostelry that dated from the days of Charles II.★

In the early years, it presented a mishmash of genres, from music hall to foreign language. In the mid-eighties, Irving made his first important London appearance as Doricourt in *The Belle's Stratagem*. Pinero's first successful play, *The Money Spinner,* opened in 1881. Despite Alexander's success with Wilde's first and last plays, the sensation of his tenure was in 1893 with Pinero's *The Second Mrs. Tanqueray.* In the title role, Mrs. Patrick Campbell triumphed when she entered Aubrey's rooms at the ubiquitous Albany, the bachelor residence of Jack Worthing in *Earnest,* and spoke the line "I love fruit when it is expensive."

Wilde wanted Lillie Langtry to play Mrs. Erlynne, the woman with a past and an adult illegitimate daughter. He assumed she would be flattered; instead, she was insulted to be considered old enough (she was thirty-nine) for such a part. Vanity was involved but also a secret: she had an eleven-year-old illegitimate daughter, who thought Langtry was her aunt, and whose father was Prince Louis of Battenberg.† Of this Wilde was unaware—Langtry was too shrewd to trust him with such a revelation. The old friends exchanged bitter words and did not speak for several

---

★The St. James's was built by the actor-singer John Braham for his wife, a large woman who disliked climbing stairs. His Covent Garden contract stipulated that she always have a ground-tier box on nights when he performed, but one night a duchess usurped her place and Mrs. Braham broke an ankle climbing to an upper box. Despite a campaign led by Vivien Leigh, the much-loved St. James's was razed in 1957 to make way for an office building.
†Battenberg was a nephew of the Prince of Wales, also one of Langtry's lovers. He was the great-grandfather of Charles Windsor, the present Prince of Wales.

years. But Wilde turned the incident into pertinent dialogue. He had Mrs. Erlynne—who was played by Ellen Terry's sister Marion—ask Lord Windermere: "How on earth could I pose as a mother with a grown-up daughter? I have never admitted that I am more than twenty-nine, or thirty at the most. Twenty-nine when there are pink shades, thirty when there are not." Wilde went around describing his work as "one of those modern drawing room plays with pink lampshades."

During rehearsals Wilde lived and worked at the Albemarle Hotel in Mayfair, beginning a long association with the hostelry. This time he did not need to manufacture an excuse, since Tite Street had been evacuated because of dangerous drainage fumes, and Constance had taken the boys to stay with friends. This was Wilde's first experience with staging a play. *Vera* and *The Duchess* had involved only long letters from London to New York. Now he saw opportunities to revise during rehearsals. That Alexander and his company worked differently never occurred to him. Arriving on time and by hansom—despite not yet earning royalties—Wilde was impeccably dressed to meet the impeccably dressed Alexander. Since Alexander played Lord Windermere, he was onstage most of the time, leaving Wilde to brood on the inadequacies of actors.

The actor's aim, Wilde believed, "is, or should be, to convert his own accidental personality into the real and essential personality of the character" and not let that personality distort a play. Anybody can act. "There are many advantages in puppets. They never argue. They have no crude views about art," he said. "They recognize the presiding intellect of the dramatist." Just as easily, he demolished the dramatist. "I do not think it makes the smallest difference what a play is if an actor has genius and power. Nor do I consider the British public to be of the slightest importance." His was a contradictory memory.

The plot centers on a woman's sudden discovery—and quick renunciation—of maternal passion. Wilde explained the psychology to Alexander: " 'This passion is too terrible,' she says. 'It wrecks my life. . . . I don't want to be a mother any more.' " Because Mrs. Erlynne manipulates the dramatic action of the play, histrionic speeches make it easier for her to reject maternal feelings. The audience ends up not taking her seriously, and Wilde escapes from melodrama into comedy. The secret that Mrs. Erlynne abandoned her daughter, now Lady Windermere, when she ran off with her lover twenty years ago is known only to the audience. Mrs.

Erlynne has returned to use this confidence to force Lord Windermere to sponsor her in society.

By revealing sooner or later who did what to whom, a dramatist shifts the balance of a play. Wilde wanted to wait until the fourth act; any earlier, he told Alexander, would reduce the dramatic effectiveness of Act Three. "The chief merit of my last act," he said, "is that it does not contain, as most plays do, the explanation of what the audience knows already, but that it is the sudden explanation of what the audience desires to know." The audience's knowledge that the self-sacrifice was made by a mother would destroy the element of surprise since sacrifice is expected of a mother. Alexander disagreed. A revelation at the end would offend the audience, making the plot a long riddle rather than a play of emotion and suspense. The issue was unresolved by opening night, when the only major change was dropping the title: *A Good Woman*. Lady Wilde bluntly told her son: "I do not like it. It is mawkish. No one cares for a good woman. *A Noble Woman* would be better."

The ending of Act Two was a problem. Lady Windermere is led to believe that her husband has betrayed her with Mrs. Erlynne. Despite his wife's protests, Mrs. Erlynne appears at her birthday party, makes a brilliant entrance, dances with Lord Windermere, and provokes his wife to seek solace with Lord Darlington. She writes a confessional letter to her husband conveniently left for Mrs. Erlynne's eyes. Realizing that she wrote the same words when leaving Lady Windermere's father, she promises to salvage her daughter's happiness. She goes to Lord Darlington's rooms, where Lady Windermere has been waiting, and pleads for her to return to her husband and save her marriage. As Mrs. Erlynne burns the incriminating letter, the two women are interrupted by the men's arrival; Lady Windermere drops her fan when she hides behind a curtain. Mrs. Erlynne pretends the fan belongs to her and Lady Windermere slips away, never knowing that she was aided by her mother.

For the curtain speech, Mrs. Erlynne asks her love interest, Lord Augustus, to keep Lord Windermere away from home. When he questions her motives, she replies: "Your reward? Your reward? Oh! ask me that tomorrow. But don't let Windermere out of your sight to-night. If you do I will never forgive you. I will never speak to you again. I'll have nothing to do with you. Remember you are to keep Windermere at your club, and don't let him come back to-night." Alexander wanted a more modern exit line, but Wilde thought Mrs. Erlynne should leave Lord Augustus in a state of bewilderment. "With regard to the new speech written yesterday personally I think it adequate," he wrote Alexander. "I want Mrs. Erlynne's whole scene with Lord Augustus to be a 'tornado' scene, and the thing to go as quickly as possible." Grudgingly Wilde wrote one line—"Well, really I might be her husband already. Positively I might"—which gives Lord Augustus the last word.

They bickered over background noise. "Every *word* of a comedy dialogue should reach the ears of the audience," Wilde complained, objecting to the duchess dropping words in her first speech to Hopper. "It should run," he explained at length, " 'Kangaroos flying about. *Agatha has found Australia on the map. What a curious shape it is!* However, it's a very young country, isn't it?' The words she left out are those I have underlined. They are the point to the remark about the young country. To omit them is to leave out the point of the climax, and in point of time nothing is saved by their omission. The words take less than ten seconds to speak." To describe the curious shape, Wilde added, "Just like a large packing case."

At the end of each day's rehearsal, Wilde insisted on a discussion. "It saves a great deal of trouble," he declared. "It would in the present instance have saved me writing this long letter, the points of which could have been more easily put forward in conversation, when I would also have had the advantage of hearing your own views on many points." Wilde feigned illness to demonstrate his determination, forcing Alexander to summon him to the theatre. They resolved the mother-daughter revelation scene. It is hinted at in the first act and disclosed in the second. Only the audience knows that the mother's identity is kept from her daughter and that the husband never knows how he nearly lost his wife. Wilde was resolving emotional conflicts about his marriage and his sexuality, but he was more interested in expressing the universality of the truth that everyone has secrets.

THE REVIEWS WERE mixed, even as they predicted a long run. Clement Scott, after William Archer London's most influential critic, made fun of Wilde's speech by putting words in the playwright's mouth: "The society that allows boys to puff cigarette-smoke into the faces of ladies in theatre-

corridors will condone the originality of a smoking author on the stage."
Wilde's bad manners outraged Scott, who thought the play cynical and
unintelligible.

James called it "infantine . . . both in subject and form." The anonymous critic of *The Illustrated Sporting and Dramatic News* complained that
he could not "reconcile the things the characters say with the things they
do." Some thought Lady Windermere such a moral person that for her to
desert her husband on the basis of gossip was illogical. The darkly serious
theme—that men are only honest with other men and women with other
women—went unnoticed. Wilde had wanted to show that heterosexual
relationships were incongruous. But critics responded to the play as yet
another version of the French well-made play, pointing to the familiar
devices of the letter and fan to drive the plot.

Shaw was amused, as were audiences enchanted by Wilde's sparkling dialogue. *Fan* contains some of his most quoted and ambiguous
lines. In conversation about how women prefer men to be bad so they can
reform them, Dumby remarks: "I don't think we are bad. I think we are
all good except Tuppy." Lord Darlington remarks: "No, we are all in the
gutter, but some of us are looking at the stars." Dumby: "We are all in
the gutter, but some of us are looking at the stars? Upon my word, you are
very romantic tonight, Darlington." Cecil Graham: "Too romantic! You
must be in love." (Darlington *is* in love—with Lady Windermere.) Lord
Darlington's observation about looking at the stars has the Irish optimism
of landing face up after too much drink.

Wilde's characters break into epigrams at emotional moments just
as modern-day musical stars burst into song. Shaw called Wilde the
"only thorough playwright because he plays with everything: with wit,
with philosophy, with drama, with actors and audience, with the whole
theatre." Both dramatists needed actors who knew how to handle long,
elaborate sentences while enacting high-society manners—such as Lord
Darlington's exchange with Lady Windermere when he remarks what a
fascinating puritan she is. "The adjective was unnecessary, Lord Darlington," she says. "I couldn't help it," he replies. "I can resist everything except
temptation." The temptation in the play is to flirt, but the line became
synonymous with Wilde's own excesses—and later a flippant excuse for
anyone.

INITIALLY MARRIAGE HAD limited Wilde's social life. He was no longer the extra man and invitations arrived for two, but when Constance was confined to bed while pregnant and then a mother caring for young children, Wilde accepted for himself. As his reputation grew, hostesses depended on him to animate their table. A married man, he lived a bachelor's life. In *Dorian Gray,* Lord Henry observes that "there are certain temperaments that marriage makes more complex. They retain their egotism, and add to it many other egos. They are forced to have more than one life." Constance accepted her husband's need to be out in society and dutifully returned to Tite Street after the premiere of *Fan*. Wilde met his friends at The Crown, a public house. A more appropriate home celebration had not been planned. Over in Fleet Street, his brother, Willie, was at *The Daily Telegraph* writing an anonymous review of *Fan:* "Mr. Oscar Wilde has spoken. He has publicly announced his complete satisfaction with his new and original play. . . . The author peoples his play with male and female editions of himself. . . . The play is a bad one, but it will succeed." Wilde had arrived as a playwright but at the expense of a fragmented family.

Willie's life had taken an unexpected turn. He declared bankruptcy in 1888 and moved in with his mother. Three years later he renewed an acquaintance with Mrs. Frank Leslie, the American widow indirectly responsible for promoting Oscar's American lecture tour. She was fifty-five, with a vague past that stretched from her illegitimate birth as Miriam Folline in New Orleans in 1836 to "the Empress of Journalism," the name given her by New York's tabloids. Mrs. Leslie exemplified a type of American woman who erased humble origins through advantageous marriages: first to a jeweler, then to an archaeologist, E. G. Squier, whom she accompanied to South America, where she met her third husband, Frank Leslie, a wealthy publisher. They married in 1874 and, following his death six years later, Mrs. Leslie took over the business.

Lady Wilde thought she had worked some Irish spell when this wealthy widow took an interest in her Willie. He was fifteen years younger, but his main attraction was his journalistic skills. In a fourth husband, she wanted a lover but mostly a business partner. Willie proposed after a week's courtship. Mrs. Leslie, acting coy, asked for time to think and left for New York. Willie was on the SS *Havre,* the next ship crossing. Wearing a charming mask, he walked down the gangplank and into Mrs. Leslie's heart, winning over her Park Avenue friends with his wit and piano improvisations. On October 4, 1891, Willie married for the first time in the Church of the Strangers on Mercer Street, ignoring advice to draw up a prenuptial agreement. The bride wore a Worth gown of pearl gray satin with a bonnet of gray velvet and pearl ostrich tips. The reception was at Delmonico's and the honeymoon at Niagara Falls. Willie spent their wedding night drunk and was seldom sober thereafter.

Instead of sitting behind an office desk, he leaned on the Lotos Club bar, entertaining members with parodies of Oscar and signing for round after round of drinks for which his wife paid. He never thought about American journalism and let the tabloids write about his antics. News of his drunken performances reached his brother, who was not amused. Lady Wilde, thoroughly misinformed about how far the marriage had deteriorated, extolled its virtues for Oscar: "I hope you wrote to Willie. He seems in radiant health, hope and happiness. . . . Her influence must work great good in him and give him the strength he wants."

Willie never had a chance. Mrs. Leslie was very demanding and, when disappointed, very angry. "A more scholarly and accomplished man never came to America," she told journalists. "I had hoped he would be of great assistance to me in my business. . . . He couldn't lead a London club life here in New York, and his attempt to do so was his chief fault." Later she admitted that "he was of no use to me either by day or by night." One newspaper headline announced: "Tired of Willie!" After six months, the estranged couple returned to England. "I'm taking Willie over, but I'll not bring Willie back," she announced. The marriage ended on June 10, 1893. Willie returned to Oakley Street, and Lady Wilde's allowance of one hundred pounds a year from her daughter-in-law ended.

Lady Wilde took a perverse delight in the divorce publicity. She saw Willie as a celebrity and supported his right not to work—that was why he had married a wealthy woman. But this first divorce in the family made her more aware of the problems between Oscar and Constance, who complained to her on every visit about her husband's long absences. Lady Wilde postponed reuniting the brothers to berate Oscar for neglecting his family. But it was too late. The son she had predicted would do "something wonderful" was in love with a bewitching young aristocrat.

THE LOVE AFFAIR of Lord Alfred Douglas and Oscar Wilde was the most scandalous homosexual relationship in Victorian letters. Not for its short-lived grand passions but for the statement it made about friendship and platonic love—and for the artistic limbo to which it relegated Wilde for nearly a century. Wilde's obsessiveness was played out in public view: it was a reckless affair. Douglas's feelings should not be underestimated. He cared deeply for Wilde, even as Wilde cared for him more. Emotionally damaged by an erratic father and a possessive mother, he was too young to make the right choices.

Called "Bosie" by his friends from a pet name his mother gave him, Douglas was vain, shallow, and, when enraged, vindictive—an entelechial family trait. By his own account, he was "rather exceptionally good-looking as a boy," with the cupid moue of a fin-de-siècle Aesthete. "That flowerlike sort of beauty must have been a horrible handicap to you," Shaw once remarked, but "it was probably Nature's reaction against the ultra-hickory type of your father."

Photographed next to Wilde, Bosie appears short and slight, but he was above average height at five feet nine inches, a muscular 126 pounds. He liked to pose for pictures like a mischievous boy, fists shoved into his trouser pockets. The myth of his incredible beauty cannot be judged by modern standards or by surviving photographs, which froze a passive, careless face when the shutter clicked. For Wilde, Douglas's blond hair and alabaster complexion, his sleepy eyes and heart-shaped mouth, personified Hellenic beauty: a marble torso come to life.

BOSIE WAS A sociable young man whom Constance welcomed into the family as she had Ross. If having young men around to talk of poetry and art made her husband happy, she made every effort to include them in family holidays. At Babbacombe Cliff in Torquay on the Devon coast, Lady Mount-Temple, a distant cousin of Constance's, owned a classic Victorian residence designed by Ruskin and decorated by Burne-Jones and Morris. Lady Mount-Temple was more than a relative; Constance addressed her as "Mia Madre" in letters, for she was the kindly mother denied her as a child. The Wildes leased the house for months at a time for a nominal fee. The Cliff was a large, rambling structure with part of the drawing room built over an archway in the carriage drive, which had a view across Lyme Bay to Exmouth. Wilde's young sons, Vyvyan and Cyril, called the outcropping "Wonderland" because it had originally been decorated with scenes from *Alice's Adventures in Wonderland*. This was Wilde's writing room. Going off to write, he announced that he was going to visit Wonderland.

From his days at Oxford, when he nonchalantly earned Firsts without appearing to study, Wilde had promoted a slothful image. "I have no sympathy myself with industry of any kind," he wrote in the short story "The Remarkable Rocket," which satirizes the narcissistic personality. "Indeed, I have always been of opinion that hard work is simply the refuge of people who have nothing whatever to do." In *Earnest,* Algernon complains, "It is awfully hard work doing nothing. However, I don't mind hard work where there is no definite object of any kind." Wilde wanted everyone to think that he was a man of fashion who wrote only when there was no better entertainment. Actually, he wrote all the time.

He wrote in his head; he wrote when he talked and later in notebooks, where he doodled and drew young faces in profile. Instead of the copy editor's upside-down caret sign to indicate insertions, he wrote inside big balloons. If words pleased him, he underlined twice, and satisfactory epigrams received a star. He wrote in ink and edited in pencil; he reworked by taking a string of words and eliminating clutter to allow the idea to breathe life, to take shape. The changes—instinctive rather than agonizing choices—were no less touches of genius. The famous line in *An Ideal Husband,* "To love oneself is the beginning of a life-long romance," began as "To love one's self is the highest note of romance." "A really well-made buttonhole is the true link between Art and Nature" started out as "A really exquisite buttonhole is the only true link between Art and Nature."

Wilde loved writing plays. He worked hard at something he liked and earned more money than he had as a critic or journalist. Being a dramatist came naturally, whereas juggling subplots in his only novel had confounded him. He was never more in control of his authorial life as at this time; he demanded the right to uninterrupted writing times in comfortable places with servants to indulge and cater to him. The history of his plays is irrevocably connected to his writing houses. A successful writer's prerogative was to complain or to blame others if unable to write. Bosie bore the brunt of the blame—perhaps unfairly—although he did complicate the progress of translating *Salomé*.

CHAPTER FIFTEEN

Translating Ecstasy

❧

Ah! I have kissed thy mouth, Jokanaan, I have kissed thy mouth.
There was a bitter taste on thy lips. Was it the taste of blood? . . .
Nay; but perchance it was the taste of love. . . .
They say that love hath a bitter taste.

—SALOME

The Jews were to be dressed in yellow, Herod and Herodias in purple, and John the Baptist in white. There would be a black floor to show off Salomé's white feet. Her special color was black, then silver, until Wilde decided on "green like a curious and poisonous lizard" standing against a violet sky. "Yes, I never thought of that," said Wilde. "Certainly a violet sky and then, in place of an orchestra, braziers of perfume. Think—the scented clouds rising and partly veiling the stage from time to time—a new perfume for each emotion" and the theatre aired out between emotions. Wilde, Charles Ricketts, and Graham Robertson talked long into the night, draping luxurious fabrics over the cast of *Salomé*.

In the spring of 1892, Wilde attended a dinner at the Lyceum's Beefsteak Room. Seated opposite him was "the serpent of old Nile," as he called the Divine Sarah, that evening resplendent in sequins and feathers, waving a long cigarette holder. "Why don't you write me a play?" she asked. "I have already done so," Wilde answered. Unhappy with her season in London, Bernhardt read the one-act script re-creating a historical moment when a king becomes the pawn of his lascivious wife and step-daughter and immediately accepted the title role.

Wilde cautioned that the central figure was the moon—admired because of its inconstancy—not the dancing princess; actually it was Herod, but Wilde chose not to confuse the temperamental actress with authorial truths. Rehearsals started in mid-June, but Bernhardt rejected the color-coordinated production and went to Henry Irving for a set and costumes. Listening to "my own words spoken by the most beautiful voice in the world has been the greatest artistic joy that it is possible to experience," Wilde said during rehearsal. How Bernhardt phrased things in French was irrelevant. "The dress, the title of the play, the order of the words may vary," Shaw said, "but the woman is always the same. She does not enter into the leading character: she substitutes herself for it."

In Wilde's perfumed Decadent dream, more representative of his imagination than any other work, he plays with the tensions between symbol, style, and substance, between art, life, and image. Language bursts into outsized symbols: "Thy mouth is like a band of scarlet on a tower of ivory," Salome says to Jokanaan. "It is like a pomegranate cut with a knife of ivory." Wilde celebrates women as described by his mother in *Social Studies*. "Woman lies at the base of all life, whether for good or evil," Lady Wilde wrote. "From Eden to Olympus, woman is the first word written on the page of every history and of every religion, and is the illuminated initial of every man's life. . . . Her power over man, whether through beauty or love, through purity or sin, is the crown and the torture, the glory or the perdition."

More recklessly than in *Dorian Gray*, Wilde here exploits voice, gaze, touch, and hunger as metaphors for desire. Merely looking at someone is enough to evoke an atmosphere of doom. Lustful gazes ravish the characters. Salome accuses Jokanaan of taking her virginity from her with his gaze, revealing the secret chambers of Wilde's imagination. Herod gazes at Salome, who desires Jokanaan, hidden in a cistern she cannot see. "It is his eyes above all that are terrible," she says. "They are like black holes burned by torches in a tapestry of Tyre." *Salomé* was a turning point in Wilde's life, a play that celebrates love as the most powerful force in human nature, written at the moment when the author embraced a perilous love. "The mystery of Love is greater than the mystery of Death," says Salome.

ALL NEW PLAYS needed the imprimatur of the Lord Chamberlain's Office, where the blue pencils were wielded by civil servants. Wilde's fate was settled by Edward F. Smyth Pigott, who held the title of examiner for nearly a half century and, in Shaw's words, was "a walking compendium of vulgar insular prejudice." Aware that there was a ban on plays depicting biblical characters, Wilde should not have been so outraged that artists and sculptors could portray biblical figures while a playwright could not. He threatened to leave the country and settle in France. "I shall take out letters of naturalisation. I will not consent to call myself a citizen of a country that shows such narrowness in artistic judgement. I am not English," he said. "I am Irish which is quite another thing." *Punch* published a cartoon of Wilde wearing military uniform laden with infantry gear, illustrating that, if he became a French citizen, he was subject to national service.

Salomé in the original French text was published by the Librairie de l'Art Indépendant in February 1893, but plans for a Paris production were unsuccessful. Dedicated "A mon ami Pierre Louÿs," it was bound in "Tyrian purple" (Max Beerbohm said "Parma violets") with letters Wilde described as "fading" or "tired" silver. Wilde bragged to Ricketts that he had become a famous French author.★ The French edition provoked passionate reactions. Edgar Saltus said it made him shudder. "It is only the shudder that counts," Wilde replied. William Archer called Salomé "an oriental Hedda Gabler," one who speaks to "that life within your life,

★The first performance in French was at the Théâtre de l'Oeuvre in Paris in 1896, when Wilde was in prison; the first London performance was privately produced in 1905; the first public performance was in 1931 at the Lyceum. The premiere of Richard Strauss's opera was in 1905 in Dresden; when he sought a license in 1909 to perform the German libretto based on Wilde's play in London, he was refused. A license was granted only after all biblical allusions were eliminated. Instead of the head appearing onstage, Salomé had to sing to a bloodstained tray. When Madame Ackle refused to sing to an empty tray, more permissions were needed for the tray to be covered with a cloth. "Only care must be taken not to build up a great heap in it, which would look suggestive," the report read.

which alone . . . is really worth living—the life of the imagination." Recently staged in London, Ibsen's play had impressed Wilde, who said afterward, "I felt pity and terror, as though the play had been Greek." *The Times* thought *Salomé* "an arrangement in blood and ferocity, morbid, *bizarre,* repulsive, and very offensive in its adaptation of scriptural phraseology to situations the reverse of sacred." To those who pointed out resemblances to Flaubert's "Hérodias," Wilde replied, "Of course I plagiarise. It is the privilege of the appreciative man. I never read Flaubert's *Tentation de St. Antoine* without signing my name at the end of it. *Que voulez-vous?* All the best Hundred Books bear my signature in this manner."

WILDE WANTED AN English version but was too involved with his next play to do it himself, and he needed an illustrator, who by right of seniority was Charles Ricketts. He focused elsewhere when he saw the work of Aubrey Beardsley in the new art magazine *The Studio*. Only twenty-one, the idiosyncratic artist was experimenting with a style based on the simplicity of Japanese woodcuts. Arousing Wilde's regard was Beardsley's drawing of the climactic scene of his play, when Salome kisses the severed head of John the Baptist. Wilde acknowledged the tribute with an inscribed copy: "For the only artist who, besides myself, knows what the dance of the seven veils is, and can see that invisible dance."

Wilde met Beardsley in the summer of 1891 at Burne-Jones's studio, where the artist appeared uninvited with his portfolio. The older artist encouraged him to continue his work and brought him out to the garden to meet the Wildes and their sons. Wilde noted that Beardsley had a face "like a silver hatchet." Diagnosed as a consumptive while still a child, Beardsley would be dead in seven years: he saw himself encumbered with "a vile constitution, a sallow face and sunken eyes, long red hair, a shuffling gait and a stoop." Through Wilde's patronage, he joined the inner circle that dined at the Café Royal, Willis's, and Kettner's. He told Wilde that he read French as easily as English, considered Balzac's characters in *La Comédie humaine* his family members, and wanted to translate *Salomé*. The publisher John Lane discouraged the idea and steered the young man back to art, promising him not only the cover but also ten full-page drawings. Working with large blocks of black ink and blank white areas to graphically define space, Beardsley set out to upset the traditional relationship between text and illustration.★ Wilde wanted to involve Bosie in some intellectual project and asked him to make the translation. Flattered by the prospect of sharing the title page with Wilde, Bosie put his inadequate French to work.

LIKE WILDE IN the mid-seventies, Beardsley was intent on being a personality and applying a decorative style to modern life. The competition between the two dandies with their lemon-colored kid gloves could overoxygenate a room. Besides taking himself too seriously, Beardsley lived with an anger at life's limits, not uncommon in people with terminal illnesses. He forged a friendship with Max Beerbohm to share the sport of challenging Wilde's authority. As he finished the drawings, Beardsley sent them by messenger to the Bodley Head office in Vigo Street. At first Lane ignored or missed some of the lewd details, but he soon returned those drawings that needed a fig leaf here or an obscurity there. While concealing some obscenities, Beardsley introduced satires of Wilde, whose bloated face appears as "the Woman in the Moon," described as a "mad," "drunken" woman "seeking everywhere for lovers."

Hostility combined with ambiguous sexuality fascinated Wilde. Beardsley, like Gide, was a young man in need of taunting. Wilde challenged his sophistication, remarking, "Dear Aubrey is too Parisian; he cannot forget that he has been to Dieppe—once!" He also attacked Beardsley's art: "When I have before me one of your drawings, I want to drink absinthe, which changes colour like jade in sunlight and makes the senses thrall, and then I can live myself back in ancient Rome, in the Rome of the later Caesars." He questioned his preferences. "Don't sit on the same chair as Aubrey, it's not compromising," Wilde once said at the Café Royal. Beardsley had a habit of folding up his long legs and perching on the arms of chairs. Then, as now, he was a puzzle, an eternal ado-

---

*Beardsley was the first innovative artist whose success was based on photogravure—a technique that enabled him to work directly from ink drawings, which were photographically reproduced, then printed straight from the block, thus destroying the distinction between an original and a copy. Beardsley earned his reputation through the publication of reproductions; few ever saw his original work.

lescent whose masturbation fantasies were sublimated in priapic art. As to homosexuality, he told Arthur Symons, "Yes, Yes, I look like a sodomite. But no, I am not one."

Bosie worked on the translation throughout the summer, more to demonstrate his dedication than to impress Wilde with his pains-taking word choices. Whatever he produced would be accepted, or so he thought; but when Wilde read it and found it full of "schoolboy faults," Bosie was insulted. Wilde should not have been surprised, he had expected too much—using the dictionary, as his mother had done as a translator, for one thing. The text was "unworthy" of the original work, he told Bosie. Tantrums followed rows, then a separation so acrimonious that Ross had to intercede on Bosie's behalf, then the reuniting—and the terms. Wilde wanted Bosie to make major revisions, and, when he refused, Beardsley wanted to step in. A four-sided squabble ensued among Wilde, Beardsley, Douglas, and Lane before Wilde wrested Bosie's version to edit himself. Retaliating, Beardsley substituted irrelevant drawings in his submissions to Lane; when he became art editor of *The Yellow Book,* he accepted on condition that Wilde was excluded as a contributor. Their paths would cross again, however, when Wilde was in exile in Dieppe.

As Wilde envisioned it, his play was the language of purple and gold, a verbal interpretation of Gustave Moreau's gilded style. Prepared for a Byzantine setting, he was shocked by the black-and-white Japanesque figures that resembled little monsters with big heads and bulging eyes; some had faunlike bodies hidden in the foliage of scaly rosebushes and exhibited genitalia. Beardsley had neither illuminated nor elevated the text; he had given his drawings a life of their own, including personal attacks on the author. They were the kinds of "naughty scribbles a preco-cious boy makes in the margins of his copybook," Wilde said. The drawings had surface appeal but not the unrestrained emotional depth that Wilde craved. They overshadowed the play and made Beardsley's reputation. Reviewing the edition, the London *Times* remarked on the graphics that the "whole thing must be a joke, and it seems to us a very poor joke!" Joyce called it "a polyphonic variation on the rapport of art and nature."

Wilde launched Symbolist drama in a vehicle in which atmosphere is everything, in which exotic language and opulent imagery create overlays of sensual evil. Enlarging artistic horizons, he flaunted his achievement in making "Drama, the most objective form known to art, . . . as personal a mode of expression as the Lyric or the Sonnet." His ambition, fluctuating since Oxford, was to be remembered not as a poet, thinker, or playwright, "but as the man who reclothed the sublimest conception which the world has ever known—the Salvation of Humanity, the Sacrifice of Himself upon the Cross by Christ—with new and burning words." These words had to wait for prison and *De Profundis*.

A NEW PERSONALITY joined Wilde's circle when Herbert Beerbohm— who added Tree to his name when he entered the theatre—introduced his elfin half brother Max around town. Called "the Incomparable Max," Beerbohm had been known to Wilde at Oxford in the mid-eighties, when he was a Merton undergraduate chumming around with Reginald "Reggie" Turner, his closest friend. Short and owlish, Max became a fixture at homosexual gatherings, his fastidious, reticent nature appreciated by the other egotists. Only Max could get away with announcing his state of mind as "Oh, I'm radiant." His was an incessant zest, and he liked to watch fires.

Turner never knew his mother and assumed he was the illegitimate son of Edward Levy-Lawson, proprietor of *The Daily Telegraph,* but his father was probably his guardian, Levy-Lawson's uncle, Lionel Lawson, who left Turner money at his death in 1879. A witty companion and a great mimic, Turner was known for his ugliness. He had a nut-shaped head, blubbery lips, a huge snoutlike nose, and a nervous habit of continually winking and blinking. Eager to be accepted, he was generous with his ample allowance. Reggie and Max were inseparable at college and remained lifelong friends, despite the complication that Turner, a homosexual, was in love with Max. Unmoved by the senses and fearful of life's coarser aspects, Max never felt passion for his men friends or for women. His late marriage by mutual agreement was probably never consummated; he told his wife, Florence, that physical love was beyond him.

Still, there was also the exception, and Turner feared that Beerbohm might be seduced by Bosie's beauty when the two became friendly at Oxford. In his offhand way, Max assured Turner that he had no reason to worry. Bosie was "obviously mad (like all his family I believe)," Max said, "and though he is pretty and clever and nice, I never judge my friends from an aesthetic, an intellectual, or an ethical standpoint: I simply like them or dislike—that is all. You are fortunate enough to have fallen into the former category."

Like a Cheshire cat, Max watched from the warmth of a distant sunlit window, noting the worst in everybody, a talent that served him well when he became a scathing caricaturist. Will Rothenstein said that "nothing escaped the clear pitiless grey eye of Max." He later regretted drawing Wilde bloated and openmouthed, looking very decadent, particularly when the picture was posted in the office of the police inspector who arrested Wilde for gross indecency.

In words and art, Beerbohm was an annoying moralist. What business was it of anyone eighteen years Wilde's junior to keep track of his drinking? "I am sorry to say that Oscar drinks far more than he ought," he wrote Turner; "indeed the first time I saw him, after all that long period of distant adoration and reverence, he was in a hopeless state of intoxication. He has deteriorated very much in appearance: his cheeks being quite a dark purple and fat to a fault." He also attacked Wilde's need for disciples in an article published in the *Anglo-American Times*. Max decided that Wilde had done "incalculable" harm by not realizing that a love of beauty for its own sake was "inborn and cannot ever be communicated." In his view the young men trying to be Aesthetes had, for the most part, failed absurdly.

Wilde read the article, told Max that his style was like a "silver dagger," and liked him all the more for his courage—few chose to take such a risk. Over dinner at Willis's, they discussed Oxford professors. Max complained that he could never hear Pater when he lectured. Wilde observed that one only overheard him. "Giving lectures for him," Max continued, hoping to trump the master, "was a form of self-communion. He *whispered* them." No wonder Wilde said that the gods had bestowed on Max "the gift of perpetual old age." Like Wilde himself, Max was a conundrum. "Tell me," Wilde asked a mutual friend, "when you are alone with him, . . . does he take off his face and reveal his mask?" The two dandies spoke the same language.

BEFORE WILDE BEGAN his second play, *A Woman of No Importance* (originally entitled *Mrs. Arbuthnot*), he and Bosie went to Bad Homburg. Much to Constance's amusement, her husband took the rest cure, demanding a strict diet and no cigarettes. That summer of 1892 he wrote at a farmhouse at Felbrigg, a village near Cromer on the coast of Norfolk. His family was at Babbacombe Cliff, and exchange visits were planned. After a few weeks of solitary writing, Wilde invited Bosie to join him. Shortly after arrival, Bosie caught a cold and took to bed, sniffling and sniveling. Wilde wrote Constance that he could not leave Bosie to visit Torquay, and she graciously offered to come and nurse: "I am so sorry about Lord Alfred Douglas, and wish I was at Cromer to look after him. If you think I could do any good, do telegraph for me, because I can easily get over to you."

In mid-September, Constance wrote to a friend that the play would be finished in a week. She said of Oscar, "He has become mad about golf and spends two or three hours on the links every day and this is good for him." One of the few games in which talking enhances a sport, golf was made for Wilde, a perfect recreation for a conversationalist. One imagines him ambling down the green in his elephantine gait, wearing tweed plus fours, distracting the other players' concentration with endless stories—most lost forever. Wilde kept his clubs leaning in the hallway corner at Tite Street, but he had more enthusiasm than skill for the game.

WILDE HANDED TREE the script of *A Woman of No Importance* on October 14 and began the nuisance of breaking in a new actor-manager. Had he collaborated again with Alexander, the process might have been easier, but the St. James's was booked and Tree had an open schedule at the Haymarket. By affecting a flippant attitude, Wilde tried to take control. "As Herod in my *Salome* you would be admirable," he told the beefy Tree. "As a peer of the realm in my latest dramatic device, pray forgive me if I do not see you." Tree reminded him that he had played the Duke of Guisebury in *The Dancing Girl*. "Ah! that's just it," said Wilde. "Before you can successfully impersonate the character I have in mind, you must forget that you ever played Falstaff: above all you must forget that you ever played a Duke in a melodrama by Henry Arthur Jones." Better still, Wilde continued, "forget you have ever acted because the part is unlike any that existed." Humoring him, Tree exclaimed: "My God! he must be super-natural." "He is certainly not natural," said Wilde. "He is a figure of art. Indeed, if you can bear the truth, he is MYSELF."

Wilde kept written notes after each rehearsal and made marginal notes on the script indicating how Tree should speak certain lines. He asked him to underplay the scene at the beginning of Act Two when Lord Illingworth is lecturing his son (although the relationship is not known) about the evils of puritanism. Lord Illingworth advises Gerald that the "wildest profligate who spills his life in folly, has a better, saner, finer philosophy of life than the Puritan has. He, at any rate, knows that the aim of life is the pleasure of living, and does in some way realise himself, be himself." A diatribe against puritanism was out of place, said Tree, particularly when the principal character is delivering a series of worldly-wise epigrams. Tree wanted the speech cut. Wilde agreed to substitute an epigram: "Puritanism is not a theory of life. It is an explanation of the English middle classes." Tree insisted on deleting the whole speech and eventually got his way.

A Woman of No Importance is "a woman's play," Wilde said. There is the woman with a past, Mrs. Arbuthnot, her illegitimate son, and the unrepentant aristocratic dandy as seducer. There is wit and melodrama, but mostly there is talk. Wilde proudly pointed out that there was absolutely no action—only conversation—in the first act. Deliberately and succinctly, he turned the most common criticism of his dramas—all talk and no action—into a virtue. Anticipating all the playwrights to come, he makes talk dramatic, and gradually, in Ibsen-like fashion, characters reveal their inner selves; he introduces flirtations in code and shows the impact of silent communication.

Trying to mix feminist theories with melodrama can be difficult, but Wilde's views are clear: the double standard is unfair. By saying that men are intellectual and heartless and women live by their emotions, Wilde explains—perhaps excuses—his own behavior. In this play he makes melodrama modern. There is a triumphant curtain line, delivered by Mrs. Arbuthnot after she has struck her former lover in the face with his own glove. Her son enters and picks up the glove, asking who had called. "Oh! no one. No one in particular. A man of no importance."

TREE SAID HE produced the play not with the assistance of the playwright but with his interference. Wilde claimed that Tree had called him "foolish," "slippery," and "deceptive." Not only did Wilde want his way with his own words—not an unheard-of prerogative—but when thwarted he attacked the little things, such as the flimsy paper used for tickets: "If I go to Charing Cross station and pay a penny to go to Westminster, I get a nicer ticket than if I bought one of your ten-and-sixpenny Stalls." When they returned to more serious matters, Tree complained that some of the dialogue was "redundant," and the heroine's name "too fluctuating—for *theatrical* purposes." Wilde wanted the part of Gerald to go to a newly discovered profile, an actor named Sydney Barraclough, but Tree refused. He wanted parts given to members of his company, in this case Ellen Terry's brother, Fred.

A Woman of No Importance opened at the Haymarket on April 19, 1893. Arrivals were dropped off at a Corinthian portico, not as imposing as the Lyceum's, but still regal. Dressed in a white waistcoat with a buttonhole of little lilies, Wilde watched from his box at stage left. When the applause and calls for the author began, he disappointed all those who expected a reprise of his speech after the premiere of *Lady Windermere's Fan*. He stood in his box, surveyed the audience from the gallery to the stalls, and made sure he was recognized before laconically announcing: "Ladies and Gentlemen, I regret to inform you that Mr. Oscar Wilde is not in the house." Afterward he was less generous with praise for the audience. "People love a wicked aristocrat who seduces a virtuous maiden," he said, "and they love a virtuous maiden for being seduced by a wicked aristocrat. I have given them what they like, so that they may learn to appreciate what I like to give them." Success was making Wilde increasingly arrogant, not that he had ever been humble.

The play had defects but was welcome entertainment. A disappointed Yeats said, "Despite its qualities, it is not a work of art, it has no central fire, it is not dramatic in any ancient sense of the word." Clement Scott, who criticized *Fan* as "a clever, immature work," praised its successor for being "pungent, observant, sarcastic, and amusing." He said that when Wilde "removes the jester's masks then he rises with his subject and elevates it at every soar." Scott called the characters "strong, poetical, sympathetic, virile," adding that if the author continued in this manner Scott would persuade himself that the stage could be made a serious platform. It has some of Wilde's best lines about relationships: "My husband is a kind of promissory note; I am tired of meeting him," says Mrs. Allonby. Whereupon Lady Caroline Pontefract replies, "But you renew him from time to time don't you?"

The idée fixe of Wilde's work was a pattern of secret and revelation, guilt and forgiveness: "The Book of Life begins with a man and woman in a garden. It ends with Revelation"; "Women have a much better time than men. There are far more things forbidden to them"; and "All the married men nowadays live like bachelors, and all the bachelors like married men." Everyone wanted to sound like a Wildean character, to sparkle with epigrams. "As far as I can ascertain," said Shaw, "I am the only person in London who cannot sit down and write an Oscar Wilde play at will. The fact that his plays, though apparently lucrative, remain unique under these circumstances says much for the self-denial of our scribes."

HIS REPUTATION SECURE in London, Wilde perversely repudiated America, where he had begun his career as a playwright, albeit unsuccessfully, with *Vera*. Elisabeth Marbury,★ now the preeminent theatrical agent for European authors, with offices worldwide, begged him to attend the first night of *Lady Windermere's Fan,* which opened in Boston in January 1893 and the following month in New York, with Maurice Barrymore—patriarch of the acting dynasty of Ethel, John, and Lionel—in the role of Lord Darlington. Wilde criticized Albert Marshman Palmer's production. Barrymore "dresses the part badly," he wrote Marbury, on the basis of secondhand reports, "and does not see that Darlington is *not* a villain, but a man who really believes that Windermere is treating his wife badly, and wishes to save her."

Wilde wanted Charles Frohman—destined to be, with David Belasco, the leading producer of the English-speaking stage—to produce *Woman* after its run at the Haymarket so that the American version would be the

---

★When Marbury started as an agent in 1890, playwrights had some legal rights, but piracy, particularly of foreign plays, was rampant. Pirates sent stenographers to the theatre to transcribe the scripts; working in the dark, they stretched string across their notes to keep the lines straight. Marbury is credited with establishing the royalty system in America.

same as the one done under his supervision. "I need not tell you," he instructed Marbury, "with your experience and artistic instinct, how a play grows at rehearsal, and what new points one can introduce." Frohman did not take the play, but Rose Coghlan, an English-born American actress, did. Again Marbury begged Wilde to attend opening night: "Your presence here would do more to advance the success of the production than anything else."

Nothing would have pleased Wilde more than a triumphant return to New York, where he had so many friends, among them Clyde Fitch. But to leave Bosie, who was busy doing badly at Oxford and needed his encouragement, might have threatened their newfound intimacy.

CHAPTER SIXTEEN

Mostly Famous

❧

Desire, at the end, was a malady, or a madness, or both.
I grew careless of the lives of others. I took pleasure where it pleased
me, and passed on. I forgot that every little action of the common day
makes or unmakes character, and that therefore what
one has done in the secret chamber one has some day to cry aloud on
the housetops.

—DE PROFUNDIS

He usually wore a frock coat and top hat and carried a silver-crested walking stick; his buttonhole was made daily by a florist in the Burlington Arcade. Now a successful dramatist, Wilde hired a hansom by the day to drop him at the theatre and wait outside until he made his nightly rounds, which usually ended at the Café Royal, where the only crime in 1890s society was not to sparkle. Seated at his favorite marble-chipped table in the Domino Room, he summoned one of the *garçons de café,* whose aprons by managerial decree covered their shoes. Ordering absinthe, he held the glass up to the light, savored its green color, and announced to all within earshot that it was Baudelaire's favorite. Whenever Wilde paused in conversation, he lit another cigarette from one of the several silver cases on the table. The first time Max Beerbohm saw the Domino Room, he looked at the gold and crimson, the mirrors and the caryatids, listened to the hum of cynical conversation broken by the clatter of dominoes on the marble tables, and said: "This indeed is life!"

When the chef appeared to make his recommendations, Wilde conferred with his guests, inquiring in French on the merits of the *sole Beaumanoir* or the *suprême de volaille à la Patti.* A celebratory life expanded his waistline, but he never saw himself as fat: fate had trapped him inside a monumental edifice. He was handsome in the way of an enormous doll. "When I am in trouble, eating is the only thing that consoles me," he said. "Indeed, when I am in really great trouble, as anyone who knows me intimately will tell you, I refuse everything except food and drink."

Sometimes Wilde and his exquisite Aeolian harps, as Max called the group that included Bosie, Ross, and Turner, made a tour of the popular music halls. In *Earnest,* Jack and Algernon discuss how they will spend the evening after dining at Willis's. "What shall we do after dinner?" asks Algernon. "Go to a theatre?" Jack replies: "Oh no! I loathe listening." "Well, let us go to the Club?" "Oh, no! I hate talking." "Well, we might trot round to the Empire at ten?" "Oh, no! I can't bear looking at things. It is so silly." "Well"—Algernon sighs—"what shall we do?" "Nothing!"

Wilde had perfected the art of talking, but listening and looking were recent enjoyments. Most evenings he was seen applauding loudly at the theatre. Michael Field observed him at a performance of *The Duchess of Malfi* and said that he "sits as if blowing bubbles of enjoyment." At *The Master Builder,* she noted his position in a box "allowing the people to see him and the silver knob of his cane." After the theatre, a late supper followed, often at the cozy Artists Room at Pagani's in Great Portland Street, a rendezvous of the Prince of Wales and Lillie Langtry, where the specialties were calf's brains and lark-and-steak pie. Along with Sarah Bernhardt, Giacomo Puccini, Richard Strauss, and Peter Tchaikovsky (who added several bars from his Fourth Symphony), Wilde signed his name on the linoleum wall. Bosie's perfect evening, Wilde said, was "a champagne dinner at the Savoy, a box at a music hall to follow, and a champagne supper at Willis's as a *bonne bouche* for the end."

For looking, Wilde enjoyed the vernissages, or private views, at the Royal Academy. He is immortalized, the tallest top-hatted figure consulting his catalog, in the painting *The Private View of the Academy, 1881* by William Powell Frith. His clubs were not comparable to those of his characters or of Douglas, who belonged to White's, which along with Boodle's was an aristocratic St. James's gentlemen's club. While at Oxford, Wilde joined St. Stephen's, a Conservative club near the Houses of Parliament; after his marriage he and Constance patronized the Albemarle, a mixed club founded in 1879. Despite support by prominent members, including an unlikely Henry James, who loathed Wilde, the prestigious Savile blackballed him in 1888. That invitations—"To meet Mr. Oscar Wilde"—inserted him between the soup and the pudding never bothered him.

BEING INVOLVED IN all aspects of theatre production introduced Wilde to a homosocial world that had existed since Elizabethan times. Uranian culture was flamboyant, theatrical, anticipating the admiration for male ballet and musical comedy dancers. Except for those who appeared in amateur drag-queen theatricals, West End actors who were homosexual were circumspect about their private lives. There was always the chance that letters (purloined or misplaced) might fall into the wrong hands, as Wilde soon discovered—even as he used such letters as plot devices for his plays. Everyone in London's homosexual underground knew the story of Stella (Ernest Boulton) and Fanny (Frederick Park), who were arrested in 1871 coming from a theatre dressed as women. Suggestive letters found in their lodgings became evidence and threatened a jail sentence. It is noteworthy that twenty-four years before Wilde's trial, when provocative letters were used as evidence, the chief justice regarded them as "no more than the romantic expression of personal admiration and affection. No doubt such feelings and attachments had existed and might exist without any evil." At that time the court preferred to pretend that homosexual feelings did not exist.

It was no exaggeration that the 1885 law under which Wilde was prosecuted was called "the Blackmailer's Charter." Dorian "had heard of rich men who had been blackmailed all their lives by some servant who had read a letter or overheard a conversation." An indiscreet letter had brought Wilde and Bosie together. After a few casual meetings, Bosie invited Wilde to visit him at Oxford. Bosie was being blackmailed and needed advice. Wilde spent the weekend in his rooms, returned to London, and handed the matter over to his solicitor, George Lewis, who retrieved the document for a hundred pounds. Bosie claims in his autobiography that Wilde was a persistent suitor, but Wilde was still seeing John Gray and was far too involved with the production of *Lady Windermere's Fan* for any intense courtship.

By May 1892, when Wilde describes Bosie to Ross as "a narcissus—so white and gold," stretched out "like a hyacinth on the sofa," the symbolism of nakedness gave Ross every reason to be jealous and to question his preeminent place in Wilde's circle. The following month, Wilde inscribes a new edition of *Poems:* "To the Gilt-mailed Boy." Intimacies paralleled Wilde's aesthetic appreciation of his lover's body.

Bosie recalled that they became lovers nine months after they met. "These familiarities were rare," he said, "but they did occur spasmodically." They stopped six months "before the final catastrophe, and were never resumed after he came out of prison." Inevitably the two developed an incompatible physical relationship. They both worshiped youth and beauty. Briefly at Trinity, Wilde's body had been muscular, but no longer. Bosie liked to romp and pose naked, completely at ease as the gilt-mailed boy. Wilde felt awkward beside him.

Wilde believed that Greek spiritual love is the highest form of love; what he wanted was not bliss or even satisfaction but contentment. "I blame myself for allowing an unintellectual friendship, a friendship whose primary aim was not the creation and contemplation of beautiful things, entirely to dominate my life." Sexual needs led to quarrels. Bosie could be "revolting," "loathsome," "offensive," and "violent," Wilde said. At some point they agreed on a platonic relationship and found sex elsewhere. "So far from his leading me astray, it was I that (unwittingly) pushed him over the precipice," Douglas later said about introducing Wilde to the homosexual underworld of rent boys.

These prostitutes, often younger than the legal age of sixteen, solicited on street corners, in public lavatories, at pubs, and in and around the promenades of the Empire, Tivoli, and Pavilion, the popular music halls. Male prostitutes sometimes called themselves "gay" to go with their female counterparts, who were known as "gay ladies." Wilde and Bosie were gentlemen who were homosexual in a country where sex was one of the few means by which someone could cut across class boundaries. Following a long tradition of gentlemen who liked to trash their own breeding in the pursuit of street boys, the two embarked on experiences

Wilde later described as "feasting with panthers." Wilde accepted promiscuity with mixed feelings: it was nonexistent in Plato's time because it was unnecessary, but evolved in modern times when free expression of desire was forbidden. Jealousy applied to marriage and was, Wilde said, an emotion "closely bound up with our conceptions of property" and "an extraordinary source of crime in modern life." As he watched Bosie leave a party with a beautiful young man, however, he must have felt some twinge of ownership.

Wilde did not meet lovers in sordid East End rooms. Usually Bosie's friend Alfred Taylor arranged introductions at Wilde's restaurants or the Café Royal; following a leisurely dinner and a mutual understanding, they left for Wilde's rooms at 10–11 St. James's Place, the Savoy, or the Albemarle, even Tite Street if the family was away. Wilde and Bosie took connecting rooms at the Savoy. The evening began with champagne dinners, then intimacies with the boys selected, followed by more champagne or hock and seltzer and talk and more talk—about sex. "Your defect was not that you knew so little about life, but that you knew too much," Wilde said of Bosie in *De Profundis*. "The gutter and the things that live in it had begun to fascinate you. . . . terribly fascinating though the one topic round which your talk invariably centred was, still at the end it became quite monotonous to me." There followed months of prodigal nights succeeded by vicious arguments redeemed only by laughter.

ALFRED TAYLOR WAS the son of a cocoa merchant and once a public school boy at Marlborough, a fact that Wilde proudly stated at his trial. Taylor lived at 13 Little College Street, behind Westminster Abbey, in a fourth-floor flat with a view of the Houses of Parliament. There he staged drag theatricals and his own mock wedding to his companion, Charles Mason. Among the young men whom Taylor introduced to Wilde was Sidney Mavor, later a Church of England priest, whom Wilde saw over a period of a year and a half; Freddy Atkins, seventeen, already a blackmailer; the brothers Charles and William Parker, unemployed gentlemen's servants, and others such as Alfred Wood, a seventeen-year-old whom Bosie tired of and passed on to Wilde.

Since these boys were already prostitutes, there was no need to seduce them, but Wilde courted them the same way he would have courted a young woman. There were champagne dinners during which he took a personal interest in their lives—one criminal talking to another; he gave them gifts, often silver cigarette cases from Thornhill's in Bond Street. Not every meeting resulted in sexual favors, but it mattered not whether there were improprieties if there appeared to be, and Wilde's behavior generated unwholesome talk. "I am one made for the exception and not for the rule," he said, claiming the right to defy established norms. "I have never posed as being ordinary, great heavens!"

THE TWO YEARS prior to Wilde's trial proved to be the most optimistic for the open debate on homosexuality. Contributing to this dialogue was Douglas's work in two periodicals: the *Spirit Lamp,* which he edited, an undergraduate Oxford publication that came out during 1892 and 1893, and *The Chameleon,* a one-issue venture in December 1894. Wilde contributed epigrams from his notebooks and called them "Phrases and Philosophies for the Use of the Young," with such wisdom as "The first duty in life is to be as artificial as possible. What the second duty is no one has as yet discovered."

In the same issue was an anonymous story, "The Priest and the Acolyte," written by the editor John Francis Bloxam, which explicitly describes pederastic interest in altar boys, a theme that the Crown made much of at Wilde's trial. Another sympathetic publication was the *Artist and Journal of Home Culture* (1888–94), edited by Bosie's friend Charles Kains Jackson. *Teleny: or the Reverse of the Medal,* an explicit homosexual novel published in 1893 by Leonard Smithers, was rumored to have many authors, of which Wilde was a likely suspect, but there is nothing in its style or content to suggest that he wrote any passages.

Bosie was an advocate for sexual freedom when few voices remained. John Addington Symonds, the grand old historian of the Renaissance who lost his chair in poetry at Oxford because of a fondness for young boys, was the closest to a crusading homosexual. He died in 1893, and that left George Ives. The illegitimate son of aristocratic parents and a Cambridge-educated poet, Ives struggled daily with thoughts about "the Cause." Most of his suffering went into a diary that grew to more than three million words. "If Bosie has really made Oxford homosexual, he has done something good and glorious," he wrote. Ives suggested the title of *The Chameleon,* a choice as interesting for its double meaning as Bunbury in *Earnest.*

Ives envisioned homosexuals from all spheres of life, working and living openly without prejudice. Somber and self-absorbed at twenty-seven, he lived at E4, the Albany, the bachelor residence immortalized in *Earnest.*★ He was not a member of Wilde's circle because he found it too exhilarating. "After going among that set it is hard to mix in ordinary society," he wrote, "for they have a charm which is rare and wonderful. I wish they were less extravagant and more real." In 1893 Ives founded a secret society, the Order of Chaeronea, modeling its rituals after the Masons'. Wilde was never a member. He lacked purpose, Ives said, noting in his diary, "Well, I shall find out in time, no one can conceal their real nature for ever." When Ives championed Greek love in print, Wilde warned, "When the prurient and impotent attack you, be sure you are right."

HOW IMPORTANT WAS Bosie's role as muse? Writing bitterly from prison, Wilde would have it that Bosie destroyed him as a writer. But the evidence shows that Wilde wrote five plays during their relationship, his most productive period. Bosie promoted Wilde's poetry of concealment, but he was not content to observe genius at work. A greedy, selfish muse, he encouraged Wilde's popular style by driving him to write for money— money to be spent on pleasures far from the writing table. But Wilde's claim in *De Profundis* that he never wrote a single line when they were together, that his life was "sterile and uncreative," is untrue. When John Gielgud met Douglas in later years, the actor was disappointed that of the genesis of *The Importance of Being Earnest* Bosie could tell him only that he had stood at Wilde's shoulder all the time (an exaggeration) he was

---

★In Act One of the original four-act version of *Earnest,* Wilde gave John Worthing the same address as Ives's, making it an insider code; before opening night he changed it to B4. He also deleted a remark by Miss Prism from an early version of Act Two when she says that Ernest must be "as bad as any young man who has chambers in the Albany, or indeed even in the vicinity of Piccadilly, can possibly be."

writing the play at Worthing. A decorative muse furnishes a room and serves a purpose.

When Wilde took rooms to work at St. James's Place, he claimed that Bosie arrived at noon and "stayed smoking cigarettes and chattering till 1:30," when he took him to luncheon at the Café Royal or the Berkeley, which "with its *liqueurs* lasted usually till 3:30." Wilde had an hour to himself while Bosie went to his club, only to reappear at teatime and stay till it was time to dress for dinner at the Savoy or at Tite Street. "We did not separate as a rule till after midnight," Wilde recalled, "as supper at Willis's had to wind up the entrancing day."

If Bosie was not hovering in plain sight, Wilde missed him, as he did at Babbacombe Cliff, when he tried to polish *A Woman of No Importance* in Wonderland. "Things are the wrong colour without gold to light them up," he wrote in March. "Are you working? I hope so. Do get a good crammer. I am rather unhappy as I can't write—I don't know why. Things are all wrong." That Bosie was the supreme, the perfect love of Wilde's life, meddlers such as Ross never understood. Wilde loved the image of the man—not the man. After prison, he admitted that "the mere fact that he wrecked my life makes me love him."

With his Greats examination scheduled for June, Bosie engaged Campbell Dodgson to tutor him at his mother's home in Salisbury. Then Wilde's yearning letter changed the schedule, and they headed for Torquay, announcing their arrival by telegram when they were halfway there. Constance left to visit her aunt in Italy, while Cyril and Vyvyan remained with their father. Wilde wrote Lady Mount-Temple that Cyril was studying French in the nursery but neglected—as he often did—to mention Vyvyan's whereabouts. Designating himself as schoolmaster, Wilde wrote the rules: compulsory hide-and-seek for headmaster, dinner with compulsory champagne, and compulsory reading in bed. ("Any boy found disobeying this rule will be immediately woken up.")

Not much tutoring occurred. Life was "lazy and luxurious," Dodgson recalled, and moral principles "lax." "We argue for hours in favor of different interpretations of Platonism," he said. "We do no logic, no history, but play with pigeons and children and drive by the sea." Of Wilde, he said, "I think him perfectly delightful with the firmest conviction that his morals are detestable." He found Bosie "beautiful and fascinating, but quite wicked." Following Baudelaire's axiom that genius is the ability to be a child at will, Wilde created an atmosphere in which the whole household became children. Bosie said Wilde "exercised a sort of enchantment which transmuted the ordinary things in life and invested them with strangeness and glamour." He told his mother that Wilde was "as simple and innocent as a child."

The carefree laughter of innocence resounded throughout the Cliff. One day there was a bad storm; the wind howled and the sea pounded against the rocks. The mood inside turned black. Something was said or done that set Bosie off on one of his tantrums, followed by his throwing clothes into valises and storming out. At such moments Wilde vowed to end the relationship. These scenes, he told Bosie, "kill me, they wreck the loveliness of life. I cannot listen to your curved lips saying hideous things to me." By the time Bosie calmed down, the train had pulled into Bristol, where he wired his apologies, begging Wilde for forgiveness. These cycles continued, with Bosie trying to prove to himself that he was lovable.

DURING THEIR MARRIAGE, Wilde avoided commiserating with Constance about her unhappy childhood, but Bosie's moods demanded he listen to stories about the horrors of being the youngest son of the Marquess of Queensberry. In 1887 Bosie's mother divorced her husband on grounds of adultery and devoted herself to her three sons, particularly Bosie. Lady Queensberry knew about Wilde and, hoping that the older writer might help her son through Oxford, invited him and Constance to visit her at Bracknell in Surrey.

Bosie's mother was less intimidating than *Earnest*'s Lady Bracknell, but she was her namesake's equal in breeding. Wilde listened as she discussed her son's vanity and extravagance. What Constance thought of being included in a discussion of how to deal with a rebellious undergraduate who monopolized her husband's time can only be imagined. Instilling a positive note, Wilde praised Bosie's poetry. During a time when attention to meter, rhyme, and classical forms was appreciated, Bosie excelled at the sonnet, his greatest skill the songs of youth. The best remembered is "Two Loves," which includes the famous lines

"Unasked by night; I am true Love, I fill
The hearts of boy and girl with mutual flame."
Then sighing, said the other, "Have thy will,
I am the love that dare not speak its name."

One afternoon at the Café Royal, Wilde chanced to meet John Sholto Douglas, whose legendary Scottish title stretched back to the Black Douglas. The marquess was a vocal atheist and amateur light boxer who gave his name to the Queensberry Rules, which conferred on boxing a new era of fairness and respectability. Stocky at five feet eight inches, a beefy boxer at his side as bodyguard, he looked like a lion on the prowl, more at home in the brawling world of the Regency than among well-behaved Victorian lords. Any conduct that he considered unvirile outraged him. Wilde and Bosie had ordered lunch when they sensed him glowering from a nearby table. Invited to join them, he fell under Wilde's charm as they found mutual interests in the sport of fishing and left understanding why Wilde had a reputation as a wit. But it was the last time he allowed positive thoughts to interfere with his plans to rescue his son.

Wilde hated the endless rows with Bosie, but he loved making up. Like many couples who fight and then embrace, they thrived on crises. Wilde told Bosie that his trust that he would always be forgiven was "perhaps the thing in you that I always really liked best, perhaps the best thing in you to like." After vowing mutual affection, Bosie expected a reward, preferably a stay at the Savoy Hotel. "I want everyone to say there goes Oscar Wilde and his boy!" Bosie said when Wilde suggested they use the side door rather than attract attention in the lobby. Built in 1889, the Savoy was London's first luxury hotel, with a view of the Thames and its bridges. It had central heating, twenty-four elevators, seventy bathrooms, and round-the-clock room service. This amenity delighted Bosie, who ordered iced champagne at any hour. The formidable Swiss hotelier César Ritz was general manager. The chef was Auguste Escoffier, who cooked for Napoléon III, created *cuisses de nymphes à l'Aurore* (cold frogs' legs in a Moselle cream jelly flavored with paprika) for the Prince of Wales and *pêches Melba* (poached peaches over vanilla ice cream covered in raspberry purée) for the diva Nellie Melba, and imported American delicacies such as canvasback duck, sweet corn, and Little Neck clams, which Wilde had enjoyed at Delmonico's tables in New York.

In April 1893, Wilde was staying at the Albemarle Hotel when Pierre Louÿs, soon to publish *Les Chansons de Bilitis* (1894), the strongest endorsement of lesbian life since Sappho, visited from Paris.* He was twenty-two and a great success with Wilde's friends, but their indiscreet behavior disturbed him. One evening Constance knocked at the door. Having brought the mail, she begged her husband to come home and see their children. Louÿs was shocked that Wilde could inflict such a humiliation on his wife. With youthful bravado, he made his friendship contingent on Wilde giving up Douglas. Wilde found this absurd. He wrote Ross that he "chose at once the meaner nature and the baser mind." Wilde could love Bosie and Constance at the same time, but he could not divide passion.

WHEN BOSIE DID not appear for his examinations, he was required to remove his name from the Magdalen roster and leave Oxford. He had no regrets; in England a title counted for more than a degree. As Lord Illing- worth tells Gerald in *A Woman of No Importance,* "Examinations are of no value whatsoever. If a man is a gentleman, he knows quite enough, and if he is not a gentleman, whatever he knows is bad for him." A summer of delicious enjoyment lay ahead. Bosie had seen a quaint thatched cottage on the river at Goring-on-Thames, an idyllic village near London, and Wilde rented it. He arrived at the station in a new white suit with his butler Arthur and the underbutler Walter Grainger, who had been a servant at Bosie's Oxford lodgings. The surroundings were serene; the Thames flowed behind the house; even the weather was good. "I have done no work here," Wilde wrote Charles Ricketts. "The river-gods have lured me to devote myself to a Canadian canoe, in which I paddle about. It is curved like a flower." He remained "divided in interest between pad- dling a canoe and planning a comedy." In an expansive mood, he invited

*Louÿs wrote in the voice of a young woman, claiming that he had translated newly discovered Sapphic writing. The second part of *The Songs of Bilitis,* entitled "Elegies at Mytilene," contains the lesbian love poems, including "The Desperate Embrace": "Love me, not with smiles, flutes, or braided flowers, but with your heart and your tears, as I love you with my breast and my lamentations. . . . Moan! Moan! Moan! Oh, woman! Eros draws us into pain. You would suffer less on the bed when bringing a child into the world than when giving birth to your love."

his brother down for the Henley Regatta weekend in July, even sending along a pound note for cigarettes, explaining that "charming people should smoke gold-tipped cigarettes or die." Willie did not join the festivities.

Bosie used Goring as a base to go back and forth to London; he returned with school friends who expected to be entertained. Not surprisingly the tranquillity was shattered with a scene, this time on the croquet lawn. Wilde said they "were spoiling each other's lives" and Bosie was "absolutely ruining" his. Since they could not make each other happy, they should part, a promise Wilde made but never kept. Bosie would hold his hand like "a gentle and penitent child," and their love, Wilde said, "passed through the shadow and the night of estrangement and sorrow and came out rose-crowned as of old."

ON HIS RETURN to Tite Street in November, Wilde secretly wrote to Lady Queensberry to advise her that her youngest son was not in good health and would benefit from a change of climate. There had been another separation. He suggested four or five months in Egypt. Wilde described Bosie's life as "aimless, unhappy and absurd," because of his lack of interest in intellectual pursuits. "I think that if he stays in London he will not come to any good, and may spoil his young life irretrievably, quite irretrievably." Wilde neglected to say that Bosie, who was recklessly consorting with young boys, had been involved in an unpleasant incident that included himself, Ross, and the sixteen-year-old son of an army colonel. Acting on the advice, Lady Queensberry arranged a stay with Lord Cromer, the consul general in Cairo, then a fashionable place for the English to spend the winter. Bosie threatened not to go unless he saw Wilde again and they reconciled, which they did, but Wilde sent no letters to Egypt.

Cairo was a paradise for street boys. Bosie had not been separated from his way of life; he had been delivered to a more exotic version. Before he met any dignitaries, he encountered Reggie Turner, whose half brother, Frank Lawson, had rented a kind of houseboat called a *dehabiyeh*—the word means "thing of gold"—which was moored in the Nile for the winter. Bosie joined them for a trip to Luxor, where they stayed at the Hôtel de Luxor; at dinner, served on long tables, they sat opposite E. F.

Benson, author of the satirical novel *Dodo* and a son of the Archbishop of Canterbury, and Robert Hichens, a music journalist with literary aspirations not yet fulfilled at the age of thirty.

They toured Luxor's temples, walked into the Valley of the Kings, and lounged around the barge on richly upholstered cushions, sipping iced drinks and indolently watching the ancient, silent feluccas drift along the Nile. More than once Bosie invoked Wilde's name. They were in the midst of an exotic world not far removed from the symbolism of the banned *Salomé*. Oscarisms dominated the competitive exchanges. Turner did hilarious imitations of Wilde when he was not inventing provocative closing lines for letters, such as "May Allah ease your urine" and "May heaven bless the sheep that bore the lamb that grew the wool which was woven into the robe of the priest who baptised you." Hichens congratulated himself for falling in with such a stimulating group. When he returned to London, he told Max Beerbohm he was writing a satire on Wilde based on the Nile stories. Max offered to help.

Wilde's silences enraged Bosie so much that he convinced his mother to act as intermediary; she sent Wilde Bosie's address in Athens, where he had gone with Benson en route to Turkey. At Lady Queensberry's urging, Cromer had offered her son a post as honorary attaché to the British ambassador in Constantinople. Bosie wanted Wilde to meet him in Paris, but during the back-and-forth with these arrangements, the ambassador had second thoughts about Douglas joining his staff, and the offer was withdrawn. Bosie appealed to Constance to advance his cause. Wilde telegraphed him: TIME HEALS EVERY WOUND BUT FOR MANY MONTHS TO COME I WILL NEITHER WRITE TO YOU NOR SEE YOU. A week later, after a barrage of telegrams, Wilde and Bosie sat down to order an expensive meal at Voison's in Paris.

NO SOONER WERE they back in London at their favorite haunts than Queensberry, now christened "the Scarlet Marquis" by Wilde, caught them lunching at the Café Royal. The Wildean charm was not as effective this time. If Bosie continued to see Wilde, he would be disowned. "I am not going to try and analyse this intimacy, and I make no charge," Queensberry wrote to his son, "but to my mind to pose as a thing is as bad as to be it. With my own eyes I saw you both in the most loathsome and disgusting relationship as expressed by your manner and expression." Bosie telegraphed back: WHAT A FUNNY LITTLE MAN YOU ARE. An angry reply arrived, followed by a waiver on the allowance, making threats meaningless. The lovers left for a trip to Florence.

The next attack came when Wilde returned to Tite Street. Queensberry arrived unannounced, waving "his small hand in the air in epileptic fury and screaming the loathsome threats he afterwards with such cunning carried out," Wilde told Bosie, who escalated the tension by threatening to shoot his father. "I think if you were dead not many people would miss you," Bosie wrote to him. Wilde watched as the child tormented the lion, waiting for the growl and the bite. "The prospect of a battle in which you would be safe delighted you," Wilde recalled. "I never remember you in higher spirits than you were for the rest of that season."

BEFORE DEPARTING FOR Cairo, Douglas gave one of his old suits to an unemployed clerk named Alfred Wood, whom he had befriended at Oxford. When Wood discovered some letters in the pockets, he realized he had found easy money. Of particular interest was a letter Wilde wrote to Bosie from Babbacombe Cliff: "My Own Boy, Your sonnet is quite lovely, and it is a marvel that those red-leaf lips of yours should have been made no less for music of song than for madness of kisses. Your slim gilt soul walks between passion and poetry. I know Hyacinthus, whom Apollo loved so madly, was you in Greek days." Dorian had received a similar letter, containing such idolatrous words as "the world is changed because you are made of ivory and gold. The curves of your lips rewrite history." As the letter passed from hand to hand, it became known as "the Hyacinth letter."

Wearing Bosie's cast-off suit, Wood met Wilde at the Café Royal in the spring of 1893; they had a drink and afterward dined in a private room at the Florence, a restaurant popular for its two-shilling five-course dinners. That evening, Wilde ordered the champagne supper and eventually presented his guest with a five-pound note. Within days, Wilde learned that Beerbohm Tree had received a copy of the Hyacinth letter. Concerned about bad publicity, Tree advised him to buy the letter back. Wilde would not consent to outright blackmail, so he gave Wood thirty-five pounds, ostensibly to help him emigrate to America. Wood handed over the packet to Wilde, who trustingly put it his pocket, only later discovering that the Hyacinth letter was missing.

An accomplice of Wood's, William Allen, called on Wilde at Tite Street. "I suppose you have come about my beautiful letter to Lord Alfred Douglas," Wilde said. "If you had not been so foolish as to send a copy of it to Mr. Beerbohm Tree, I would gladly have paid you a very large sum of money for the letter, as I consider it to be a work of art." "A very curious construction can be put on that letter," Allen said. "Art is rarely intelligible to the criminal classes," replied Wilde. "A man has offered me sixty pounds for it." "If you will take my advice, you will go to that man and sell my letter to him for sixty pounds. I myself have never received so large a sum for any prose work of that length: but I am glad to find that there is someone in England who considers a letter of mine worth sixty pounds." "The man is out of town." "He is sure to come back," added Wilde.

Finally Allen admitted that he needed money. Wilde gave him half a sovereign with the comment "The letter is a prose poem, will shortly be published in sonnet form in a delightful magazine, and I will send you a copy of it."★ Allen left, and in a few minutes his cohort, Robert Clibborn, appeared at the door and handed Wilde the original of the letter. Wilde examined it and noted that it was soiled. "I think it quite unpardonable that better care was not taken of this original manuscript of mine." Wilde gave him another coin. "I am afraid you are leading a wonderfully wicked life," said Wilde. "There is good and bad in every one of us," said Clibborn. Wilde kept the letter in some safe place, but a copy later surfaced and was read aloud at the Old Bailey.

WHILE HICHENS WORKED on his satire, to be called *The Green Carnation,* a literary publication that would become celebrated was being planned. During the 1890s, the Victorians needed to construct a new world to replace what had existed when Queen Victoria, now ap-

---

★Wilde sensed there might be more trouble and probably asked Pierre Louÿs to turn the letter into a French sonnet. It was published in the *Spirit Lamp,* and Wilde used the defense at his trial that the letter was a work of art.

proaching her diamond jubilee, ascended the throne. The decade has been variously labeled "the Naughty Nineties," "the Yellow Nineties," "the Mauve Decade," and "the Age of Decadence." Wilde and the Yellow Nineties were the most synonymous: yellow was the color of his walls and his wine, the color of sunlight and sunflowers. Lord Henry remarks wistfully in *Dorian Gray* that "yellow satin could console one for all the miseries of life." The color had been favored by Rossetti, Morris, and Burne-Jones. Whistler used yellow in his Japanese paintings. Beardsley painted the walls of his studio yellow with black moldings. But the label "the Yellow Nineties" owes more to the publication and demise of *The Yellow Book* than to any one artist's color sense.

Aubrey Beardsley started the quarterly with Henry Harland and John Lane; all decided to exclude Wilde from participation. They had not forgotten the three-way disagreements over *Salome* and feared more of the same. The new publication appeared in April 1894, bound like a book, with a sense of mission and permanence that impressed the public. The contents page listed such figures as Henry James, Max Beerbohm, Arthur Symons, Richard Garnett, and Edmund Gosse. "A mixture of English rowdyism and French lubricity," *The Times* said. "Have you seen *The Yellow Book*?" Wilde asked Ada Leverson. "It is horrid and not yellow at all." He told Bosie: "It is dull and loathsome: A great failure—I am so glad." When Charles Ricketts tried to praise it, Wilde stopped him and told how he had been trying to "lose" his copy—only to have it continually returned to him by overzealous cabbies and railway guards. It was Beardsley's Decadent style, a reminder of the *Salome* illustrations, that nonetheless linked the book with Wilde. More subdued artists—John Singer Sargent, Wilson Steer, and Sir Frederick Leighton—went unnoticed.

Two months after *The Yellow Book* appeared, the rarest of Wilde's books, *The Sphinx,* a poem in progress since Oxford, was published. Ricketts outdid himself with a beautiful vellum book that allowed the interplay between illustration and text to work like that in a medieval manuscript. He considered the ten full-page drawings, delicate with wavy lines, his best. Wilde complained that the drawings were conceived through his intellect, not his temperament. Ricketts was angry. Not knowing where to lash out, he attacked Wilde's inscription: an aggressive example of his eccentric signature, which ended in a sprawling straight-lined *Z*. Ricketts tore out the page on which it was written and returned it to Wilde. But the *succès de scandale* of Beardsley's illustrations for *Salome* overshadowed *The Sphinx,* and, like *A House of Pomegranates,* it was remaindered. Most of the two hundred first-edition copies, whose entire text was printed in capital letters, went unsold, and those were destroyed in a fire at the Ballantyne Press in 1899.

CHAPTER SEVENTEEN

A Broken Line

❧

*We can have in life but one great experience at best, and the secret of
life is to reproduce that experience as often as possible.*

—THE PICTURE OF DORIAN GRAY

Wilde believed that the imagination shapes reality to its will,
and he lived uneasily with the uncanny ability to write his
life and then live it, authenticating his philosophy that life
imitates art more frequently than art imitates life. He trusted in fortune-
tellers to confirm his sense of destiny; rather than the tarot, he preferred
chiromancy, the ancient art of palmistry, taught by Anaxagoras and practiced by Aristotle. London's foremost chiromancist was Count Louis
Hamon, known as Cheiro, who wrote one of the first textbooks on palmistry and predicted Wilde's fate at a party after the opening of *A Woman of
No Importance* where guests anonymously put their hands through a
curtain. "I little thought when his rather fat hands were passed through
the holes in the curtain that such hands could belong to the most talked
of man in London at that moment," he wrote when Wilde's future was
long past. Wilde's left hand—the hand that records what one is born
with—reflected the nobility and intelligence inherited from his parents;
his right hand—the hand that reveals what one does with that legacy—
showed "brilliance and uninterrupted success." It was the hand of a king,
Cheiro said, but the hand of a king who would send himself into exile.

"At what date?" Wilde asked.

"A few years from now . . . between your forty-first and forty-second year."

Wilde noted the prophecy and left but returned for a private reading. Asked to sign Cheiro's visitors' book, he wrote, "The mystery of the world is the visible, not the invisible," a point made in *Dorian Gray* when Lord Henry remarks to Dorian, "It is only shallow people who do not judge by appearances. The true mystery of the world is the visible, not the invisible." At the next appointment with Cheiro in Half Moon Street, Wilde asked, "Is the break still there?" It was. "But surely," responded Cheiro, "[your] Destiny could not be broken." Wilde replied: "My good friend, you know well Fate does not keep road-menders on her highways."

In July 1894, he consulted Mrs. Robinson, whom he called "the Sibyl of Mortimer Street." She told him that he would take a journey at the beginning of the year but warned, "I see a very brilliant life for you up to a certain point. Then I see a wall. Beyond the wall I see nothing." Wilde thought she might have foreseen Lady Wilde's death. In failing health and bedridden, his mother received daily visits from Constance, who ran errands for her. "Death and Love seem to walk on either hand as I go through life," Wilde told Bosie after visiting his invalid mother. "They are the only things I think of, their wings shadow me."

Willie married for the second time on January 11, 1894, and moved into Oakley Street with his bride, Sophia Lily Lees, a Dublin girl of thirty-six who surrendered a two-thousand-pound dowry by marrying the forty-three-year-old Willie. Wilde's absence from the wedding provoked one of his mother's motivational letters: "I am truly sorry to find that you and Willie meet as enemies. Is this to go on to my death? Not a cheering prospect for me, to have my two sons at enmity, and unable to meet at my deathbed. I think, to please me, you might write the 8 words I asked—'I forget the enmity. Let us be friends. Signed Oscar.' *8 words!* Can you do it to oblige me? There need be no intimacy between you but at least *social civility.*" Wilde replied in *Earnest* with Gwendolen's remark to Cecily: "Now that I come to think of it, I have never heard any man mention his brother. The subject seems distasteful to most men." Wilde never mentioned Willie, but Willie made an avocation of mentioning him.

WILDE WROTE PLAYS to elicit laughter and surprise. No tears. The need to disguise the sexual aspects of his life while revealing emotional truths deepened his plays and opened them up to a wider audience. By expressing emotions subtextually, he rendered them all the stronger. In some way, all of Wilde's characters are dandies. Onstage the dandy is a heterosexual philanderer encoded as a third sex, with the manners and morals to move in or outside society. Wilde was most comfortable in the liminal zone between masculinity and femininity. In the three social comedies leading up to *Earnest,* women are bought and sold, but it is the woman who suffers while the man goes free. His women characters—Mrs. Cheveley, Mrs. Erlynne, Lady Bracknell—chattering away on fashion and behavior, are women acting like men being dandies. By using foundlings, orphans, or mysterious births (Jack Worthing's only proof of birth is a handbag found at Victoria Station), Wilde responded not only to his family background, which included three illegitimate half siblings, but to plotlines from the literature of the time.

During 1894 he worked on a variety of scenarios that he variously completed, left in fragments, or let evaporate in talk. *Salomé* led to scribblings about a biblical drama *La Sainte Courtisane,* subtitled *The Woman Covered with Jewels.* He began work on a more mature blank-verse drama, *A Florentine Tragedy,* imagined *A Woman's Tragedy,* yet another "good woman" play, and jotted down sketches for *Constance.*★ He returned to a medieval drama in *The Cardinal of Avignon,* conceived during the American tour, and sent it off to George Alexander. The questions—Can a man ever be good? Can a woman be anything else?—preoccupied him as he worked on *An Ideal Husband,* with the fateful line "As a rule, everybody turns out to be somebody else."

Wilde did not stay at the St. James's Theatre with Alexander, whom he thought not up to his dandy roles. Despite criticism that Alexander only played himself, he saw each role as an individual challenge and was a far better actor of Wildean parts than Beerbohm Tree. But Wilde balked at Alexander's sincerity and went after the highest bidder. He gave first re-

---

★Wilde wrote the scenario at Worthing while he was working on *Earnest. Constance* starts out as another "good woman" play, but by the end the title character loves another man and has hastened her husband's suicide. Wilde told George Alexander that he wanted "the sheer passion of love to dominate everything." Frank Harris later dramatized Wilde's scenario as *Mr. and Mrs. Daventry.*

fusal to John Hare of the Garrick Theatre, who rejected the script because he did not like the last act. He went to Tree, who was touring America and had leased the Haymarket to Lewis Waller and H. H. Morell. They took the play, originally called *Mrs. Cheveley,* and rehearsals began in December.

An Ideal Husband is an adult fairy tale that has a magic charm—a stolen diamond brooch that leads a double life as a bracelet—and a happy ending, where everyone gets dressed up and walks arm in arm into dinner. Deliciously absurd, morally serious, profoundly sentimental, and wickedly melodramatic, it is primarily a comedy of manners about politics, corruption, and love. It pounds away at a basic hypocrisy of English life: the secret of public success is not to be found out. Wilde finally had the opportunity to show that ideal husbands, like Renaissance silversmiths, can be criminals. This time the man has a past, the woman is an adventuress, and the puritan wife more dangerous than the scheming blackmailer, Mrs. Cheveley, who observes Lady Chiltern's handwriting and says, "The ten commandments in every stroke of the pen!"

Written when Wilde was being blackmailed over the Hyacinth letter and six months before he went to prison, it is a well-made play that satisfies for being so contrived that the audience scarcely notices how subversive it really is. It captures the contradictory essence of its author even more than *Dorian Gray* by introducing the most fully realized of Wilde's pantheon of dandies in the character of Lord Goring. "There is something entertaining in the picture of the rather elderly young fop," one critic noted of the role, "who makes one doubt whether he is a fool with some cleverness and good sense, or a clever fellow who affects folly." The same could be said of Wilde.

Lady Chiltern's husband has made his fortune through a youthful indiscretion that now threatens his marriage. When she learns that he has sold state secrets, she cruelly declares: "One's past is what one is." Wilde did not give her Constance's generosity to love her husband more in adversity. That this error has enabled Sir Robert to have a useful career in public life underscores Wilde's defense of sin on philosophical grounds. But Sir Robert resists being stereotyped. He sees his acceptance of a bribe as a mark of "strength and courage," not weakness. Wilde will not allow him the traditional punishments: poison or pistol or cultivating his garden. Instead he accepts a cabinet position: his treason leads to good, but only through concealment and the threat of retribution. H. G. Wells, a new critic at the *Pall Mall Gazette,* wrote knowingly that Wilde was "working his way to innocence."★

On opening night, January 3, the audience wondered whether Wilde would top his cigarette speech at the premiere of *Lady Windermere's Fan.* Instead he formalized it, with no risks taken. At the curtain call, he bowed and said, "I thank you for the kind attention you have given to my play, and I thank the clever company for its interpretation of this airy familiarity with an audience usually lenient and good natured." Not so good-natured two nights later was Henry James, who sat gloomily in the stalls when he should have been at the St. James's for the opening of his play *Guy Domville.* To appease his nervousness, he decided to condemn *An Ideal Husband* as "so helpless, so crude, so bad, so clumsy, feeble and vulgar."

When James called Wilde "Hosscar," contempt dripped with each hissing sibilant. His dislike for Wilde had not mellowed since their only meeting at a Washington reception during Wilde's American tour in 1882. Exuberant over the publishing success of *The Portrait of a Lady* and *Washington Square,* he mentioned his nostalgia for London. "Really? You care for *places?* The world is my home," Wilde replied. James took it as a rebuff, perhaps a threat to his suspect sexuality. At the mention of Wilde's name, James broke into declamations of him as "a fatuous fool, tenth-rate cad," "an unclean beast," and an "unspeakable animal."

The only form in which James had not excelled was the drama. He saw plays as the novel intensified. Lacking the distinction of "successful playwright," he felt incomplete. As much as he despised Wilde, it was masochistic of him to sit through Wilde's play on his own first night, leaving with the echo of enthusiastic applause, which he said gave the appearance "of complete success" and gave him the "most fearful apprehension." A solitary James walked across St. James's Square, stopping in the middle to ask himself: "How *can* my piece do anything with a public

---

★When Wilde wrote the play, in 1894, Sir Robert's crime referred to Benjamin Disraeli's purchase of shares in the Suez Canal. The Argentine canal project (a speculators' swindle) in which Mrs. Cheveley invests had no counterpart in reality then, but it does now with the Hidrovia waterway scheduled to open up South America's heartland to commerce in 2000. A similar plot was seen in Pinero's 1890 *The Cabinet Minister,* where an unscrupulous financier blackmails the wife of a cabinet minister into giving him inside information about the Rajputana canal project.

with whom *that* is a success?" He arrived at the St. James's for the final curtain of *Guy Domville*. There were cries of "Author! Author!" Hoping for the best, Alexander escorted James onstage, but to the sounds of hoots, jeers, and catcalls. For years afterward James dreamed of hostile faces, white against the dark background of the gallery, screaming at him. He returned to novels and never again wrote for the stage. "I have come," he said, "to *hate* the whole theatrical subject."

Outrage over Wilde's success at his expense never left James. He reveled in the Crown's prosecution during the trials, which he followed with ill-disguised fascination, calling the turn of events "hideously, atrociously dramatic, and really interesting." Wilde's fall, James told Edmund Gosse, "from nearly twenty years of a really unique kind of 'brilliant' conspicuity (wit, 'art,' conversation—'one of our two or three dramatists, etc.') to that sordid prison-cell and this gulf of obscenity over which the ghoulish public hangs and gloats—it is beyond any utterance or irony or any pang of compassion! He was never in the smallest degree interesting to me—but this hideous human history has made him so—in a manner."

IN JULY 1894, Alexander gave Wilde £150 for the right of first refusal on his new farcical comedy. Wilde started work at Worthing, a seaside resort in Sussex, and in only twenty-one days produced the first draft of the wittiest comedy in the English language. Worthing was middle-class and affordable, a lazy place where families sat on wooden benches and strolled along the promenade. Brighton's Georgian diversions were a twenty-minute hansom ride away along the uncobbled Brighton road. The months of August and September passed pleasantly at 5 The Haven, Esplanade, an undistinguished Victorian row house overlooking the beach.

Never before did Wilde write so quickly and easily. As he completed each act in longhand, it was recopied into an exercise book and sent to Mrs. Marshall's Typewriting Office in the Strand. Wilde saw these new establishments as omnivorous beasts eating up pages pushed through the mail slot. To avoid any revelations about the plot's twists and turns (different typists worked on the script), Wilde submitted it under the name of *Lady Lancing: A Serious Comedy for Trivial People* and withheld the crucial last line. Back came a clean draft to be trimmed, tightened, and polished. No one eliminated meaningless words better than Wilde.

His dialogue soars onstage because he understood the importance of timing.

That summer was the last the family spent together. Wilde was astonished to meet the "ugly Swiss governess" who had been caring for Cyril and Vyvyan for a year, an indication of his prolonged absences from Tite Street. Frequent reports reached Bosie. "I have been doing nothing here but bathing and playwriting," Wilde wrote. "My play is really very funny: I am quite delighted with it. But it is not shaped yet. It lies in Sibylline leaves about the room, and Arthur has twice made a chaos of it by 'tidying up.' The result, however, was dramatic." Wilde said the "first act is ingenious, the second beautiful, the third abominably clever." There comes a point when one must stop being someone else and discover who one is—that was *Earnest*'s message.

One day on the beach, a young man named Alphonso Conway helped Wilde launch a boat from the shore. "He led a happy, idle life," Wilde said later when Conway's name came up during his trial. The eighteen-year-old was his companion for six weeks, often seen on the beach with Wilde's sons. Wilde promised to take him on a trip as a token of his appreciation; he bought Conway a blue-serge suit and straw boater and they went to Brighton. Wilde socialized below his class because of the pleasure that came from "being with those who are young, bright, happy, careless, and free. I do not like the sensible and I do not like the old."

Vyvyan, eleven at the time, recalled this Worthing holiday as a happy one. He admired the power of his father's swimming as he "ploughed through the waves in a rough sea like a shark." The boys preferred their father in fanciful moods and liked it when he built sand castles with them. Dressed in a Norfolk jacket, knickerbockers, and a large-brimmed gray hat like the one favored by Walt Whitman, Wilde made a striking barefoot figure as he crawled around his ephemeral property. Vyvyan said his father built "long rambling castles" with "moats and tunnels and towers and battlements, and when they were finished he would usually pull a few lead soldiers out of his pocket to man the castle walls."

WILDE WAS AMAZED to have a book called *The Green Carnation* land on his desk at Worthing. The anonymous author was Robert Hichens, who had listened well to tales told about Wilde during the Nile cruise with Bosie and Reggie. Wilde appreciated its humor as a satire, since he was one of the presumed authors, along with his friend Ada Leverson, the novelist Marie Corelli, and Alfred Austin, soon to follow Tennyson as poet laureate. Turning rumors to his advantage, he denied authorship. "I invented that magnificent flower," he wrote to the *Pall Mall Gazette*. "But with the middle-class and mediocre book that usurps its strangely beautiful name I have, I need hardly say, nothing whatsoever to do. The flower is a work of art. The book is not." Queensberry read the novel with distaste.

Hichens put on record Wilde's homosexual life in the obvious relationship between Esmé Amarinth (Wilde) and Lord Reggie Hastings (Turner with a patina of Douglas). Amarinth talks brilliantly in Wilde's epigrammatic style, and Lord Reggie mesmerizes a choirboy with his green carnation buttonhole. Imitating the style of *Dorian Gray,* the novel came perilously close to depicting living people in a libelous manner. In one of its lighter moods, *The Athenaeum* suggested that with lines such as "I love drinking Bovril in secret. It seems like a vice," the novel was "apparently an elaborate advertisement" for the beef-soup base. Two weeks later it reported that the "Bovril Company informs us that it had nothing to do with the writing of *The Green Carnation,* so that the object of the writer in producing so silly a book seems unexplained."*

The Green Carnation had been a welcome interruption, an excuse to write a letter to the editor, one of Wilde's favorite amusements. Returning to *Earnest,* he edited and added coded references to homosexuality. Most of the audience did not know that "earnest" was Victorian slang for homosexuality ("Is he earnest?" was a familiar question). Introduced into the subculture in 1892, three years before Wilde's play, the pun appears in a volume of sonnets entitled *Love in Earnest* by the young schoolmaster John Gambril Nicholson. *Cecily* was a word used for rent boys. *Bunburyism,* which concealed a lewd pun, meant an alibi indicating the double life necessary for seeking forbidden pleasure. The word *shame* was open to interpretation. Bosie's poem "In Praise of Shame" includes the line "Of all sweet passions Shame is loveliest."

Much attention is paid to food, particularly food eaten by men. In one of Wilde's better gender paradoxes, Gwendolen praises her father for con-

---

*In an early draft of *Earnest,* Wilde has Lady Brancaster (later Bracknell) look at a book called *The Green Carnation* and pronounce it "a morbid and middle-class affair."

ceding that a man's place is in the home and that public affairs may be safely entrusted to women: "The home seems to me to be the proper sphere for the man. And certainly once a man begins to neglect his domestic duties he becomes painfully effeminate, does he not? And I don't like that. It makes men so very attractive." Wilde's art of inversion reaches a comic high when Algy becomes Bunbury; Jack becomes Ernest; women read philosophy; and men eat dainty cucumber sandwiches.

Bosie arrived in Worthing, sneered at the surroundings, and made clear that it was not up to his standards. Constance and the children returned to London, and Wilde took him to the Grand Hotel overlooking the Brighton pier. The chill October weather led to a bad case of influenza, and Bosie took to his bed, sulking. Wilde nursed him until he felt better and they moved to less expensive lodgings. When Wilde fell ill, Bosie turned away, disgusted with his snuffling and sneezing. Bosie complained when Wilde did not feel well enough to go out on the town, escalating a tantrum delivered in full force the next morning. "When you are not on your pedestal you are not interesting," he screamed and left for the Grand. "The next time you are ill I will go away at once." It was Wilde's fortieth birthday.

Wilde returned to London three days later, determined to end the relationship. He picked up the newspaper and read that Bosie's brother Drumlanrig had been killed in a gun explosion. Suicide was suspected because of threatened revelations of a homosexual relationship with Lord Rosebery, the foreign minister (soon to be prime minister), for whom Drumlanrig was a private secretary. This tragedy, Wilde wrote to Ives, was "the first noble sorrow" of Bosie's life, and he had to be "the sharer of his pain." He rushed to Bosie's side, all bad behavior forgiven. The incident convinced Queensberry not to let scandalous gossip touch another son.

MEANWHILE, WILDE LIVED with palpable tension and mounting debts. He had outstanding bills at several hotels and owed hundreds of pounds for cigarettes and the silver cases he handed out as gifts. "I am sorry my life is so marred and maimed by extravagance," he told Alexander. "But I cannot live otherwise. I, at any rate, pay the penalty of suffering." In October, Wilde sent Alexander the polished first draft of *Earnest,* asking for an advance; when the actor noticed that there was no leading role for him, he rejected the four-act version. The parts "are equally good," Wilde told him, the "plot is slight, but I think, adequate" with "lots of fun and wit." Elisabeth Marbury, who had sold a first option in America for three hundred pounds to Charles Frohman, had the right idea about the play. "I think it would be a mistake for you to sell outright," she said, "because it really seems to me that this piece will make some money for you."

When *Guy Domville* folded after thirty-one performances, Alexander felt differently about *Earnest* and set out to create his play by collapsing four acts into three. Minor characters disappeared; one scene was eliminated and others shortened. Jack Worthing became a romantic role, more likable and less cynical, more suitable for Alexander. With the hilarious Gribsby scene from Act Two (when the solicitor Gribsby arrives to arrest Algy for nonpayment of debts) chopped off, the play's trivial center was strengthened. "This scene that you feel is superfluous," Wilde tersely told Alexander, "cost me terrible exhausting labour and heart-rending nerve-racking strain. You may not believe me, but I assure you on my honour that it must have taken fully five minutes to write." Rehearsals did not go smoothly; there were too many revisions to be smoothed out. An exasperated Alexander begged Wilde to get out of town: "I'll send you a box for the first night and see you again after the performance."

CAIRO WAS WILDE'S choice, but Bosie demanded Algeria, where Lord Henry and Dorian had gone for the beautiful Arab boys. "I fly to Algiers with Bosie tomorrow," Wilde nonchalantly told Ada Leverson. "I begged him to let me stay to rehearse, but so beautiful is his nature that he declined at once." By 1895 Algeria had become a fashionable winter destination in tandem with Egypt. Although it offered none of the great monuments of antiquity, it had oasis resorts like Biskra, where André Gide and a friend had spent the previous winter, and Blida, the walled city known as "the desert rose," aromatic with the fragrance of orange and lemon groves. In the Arab quarter, with its teeming souks and suggestive smells of spices, sweat, and dung, an exotic world awaited male visitors. The Kabyle boys showed their availability by scrambling up the men's trousers.

Wilde and Bosie registered at the Grand Hôtel d'Orient in Blida. Gide had been there for some days but found the January grayness too depressing and planned to move to Biskra. He was paying his bill when he glanced at the slate on which the names of guests were written in chalk and noted the new arrivals. Impulsively, he erased his name from the top of the list but reconsidered his decision halfway to the rail station. What good could come from such a snub, Gide reasoned, and admonished himself for being so intimidated. He returned to the hotel and read *Barnaby Rudge* in the lobby until Wilde and Bosie returned from their walk.

It had been two years since Gide and Wilde had talked at length in Paris. Gide found him changed. "One felt less softness in his look," he recalled, "something raucous in his laughter and something frenzied in his joy. He seemed both more sure of pleasing and less ambitious to succeed in doing so; he was bolder, stronger, bigger." Since Paris, when Wilde's taunting of his monastic attitudes had panicked him, Gide had recognized his own bisexuality but practiced homosexuality more surreptitiously than Wilde.

On one walk outside the walls, Wilde confided to Gide the sorry state he was in with Queensberry. Gide advised prudence. "Prudence!" Wilde exclaimed. "But can I have any? That would be going backwards. I must go as far as possible. . . . I cannot go further. . . . Something must happen . . . something else." Wilde changed the subject and memorably asked: "Would you like to know the great drama of my life? It's that I've put my genius into my life; I've put only my talent into my works." They entered the native quarter, and Wilde strode purposefully around until he found a suitable guide and asked to see some Arab boys "as beautiful as bronze statues." "I hope to have quite demoralized this city," he told Gide.

Ross received a letter extolling hashish—"quite exquisite: three puffs of smoke and then peace and love"—and the boys—"the beggars here have profiles so the problem of poverty is easily solved." Bosie shocked Gide by announcing, "I hope you're like me. . . . I only like boys." The evening provided only a café fight, and Gide set off to Algiers the next morning. "It's impossible to gauge what is the young Lord's intrinsic worth," he wrote his mother. "Wilde seems to have corrupted him to the very marrow of his bones." Bosie's dreamy demeanor made it difficult for others to see him as a debaucher.

Alone with Gide in Algiers—Bosie stayed in Blida to be with a young boy—Wilde arranged an evening in a Moorish café known for its music and its enticing waiters, one of whom joined them and began to play the flute. Transfixed by the sounds and the boy's gentle movements, Gide watched silently until Wilde motioned for them to leave. Outside there was a conference with the guide. Wilde asked Gide if he would like the flutist. Gide could barely utter "Yes." Wilde assumed that he had arranged for Gide's initiation.* In his autobiography, *Si le grain ne meurt,* Gide noted that the "great pleasure of the debauched is to lead others to debauchery." Offering no explanations, Wilde led Gide to the European bar of the Oasis Hotel, where they drank until an appointed hour and left to meet the guide at a small hotel. Wilde produced a key, Gide entered the room, and the guide appeared with the flute player, with whom Gide boasted he took his pleasure five times and was disappointed when the boy was not impressed.

THE NEXT MORNING Wilde began an arduous and lonely journey back to London. There had been many rows on this trip. Because he was preoccupied with the opening of *Earnest,* Wilde's enthusiasm for sexual conquest had not matched that of Bosie, who decided to stay on with a beguiling coffee server named Ali. It was snowing when Wilde departed; no one was there to say good-bye or wish him success for *Earnest's* opening night. His ferry across the Mediterranean was delayed for twenty hours. He had time to ponder the truth of his remark that "there is no such thing as changing one's life, one merely wanders round and round within the circle of one's own personality."

For the past two years, when Wilde lived in rooms or hotels, he returned infrequently to Tite Street. He missed Cyril and Vyvyan but was weary of lying to his wife. The positive attitude Constance maintained toward her marriage cannot be explained by traditional concepts of wifely love. Her devotion transcended the usual marital loyalties. During

---

*By Gide's own account, he actually lost his virginity to a boy at the end of 1893 in Sousse in Tunisia and the next year had his first heterosexual experience with a prostitute in Biskra.

their engagement, she had pledged to love her husband with such devotion that he would never leave or love anyone else as long as she could love and comfort him. That she had done and in all likelihood would have continued; in her mind, loving the sinner was more important than the sinner's transgressions.

Cyril and Vyvyan were both in school, beyond intensive mothering. Constance regularly visited her mother-in-law, who suffered from all the aches and pains that beleaguer a woman of seventy-three. She helped the working poor, particularly women with small children, through the Chelsea Women's Liberal Association. She had given up the editorship of *The Gazette* for the Rational Dress Society but maintained a relationship with the manager of Hatchard's, a popular Piccadilly bookstore that published the magazine. His name was Arthur Lee Humphreys; he was six years her junior and married.

They were brought together again in the summer of 1894 through a proposal made by Wilde. After reading *The Green Carnation,* he decided to curb fictional characters speaking like him. It was time to copyright his words. Wilde asked Constance to collate a selection of epigrams and sayings and gave Humphreys permission to quote from the copyrighted material for fifty pounds. (Later in the year, "A Few Maxims for the Instruction of the Over-Educated" appeared in *The Saturday Review* and "Phrases and Philosophies for the Use of the Young in *The Chameleon.*)

Wilde was at Worthing preoccupied with *Earnest* and Bosie and did not see Constance's choices until they were set in type. He wrote Humphreys that the book is "so bad, so disappointing, that I am writing a set of new aphorisms, and will have to alter much of the printed matter. The plays are particularly badly done. . . . After the *Green Carnation* publication, this book of 'real Oscar Wilde' should be refined and distinguished: else, it will look like a bit of journalism." Fifty copies of *Oscariana,* the first of many volumes of Wilde's sayings, appeared in January 1895, and another edition was released in May. Wilde must have been pleased, for he sent Humphreys a ticket for the first night of *Earnest*. And Constance fell in love with Humphreys.

His affection can only be surmised from Constance's few letters to him in which she unburdened herself. She had adored her father, who abandoned her, as much as she adored Wilde. In his position as a prominent bookseller, Humphreys would have heard gossip about Wilde and his young boys; he was wise enough to understand that when Constance spoke of her parents, she spoke also of herself. She wrote Humphreys that she had "stepped past the limits perhaps of good taste in the wish to be your friend and to have you for my friend. I spoke to you very openly about myself, & I confess that I should not like you to repeat what I said about my childhood." Talking about his marriage was a way to show dissatisfaction with her own. Constance told him she thought him an "ideal husband" and emphasized the point by writing that he was not only an ideal husband but "not far short of being an ideal man!" She continued, "I liked you & was interested in you, & I saw that you were good, and it is rarely that I come across a man that has that written in his face."

Constance wanted to worship her husband, but he eluded her. Humphreys did not. "I am the most truthful person in the world," she wrote, "also I am intuitive, and it is perfectly true that after I parted from you yesterday I knew as clearly as I do to-day that you stand on a pinnacle high above me, and that your marriage was made for the sake of good, was the result of your character, and so was ideal." Another letter beginning "My Darling Arthur" and ending "Your always devotedly loving Constance" declares "how much I love you, and how dear and delightful you have been to me today. I *have* been happy, and I *do* love you dear Arthur. Nothing in my life has ever made me so happy as this love of yours to me has done. . . . I love you just because you ARE, and because you have come into my life to fill it with love and make it rich." Constance thanks him for being "dear to the children, and nice to Oscar too."

They often met at the London Library. Following one conversation about the low minimum wage of sixpence an hour, she wrote that they "must not talk of subjects that we do not agree upon. You have a very strong nature, and it is perhaps natural that you should have no sympathy with the unfortunate of the world." She asks that they do not "speak of it again; it is a subject—that I feel most deeply on, and that is not serious to you." Brief though this affair would have been, since Constance soon injured her back and Wilde's trials became the center of her emotional life, it is pleasant to think of these two arguing about labor issues on a park bench, embracing, then going their separate ways. Now Mrs. Oscar Wilde had her own intimate secret.

PART FIVE
(1895–1900)

Reconciling

Some kill their love when they are young,
    And some when they are old:
Some strangle with the hands of Lust,
    Some with the hands of Gold:
The kindest use a knife, because
    The dead so soon grow cold.

Some love too little, some too long,
    Some sell, and others buy;
Some do the deed with many tears,
    And some without a sigh:
For each man kills the thing he loves,
    Yet each man does not die.

    —The Ballad of Reading Gaol

CHAPTER EIGHTEEN

The Last First Night

❧

ALGERNON: A man who marries without knowing Bunbury has a very tedious time of it.

JACK: That is nonsense. If I marry a charming girl like Gwendolen, and she is the only girl I ever saw in my life that I would marry, I certainly won't want to know Bunbury.

ALGERNON: Then your wife will. You don't seem to realize, that in married life three is company and two is none.

—*THE IMPORTANCE OF BEING EARNEST*

On February 14, the first night of *The Importance of Being Earnest,* London had one of its infrequent snowstorms. The weather provoked as much comment as Wilde's play. Early morning flurries dusted the city, then turned to windswept snow by early evening, when skittish horses drawing broughams, hansoms, and bespoke carriages crowded into narrow King Street and the entrance of the St. James's Theatre. Young men wore buttonholes of lilies of the valley. An enthusiastic crowd hailed Wilde's arrival with Constance on his arm. Asked if he thought the play would be a success, the author replied, "The play *is* a success. The only question is whether the first night's audience will be one."

At nine o'clock, having shed damp wraps and capes, the audience impatiently waited for the curtain, which rose fifteen minutes late. Observing Aubrey Beardsley seated in a box with his sister, Wilde said:

"Mabel a daisy, Aubrey the most monstrous of orchids." A dutiful, hard-working, puritanical—in short, earnest—audience saw a play in which earnestness is trivialized and the name Ernest taken seriously (Cecily and Gwendolen will only marry a man named Ernest). A farce should be a mosaic, a friend told Wilde. "No," he contradicted, "it must be like a pistol shot." Sir John Gielgud, who played Jack Worthing many times, said the play is like chamber music. The punning last line withheld from Strand typists brought down the house. Lady Bracknell accuses Jack of "display-ing signs of triviality," to which Jack responds, "On the contrary, Aunt Augusta, I've now realised for the first time in my life the Importance of Being Earnest." (Wilde added *vital* before *Importance* in 1899, when the play was first published.)

Wilde took a curtain call with Alexander but made no speech. He had stunned the audience after *Lady Windermere's Fan,* been silent after *A Woman of No Importance,* and humble after *An Ideal Husband.* There was nothing more to say. He found Alexander in his dressing room. "Well, wasn't I right? What did you think of it?" the actor asked. Wilde's ironic gaze commanded silence until he replied: "My dear Aleck, it was charm-ing, quite charming. And, do you know, from time to time I was reminded of a play I once wrote myself, called *The Importance of Being Earnest.*" H. G. Wells and George Bernard Shaw were amused, but Shaw thought the play insignificant. William Archer worried that it raised no moral prin-ciples except the author's witty personality.★

Few knew of the backstage drama. Responding to rumors that Queensberry planned to address the audience about his son's relationship with Wilde, Alexander called the police and canceled Queensberry's ticket. It was said that he arrived with a bundle of turnips and carrots, which he hurled at the backstage door when security officers barred him from entering the lobby. Wilde wrote Bosie that his father had "left a grotesque bouquet of vegetables for me! I had all Scotland Yard—twenty police—to guard the theatre. He prowled about for three hours, then left

★The four-act play was forgotten. Charles Frohman, who had both versions, used the London text when he opened in New York at the Empire Theatre on April 22, and this became the revival standard. It was not until November 15, 1985, that the original version was staged at John Carroll University, a Jesuit university in Cleveland, Ohio.

chattering like a monstrous ape." Wilde was touched that Bosie rushed home, even though his eagerness had more to do with wanting filial revenge than with concern over Wilde's reputation.

WILDE CONSULTED HIS solicitor in May and again in July 1894 to discuss what steps could be taken to stop Queensberry's harassment. Wilde considered Queensberry's invasion of his private home, when he "stood uttering every foul word his foul mind could think of," and his public display at *Earnest*'s premiere sufficient grounds for legal action. But there had to be witnesses. Prosecution was impossible without the testimony of George Alexander and his staff. At the same time, Queensberry brought Wilde's suggestive letters to his solicitor, asking what he could do, and was told nothing.

Planning his next move, Queensberry prowled about Wilde's favorite restaurants looking for him. His emotional state was precarious. Not only had he been agitated by thoughts of homosexual conspiracies since his elder son's suicide but he was also mortified by the recent annulment of his brief second marriage for reasons of impotence. He hated his father-in-law, the effeminate Alfred Montgomery, and was convinced that his first wife's family had passed homosexual traits on to their sons.

At the Avondale Hotel, Wilde's grip on reality was no better. He refused Bosie's whim to invite a young boy to stay at the hotel. Bosie stormed out, stranding him with a £140 bill. Wilde considered fleeing to Paris, but the hotel had impounded his luggage. On February 28, he went to the Albemarle Club on Dover Street to collect his mail. The hall porter handed him an envelope with a calling card left ten days earlier by Queensberry on which the porter had noted the exact date and time. Wilde turned the card over and over, inspecting each side, calculating the date, then glancing at the porter, who obviously had read the message. The handwriting was difficult to decipher. Did it say: "To Oscar Wilde, posing as a somdomite [*sic*]"? Or "To Oscar Wilde, posing somdomite"? Was the marquess's misspelling deliberate, hasty, or in ignorance? Wilde now had evidence of probable libel.

Before communicating with Bosie, he wrote Ross. "I don't see anything now but a criminal prosecution," he said. "My whole life seems ruined by this man. The tower of ivory is assailed by the foul thing. On the sand is my life split." Ross and others advised him to ignore the card, tear it up, and leave for Paris. Wilde would not be swayed; he wanted his life back. Going to court seemed the only way. Once he put "into motion the forces of Society," he said, "Society turned on me and said, 'Have you been living all this time in defiance of my laws, and do you now appeal to these laws for protection? You shall have these laws exercised to the full. You shall abide by which you have appealed to.' "

Events moved quickly. Wilde telegraphed the headmaster of Cyril's school, canceling plans for his son to come home. He met with Constance and told her that he was not a "posing sodomite" and there was no justification for Queensberry's libel. There was no reason in Wilde's mind because he was not pretending to be a homosexual—he was one. His wife never doubted him and wanted to help despite her ill health. During the summer, when Wilde had been in Brighton with Bosie, Constance had injured her back in a fall down the stairs at Tite Street. Lady Mount-Temple invited her to Babbacombe Cliff to recuperate, but she was overdrawn at the bank and had no funds to travel. She had to plead with Ross to locate her husband and ask him for money. Now, with Wilde's decision to sue, the couple were reunited but under crisis circumstances.

AT THE MARLBOROUGH Police Court on March 1, Wilde swore out a warrant for the arrest of the Marquess of Queensberry on the charge of publishing a libel against him. Confident that his father soon would be punished for an innocent libel, Bosie pledged that his mother and brother would pay Wilde's court costs. Wilde sat in his solicitor's office and told, as he later recalled, "serious lies to a bald man," C. O. Humphreys, his legal adviser by default. His own solicitor, George Lewis, who had made Bosie's blackmail problems at Oxford disappear, had been preempted by Queensberry. Asked by Humphreys if there was any basis to the charges, Wilde denied everything.

Humphreys persuaded the eloquent Sir Edward Clarke to be Wilde's barrister; the eventuality of rent boys testifying against his client never occurred to him. Lewis withdrew from the case out of friendship for Wilde and was replaced by Charles Russell and the barrister Edward

Carson. A fellow student of Wilde's from Trinity, Carson was convinced to take the case only when he saw the damaging dossier collected on Wilde's relationships. "No doubt he will perform his task with the added bitterness of an old friend," Wilde remarked.

At this difficult time, Bosie goaded Wilde into taking him to Monte Carlo, where he neglected him in favor of losing his money at the casino. Wilde had time to reflect on his situation but did not waver in his decision when he returned to London, the holiday cut short because the two were recognized and asked to leave the hotel. The impending libel trial had attracted the attention of the European press.

On March 23, Wilde consulted Frank Harris and arranged to meet him the following day at the Café Royal, where Harris was lunching with George Bernard Shaw. By the time Wilde arrived, Harris and Shaw had concluded their business. Shaw, who barely knew Wilde and had never met Bosie, ended up witnessing a crucial scene in Wilde's downfall.

Wilde asked Harris to be a literary expert and testify as to the artistic merit of *Dorian Gray*. Harris ignored the request and launched into the reasons why Wilde should drop the libel action and flee to France until all was forgotten. Into the fray strode Bosie, uninvited and worried that antagonistic forces were working against him. Wilde tried to convince Harris that if Bosie swore to the brutishness of his father, all would be well. Harris correctly argued that a son's views on his father were irrelevant to the libel against Wilde. A bemused Shaw nodded in agreement. Infuriated, Wilde attacked Harris for not supporting him. "It is not friendly of you, Frank. It really is not friendly," he said and turned his back on the Café Royal forever.

All his life he had wanted to do something unequivocal. He was the bravest of men in his refusal to pretend to be other than what he was and in his insistence that he would not run away. Unwilling "to be dogged by a maniac" and secretly wanting a platform to justify the right of the artist to live as he wanted, Wilde saw that the central conflict—as in his plays—was between the individual and society. In the tradition of Baudelaire and Zola, he wanted his day in court, wrongly assuming that his personality, not his private sex life, would be the center of attention. The marquess entered a plea of justification, which ran to thirteen counts of "acts of gross indecency." Two additional counts addressed the alleged immorality of *Dorian Gray* and the maxims published in *The Chameleon*.

THE LIBEL TRIAL opened at the Central Criminal Court, known as the Old Bailey, on April 3, 1895, and lasted three days. The small public gallery was filled with men. No women queued for admittance. Though Wilde was the prosecutor, it was evident that he was the one on trial. Clarke, who grew in confidence through three trials, made the opening speech, defending Wilde's reputation. He described the Hyacinth letter, which he rightly assumed would be brought up by the defense, as a prose sonnet and stressed that its interpretation had nothing to do with the plea in question. Bosie was not called as a witness; the only witness beyond the Albemarle Club's porter, to whom the libel was published, was Wilde, who, in an unconscious slip into vanity, identified himself as thirty-nine years old. Carson, who made his reputation in this so-called trial of the century, looked sharply at his old classmate and made a notation. Carson knew Wilde to be forty and used the fact that he had lied to undermine his credibility as a witness.

Brilliantly setting the tone of the cross-examination with his first question, Carson said: "You stated that your age was thirty-nine. I think you are over forty. You were born on the sixteenth of October 1854?" Then Carson held up a copy of Wilde's birth certificate. "I have no wish to pose as being young," Wilde replied, smiling at the double meaning. "You have my certificate and that settles the matter." "But being born in 1854 makes you more than forty?" Carson persisted. "Ah! Very well." Wilde sighed and allowed Carson the satisfaction of doing simple mathematics.

Now Carson could emphasize how much older Wilde was than Bosie—his lover had been twenty and Wilde thirty-six when they met—and the young men whose names were introduced. Ultimately, it was as a malicious seducer of youth and a man who shamelessly corrupted the boundaries between the classes by giving street boys champagne dinners and cigarette cases that Wilde was made to seem the most dangerous to the public, although none of the boys mentioned was under the statutory age of sixteen.

Carson went on to analyze *Dorian Gray,* probing for its homosexual content, hoping to prove Wilde an immoral author, putting him in the awkward situation of defending dialogue he had written for fictional characters. Wilde answered too wittily when he should have kept the examination to a discussion of literary and aesthetic issues. Carson read aloud a piece of verse from one of Wilde's articles and asked whether Wilde was the author. Wilde considered the question. There was a prolonged pause. "Ah no, Mr. Carson, Shakespeare wrote that." Having bested his former school friend, Wilde forgot that he was in the witness box. Carson read another piece of verse and asked, "And I suppose Shakespeare wrote that also, Mr. Wilde?" "Not as you read it, Mr. Carson," Wilde replied and turned his back on the noise, arms folded over his chest, staring at the ceiling. The judge ordered silence and threatened to clear the courtroom.

The game was afoot. Carson would not be humiliated again. He poked and probed at Wilde's contradictory elitism, questioning his friendships with what Carson termed shiftless and homeless boys. The Hyacinth letter, stolen and retrieved for thirty-five pounds, returned to haunt Wilde. Denying any improper behavior, he invoked artistic freedom in his choice of enjoying the company of unsavory young men and writing poetic letters. On the second day, Carson resumed his cross-examination by asking questions about Alfred Taylor, alleged to have introduced Wilde to young men at his Little College Street rooms. Wilde said he was unaware of any such connections, describing Taylor as "a man of great taste and intelligence" who "was brought up at a good English school." Carson interrogated Wilde on all the boys who had given pretrial depositions: the Parker brothers, Fred Atkins, Ernest Scarfe, Sidney Mavor. Then he introduced the name of Walter Grainger, a former servant of Douglas, who was hired as underbutler at Worthing. Wilde admitted knowing him but said he had never dined with him as he had the others.

"Did you ever kiss him?" Carson asked. Wilde was caught off-guard. "Oh, dear, no," he replied. "He was a peculiarly plain boy. He was unfortunately extremely ugly. I pitied him for it."

> Carson: Was that the reason you did not kiss him?
> Wilde: Oh, Mr. Carson: you are pertinently insolent.
> Carson: Did you say that in support of your statement that you never kissed him?
> Wilde: No. It is a childish question.
> Carson: Did you ever put forward a reason why you never kissed the boy?

Wilde: Not at all.

Carson: Why, sir, did you mention that this boy is
   extremely ugly?

Wilde: For this reason. If I were asked why I did not kiss a
   door-mat I would say because I do not like to kiss
   door-mats.

Carson hammered away at the question: "Why did you mention his ugliness?" His harangue had Wilde confused. He started but never completed sentences; finally, he addressed his former classmate with the tone of an injured child: "You sting me and insult me and try to unnerve me—and at times one says things flippantly when one ought to speak more seriously I admit it."

"Then you said it flippantly?" Carson asked.

"Oh, yes," Wilde said, "it was a flippant answer."

The implication that he would have kissed the boy if he had been attractive destroyed Wilde's case against Queensberry. The outburst authenticated the relationship between Aestheticism and sexual appetite, even as Wilde had pretended that the two had nothing in common.

CLARKE'S ONLY REBUTTAL was the contents of Queensberry's insulting letters, which included a malicious passage that hinted at Bosie's illegitimacy. Introducing the letters was a mistake, for they revealed the irrational mind of the marquess and inadvertently put into the record—and into the newspapers—the names of Rosebery and Gladstone and made Wilde a scapegoat for homosexual rumors about Rosebery. Any hope that the establishment would intervene to aid Wilde's acquittal was lost.

By introducing the letters, Clarke gave Carson the right to cross-examine Wilde again. Clarke had a premonition that his client had been less than truthful when Wilde, realizing his vulnerability, asked if Carson could question him about an incident when he and a boy were turned out of the Albemarle Hotel in the middle of the night. At this point Clarke rested his case for the Crown. For the defense, Carson stressed that Queensberry only wanted to free his son from Wilde's immoral influence. Then, in a surprise move, Carson announced that he was going to bring forward the young men named in the plea of justification, who would testify to indecent acts with Wilde.

Clarke advised Wilde to withdraw and consent to the charge and told him he hoped he would leave the country before he was arrested. Wilde would not abscond like a common criminal, but on the morning of April 5 he was not in court for the finale. As Carson read out the already familiar names of those who would be called to testify, Clarke tugged on the barrister's black cloak. A bewigged head looked down. The case was over. Carson insisted on the whole plea, and Wilde accepted that Queensberry was entitled to call him a posing sodomite in the public interest. At the judge's instruction, the jury returned a verdict of not guilty. Queensberry made sure that the rent boys' statements not used in the libel trial reached prosecutors. "If the country allows you to leave," he wrote Wilde, "all the better for the country! But, if you take my son with you, I will follow you wherever you go and shoot you!"

WILDE LEFT THE Old Bailey for the Cadogan Hotel in Chelsea accompanied by Ross and Bosie, who had been in court every day. He knew that he would be arrested, but then again he might not. He sat slouched in his chair, mesmerized, sipping hock and seltzer, a half-packed suitcase on the bed. Ross saw Constance, who had been unaware of her husband's double life until the libel trial, and told her the situation. "I hope Oscar is going away abroad," she said.

But Wilde had an intractable nature. While others argued over his future, he ordered more to drink, repeating that he would stay and serve whatever sentence he was given. The arrest warrant, requested from the Bow Street magistrate at 3:30 P.M., was not issued until 5:00, when it was too late for the last boat train to France. The delay was either deliberate, to allow Wilde to leave quietly, or the result of bureaucratic paper handling. Shortly after 6:00 the men from Scotland Yard knocked on the door of Room 53. Wilde put on his overcoat, picked up his gloves along with a yellow-bound French paperback novel, and left Sloane Square to be booked. Newspaper headlines reported that he was arrested with a "Yellow Book under his arm," wrongly assumed to be *The Yellow Book*. Wilde made it notorious without ever having published a word in it.

Was another trial necessary? An argument has been made that

Queensberry convinced the government to prosecute Wilde by threatening to implicate Lord Rosebery. Even without that incentive, the prosecutors were within the law to continue the case based on the evidence not
presented. Wilde always said that one should be careful in one's choice of
enemies. Through years of posturing, he had more than his share of jealous rivals. Surprisingly, the one to seek revenge was a minor actor named
Charles Brookfield, who held a grudge over a flippant remark Wilde had
made about his keeping his gloves on at a tea party and wearing the wrong
kind of suit off the stage. In 1892 Brookfield had collaborated with J. M.
Glover on the musical parody of *Lady Windermere's Fan* called *The Poet and
the Puppets,* which Wilde tolerated in his good-natured way, always pleased
with attention even if hostile.

Two years later Brookfield took the role of Lord Goring's servant in
An Ideal Husband, explaining that he did not want to learn many of
Wilde's lines. During rehearsals Wilde insisted that the cast work on
Christmas Day. Brookfield protested. "Don't you keep Christmas, Oscar?"
he asked. "No, Brookfield," replied Wilde, "the only festival of the Church
I keep is Septuagesima. Do you keep Septuagesima, Brookfield?" "Not
since I was a boy." "Ah, be a boy again," said Wilde.

When the libel trial was announced, Brookfield volunteered to collect
evidence against Wilde and celebrated Queensberry's not guilty verdict at
a party following his performance in Wilde's play. (A final irony, Brookfield was made examiner of plays in 1912.)

WILDE ENTERED THE prisoner's dock on April 26 charged with the
commission of acts of gross indecency in private with members of his
own sex. Under the 1885 Labouchere Amendment, conviction carried
the maximum sentence of two years' imprisonment. Creating the first
non-religious category for such sexual offenses, this amendment shifted
the focus of the law from sodomy—a crime based on a specific act—to a
crime against gender. Technically, Wilde was never on trial for sodomizing
boys; he was tried for violations against the male sex. His trial tested not
only the standards of indecent acts between men but the extent to which
private sexual behavior could become publicly regulated. He walked into
the Old Bailey a sodomite under the old law and emerged a newly
defined homosexual.

Denied bail, he spent two weeks in Holloway Prison, shuttling back and forth to Bow Street court for hearings, until his criminal trial opened. In *Earnest's* Gribsby scene, Jack complains about being imprisoned in Holloway because it is in the suburbs. Gribsby assures him that, although middle class, it is "fashionable and well-aired." The papers described it during Wilde's stay as "dirty, dingy, damp and unwholesome . . . hardly fit for a cat to live in."

Bosie visited Wilde daily until the day before the trial, when Clarke advised him to leave for France and avoid the risk of being cross-examined in court. It was rumored that Bosie would be arrested, but authorities claimed there was no evidence against him. His father had made sure of that. Wilde missed the visits. "A slim thing, gold-haired like an angel, stands always at my side," he wrote to Ada Leverson. "His presence overshadows me."

For the second trial, Carson was replaced by Charles Gill, also a Trinity man and no friend of Wilde. Clarke volunteered for the defense and waived any fees. Alfred Taylor, whose reputation for procuring had figured prominently in the first trial, was offered immunity for testifying against Wilde but refused; he was, as Wilde had told the court, a Marlborough boy and a man of taste. To Wilde's detriment, they were to be tried together on the same charges as well as a charge of conspiring with each other to commit indecent acts, which implied sodomy.

To paraphrase Macaulay, it is always a ridiculous spectacle to observe the British in a fit of morality. No one reached out to help Wilde. The evil joy that feeds on scandal and a man's downfall increased in intensity. No one behaved well—not the press or the middle class at whom Wilde scoffed or the aristocrats whom he satirized. "Everyone," recalled Frank Harris, "tried to outdo his neighbour in expressions of loathing and abhorrence." Yeats rightly pointed out that the rage against Wilde was the rage of the British against art and the artist, a hatred generally dormant until the artist trespasses into foreign territory.

WILDE WAS SLEEPING on a prison cot at the same time that his income was at its peak. He had two plays running in the West End. He was being talked about as the century's most brilliant writer of comedy. After his arrest on April 5, *The Importance of Being Earnest* continued production, although the author's name was removed from advertisements on the hoardings and from the programs. To prolong the run and help Wilde pay his debts, George Alexander kept the play onstage until May 8, its eighty-third performance, before replacing it with *The Triumph of the Philistines*, an unfortunate title, considering the circumstances.★ *Earnest's* New York production opened on April 22 and closed in little more than a week, the victim of scandal, poor reviews, and empty seats. *An Ideal Husband* trans-ferred from the Haymarket on the day of Wilde's arrest to the Criterion, where it lasted two weeks. Wilde's books were removed from most publishers' lists and bookshop shelves.

Constance removed Cyril and Vyvyan from school to shield them from publicity. Later a French governess took them to Switzerland while Constance remained in London to be by her husband's side. She paid what outstanding bills she could afford, sending a guinea to the Sibyl of Mortimer Street, who had predicted good fortune only months ago. "What is to become of my husband who has so betrayed and deceived me and ruined the lives of my darling boys?" she asked the fortune-teller. "Can you tell me anything? You told me that after this terrible shock my life was to become easier but will there be any happiness in it, or is that dead for me? And I have had so little. My life has all been cut to pieces as my hand is by its lines." The sibyl was silent. But Lady Windermere under-stood: "Misfortunes one can endure—they come from outside, they are accidents. But to suffer for one's own faults—ah!—there is the sting of life."

More humiliation followed. On April 24, bailiffs arrived at Tite Street to auction the contents of "the House Beautiful." The sale was held in the drawing room, under the Balzacian eye of Harper Pennington's full-length portrait of Wilde, bought for fourteen pounds by Ada Leverson. Everything, including the children's toys and Thomas Carlyle's writing desk, on which little literary work was done, was knocked down. A cir-

---

★The author was Henry Arthur Jones, whose greatest success was in 1898 with *The Liars,* a play sometimes attributed to Wilde. It was rumored that after *The Ballad of Reading Gaol* Wilde wrote a final dramatic masterpiece and Jones offered the use of his name to have it produced—a curious but unlikely story since there is no mention of it in Wilde's letters to Smithers or Ross. Even if good money had been involved, would Wilde have bowed so low? Wilde respected Pinero but ignored Jones: "I know and admire Pinero's work," he wrote to George Alexander, "but *who is* Jones?"

cus atmosphere prevailed. The curious elbowed each other up and down the stairs, peering at the bedroom, pulling open drawers. Personal letters were exposed, and some original manuscripts vanished. French readers greedily digested a copy of *Le Latin mystique.* No attempt was made to bid up the prices; it was as if Wilde's personal effects—from his beloved blue china to paintings by Shannon and Ricketts—had no value because of the indictment against the owner.

WILDE ARRIVED AT the Old Bailey wearing a dark chesterfield coat, silk hat, dark tie, and no buttonhole. He was thinner after his stay in Holloway Prison. *The Illustrated Police News* reported that the defendant's "face looked almost bloodless, and his eyes heavy and weary." He entered the dock, a high box with glass panels on each side and a narrow oak plank that served as a seat. Next to him sat Alfred Taylor. The same names heard in the Queensberry trial were introduced, except that now there was a face and voice behind the accusations.

The first witness was Charles Parker, who gave his age as twenty-one and his occupation as gentleman's valet. Admitting that he sold sexual favors, he described how he met Wilde at Solferino's restaurant and went with him to the Savoy, where with his consent Wilde "committed the act of sodomy upon me." Afterward he received two pounds. His brother William, a groom, added more details about the dinner meeting, testifying how Wilde fed his brother preserved cherries from his own mouth. Landladies who had rented to Taylor and Charles Parker were questioned. The blackmailer Alfred Wood was the only witness to mention Douglas's name. Gill moved quickly to discredit this connection, getting Wood to admit that Douglas introduced him to Wilde not in person but by telegram.

Fred Atkins, a twenty-year-old former billiard marker and bookmaker's clerk, testified that Wilde took him to Paris for a weekend at the Grand Hôtel on the boulevard des Capucines. One night he attended the Moulin Rouge on his own and returned to the hotel to find Wilde in bed with Maurice Schwabe, nephew of the wife of the solicitor general, Sir Frank Lockwood, whose name had been carefully kept out of the libel trial by Carson. Clarke's cross-examination concentrated on Atkins's reputation as a blackmailer and the other boys' background as prostitutes. The exception was Edward Shelley, the clerk from the Bodley Head, who told the court how Wilde's advances made him feel "degraded," how he "objected vigorously" to them, and had left his position because colleagues called him "Mrs. Wilde" and "Miss Oscar." There was sufficient evidence to prove that Shelley was unstable.

On the fourth day the defense's case opened, and Clarke called Wilde to the witness stand. Familiar ground was covered as to Wilde's literary work. He was asked to swear that the evidence he gave at the Queensberry trial was true and that there was no truth in any of the allegations in the present case. Gill returned to *The Chameleon,* in particular the two ambiguous poems written by Douglas. Wilde's finest moment came when he was asked to explain "the love that dare not speak its name," the last line of "Two Loves." Wilde wanted to defend the artist's right to freedom, which included sexual freedom, but to protect himself he had to pretend that he was not sensual, which contradicted his aesthetic ideals of enjoying pleasure. He gave a tribute to Greek love, to the misunderstood relationship that "repeatedly exists between an elder and a younger man, when the elder man has intellect, and the younger man has all the joy, hope and glamour of life before him." Applause from the public gallery was accompanied by hisses.

From his perch in the gallery, Max Beerbohm called the speech "simply wonderful." Wilde, he said, was "perfectly self-possessed, dominating the Old Bailey with his fine presence and musical voice. He has never had so great a triumph, I am sure, as when the gallery burst into applause." Of his contemporaries, George Ives was the most responsible for elevating Wilde to homosexual martyr, recording in his diary that Wilde was one of those who "though they may have erred, at least created no actual victims or sorrow." The plight of Constance and the boys mattered to few.

As the trial progressed, there was damaging evidence from several of the young men implicated in the crimes and from chambermaids at the Savoy who thought they found fecal stains on bedsheets alleged to be from Wilde's room (Wilde later told Frank Harris the sheets were Bosie's). In his turn, Clarke challenged the credibility of the witnesses. The conspiracy charge was dropped, a paradoxical move in retrospect, since it denied the existence of a community of men who took sexual pleasure in other men, despite the fact that the trials described that community in detail. It was now a question of whether Wilde was guilty of indecent acts.

After three hours of deliberation, one juror continued to hold out for acquittal. No verdict meant another trial. Bail was denied until the Reverend Stewart Headlam and Percy Douglas provided £1,250 each as surety.

ON MAY 7, Wilde was freed for three weeks. He and Percy drove to an out-of-the-way hotel near St. Pancras, where he was asked to leave almost immediately after registering. Queensberry and his gang made sure that no hotel would admit him. Home was the last resort. Now seventy-four and as imperious as ever, Lady Wilde still lived at Oakley Street with Willie and his second wife, Lily. The two brothers had not spoken for nearly two years. Willie said his brother "came tapping with his beak against the window-pane, and fell down on my threshold like a wounded stag." There was talk about whether Wilde should leave the country. His mother royally told him, "If you stay, even if you go to prison, you will always be my son, it will make no difference to my affection, but if you go, I will never speak to you again." Yeats later said that Wilde "made the right decision" and "owes to that decision half of his renown."

Willie exulted in his brother's vulnerability. Wilde spent the night on a camp bed in a corner near the fireplace like a stray dog. Willie drank too much and muttered, "At least my vices were decent." Robert Sherard visited and found Wilde agitated and flushed with fever. One of the few times he left the house was to dine with the Leversons. Wilde called Ada Leverson "the Sphinx," one of his more endearing pet names. Well-married to the son of a diamond merchant, she was a woman of spirit and brilliance, a humorist—for *Punch*—at a time when women were not encouraged to publish wit. It appealed to Wilde that she resembled Sarah Bernhardt, particularly in the way she wore her frizzy hair piled on top of her head. The Leversons took one look at Wilde and invited him to stay with them. They informed their servants they could leave with a month's wages if they did not want to stay in the house with a notorious man—but none left.

Wilde took over their son's nursery and insisted that the toys remain. His old hairdresser from happier days called daily to shave and wave his hair. He ate his meals in the nursery and joined the Leversons later formally dressed and wearing a buttonhole, amusing them with his remark about Dickens that "one must have a heart of stone to read the death of

Little Nell without laughing." He talked about everything, including the effects of absinthe, except his problems. He recalled that once in Paris he drank absinthe for three nights straight, priding himself on his sobriety until the waiter came to water the sawdust. Then he saw tulips, lilies, and roses sprout and grow to make a garden in the café.

Constance visited him in the nursery, where he greeted visitors; for two hours she pleaded with him to leave the country. Few of Wilde's friends considered how awful it was for her to learn the truth about her husband's fondness for young men, then to see her friends turn away. She faced many decisions about her life and that of her children. Still, there she was holding Wilde's hand amidst the rocking horse and building blocks, offering the only advice a wife could give: save yourself.

WHEN WILDE'S TRIAL opened on May 20, Clarke successfully argued that since conspiracy charges had been dropped in the previous trial, the two defendants be tried separately, but he failed to have Taylor, whom he knew would be convicted, tried last. After a day and a half of testimony, the jury deliberated for forty-five minutes and found Taylor guilty.

Wilde entered the dock to stand trial for the second time on May 22. Replacing Gill was Sir Frank Lockwood, the solicitor general, an indication that the Crown was seeking to convict. The same witnesses were heard and the same letters dissected. On the third day, when Clarke called Wilde to the witness box, he looked tired; there were dark circles under his eyes, and his clothes were disheveled. He had the look and hollow sound of a defeated man. But when Clarke asked him whether there was any truth in the accusations against him, he answered in a determined voice, "None whatsoever." Clarke's defense strategy was to make his client an obvious scapegoat of British hypocrisy. "This trial," he told the court, "seems to be operating as an act of indemnity for all the blackmailers in London." To no avail, he argued that the accusers should be the accused. The jury deliberated for two hours before rendering a guilty verdict.

An added insult throughout the proceedings was the conspicuous presence of Queensberry. Wilde bitterly described to Bosie how his father attracted attention with his "stableman's gait and dress, the bowed legs, the twitching hands, the hanging lower lip, the bestial and half-witted grin."

Sacrificing Wilde to Victorian homophobia calmed the puritans: there were no more arrests. The aristocrats sacrificed Wilde because he had attempted to rise above his proper station; the legal system punished him because he had perverted the law by lying about his homosexual acts. He had wanted to punish Queensberry to please Bosie but only punished himself. He had put on an extraordinary performance in the dock and truly believed that, like Sir Robert Chiltern in *An Ideal Husband,* he would triumph over the past and start life anew.

During sentencing, Sir Alfred Wills upheld centuries of prejudice with his declaration: "People who can do these things must be dead to all sense of shame, and one cannot hope to produce any effect upon them. It is the worst case I have ever tried. That you, Taylor, kept a kind of male brothel it is impossible to doubt. And that you, Wilde, have been the centre of a circle of extensive corruption of the most hideous kind among young men, it is equally impossible to doubt." That the Crown never proved that Wilde was a corruptor went unnoticed.

"And I? May I say nothing, my lord?" Wilde inquired. Affronted, Wills motioned for the warders to take the prisoner away.

CHAPTER NINETEEN

Touching Sorrow

✎

*Clergymen, and people who use phrases without wisdom, sometimes
talk of suffering as a mystery. It is really a revelation. One discerns
things that one never discerned before. One approaches the whole of
history from a different standpoint. . . .
I now see that sorrow, being the supreme emotion of which man is
capable, is at once the type and test of all great Art.*

—DE PROFUNDIS

The gulf between Wilde's crime and his punishment was enormous. Of suffering, he had only idealistic notions. On his American tour, when he visited a prison in Lincoln, Nebraska, he had found the inmates "mean-looking." That pleased him. "I should hate to see a criminal with a noble face," he wrote Nellie Sickert, describing to her the "little whitewashed cells, so tragically tidy, but with books in them." When he saw a translation of Dante, he wondered how the words of an exiled Florentine could soothe the sorrow of a modern prisoner.

In "The Soul of Man Under Socialism," he imagines that "even in prison, a man can be quite free. His soul can be free. His personality can be untroubled. He can be at peace. . . . He may commit a sin against society, and yet realize through that sin his true perfection." Wilde tried to prove in *De Profundis* that his personality had undergone similar changes, but prison never brought peace of mind or perfection.

After his conviction, Wilde was taken to Pentonville Prison and put in a single lime-washed cell thirteen feet long by seven feet wide with a nine-foot ceiling. He passed the cursory medical examination and was declared fit for hard labor. He wore the standard drab gray uniform with thick black arrows and a cap with a face flap, which he had to lower whenever he met another prisoner. He was issued a blanket and a hard pillow and slept for the first months on a plank bed, the object of which he said was to produce insomnia. The prisoner gets used to not sleeping and, even when issued a hard mattress later in his term, still suffers from insomnia. "For sleep," Wilde wrote, "like all wholesome things, is a habit."

Beyond a small table for his personal and eating needs, nothing was permitted. No pictures. No books. No toilet (drainpipes made communication easier). A tin chamber pot could be emptied three times a day, but access to prison lavatories was restricted to the one hour daily for exercise. For a man of Wilde's fastidious nature to be squatting on a pot in a darkened cell throughout the night when he had chronic diarrhea was torture. He lost twenty-two pounds. By shedding the fat gained from the richness of the Café Royal's menu, his face regained its angular features. Visitors commented on how fit he looked.

He was up at six and in bed by seven. The first rule that unnerved him was daily inspection, when utensils had to be precisely arranged. "I had to keep everything in my cell in its exact place," he said, "and if I neglected this even in the slightest, I was punished." One warder recalled how Wilde would arrange his tins and then "step back and view them with an air of childlike complacency."

Wilde was a physically powerful man, which helped him survive the severities of prison. Otherwise, he would have withered and died, for imprisonment is a form of erosion as the prisoner consumes himself with trying to understand his abandonment. Wilde slid backward, becoming a child again, helpless and abused. Nothing is more moving than his letters of protest on behalf of the children imprisoned beside him. "The terror of a child in prison is quite limitless," he wrote in a letter to *The Daily Chronicle,* where he described a boy in the opposite cell: "The child's face was like a white wedge of sheer terror. There was in his eyes the terror of a hunted animal. The next morning I heard him at breakfast time crying, and calling to be let out. His cry was for his parents."

It took Wilde many months to adjust to the prison diet of gruel, beans, soup, and cold meat once a week. Diarrhea was so endemic that the smell made the warders ill when they opened up the cells in the morning. Wilde's first visitor, R. B. Haldane, a Liberal politician, arranged for him to have access to books other than those in the prison library, which Wilde described as consisting chiefly of "third-rate, badly-written, religious books, so-called, written apparently for children, and utterly unsuitable for children or for anyone else."

To do nothing is difficult. In "The Critic as Artist," Gilbert talks about contemplation—Plato's noblest form of energy—and concludes that modern man is "too critical, too intellectually subtle and too curious of exquisite pleasures, to accept any speculations about life in exchange for life itself." Prison life was about being, not doing, about memory, "the diary that we all carry about with us," as Cecily says in *Earnest*. Nothing prepared Wilde for the realization that in prison he had to learn to communicate with himself in a vastly different way.

Previously Wilde's moments of solitude, whether in the bath or lying on the sofa thinking of epigrams, were in preparation for talk with others. Family, friendship, art, work—things that he had taken for granted—were the exceptions in prison, where disappointment and pain are everyday emotions. Now interior monologues led to bitterness toward Douglas, but Wilde remained loyal to his principles. "To have altered my life would have been to have admitted that Uranian love is ignoble," he wrote to Ross. "I hold it to be noble—more noble than other forms." Only when Wilde understood ruin could he accept those imperfections he had shunned. Retreating from un-Christian positions, he became humane: illness and ugliness no longer revolted him.

On June 21, a representative of Queensberry's solicitor arrived to serve Wilde with a bankruptcy notice. The marquess wanted his £677 in costs for the libel trial, which Bosie had promised would be paid by his mother and brother. A new friend—malice—joined him in his solitude. On July 4, perhaps through Haldane's intercession, Wilde was transferred to Wandsworth Prison. He hated it more than Pentonville. The food was worse. "It even smelt bad," Wilde said. "It was not fit for dogs." Put on the treadmill to grind flour six hours a day (twenty minutes on and five minutes' rest), he stood in a cubicle holding on to iron circular handles; his left foot was placed on the higher step, the right foot on the lower, and in that position he paddled and moved the treadmill, making an ascent of six thousand feet. After three days, his diarrhea was so bad that he was moved to the infirmary.

After his release from the hospital, which he quite enjoyed since there he was allowed to talk with the other patients, Wilde was taken off the treadmill and assigned work in his cell. He was supposed to pick four pounds of oakum daily. His long fingers became scarred from separating loose fibers by untwisting old ropes, which were then mixed with tar to caulk the seams of ships. But he had books. Haldane provided editions of some of his favorite authors: Pater, Cardinal Newman, and St. Augustine. *Madame Bovary,* which he requested, was judged inappropriate.

Wilde had served three months at Wandsworth and was entitled to receive and send one letter and to have one visitor. He put family responsibilities over Bosie and accepted a letter from his brother-in-law, who hinted at a reconciliation with Constance if Wilde showed repentance. Wilde wrote his wife a tender, penitent letter that moved her to apply for a special visit, since Robert Sherard had been first. Visits from family and friends, allowed only four times a year and for only twenty minutes, were medieval in atmosphere and left the inmates more depressed than ever. "The prisoner," Wilde said, "is either locked up in a large iron cage or in a large wooden box, with a small aperture, covered with wire netting, through which he is allowed to peer. His friends are placed in a similar cage, some three or four feet distant, and two warders stand between, to listen to, and, if they wish, stop or interrupt the conversation such as it may be."

Proceedings for Wilde's bankruptcy necessitated his leaving Wandsworth for hearings at Bankruptcy Court in Carey Street, where he was handcuffed and paraded before waiting crowds. One day he turned his head in chapel, and his mattress was removed as punishment. Another morning he was too weak to dress himself and fell on the stone floor of his cell, striking his right ear. "One of the tragedies of prison life," said Wilde, "is that it turns a man's heart to stone. The feelings of natural affection, like all other feelings, require to be fed." Used to living in a world where nothing was what it seemed, Wilde learned in prison, he said, "that things are what they are and will be what they will be."

On November 20, 1895, he was transferred from Wandsworth to Reading, largely thanks to Haldane's concern. Wilde had received no preferential treatment at Pentonville or Wandsworth, but his idleness at oakum picking and infractions of the silence rule militated for a change. At Reading he worked in the library (he enjoyed putting brown wrappers on the books) and tended the garden. Rather than be transported in a prison vehicle, Wilde was taken handcuffed and in prison uniform by train. He had to wait half an hour on the platform at Clapham Junction, where he was recognized and ridiculed. It was a humiliation that he never forgot.

READING WAS A small county prison, similar to many built in the mid-nineteenth century. Cruciform in shape, with four wings, it opened in 1844 on the site of a jail dating from 1571 and housed men from children to the aged and some women. At Wilde's time there were 13 women out of 170 inmates. The chapel, with opaque leaded windows and a cathedral ceiling, had seating arranged so that prisoners could see only the chaplain. At Reading, Wilde learned to obey the rules and criticize the system. His long, wavy hair was cut to a regulation length. His warder recalled him asking, " 'Must it be cut? You don't know what it means to me,' and tears rolled down his cheeks."

His cell number was C.3.3., indicating the third cell on the third landing of C block. For the next eight months, until he was transferred, the governor, Lieutenant-Colonel Henry Isaacson, made Wilde's existence no less miserable. "He had the eyes of a ferret, the body of an ape, and the soul of a rat," Wilde said. It was said that Oxford students going back and forth to London saw the turrets of Reading as they passed by and yelled "Hi, Oscar!" from the windows of the train.

Recognized as a new inmate because he had not learned to talk without moving his lips, Wilde spent his first six weeks in silence until one exercise hour, when the prisoner behind him said, "Oscar Wilde, I pity you, for you must suffer more than we do." Wilde whispered, "No, my friend, we all suffer alike." Wilde later told Gide that from that moment he no longer thought of killing himself. Once he learned to communicate, Wilde befriended prisoners. Always fascinated by the criminal element, although from a distance, he now took a personal interest in the lives of his fellow inmates and arranged to have money sent to them when they were released.

Gradually, through the loss of speech and audience response, Wilde suffered the loss of imagination: his storytelling talents stopped. "I like hearing myself talk," he often said. "It is one of my greatest pleasures." Once afflicted with laryngitis, he regretted that without voice he could not even listen with appreciation. Observed talking, Wilde took responsibility for starting the conversation and was given two weeks' solitary confinement. Another time he broke the rules when he responded to a prisoner who made "the sign of the widow's son," an appeal from one brother Mason to another, which cannot be ignored. Isaacson had his books removed for minor infractions. Wilde began a parallel identification between Christ's sufferings and those of prisoners.

Salomé was staged in Paris at the Théâtre de l'Oeuvre on February 11, 1896, and praised in the English press. Wilde said that Isaacson treated him with more deference thereafter, but he always saw the governor as the kind of man who could not eat his breakfast until he had punished someone. That Wilde wanted to write more than authorized letters did not move Isaacson. Verlaine, who served two years in a Belgian prison for shooting his lover Rimbaud, wrote poetry on scraps of paper and ground coffee, a more pleasant task than picking oakum. The Marquis de Sade, who spent many years off and on incarcerated, produced his best writing from a cell, but he also received unlimited writing supplies for his plays and stories.

WILDE WAS AWARE of Constance's efforts to rebuild her life in Switzerland, Germany, and Italy. She had good friends in the Carlos Blackers, who lived in Switzerland, and Lady Margaret Brooke, the Ranee of Sarawak, who had a villa near Genoa; it was Lady Brooke who had urged her friend Haldane to visit Wilde in prison. Reconciliation was very much on Constance's mind after she received Wilde's letter. She wrote Emily Thursfield that, because he was "very repentant," she was willing to humble herself. "By sticking to him now," she said, "I may save him from even worse and I believe that he cares now for no-one but myself and the children." She rationalized that "if I find it impossible to live with him I can always leave him."

No less than when she married, Constance believed in the healing power of love. "I think we women are meant for comforters," she told Emily, "and I believe that no-one can really take my place now, or help him as I can." However, her health problems persisted; a second operation in January 1896 restored partial mobility and increased hopes of reconciliation. In a nostalgic mood, Constance told Emily that she wanted her husband to take her again to the place where she "first heard a nightingale's song. I have never forgotten the magic of it all."

During this time, Cyril and Vyvyan attended several European boarding schools until they were placed in separate academies. Cyril knew his father was in prison because he had read the newspapers at a relative's house, and he may have known the charge, but he never discussed it with his younger brother. In *Son of Oscar Wilde,* Vyvyan recalls many idyllic periods during their exile. The boys learned German and Italian, while in prison their father taught himself the same languages; they knew the pasta maker and the wine maker, and they had far more freedom to explore and get into trouble than they would have had living in England.

Wilde realized that his ailing mother would not live to see him released from prison. His sister-in-law, Lily, visited him with the news, a gesture Wilde appreciated since his brother had not asked to see him. Wilde paid for her confinement when his niece, Dorothy Ierne Wilde, was born on July 11, 1895. Lady Wilde had asked the prison authorities if Oscar might see her, but the request was denied. When told, she said: "May the prison help him!" and turned her face to the wall. Lily wrote Constance that Lady Wilde died on February 3, 1896; Oscar was not told. Constance wanted to be the one to break the sad news. Negotiating with the prison authorities for a special visit took ten days and the journey four. She wrote Lily that she was on her way, that "such a terrible thing could not be told to him roughly."

Aware of the circumstances, the governor arranged for the couple to meet in a private room. Constance began to talk, but Wilde interrupted her. "I knew it already." On the night his mother died, he said he heard the cry of the banshee and saw a vision of her dressed to go out. Oscar had lost the best of himself. This was the last time that Constance talked with her husband. Lady Wilde failed to reunite Willie and Oscar before her death. And Willie never wrote or visited his brother in prison. "For many reasons he wd [would] not want to see me," Willie wrote More Adey. (One reason was Wilde's anger that Willie had sold his beloved fur coat from the American tour.)

Adey sent a wreath from Wilde's friends, one of the many selfless acts that he took on while Wilde was in Reading. A friend of Ross and a translator of Ibsen, Adey volunteered to draft petitions to the home secretary for Wilde's release on grounds of ill health. Lily Wilde gave Oscar's possessions, including manuscripts that Willie had not disposed of, to Adey for safekeeping. But the fact that he visited Wilde caused some problems when Constance found out, because Oscar had promised not to see his homosexual friends.

Hounded for court costs by Queensberry's solicitor, Wilde had only a half interest in Constance's dowry with which to negotiate. An agreement was struck for him to receive £150 pounds annually from his wife and one-third the life interest, with the rest to go to their sons in the event of her death. There was one stipulation: he forfeited payments if he returned to Bosie or any of his disreputable friends. Constance believed that if Oscar and Bosie were kept apart her husband would return to her after prison. In the interim she changed the family name to Holland, which had belonged to Holland Watson, Constance's great-great-grandfather. Vyvyan dropped his middle name, Oscar. As time passed, reconciliation seemed less likely and divorce more difficult. Constance might be asked to produce new evidence of her husband's infidelities. She decided on a legal separation.

IN PARIS SINCE the criminal trials, Bosie resumed his old life of reckless pleasure. Advised to stay away from England for at least two years, he nursed a wounded vanity and, when it was to his advantage, suffered the guilt of the survivor. He wanted his side of the case to be heard. The *Mercure de France* asked him to write an article in which he decided to quote from three of Wilde's love letters written to him during the trial. He interested the magazine's publishing company in a new edition of his poems dedicated to Wilde. Since he had not heard from Wilde, he interpreted the silence to mean that Wilde no longer loved him, despite the fact that he was still protecting Bosie from scandal.

If the letters revealed details about the relationship, it would be clear that Wilde had lied in court. Horrified, Wilde told Ross to stop such "revolting and grotesque" folly. Wilde turned against Bosie, promising to "have nothing to do with him." When Ross was instructed to ask him for the return of all gifts and letters, Douglas refused. "If Oscar asks me to kill myself I will do so, and he shall have back the letters when I am dead," he replied. Bosie would not be ignored and launched an article in *La Revue blanche* entitled "Introduction to My Poems, with some remarks on the Oscar Wilde case." Enjoying himself in Capri, he sent a message through Adey: "Tell him I know that I have ruined his life, that everything is my fault, if that pleases him. I don't care. Doesn't he think that my life is just as much ruined as his and so much sooner?" Bosie realized that Ross had taken the opportunity of his absence to reestablish his position as intimate friend.

Halfway though his sentence, Wilde was so desperate that he discarded his principles and aligned himself with current theories, which held that homosexuality was a medical condition, a kind of madness was the way Constance referred to it. Wilde knew this to be untrue; his nature was homosexual. But by admitting to sexual madness, a disease to be cured, not a crime to be punished, Wilde built the argument that prison was aggravating his madness. The prison surgeon did not, however, agree, and the petition was denied.

In July 1896, Isaacson was replaced by Major James Osmond Nelson, who "altered every man's life in this place," Wilde's in particular. The writer was given a light in his cell as late as he wanted, and the warders were much kinder, in particular Thomas Martin. Four months before his term ended, he was permitted an unlimited supply of writing materials. The governor agreed, in order to circumvent prison rules, that Wilde would be allowed to write a long letter for medicinal purposes. Between January and March 1897, he wrote *De Profundis* on thin blue prison paper under "that little tent of blue," as he called his cell window in *The Ballad of Reading Gaol*. Each page was supposed to be taken away when it was completed; only at the end was the author allowed to read successive pages and make revisions. Shaw said that "no other Irishman had yet produced as masterful a comedy."

Wilde wanted to write an epistle, to tell the gospel according to Oscar

Wilde, an apologia *pro vita sua* in which he would draw up a statement of account, both for himself and for the public, concerning his relationship with Douglas, the reasons for his downfall, and his past, present, and future position in art and in life. In *De Profundis,* Bosie is cast as the villain and Wilde as a well-meaning intellectual entrapped by the young lord to punish his mad father: "It was the triumph of the smaller over the bigger nature." As a piece of writing, the work is an intriguing example of the memoir genre. As an account of his relationship with Bosie, it is too clouded with anger to be reliable. As evidence that Wilde had been reborn in suffering and sorrow, it is deceptive.

At its best, *De Profundis* is a meditation on the metaphysical aspects of art and memory. Deprived in prison of the amoral Greek worship of the visible world, Wilde lost his muscular voice and became sentimental. Deprived of enjoying pleasure, he embraced suffering. "There is a luxury in self-reproach," Dorian observes. "When we blame ourselves we feel that no one else has a right to blame us. It is the confession, not the priest that gives us absolution." The process cleansed him of "much perilous stuff," he told Ross.

THREE DAYS BEFORE Wilde's release, Charles Ricketts visited him at Reading. Wilde's friends had started a fund, which grew to eight hundred pounds, to help him get started in France, and Ricketts, when he could barely afford to, contributed one hundred pounds. He recalled the surroundings with the eye of an artist—the small putty-colored waiting room decorated with a chocolate dado and an ebonized clock, the ocher corridors, the green-baize-covered table at which Wilde sat with his back to the window. He talked about entering a monastery, but Ricketts suggested Venice as the place for work and privacy. "No!" Wilde exclaimed. "Privacy! Work! my dear Ricketts. I wish to look at life, not to become a monument for tourists. . . . France understands the value of an artist for what he is, not for what he may have done."

But the French literati who had welcomed Wilde during his Paris sojourns had not rallied for him; a petition circulated in his defense failed to secure enough signatures. Numerous journal articles had protested the verdict. Rachilde (Marguérite Eymery), whose novel *Monsieur Vénus* dealt with male homosexuality, protested Wilde's imprisonment with an article in *La Revue blanche.* Entitled "Questions brûlantes" (Burning Questions), it criticized hypocritical British morality and endorsed the right to express same-sex love, but ultimately took refuge in the familiar rhetoric of idealized platonic love.

Wilde had one other visitor before his release. His solicitor Arthur Hansell arrived with papers for him to sign, turning over the guardianship of Vyvyan and Cyril to Constance and her cousin Adrian Hope. Wilde looked at the documents and signed, unaware that Constance was in the next room. She asked the warder to let her have "one last glimpse" of her husband. He moved away from the glass portion of the door he was guarding. Constance took a brief final look and wept.

When Wilde left Reading Prison on the evening of May 18, 1897, Nelson handed him the packet containing *De Profundis,* eighty close-written pages on twenty folio sheets. His reactions to the death of a fellow prisoner inspired *The Ballad of Reading Gaol,* written over six months in France and Italy. On July 7, 1896, Charles Thomas Wooldridge, a thirty-year-old trooper in the Royal Horse Guards, was hanged in Reading Prison. He was convicted of the premeditated murder of his twenty-three-year-old wife, whose throat he slit three times with a razor. The refrain that haunts the poem—"For each man kills the thing he loves"— formed in Wilde's mind as he watched the hangman cross the courtyard. A political tract and a humanist plea, the *Ballad* celebrates an individual's desire for freedom and is remarkable for the content of selected stanzas rather than its metrical cleverness.

Wilde wrote two letters to *The Daily Chronicle* condemning the prison system, one when he was in Dieppe and the other in Paris. He wrote them quickly and with the same energy that had produced his sonnets to Lillie Langtry and Ellen Terry. The first, published on May 28, 1897, took issue with the dismissal of Warder Martin, who by his repeated kindnesses had made Wilde's last months in Reading bearable. His infraction was giving a few biscuits to a hungry child. Poignantly Wilde described the hardships a child endures in prison. The second letter, dated March 23, 1898, objected to a proposal of the home secretary to appoint more prison inspectors. Wilde viewed such reform as useless. Inspectors visit prisons, he wrote, only to see that regulations are followed, to enforce

an inhuman code. "No prisoner has ever had the smallest relief, or attention, or care from any of the official visitors." Reform, he pleaded, should
be directed toward alleviating the three punishments authorized by law:
hunger, insomnia, and disease.

WILDE HAD SERVED every day of his sentence; a petition for release a
few days early to avoid the newspaper reporters had been denied. Accompanied by two prison officers, he was taken by cab to Twyford Station and
boarded the London train; they left the train in Westbourne Park and
went the rest of the way to Pentonville Prison by cab. Only two reporters
were at Reading to record his departure, and the rest of the trip was without incident. Wilde had to spend the night at Pentonville because rules
called for a prisoner to be released from the prison to which he was
admitted.

At 6:15 A.M. More Adey and the Reverend Stewart Headlam, who
had put up part of Wilde's bail, met him with a cab and went to Headlam's home in Bloomsbury. Wilde was exhausted, but he knew what was
expected of him: to be the Oscar of old, to put everyone at ease, to pretend
that life would go gaily on. He appeared in new clothes, cigarette in hand,
buttonhole in place, and had his first cup of coffee in two years. Ada and
Ernest Leverson arrived to see Wilde emerge anew "with the dignity of a
king returning from exile." Wilde saluted the Sphinx with his memorable
greeting: "Sphinx, how marvellous of you to know exactly the right hat
to wear at seven o'clock in the morning to meet a friend who has been
away! You can't have got up, you must have sat up."

Headlam was not a close friend but a clergyman who felt he had to
step forward when Wilde was denied bail. Suddenly Wilde changed the
subject to religion, perhaps in deference to his host. "I look on all the
different religions as colleges in a great university," he said. "Roman
Catholicism is the greatest and most romantic of them." He then sent off
a letter to the Jesuits asking to be admitted for a six-month retreat. The
messenger delivered the request to the rectory at Farm Street and waited
for a reply. There must have been an initial shock when the priests realized who was making the request. They replied that Wilde could not be
accepted without at least a year's deliberation. That there was such a rule

for a short-term stay seems doubtful. When Wilde realized that there was no alternative to exile, "he broke down and sobbed bitterly," Ada Leverson recalled.

The last time Wilde missed the boat to France, he was arrested at the Cadogan Hotel and taken to prison. To miss the last boat now would disappoint Robert Ross and Reggie Turner, his remaining best friends, awaiting his arrival at Dieppe. Wilde met with some more well-wishers, took a cab to the station, and boarded the Newhaven train. His thoughts were only of Bosie.

CHAPTER TWENTY

Misbegotten Yesterdays

❧

It is only shallow people who require years to get rid of an emotion. A man who is master of himself can end a sorrow as easily as he can invent a pleasure.

—THE PICTURE OF DORIAN GRAY

Years earlier Cheiro had read Wilde's palm and foretold that he had the hand of a king who would send himself into exile. Leaving England forever, Wilde forfeited reputation, family, marriage, and country. His few close friends could afford to visit him only if he stayed close to shore. In five months he would be forty-three. His body was as trim as it had been when he arrived from Dublin on his way to Oxford, but he looked older. His hair was streaked with gray, and there was the beginning of a bald spot on the crown; his complexion, never robust, was ashen, his eyes dull, his hearing impaired by the fall in prison. Inside he wanted to feel young again. He immediately went below, avoiding the traditional farewell to Newhaven's chalk cliffs, insignificant beside those of Dover but still inspiring sadness for those never to return. His only wish was not to be recognized. Speech, after a long silence, startled him. He was not used to the sound of his own voice and wanted no conversation with strangers.

He had made this channel crossing many times. As a young man, he had visited Walter Sickert and his sister Nellie at their home. He had ended his honeymoon in Dieppe and returned a happily married man. There had been visits to the casino with Bosie, and overnight revels with other poets. The Rhymers, when not meeting at the Cheshire Cheese off Fleet Street, had often gathered at Dieppe, sometimes walking around London waiting to catch the early-morning boat train to Newhaven. The Normandy resort catered to the Anglo-French, with salons for the wealthy and cafés for the artists.

As the ferry arrived at 4:00 A.M. on May 20, dawn silhouetted the citadel and the Arques hills. From the jetty, Ross and Turner saw Wilde's towering form outlined in the translucent light. They waved and ran along the quay to greet him as he walked down the gangplank, clutching the original copy of *De Profundis.* He unburdened himself of the manuscript, giving Ross the responsibility for making copies and sending the original to Bosie. (Fearing that he might destroy the original, Ross sent him a copy.) The letter began "Dear Bosie" and ended "Your Affectionate Friend."

A room was reserved under his nom de plume Monsieur Sebastian Melmoth at the Hôtel Sandwich, behind the promenade on the rue de l'Hôtel de Ville. In the French tradition, the hotel was a bar where the patron let some rooms. Wilde's new luggage, a gift from Reggie Turner, bore the initials "S.M." Considerable thought was given to what name to use so as not to frighten the mailman. The symbolism was more inspired than Wilde realized: Sebastian for the patron saint of the plague, and Melmoth from his great-uncle's book *Melmoth the Wanderer.*

Wilde saw himself not as the Sebastian with too many arrows but as the Sebastian who cheated death, as he had in prison. He had early recollections of the Christian martyr—his body tied to a tree and pierced by arrows—from portraits by Ribera and Giordano in the permanent collection at the Dublin National Gallery. After his first trip to Italy, he often mentioned the Guido Reni at Genoa's Palazzo Rosso.* The Melmoth

---

*Sebastian was condemned to death for converting soldiers in his ranks, but he did not die as depicted; the archers left him for dead and a widow nursed him back to health. He presented himself before Emperor Diocletian, who condemned him to death again—by beating. His body was thrown into a sewer and found by another pious woman, who dreamed that Sebastian told her to bury his remains near the catacombs. Reni's iconography made his St. Sebastian series popular with homosexuals; twentieth-century writers such as Evelyn Waugh, in *Brideshead Revisited,* and Tennessee Williams, in *Suddenly Last Summer,* named characters of ambiguous sexuality Sebastian.

Wilde identified with roams the earth looking for someone so eager to get away from worldly tortures that he will sell his soul to the Devil in order to rid himself of earthly miseries. Melmoth drives men to despair and then asks his victims: "Will you take my place in Hell for all eternity if I rescue you from Hell on earth here and now?"

Wilde arrived in Dieppe with an £800 collection from friends to set up a new life. He could count on £150 a year from Constance, and beyond that he was dependent on Ross. Once a lover and then a friend, Ross became Wilde's financial adviser and banker. Always jealous of Douglas, he now had the power to keep the former lovers apart. Throughout Wilde's exile, Ross nagged him like a stern nanny to be prudent; he liked to be the jockey reining him in whenever Wilde wanted to express or enjoy himself. Wilde thought that the coffers would be replenished by anonymous friends, but Ross doubted that their small band could afford to adopt long-term debt to keep Wilde living beyond his means. Wilde was furious when Ross reluctantly distributed a total of £20 to his warders and fellow prisoners.

Ross and Wilde's friendship was complex and control-driven. Each used and exploited the other. Following Wilde's death, Ross told Will Rothenstein that he "had grown to feel, rather foolishly, a sort of responsibility" for Wilde, "for everything connected with him except his genius." Wilde had become to him like an "adopted prodigal baby." Wilde suggested that Ross join him in exile. Ross led an active homosexual life despite his devout Catholicism and his vulnerability to the same law that had sent Wilde to prison. Wilde might not fall in love again as he had with Bosie, but he would become smitten with younger boys. Ross could never sparkle in Paris.

DIEPPE WAS NOT a large enough place for Ross, Turner, and Wilde. Everybody met everybody else, morning, noon, and night. Ignoring the disdain of the English who recognized him, Wilde went to his favorite haunts. He had coffee in the morning at the quayside Café Suisse spread out under five eighteenth-century arches, and aperitifs in the evening at the Café des Tribuneaux in the central square. He was seated at the Suisse when he saw Aubrey Beardsley walking along the dock with his fellow illustrator Charles Conder. Panicked at the sight of Wilde, Beardsley shoved Conder into a side street. Beardsley found himself in an uncomfortable situation. His patron was André Raffalovich, who demanded as he had with John Gray that no friend of his could be one of Wilde's.

"He is sure to make trouble here," Conder told a friend. "He'll harangue the ignorant under the Arcades. He'll use the Café Suisse as his platform and he'll make an exhibition of himself." Wilde was nearly arrested after a drunken party with visiting French poets at the Café des Tribuneaux. The police warned him that he would have to leave Dieppe if he sponsored another riotous evening. But Wilde wanted to feel joy. "Laughter is the primeval attitude towards life," he said, "a mode of approach that survives only in artists and criminals!"

Wilde's drinking habits changed after prison. He had spent several decades as a heavy drinker, aided by a prodigious tolerance that impressed even the Colorado miners. He was seldom perceived as drunk. The term *alcoholism* was not in general use in his time; in fact, there was no understanding of alcoholism as an addiction or as a serious, often inherited, disease. Wilde might have shared a genetic predisposition. His brother was an alcoholic by the standards of denial, binges, and blackouts. Willie had mood changes associated with alcoholism, terrifying his mother by stamping his foot and swearing at her if she hesitated to advance him money. Sir William was rumored to have become a compulsive drinker after the Mary Travers libel trial, but there were no public incidents. During Wilde's stay at Oakley Street between his trials, Robert Sherard observed Willie drunk and Lady Wilde taking to her bed with a bottle of gin. He reported the goings-on to Edmond de Goncourt, who wrote in his diary: "Pitiful family, where the mother of the two brothers is always drunk, the bottles of gin filling her room." Before prison Wilde drank to celebrate life, not to forget it. As a successful poet and playwright, he had no need to create an alternative reality to feel good or normal—until imagination failed him.

IN DIEPPE THERE was some artistic hospitality on Wilde's arrival. The Arthur Stannards (Henrietta wrote popular novels under the pseudonym John Strange Winter) had him to their salon in the former residence of the Duchess de Berri, near his hotel. The Norwegian landscape painter Fritz von Thaulow invited him to the Villa des Orchides in the Faubourg de la

Barre, a meeting place for local and visiting artists. One evening Thaulow asked what Wilde was working on. "I'm writing an essay called, 'A Defence of Drunkenness.' " "Good gracious, my dear Wilde, why always such provoking titles?" Thaulow asked, remembering "The Decay of Lying."

Wilde replied that the soul can be liberated only by drunkenness or "the Great Silence." He went on to describe how a waiter brings the silence in a glass of opalescent liquid. "Knock, and the door will always open, the door of *le paradis artificiel*."★ Consorting with the "green fairy" became more of a need. Soon Wilde had absinthe in the morning to induce a few hours of blessed sleep. "Alcohol, taken in sufficient quantities," he said, "produces all the effect of intoxication, but the only proper intoxication is conversation." The difference between a glass of absinthe and a sunset was less important in exile.

AT THE END of May, Wilde moved to the Hôtel de la Plage, where he took the two best rooms. The hotel was in Berneval-sur-Mer, a village with only twenty homes, ten miles from Dieppe. The only other guest was an elderly gentleman who went to bed at eight o'clock every evening because there was nothing else to do. Wilde aligned his few possessions precisely on the bedroom dresser (prison had made him a compulsive orderer), but there were so many things he needed: cigarettes, *The Daily Chronicle,* pictures for the wall—and always books. Those he had received in prison had to be left behind in the Reading Library.

He was delighted to receive Max Beerbohm's *The Happy Hypocrite,* an homage to *Dorian Gray.* He read the satire, he wrote Turner, "beginning at the end, as one should always do" because the end of art is the beginning. Beerbohm reversed the action of Wilde's novel: the main character, Lord George, is saved by love while Dorian is destroyed by selfishness. "I had always been disappointed," Wilde wrote Beerbohm, "that my story had suggested no other work of art in others. For whenever a

---

★Wilde was referring to Baudelaire's *Les Paradis artificiels* (1860), wrongly considered a celebration of decadence, when Baudelaire meant it as a condemnation of drugs and alcohol by someone who had discovered the perils too late. "I have come to loathe all stimulants because of the way they expand Time, and of the exaggerations with which they endow everything."

beautiful flower grows in a meadow or lawn, some other flower, so like it that it is differently beautiful, is sure to grow up beside it."

Wilde found new friends among the Dieppois—the waiters and fishermen and Monsieur O. J. Bonnet, the patron of his hotel, who distracted him with the idea of buying a parcel of land and building his own chalet for five hundred pounds. What he missed was the other society he had in London, artists, poets, his homosexual friends. "I begin to realise my terrible position of isolation," he wrote Ross. "I thought I was accepting everything so well and so simply, and I have had moods of rage passing over my nature." He survived by writing detailed, witty, and haranguing letters, rich in the observations that had formerly delighted habitués of the Café Royal. One day he picked up his mail at the Hôtel Sandwich, met Beardsley, and enjoyed an evening with him at the Thaulows'. Later they went shopping. "I have made Aubrey buy a hat more silver than silver: he is quite wonderful in it," Wilde wrote Turner. In the last stages of consumption, Beardsley was coughing up blood.

THE ONLY THING that captured Wilde's imagination was the thought of his own chalet. Ross received a letter in early June full of optimistic plans. "I adore this place. . . . If I live in Paris I may be doomed to things I don't desire. . . . I am frightened of Paris. I want to live here." He drew Ross a floor plan: three bedrooms, a view of the sea. He casually announced that he was working. "I have begun something that I think will be very good," he wrote, meaning *The Ballad of Reading Gaol*. Wilde needed to live like a man of letters, not like a Balzacian lodger. A chalet would provide such a setting.

He waited for friends to make a "pilgrimage to the sinner." He had grown fond of Ernest Dowson, a poet from the Rhymers' Club and one of the few who had visited him at his mother's house in Oakley Street when he was released on bail. Wilde may have heard from Lionel Johnson some talk about Dowson's obsessive love for Adelaide, a young waitress who married another that year. Dowson was living out his few remaining years as an absinthe addict. A friendship between the two lonely people began and deepened. "I want to have a poet to talk to . . . tonight I am going to read your poems—your lovely lyrics—words with wings *you* write always. It is an exquisite gift, and fortunately rare in an age whose prose is more poetic than its poetry." Wilde delighted in Dowson's company, called him "le Poète," praised his verses, and probably had a crush on him. "Why are you so persistently and perversely wonderful?" he asked when inviting him to visit.

Constance sent Wilde photographs of his sons ("such lovely little fellows in Eton collars") but wrote nothing about their father seeing them or a reconciliation. If Wilde saw Bosie—and he wanted to—he would forfeit his allowance and his wife's goodwill. Reading a challenging book, visiting with a friend, or writing a long letter exhausted him. Unless consoled by alcohol, Wilde battled insomnia nightly. Not feeling up to the challenge of intellectual battle, he missed his emotional life as a husband and father. Regardless of time spent at Tite Street, his family was an irreplaceable anchor. "I have now no *storage* of nervous force," he wrote Frank Harris.

FROM PARIS, BOSIE denounced Wilde and his friends for not allowing him to visit Dieppe. "I feel him as an evil influence," Wilde wrote to Ross, attempting to appear resolute. "To be with him would be to return to the hell from which I do think I have been released. I hope never to see him again." But Wilde was thinking about how he could meet Bosie without reprisal and gave away his intentions by groveling. "You are made to help me," he told Ross. "I weep with sorrow when I think how much I need help, but I weep with joy when I think I have you to give it to me." Ross sniffed a change in the wind.

In June, Bosie received his first letter since the trials. Wilde tried to keep to literary topics. All that is left, he said, "is the knowledge that we love each other." Filled with "the strange new joy of talking to you," Wilde wrote daily. "I am so glad you went to bed at seven o'clock," he wrote. "Modern life is terrible to vibrating delicate frames like yours: a rose-leaf in a storm of hard hail is not so fragile. With us who are modern it is the *scabbard* that wears out the sword."

When Gide made a special trip to pay his respects, he found Wilde arranging a celebration for Queen Victoria's Diamond Jubilee on June 22. He was relieved that Wilde was "no longer the lyrical madman of Algeria, but the gentle Wilde of before the crisis." In his room, Gide noticed the woodcut of Queen Victoria with her dog from the recent issue of the *New*

Review and his *Nourritures terrestres,* whose character Ménalque resembles Wilde. "One should never go back to the same existence," he told Gide. "My life is like a work of art; an artist never stars in the same thing twice . . . or if he does, it's that he hasn't succeeded. My life before prison was as successful as possible. Now it's something that's over." Repeatedly Wilde said that he was never going to write another play, but his friends refused to listen. After *A Woman of No Importance,* he told a journalist that he had given the audience what they liked—a virtuous maiden seduced by a wicked aristocrat—so they would appreciate what he liked to give them. That audience no longer existed, and Wilde knew he was not in any position to create a new one. Failure as a poet was better than failure as a playwright.

Fifteen "little *gamins*" arrived at the Café de la Paix in Berneval for the Jubilee fête. Wilde was as excited that the dear queen had reigned so long as he was to be paterfamilias. It was an occasion for excess, for strawberries and cream, chocolates, and an iced cake inscribed to the queen in pink sugar. The boys had their pick of accordions, trumpets, or clarions. They sang the Marseillaise and "God Save the Queen," and danced a ronde, waving small British flags. Toasts saluted the queen and Monsieur Melmoth, whom the boys called "the Président de la République." This was the life Wilde wanted—except with grown-ups. One of the many pleasures he had lost was that of being a host.

SINCE WILDE HAD no prospects of earning money to build a châlet, he decided to rent one—thirty-two pounds for the season. The Châlet Bourgeat was a short walk from the hotel where he took his meals. He hired a valet for thirty-five francs a month and felt more like a literary gentleman. Charles Wyndham visited to ask him to adapt Eugène Scribe's *Le Verre d'eau,* set in the court of Queen Anne. Wilde was excited, then anxious, finally declining, explaining that he had "no heart to write clever comedy." He wondered if he could write in Italy. "I am not in the mood to do the work I want, and I fear I shall never be," he wrote Will Rothenstein. "The intense energy of creation has been kicked out of me. I don't care now to struggle to get back what, when I had it, gave me little pleasure." The exception was writing the *Ballad.*

Through Dowson, Wilde met Leonard Smithers, who was Beardsley's publisher and had launched *The Savoy* in 1896, when Beardsley was dismissed from *The Yellow Book* following Wilde's arrest. Wilde knew about Smithers, a Sheffield solicitor turned bookseller and publisher with a penchant for pornography. One of his titles had been the homosexual novel *Teleny*. "I will publish," he told Vincent O'Sullivan, "anything the others are afraid of." Wilde called him "the most learned erotomaniac in Europe." Smithers agreed to publish Wilde's work in progress, receiving at the end of August a partial draft to be typewritten. But Wilde still had no advance. Smithers was, Wilde told Dowson, "personally charming, but at present I simply am furious with him, and intend to remain so, till he sends me the money." This would be a familiar refrain in his dealings with the amenable but tightfisted Smithers.

Bosie's planned arrival in Dieppe was abruptly canceled when Wilde's solicitor intervened, warning that Queensberry would raise a new scandal if he discovered them together. A meeting in Rouen a month later was postponed because Bosie claimed he had no money for the train fare. "I am greatly hurt by his meanness and lack of imagination," Wilde told Ross. The momentous date became August 28, 1897. "Poor Oscar cried when I met him at the station," Bosie recalled. "We walked about all day arm in arm, or hand in hand, and were perfectly happy." They spent the night at the Grand Hôtel de France, parting the next morning with pledges of mutual love.

Wilde wanted to be with Bosie; no further meetings were necessary to test his feelings, once so bitter in prison. "I feel that my only hope of again doing beautiful work in art is being with you," he wrote him. "It was not so in old days, but now it is different, and you can really recreate in me that energy and sense of joyous power on which art depends. Everyone is furious with me for going back to you, but they don't understand us." Wilde begged Bosie: "Do remake my ruined life for me, and then our friendship and love will have a different meaning to the world." Tersely he informed Ross, "Yes: I saw Bosie, and of course I love him as I always did, with a sense of tragedy and ruin."

Bosie was not one to remake anyone's ruined life. Constance was, but she had wavered, listened to her counselors, and waited to see if her husband had reformed. When she waited too long, Wilde chose Bosie over his sons. He had lied to himself about enjoying French provincial life. As fall came, he was bored and cold in his châlet. On September 14, he left for Paris and a few days later met Bosie in Aix-les-Bains, where they caught the overnight train to Naples. The Normandy exile had lasted less than four months.

Lovers imagine they can live on love. Wilde and Bosie were no exception, escaping family and society, hoping to keep on breaking the rules. Wilde had an allowance of three pounds a week from his wife, with a termination clause if he returned to Bosie. Bosie had eight pounds a week from his mother and a warning to stay away from Wilde. In the beginning they were kind to each other. Bosie had not read the hateful parts about him in *De Profundis* and would not, by his account, until twelve years after Wilde's death. Using Bosie's title, they established credit at the Hôtel Royal des Étrangers and went off to rent a furnished villa.

THE FASHIONABLE AREA of Posillipo curves around the Bay of Naples north of the city. Pine and palm trees frame the terraced villas hugging the rocky cliffs, looking out to the astonishing view of Mount Vesuvius. At the Villa Giudice—the most beautifully situated of Wilde's writing houses, rivaling Babbacombe Cliff—the two would write poetry and be happy together. Wilde had put together £120 to cover rent and servants; £100 was a commission from the composer Dalhousie Young, who had visited in Berneval. Wilde affected a schoolmaster's role, hoping to direct Bosie's imagination toward something other than sex. Arising in the morning, he announced, "I think I'll do a libretto for an opera on 'Daphnis and Chloe'—and you'll help me." Bosie was not without musical talent, and the villa had a piano, but the two produced only a few lyrics, not a libretto. Wilde began lessons in Italian conversation, mixing his Dante with modern slang. He engaged his teacher to translate *Salome*. Working on the terrace, shading his downy good looks from the sun like a blond Byron, Bosie composed three sonnets. Wilde christened them "The Triad of the Moon."

Reporting Wilde's whereabouts, the French papers made it sound as though the villa belonged to Douglas when, in fact, Wilde was paying for everything. They hired four servants to cook and clean but continued to take evening meals on credit at the hotel. Wilde did not need bliss, only contentment and companionship. He kept working on the *Ballad,* eager to have money from Smithers. "He laboured over it in a manner which I had never known him to labour before," Bosie recalled. "Every word had to be considered; every rhyme and every cadence carefully pondered. I had *The Ballad of Reading Gaol* for breakfast, dinner, and tea and for many weeks it was our sole topic of conversation."

Wilde justified his actions to Turner, writing that Bosie loved him "more than he loves or can love anyone else." Going back to him "was psychologically inevitable." To Ross he explained: "I cannot live without the atmosphere of Love. I must love and be loved, whatever price I pay for it. I could have lived all my life with you, but you have other claims on you . . . and all you could give me was a week of companionship." As for his wife, he wrote to Carlos Blacker: "I must remake my maimed life on my own lines. Had Constance allowed me to see my boys, my life would, I think have been quite different." Wilde should have been patient and waited longer before seeing Bosie, if seeing his sons was that important to him.

Easily bored, Bosie sought out his friends on Capri, arranging for lunch at Axel Munthe's villa at Anacapri. Munthe was a Swedish doctor who had treated the foreign colonies in Paris and Rome. He fell in love with Capri on his honeymoon in 1880 and spent the rest of his life building his home on a mountaintop of volcanic rock, an act of endurance that made him a revered figure on the island. He knew anyone of importance who had ever needed a doctor while on the Grand Tour, and he never hesitated to mention that he was one of five present at the opening of the tomb of Tutankhamen. "A wonderful personality," said Wilde after viewing Munthe's extensive Greek collection, giving his host the highest praise. Guests made the arduous climb to Anacapri for conversation, not feasting. Munthe believed that eating was a physiological need, not a pleasure. He set his table as if for a banquet with antique Venetian glasses but served macaroni or a kind of hash composed of eggs, potatoes, and vegetables. Wilde and Bosie were not tempted to duplicate such abstemious fare at the Villa Guidice.

Naples was known for its *ragazzi di vita,* boys of the street. The Greek bronzes of Naples rest by day in the museums, Wilde remarked, and are seen on the streets at night. Names of supposed conquests tumbled out in letters to Ross and Turner. "I am engaged to a fisherman of extraordinary beauty, age eighteen." Didaco had "a face chiselled for high romance." Pietro was "like a young St. John. One would have followed him into the desert." Wilde did not lack for Ganymedean muses, but they inspired no writing. Wilde and Bosie had re-created their London life as it was before the trials.

When she learned about his living arrangements at the villa, Constance stopped Wilde's stipend. More Adey was caught in the middle when he told Wilde that his wife was acting within her rights. Wilde launched a semantic battle about Bosie not being a "disreputable person" because he had never been convicted of anything. He rebuked Constance for a "terrible letter" and for using words such as "forbid," "require," and "not allow." "How can she really imagine that she can influence or control my life?" he stormed to Ross. "She might just as well try to influence and control my art. . . . Women are so petty, and Constance has no imagination. Perhaps, for revenge, she will have another trial: then she certainly may claim to have for the first time in her life influenced me. I wish to goodness she would leave me alone." And she did.

THE MONEY RAN out and Bosie left. Wilde was too exhausted to ask Ross for a loan, which he could never have repaid anyway. There were scenes and tantrums but modulated, unlike those that drove Wilde to despair in the old days. Bosie had achieved his goal—getting Wilde back. That obstacle cleared, there was little excitement in their day-to-day existence. It was a quiet rather than a chaotic ending. Douglas told his mother that he had "lost that supreme desire for his society which I had before, and which made a sort of aching void when he was not with me. . . . If I hadn't rejoined him and lived with him for two months, I should *never* have got over longing for him." Of course, the society he had had with Wilde was lost forever because Wilde's position was no longer that of a married, successful playwright. Wilde understood. Bosie felt the same as Dorian had when he reproached Sibyl: "I loved you because you were marvellous, because you had genius and intellect, because you realized the dreams of great poets and gave shape and substance to the shadows of art." Without her art, she was "nothing."

Oscar behaved like a perfect gentleman, Bosie assured his mother. "He has been sweet and gentle and will always remain to me as a type of what a gentleman and a friend should be." Bosie could not stand the reflected infamy: "I am tired of the struggle and tired of being ill-treated by the

World." Pleased that her son had fled, Lady Queensberry opened her purse; she paid the rent on the villa, the unpaid Naples hotel bill, and two hundred pounds toward trial costs. Wilde considered payment of the five-hundred-pound court costs for which he had been bankrupted a debt of honor. Intellectually Bosie agreed, but he believed that gentlemen commonly do not pay debts of honor and no one thinks anything the worse of them. The two hundred should have gone to what Wilde spent on Bosie in Naples.

In December, Eleonora Duse, known as La Duse, came to the magisterial Teatro Mercadante. Wilde saw her in *Magda* and an Italian adaptation of Pinero's *The Second Mrs. Tanqueray.* He hoped she might play Salomé, although she was no Bernhardt. The two actresses could not have been more different. Duse created characters with simplicity—no gesticulating or declaiming. Small and unprepossessing, she had a soft voice but played tortured and betrayed women. It was said that she could blush on demand. A *no* or a *pouah*—just one word—was done with such interpretation that it inspired unanimous applause. Duse read *Salomé,* but she did not see herself as the lurid princess. It was a narcissistic part better suited to Bernhardt.

Fitful after Bosie's departure, Wilde accepted the invitation of a newly met friend described as a "Russian Elder" to visit Taormina in Sicily. There he spent Christmas and New Year's, and met Baron von Gloeden, whose photographs of Sicilian youths in the costumes of Theocritan goatherds or shepherds he obliquely refers to in *Dorian Gray:* Lord Henry collects photographs of Dorian posing as such homoerotic icons as Antinoüs, Adonis, and Narcissus. The baron had settled in Taormina in the nineties and became a photographer to support himself when he exhausted the family fortune. His nude Sicilian boys posed like Greek statues delighted Wilde, who reciprocated with a copy of the *Ballad.*

Wilde returned to Posillipo to discover that the servants had stolen everything. He mourned the loss of a pastel portrait of him in a red vest done in Paris in 1891 by Will Rothenstein, then nineteen and destined to become principal of the Royal College of Art. The burglary provided an excuse to leave the Villa Giudice, with its memories of happy, sunny days. He moved to the Palazzo Bambino, at 31 Santa Lucia in Naples, and planned his entry into Paris.

Since finishing the *Ballad,* Wilde had methodically corrected proofs, enjoying as he always did the process of editing. Before he left for Sicily, he told Leonard Smithers that he was overcome by "the *maladie de perfection*" and wanted no more proofs. He approved the type (thick font) and design (a cinnamon-colored spine) and fought with Smithers about the publisher's name on the page being larger than the author's, identified as C.3.3. A major disappointment was the lack of interest in America, which Wilde interpreted as a rejection of himself and his work. He had wanted three hundred pounds for newspaper publication, but the only offer was one hundred dollars from the *New York Journal*. Elisabeth Marbury apologized: "Nobody here seems to feel any interest in the poem. The *World* refuses to give us anything and no syndicate will handle it." The coolness probably had more to do with the subject matter than with Wilde's infamy.

On February 13, 1898, when the *Ballad* was published, Wilde was in Paris, settled into the Hôtel de Nice, 4 rue des Beaux-Arts. The same day Americans read about Reading Gaol in the daily newspaper. In England everyone knew the author's identity, paying to read about his suffering. One shop sold out its fifty copies on the morning of publication. Few review copies were sent out, so there was little press recognition. *The Daily Telegraph* described it as "a moving piece of work, without doubt, despite its tone," and as having "already had a certain vogue, not merely for the reason that it is a strikingly vivid and realistic description of prison life, but also because everyone is ready with a suggestion as to who the anonymous really is." Constance received an uninscribed copy and wrote her brother, "It is frightfully tragic and makes one cry."

Within a month, the tragedy was Constance's sudden death. Wilde learned that his wife had died in Genoa on April 7, 1898, at the age of forty. Her chronic back problems had forced a second operation on her spine, and she did not recover. Bosie was sympathetic. Constance had always treated him kindly when he visited Tite Street. Wilde cabled to Ross, AM IN GREAT GRIEF, and asked him to come to Paris. Ross rushed over and found his friend in laudable spirits. He wrote Smithers that Oscar "did not feel it at all." Such a remark was typical of Ross, who saw Wilde as only a lover of men. "My way back to a new life ends in her grave," he told Frank Harris. "Everything that happens to me is symbolic and irrevocable." Wilde's feelings were complex but no less poignant. He called his wife's death a tragedy, and that was true for her as well as for him. As long as Constance lived, there was a hope that he could see his sons. Now her family closed ranks against him. "If we had only met once, and kissed each other," he wrote Carlos Blacker. "It is too late. How awful life is."

The following month, Wilde celebrated the French translation of *The Ballad of Reading Gaol*. Now the French had something of his to read beyond *Salomé*. As the *Ballad* was going into its fifth English edition, Smithers took out an advertisement in *The Athenaeum* with the headline "3000 Copies Sold in Three Weeks." "When I read it," Wilde told George Ives, "I feel like Lipton's tea!" It seemed that the positive response might open a new literary chapter. Instead, it ended Wilde's artistic period and began a new existence as an overt homosexual.

CHAPTER TWENTY-ONE

Stealing Happiness

❧

O we are wearied of this sense of guilt,
Wearied of pleasure's paramour despair,
Wearied of every temple we have built,
Wearied of every right, unanswered prayer.
For man is weak; God sleeps, and heaven is high;
One fiery-coloured moment: one great love;
and lo! we die.

—"PANTHEA"

Even for the author of *Salomé,* Paris was not a homecoming. Wilde's last extended stay in the city had been in 1891, when he was welcomed by artist-aristocrats who no longer dominated the salons. Verlaine had died while Wilde was imprisoned, and Mallarmé would be dead in six months. Louÿs had married and forgotten old recriminations. To absolve himself of guilt, Gide made his courtesy call in Berneval, but he saw Wilde only once afterward, when Wilde hailed him from an outdoor café. Wilde insisted that Gide sit beside him. "I'm so alone these days," he said, adding that he had not even a sou. Gide gave him some money and lied about another meeting. "I have lost the mainspring of life and art, *la joie de vivre;* it is dreadful," Wilde wrote Frank Harris. "I have pleasures, and passions, but the joy of life is gone. I am going under: the morgue yawns for me. I go and look at my zinc-bed there. After all, I had a wonderful life, which is, I fear, over." He had learned "a curious and bitter lesson," he said, almost surprised by the insight. "I used to rely on my personality: now I know that my personality really rested on the fiction of *position*. Having lost position, I find my personality of no avail."

By necessity, Wilde's exile on the Left Bank was spent with the lower rung of artists, who had not yet made a reputation that could be tarnished by association with him now that he had decided to live openly—and without fear—as a homosexual. When he threw away the mask and stopped the lies, he was strangely happy. In this new sensual life, there was no room for intellectual Greek love. He could not be arrested for soliciting in Paris, but he would be talked about. That was fine: Wilde needed to be talked about. "A patriot put in prison for loving his country loves his country," he said, "and a poet in prison for loving boys loves boys." Every day in Paris, he wanted to be in love with a beautiful boy.

This was no new artistic manifesto comparable to Aestheticism, Decadence, or platonic love. It probably went unnoticed that Wilde was making a statement about himself, his nature, and his life as a work of art. He had no guidelines, no thoughts about his identity as a homosexual or his place in a nonexistent homosexual culture. He knew he would never see his children again. There was no one left to outrage except himself and a few old friends.

Will Rothenstein took him to dinner at an outdoor restaurant that featured an orchestra. Wilde insisted on being seated near the musicians and flaunted his interest in one of the players. Uncomfortable, Rothenstein decided not to keep in touch. On his next visit to Paris, he saw Wilde walking along the boulevards. He later wrote, "I saw at once that he knew we had meant to avoid him. The look he gave us was tragic, and he seemed ill, and was shabby and down at heel."

WILDE ENJOYED BEING in his old neighborhood. The Hôtel Voltaire, where he had written *The Duchess of Padua* and *The Sphinx,* was a short walk from where he stayed on the rue des Beaux-Arts, which paralleled the rue Visconti, where Balzac had his printing shop. Poverty did not ennoble Wilde, nor did it inspire him. Being hungry was romantic only when one was young. Twenty years earlier, he had never scribbled at the tables of the Brasserie Lipp or Les Deux Magots, popular cafés on the boulevard St.-Germain where the rue Bonaparte starts down toward the Seine. The ubiquitous circular table was for drinking and meeting friends, for reading the *Chronicle* with much rustling of the pages, and for writing letters, particularly if the café provided stationery and ink. At the Café Procope he made friends with Marcel Legay, a songwriter, and J.-B. de Bucé, editor of a small literary journal. One evening, Jean Lorrain, a Decadent novelist, and Wilde had a good-natured squabble about who was the better poseur. Wilde's passion for *blague,* or humbug, never abated.

No longer able to be a generous host, he learned to sit and wait until someone else paid. "I live a very ordinary life," he somberly wrote Ross. "I go to cafés like Pousset's where I meet artists and writers. I don't frequent places like the Café de la Paix [on the boulevard des Capucines]. I dine in modest restaurants for two or three francs. My life is rather dull. I cannot flaunt or dash about: I have not got the money, nor the clothes. When I can I go to the Quartier Latin under the wing of a poet, and talk about art."

Since he was constantly borrowing and begging, Wilde made it impossible for anyone to calculate how much money he had to spend, but he was never as poor as he said he was when asking for a handout. His quarterly allowance, doled out by Ross, was £37.10, the equivalent of 925 francs. He tried to live on 250 francs a month, and his hotel cost 70. In addition, he earned royalties on the *Ballad* because, he said, "the public liked to hear of my pain." He sold publication rights for *An Ideal Husband* and *Earnest* to Smithers for £30, paid out in increments of £5. Wilde's cycles of frugality, as reported to Ross, were not without humor. He found a restaurant where for 80 francs a month "one can get nothing fit to eat— two chances a day." He discovered that "one can't get railway-tickets on credit. It is such a bore!"

Getting money from London was a constant irritation. As an expatri- ate, Wilde could have opened a bank account, but he was living under the assumed name Sebastian Melmoth, with only a gentleman's calling card for identification. Funds were wired to Thomas Cook's at the place de l'Opéra, long the Englishman's connection to home. "I have been *seven* times to Cook's," he wrote Smithers, "and also went at seven o'clock, two hours after their bank closes, and woke them up. Of course nothing at all had arrived, so I have had no dinner." While in the area, he browsed around Brentano's, the English and American bookstore at 37 avenue de l'Opéra. He had to pay cash, and his last purchases were four volumes of Tennyson and seven popular novels, curiously entitled *Colonel Harbottle's Client, March Hares,* and *A Protegée of Jack Hamlin.*

Bosie's income was even more mysterious. He went from having no money in Naples to leasing an apartment on avenue Kléber, one of Baron Haussmann's fashionable thoroughfares radiating from the Arc de Triomphe. Wilde helped him select furniture, including a green bed in honor of Baudelaire. Bosie continued to gamble heavily on horse races, and once had to pawn his cuff links for train fare to Paris. No one changed, as Wilde had astutely observed: people just kept rattling about in their old personalities. When Ross sent some new clothes, Wilde complained that the trousers were too tight in the waist. He was gaining weight because of cheap food. "Nothing fattens so much as a dinner at 1 fr. 50," he said.

The former lovers enjoyed each other's company as much as ever, but Wilde's heart no longer quickened when they met. At twenty-seven, Bosie looked years younger, but his Apollonian aura was tarnished through use. Money remained an issue between them. A hopeless handicapper, Bosie usually lost heavily at the races, but when he won twelve hundred pounds, Wilde asked him to settle his debt of honor. Bosie was outraged. "I can't afford to spend anything except on myself " was a typical reply. As they were sitting at a table outside the Café de la Paix, Wilde let the matter drop.

WILDE WAS KNOWN to many boys along the boulevards. "Of course I cannot bear being alone," he wrote Ross, "and while the literary people are charming when they meet me, we meet rarely. My companions are such as I can get, and I of course have to pay for such friendships." His letters to Ross and Turner listed many a boy. There was Ashton, Edmond, Léon, a Russian named Maltchek Perovinsky, and Giorgio, a Corsican who worked at the Restaurant Jouffroy, Eugene, who was "the harvest-moon," and Alphonse, who was "quite an imp." At the Café d'Égypte, there was a slim brown Egyptian waiter "rather like a handsome bamboo walking-stick." The beauty of the French fauns gave Wilde something to write home about, but he was really bored "by the lack of intellect," for which he admonished himself. "I attribute it to Oxford. None of us survive culture."

One companion brightened his exile: Maurice Gilbert. Described by Wilde in adjectives redolent of Bosie, Gilbert had an upper lip that was more "like a rose-leaf than any rose-leaf I ever saw." Half English and half French, he had been a soldier in the marine infantry and did odd jobs around Paris, particularly for Rowland Strong, a friend of Wilde who was Paris correspondent for the *Observer*. Gilbert was generous and patient; he played bezique, a pinochle-like game, hour after hour because it amused Wilde. "Maurice has won twenty-five games of bezique and I twenty-four," Wilde reported, "however, as he has youth, and I have only genius, it is only natural that he should beat me." When the seventh edition of the *Ballad* was issued with Wilde's name—enclosed in brackets—below his cell number, C.3.3., Gilbert copied Wilde's extravagant signature onto presentation copies because the author was too tired to sign his final work.

Also Bosie's boy, Gilbert returned to Bosie during the racing season. He traveled to London to share the affections of Ross and Turner, expenses presumably paid by Turner, the only one who could afford such gestures. When he is away, Wilde teases Ross: "So you love Maurice?" And asks Turner, "How is my golden Maurice? I suppose he is wildly loved?" As a lover to the whole group, Gilbert linked them together and symbolized how homosexual love could germinate without jealousy.

Inevitably, Wilde established friends in the theatre. Georgette Leblanc, mistress of the dramatist Maurice Maeterlinck and the leading actress at the Opéra Comique, gave him seats for her performances. He visited the actress's house near the Bois de Boulogne, decorated to Wilde's taste with white walls and Burne-Jones photographs. He met Maeterlinck, dubbed "the Belgian Shakespeare" in 1889 after the production of his first play, *La Princesse Maleine*. Maeterlinck had given up playwriting, prompting Wilde's remark that he "rests his hope of humanity on the Bicycle." André Antoine, a French actor, gave Wilde a box seat to see *Les Tisserands,* a translation of Gerhart Hauptmann's socialistic drama *Die Weber,* based on the incidents of the weavers' revolt in 1844.

Wilde said it "was rather like a public meeting, and should be called *The Triumph of the Supers.*"

The annual May Fête des Fous distracted him. "A delightful evening," he wrote Turner, "the whole Quartier Latin was bright with beauty and wine, and the students in their mediaeval costumes picturesque and improbable and gay." Beyond frequenting poetry readings at Montmartre cafés, Wilde found friends at places catering to homosexuals. His favorite was the Calisaya, on the boulevard des Italiens, where he knew the bartender and met Ernest La Jeunesse, a journalist. Sometimes his old friends Jean Lorrain and Maurice Du Plessys joined them. It was a comfortable spot to end the evening with *petits verres.* Vincent O'Sullivan warned him that the bar was filled with "sodomist outcasts, who were sometimes dangerous in other ways." But Wilde liked the atmosphere.

IN DECEMBER, THE irrepressible Frank Harris appeared with the offer of three months in the fishing village of La Napoule near Cannes, enough time, he thought, for Wilde to produce "a work of art." Harris had sold *The Saturday Review* and was going into the hotel business in Monaco.* "Frank insists on my being at high intellectual pressure," Wilde told Ross, "it is most exhausting; but when we arrive at La Napoule I am going to break the news to him—now an open secret—that I have softening of the brain, and cannot always be a genius." Wilde settled into the Hôtel des Bains on the Golfe Juan, but Harris, with whom he had expected to celebrate Christmas, did not appear for several weeks.

In the interim Wilde met Harold Mellor, the twenty-six-year-old son of a British industrialist who was staying at Cannes with his mother. Wilde learned that Mellor had been sent down from Harrow at fourteen for being loved by the captain of the cricket eleven. He was often accompanied by Eolo, a young Italian bought from his father for two hundred

---

*Harris ended up appropriating from Wilde a short story, "The Irony of Chance," and the scenario for *Mr. and Mrs. Daventry.* Wilde had the idea for *Daventry* as early as 1894, when he offered it to George Alexander. Harris took the idea and wrote the play on his own, but not before Wilde sold options to at least five other people: Mrs. James Brown-Potter, an American socialite; Horace Sedger; Ada Rehan; Louis Nethersole, a theatrical manager; and Smithers.

lire, a kind of slave. The incongruous threesome celebrated Boxing Day with plum pudding and Pommery-Greno, a champagne that brought Wilde back to "the exquisite taste of ancient life." How Wilde celebrated the new year of 1899 was not recorded. He was with Mellor in Nice to see Sarah Bernhardt in *La Tosca*. Afterward he visited backstage; she embraced him, and there was weeping all around. Forgotten was her refusal to buy the rights to *Salomé* when he was bankrupt.

IN MID-FEBRUARY, Wilde moved from La Napoule to the Hôtel Terminus in Nice. Since he was doing no writing, Harris wanted him to inspect villas to rent. Soon he was trapped in a typical financial muddle. At most hotels Wilde charged his room and meals until presented with the bill, when some payment was required. He found the German food at the Terminus loathsome; the English residents objected to his presence. Every day a bill was delivered with morning coffee. He wrote, "My dear Frank, you must come down and see me here for a few moments. You cannot, and you will not, abandon me. I won't go to the Palace, because it would not be good for your hotel for me to be seen there." An oblique threat and the bill was paid, and Wilde's three months on the Riviera ended. Adrift, he went to stay at Mellor's villa on Lake Geneva. "I hope to be happy there: at any rate there will be free meals," he told Ross, "and champagne has been ordered, though the Nice doctor now absolutely forbids me to take any, on account of gout."

On the way to Switzerland, Wilde made a detour to Genoa to say farewell to his wife. He left flowers on Constance's grave, marked with a marble cross inlaid with dark ivy leaves, at the Protestant Cemetery. "It was very tragic," he wrote Ross, "seeing her name carved on a tomb—her surname, my name not mentioned of course—just 'Constance Mary, daughter of Horace Lloyd, Q.C.' and a verse from *Revelations*. I was deeply affected—with a sense, also, of the uselessness of all regrets. Nothing could have been otherwise, and Life is a very terrible thing."★

There were others to mourn. A month before Constance's death, Wilde learned that Aubrey Beardsley had died at Mentone at the age of twenty-five. "There is something macabre and tragic," Wilde wrote

★ "Wife of Oscar Wilde" was added in 1963.

Smithers, "in the fact that one who added another terror to life should have died at the age of a flower." When he arrived in Switzerland, he learned that Willie had died on March 13, 1899, at the age of forty-six. Wilde regretted the "wide chasms" between them but saw his brother's death as inevitable because of his excessive drinking. "One has always sad memories of what Willie might have been," his widow wrote Wilde, "instead of dying practically unknown & leaving his child to be supported by my sister. She is in a country convent & I think will have a good share of the family brains." Wilde's niece, Dorothy, was nearly four years old.

WILDE FOUND SWITZERLAND's natural beauty impressive but the young men disappointing. "Swiss people are carved out of wood with a rough knife, most of them; the others are carved out of turnips," he wrote. With Mellor, as with others who offered hospitality, Wilde accepted his role as court jester. He took no offense about singing for his supper, as long as he was well-fed and champagne flowed. Soon his thirst for champagne was tempered by cheap Swiss wine and then beer. "Mellor carries out the traditions of the ancient misers," Wilde observed. "If I ask him to lend me five francs he grows yellow and takes to his bed. Every day I discover some new fault in him." He asked Smithers for five pounds to escape to Italy. "The chastity of Switzerland has got on my nerves," he wrote.

He spent April on the Ligurian coast, using Santa Margherita as a base to explore Rapallo and Portofino. He begged Ross to join him: "Whatever I do is wrong: because my life is not on a right basis. In Paris I am bad: here I am bored: the last state is the worse." Ross did visit and brought Wilde back to Paris in late May. Before returning to the Alsace, Wilde exhausted his credit at several small Right Bank hotels. The Hôtel de la Néva on the rue Monsigny let him stay only a few weeks; then he moved to the nearby Hôtel Marsollier on the rue Marsollier, where he spent June and July, until presented with a bill. "Life is rather dust now, and water-wells are rare in the desert," he wrote Harris, asking for a "tenner." Wilde likened himself to St. Francis of Assisi, wedded to poverty but in an unsuccessful marriage, living on echoes with no music of his own.

Friends marveled at how Wilde kept on begging, using different words, although sometimes the same excuses, in each letter. Typically he wrote Ross that he had subsisted on only breakfast served at the hotel. "I have had a very bad time lately, and for two days had not a penny in my pocket, so had to wander about, filled with a wild longing for *bock* and cigarettes: it was really like journeying through Hell." There was no moral disgrace in begging; his genius had brought him to this point, and genius should be fed. Wilde stood by his words in "The Soul of Man Under Socialism" that artists should be freed from financial worries. He was educating the public and believed that the Frank Harrises of the world should share with those less fortunate, as he had done when successful. Invoking Balzac in one letter, he observed that "it is always a bore to find oneself without pocket-money. Balzac's *héros métallique* still dominates our age, as do indeed all Balzac's heroes; and the French have not yet realised that the basis of all civilisation is unlimited credit. Empires only fall when they have to pay their bills: at the moment the Barbarians arrive."

GEORGE IVES VISITED and skulked about Paris trying to be invisible. Here was the so-called voice of the movement—his second volume of Uranian verse, *Book of Chains,* was published in 1897—afraid to compromise himself by being seen with Wilde. He would call the Hôtel d'Alsace and leave a message without giving his address. "Don't have with *me* the silly mania for secrecy that makes you miss the value of things," Wilde told him, "to you it is of more importance to conceal your address from a friend than to see your friend. . . . On the whole, George, you are a great baby. One can't help being angry with you." Since Wilde's hearing was getting worse, Ives preferred to talk privately at his hotel, where he could raise his voice without eavesdroppers. Wilde wanted to be seen on the boulevards. The cafés did not tempt Ives, who was still drinking hot milk to protest Wilde's imprisonment.

When they talked of "the movement" and how long acceptance of homosexuality would take, Wilde said, "I have no doubt we shall win—but the road is long, and red with monstrous martyrdoms. Nothing but the repeal of the Criminal Law Amendment Act would do any good. That is essential. It is not so much public opinion, as public officials that need educating." "Oscar *meant* well, to all," Ives wrote in his diary. "He had not the gift of responsibility, he could not estimate consequence, he was all Art, and all Emotion, and I looked up to him as to a superman, and do still, while utterly disagreeing with his written philosophy, and even with his life, on many sides."

DURING THE SIXTEEN months that Wilde lived intermittently at the Alsace, he stayed in different rooms depending on his finances. He lived first in two rooms on the third floor, moved to the fourth floor, and died on the second floor. "It is a poor little Bohemian hotel, only suited for those Sybarites who are exiled from Sybaris," he said. Comfortable but not squalid, as sometimes reported, the Alsace was no different from other small hotels where Wilde established credit during his exile in Paris. The difference was the kindness of the proprietor, Jean Dupoirier, who liked Wilde and did not press him to pay. Dupoirier paid his bill of twenty pounds at the Hôtel Marsollier and rescued his confiscated possessions. That Dupoirier, a hotelier trying to make ends meet, with no knowledge of Wilde's works, became Wilde's guardian angel during his last days can only be explained by Wilde's ability to charm.

The hotel's distinguishing feature was a courtyard dominated by a fig tree. Wilde had his own table placed under the tree and each morning awoke there with coffee. At other hours, he sat staring into the middle distance, drinking absinthe, accumulating saucers. His rent ranged from forty to sixty-five francs a month. He ate the same food every day: a breakfast of coffee and a roll with butter at eleven and a lunch of two chops and two soft-boiled eggs at two. At five he walked across the Pont Royal to the Café de la Régence for an aperitif and then to the Café de Paris for dinner, ending the evening at what he called the "literary resort of myself and my friends," the Calisaya. Dupoirier went to the avenue de l'Opéra to replenish Wilde's weekly supply of Courvoisier—four bottles at twenty-eight francs, more than his room. Drinking was the only way Wilde could sleep.

One day at the Café Vieille Rose, near the place de l'Opéra, Wilde was dining on ortolans with Ross and Laurence Housman when the name of

Robert Burns changed the conversation. "God saved the genius of Burns to poetry by driving him through drink to failure," Wilde told Housman. "Riotous living and dying saved him from that last degradation of smug prosperity which threatened him." As much as Wilde wanted his dining companions to see the parallels between his life and Burns's, the name under discussion should have been that of the Irish playwright Richard Brinsley Sheridan, who also challenged English hypocrisy and was generous to the point of prodigality; both sought fame and ended life in poverty, drunkenness, and apparent failure.

WILDE'S FAREWELL TO the eighteen hundreds was uneventful—a "very pleasant Christmas," he wrote Ross. Across the channel on New Year's Eve, fires were lit on every hilltop from the South Downs to the Scottish border, and bells rang from every church with a belfry. In Westminster Abbey, a future bishop of Oxford, Charles Gore, declared: "Our present-day literature is singularly without inspiration. There is no Carlyle to whom all men naturally turn to find some answer to their chaotic yearnings; there is no Tennyson . . . there is no prophet of the people." Once there had been Wilde, a self-proclaimed prophet who taught that art and life are interchangeable.

In February, Wilde was bedridden with a throat infection that the doctor appeared unable to treat. "My throat is a lime kiln, my brain a furnace and my nerves a coil of angry adders," he complained as he continued to smoke harsh French cigarettes. He ate some bad mussels, which gave him an itchy rash. "Poisoning by mussels," he told Ross, "is very painful and when one has one's bath one looks like a leopard." But an itchy rash—as Ellmann notes—is not a symptom of syphilis. This rash became the only noticeable evidence that Wilde was syphilitic, even though a rash is characteristic of secondary syphilis and by this time Wilde would have been in the tertiary stage, with such classic symptoms as mental deterioration or an unsteady gait called "ataxia." He exhibited none of these. In March, Wilde described "a sort of blood poisoning," blaming the "insanitary state" of the hotel, and spent ten days in a hospital.

Admittedly neurasthenic—a Victorian term for listlessness more mental than physical—Wilde did not like lolling in bed. It took a great deal of energy to be charming "when one is cooped up in a wretched hotel," he said. The sudden death of Ernest Dowson on February 23 at the age of thirty-two saddened him; he called Dowson "a sweet singer, with a note all the lovelier because it reminds us of how thrushes sang in Shakespeare's day." Also deceased was the Marquess of Queensberry, who died on January 31, leaving Bosie twenty thousand pounds. Bosie again refused to settle his debt of honor.

To the rescue once more, this time driving a motorcar, came Mellor, who offered Wilde a modest stipend of fifty pounds to accompany him to Italy. Wilde asked Ross to meet him in Rome. "It will be delightful to be together again, and this time I really must become a Catholic." Wilde arrived in Rome on Good Friday; through a "miracle" he obtained a ticket for St. Peter's on Easter Sunday and received Pope Leo XIII's blessing. During recent visits to Europe, Ross had avoided seeing Wilde in Paris. This time, although as close as Milan, he did not come to Rome, even when taunted by Wilde's imminent conversion. Ross was a Papist snob. He felt his brand of faith and confession superior to Wilde's love of pageantry and ritual.

Agreeing with Byron that it is "the only city of the soul," Wilde fell in love all over again with Rome. He had a better time alone, not being bothered by Ross's autocratic notions. He culled boys on the Corso and in the Borghese Gardens and collected blessings—seven in all—from the Pope: "I do nothing but see the Pope: I have already been blessed many times, once in the private Chapel of the Vatican." It delighted Wilde's childish side that the Pope wore a different chasuble and maniple every time he received a blessing. "I really must become a Catholic," he told Ross, "though I fear that if I went before the Holy Father with a blossoming rod it would turn at once into an umbrella or something dreadful of that kind." He bought a Kodak camera and was so pleased with the results that he considered becoming a photographer.

Back in Paris for the April opening of the Exhibition of 1900, in its opulent crystal-domed building, Wilde attended almost daily until his health began to fail, enchanted by the exhibits, particularly Rodin's daunting statue of Balzac. Ernest La Jeunesse said that Wilde loved the fanfare and "built again his own palace of fame, riches and immortality."

. . .

ON OCTOBER 10, Wilde had an unspecified operation on his right ear, the one injured from the fall in prison, which was performed in his hotel room by a French surgeon, Paul Cleiss. The next day he telegraphed Ross: TERRIBLY WEAK. PLEASE COME. The doctor from the British embassy, Maurice à'Court Tucker, made frequent visits, a total of sixty-eight. With the onset of meningitis, Wilde had a round-the-clock nurse and a brain specialist. Food arrived from a restaurant. Dupoirier moved him to the second floor to avoid too many steps. Number 8 was a suite of two rooms with a heavy, round mahogany table and chairs, an old gilt clock on the mantelpiece, and fading flowers on the wallpaper. A thick velvet curtain enclosed the bed. Books were everywhere, the table littered with papers, and a bowl filled with crumbling cigarette ashes of the cheap French variety, since Wilde could not afford his favorite gold-tipped Russians. A bottle of absinthe was on the washstand and an open copy of Gautier's *Émaux et Camées.*

Ross arrived on October 17, the day after Wilde's forty-sixth birthday. Wilde had celebrated in bed, drinking champagne, which the doctors allowed him throughout his illness. "Ah! Robbie," he said, "when we are dead and buried in our porphyry tombs, and the trumpet of the Last Judgment is sounded, I shall turn and whisper to you, 'Robbie, Robbie, let us pretend we do not hear it.' " By the twenty-ninth, he felt well enough to get out of bed for the first time. He and Ross dined in the Latin Quarter, and Wilde drank absinthe. The next afternoon they went for a drive in the Bois de Boulogne and stopped at nearly every café for an absinthe. Ross warned Wilde that he would kill himself if he kept on drinking. "And what have I to live for, Robbie?" he asked and talked constantly of paying off his debts before he died.

He could not complain of being alone. Dupoirier fussed over him, popping in whenever he finished a task around the hotel. Turner was there; Wilde's sister-in-law, Lily, and her new husband visited. "I will never outlive the century," he told them. "The English people would not stand for it." Despite Wilde's protestations and tears, Ross left to join his mother in Nice on November 12, a trip that could have been postponed. Ross convinced himself that Wilde was not that ill, but his finicky nature was incompatible with the unpleasantness of the sickroom.

It became Turner's responsibility to monitor the drinking. "You are qualifying for a doctor," said Wilde. "When you can refuse bread to the hungry and drink to the thirsty, you may apply for your diploma." One morning he awoke and said, "I have had a dreadful dream. I dreamt that I was dining with the dead." Turner remarked, "My dear Oscar, I am sure you were the life and soul of the party."

When delirious, Wilde talked in French and English and recited lines in Greek and Latin; at other times he was capable of lucid conversation. Turner sent Ross daily reports: "He has not once hinted he thinks he is in danger nor did he before the delirium began. He was only anxious to be out of pain. . . . He is very difficult & rude." Turner tricked Wilde into taking some nourishment by turning out the lights and substituting milk for water. He held an ice pack on his head for forty-five minutes to lower his temperature until Wilde snapped, "You dear little Jew, don't you think this is enough." He refused to have mustard plasters applied to his feet. The doctors wanted to have his hair cut, but Turner told Ross he doubted that "Oscar will allow it."

When there was little change in Wilde's condition after ten days, Tucker and Cleiss wrote and signed a report, describing Wilde's worsening condition without mentioning syphilis: "The diagnosis of encephalitic meningitis must be made without doubt. . . . Surgical intervention seems impossible." The abscess in his ear had spread to the brain and he was dying of cerebral meningitis, an infection of the lining of the brain. His face was florid from an unbroken fever, his breathing labored. Leeches were placed on either side of the forehead to relieve pressure on the brain. Now it was simply a matter of waiting and watching. Ross arrived on November 29, after receiving Turner's telegram that Wilde's state was ALMOST HOPELESS. The pain was so great that when Wilde tried to speak to Ross he jammed his fist into his mouth to stifle a cry.

Some sign might have passed between them to have Ross rush to bring Father Cuthbert Dunne of the Passionist Order from St. Joseph's in Paris to Wilde's bedside. Ross judged that Wilde was never serious about converting, but he had promised to bring a priest if Wilde were dying. Wilde called Ross "the cherub with the flaming sword, forbidding my entrance into Eden." Wilde affirmed his wish to be received into the Catholic Church and was baptized. The following day, Father Dunne administered Extreme Unction, the last rites. Since he was in and out of coma and could not swallow, Wilde was unable to take Holy Communion. Father Dunne wrote that "when roused Wilde gave signs of being inwardly conscious" and knew that he was being received into the church. When the priest repeated the Acts of Contrition, Faith, Hope, and Charity close to his ear, Wilde tried to say the words after him.

On the afternoon of November 30, he struggled for air, and Dupoirier helped him to sit up. Just before two o'clock, he gasped, sighed, and sank back on the pillow. Catholicism was not a religion Wilde could live in, but Ross was right in assuming that it was the religion he wanted to die in. His decision was probably the best he ever made for his friend. Wilde's conversion also made possible a Catholic funeral.★

Maurice Gilbert photographed Wilde laid out in white, holding a rosary, surrounded by lilies and palm branches. He looked peaceful, like a child taking a nap after Holy Communion. "Oscar's end was as quiet and peaceful as that of an innocent child!" said Turner. There were no last words. Days earlier Wilde had told visitors that he was dying above his means and fighting a duel to the death with his wallpaper.

BOSIE ARRIVED FOR the funeral on December 2. He paid all expenses but selected an ordinary sixth-class internment. At nine o'clock the funeral cortege left the hotel, making its way along the rue Bonaparte to the church of St.-Germain-des-Prés. Black horses pulled an unadorned hearse topped with lilies, orchids, and roses. A low Requiem Mass, without music or choir, was said in the chapel by the church's vicar and Father Dunne. The church itself, the oldest in Paris, was special to Wilde. Situated across from the Café Les Deux Magots, it was a convenient retreat. The purple and gold of Catholicism had always greeted his imagination when he entered and sat in the coolness, thinking, perhaps praying.

Following services, a group of fifty walked behind the four carriages and the hearse, which bore the number thirteen, to the burial in suburban Bagneux Cemetery. There were wreaths from close friends and one from Dupoirier, inscribed *"À mon Locataire."* Many French friends, old

---

★Entry 547 in the register of St. Joseph's Church on the avenue Hoche in Paris reads: "1900: Nov. 29. Today Oscar Wilde, lying *in extremis* at the Hôtel d'Alsace, 13 rue des Beaux-Arts, Paris, was conditionally baptised by me. Cuthbert Dunne. He died the following day, having received at my hands the Sacrament of Extreme Unction."

and new, were in attendance. Wilde once told a friend that "if a man needs an elaborate tombstone in order to remain in the memory of his country, it is clear that his living at all was an act of absolute superfluity." At Bagneux, he had a simple stone with an iron railing around it and an inscription in Latin from the Book of Job that translates: "To my words they durst add nothing, and my speech dropped upon them."

Epilogue

࿇

Nine years after his death, Wilde's remains were moved from Bagneux to a grave at Père-Lachaise Cemetery. Ross received a gift of two thousand pounds from one of Wilde's friends, Mrs. Helen Carew, mother of Sir Coleridge Kennard, to erect an elaborate monument on the site. Will Rothenstein recommended the American-born sculptor Jacob Epstein for the commission. Inspired by Assyrian and Egyptian depictions of the sphinx, Epstein carved a flying demon-angel across the stone's face. On the back are lines from *The Ballad of Reading Gaol:*

And alien tears will fill for him
    Pity's long-broken urn,
For his mourners will be outcast men,
    And outcasts always mourn.

Regulations required that disinterment be in a case made in the workshops on the Bagneux Cemetery premises, although Ross had an elegant casket available. The coffin was plain oak, with a silver plate on the lid, on which was engraved OSCARD WILDE 1854–1900. Once again Wilde's name was given a new twist—this time rhyming with *discard*. Ross exploded when he noticed the mistake, and the undertaker chiseled out the D. When the tomb was erected in 1912, French officialdom stepped in and banned public viewing because of the figure's prominent genitalia, which were subsequently covered in plaster, and the entire work was hidden under a tarpaulin. Epstein refused to modify the carving or hide its sexuality with a fig leaf. It remained wrapped until the outbreak of World War I.

Ross returned to London after Wilde's death and opened the Carfax Gallery in St. James's, exhibiting the work of Max Beerbohm and Aubrey Beardsley and enhancing his reputation as an art dealer and critic. In 1912 he was appointed assessor of pictures and drawings for the Board of the Inland Revenue, with the responsibility of visiting estates to estimate the value of art for death duties; in 1917 he was selected a trustee of the Tate Gallery.

As Wilde's literary executor, Ross published an abridged version of *De Profundis* in 1905; by the following year he had rescued the estate from bankruptcy. He died in his sleep on October 5, 1918, at the age of forty-nine. His will instructed that his ashes be placed in a special compartment he had asked Epstein to design on the back of Wilde's tomb. This ceremony was delayed until after Bosie's death; it took place in 1950, on the fiftieth anniversary of Wilde's death. There was no provision for an inscription.

Bosie lived a long and litigious life, dying on March 20, 1945, at the age of seventy-four. He had converted to Catholicism and renounced homosexuality, wed the poet Olive Custance, had a son, and separated after ten years of marriage. He was the editor and owner of the literary magazine *Academy* and published three books (one ghostwritten) that deal unevenly with the Wilde years.

In 1918 he testified in the sensational libel trial brought by Maud Allan, an erotic dancer who was appearing in private performances of Wilde's *Salome,* against the Independent member of Parliament Noel Pemberton Billing. Billing had published in his newspaper, *The Vigilante,* an article alleging the existence of a Black Book containing the names of 47,000 perverts in high places. He suggested that the police might find several of that number, who shared Wilde's sexual inclinations and therefore were susceptible to blackmail by German agents, watching Salome do her dance of the seven veils.

Billing brought to court—among others—Bosie, who self-righteously seized the opportunity to reproach Wilde. "I think [Wilde] had a diabolical influence on everyone he met. I think he is the greatest force for evil that has appeared in Europe during the last 350 years," he told the court. "He was the agent of the devil in every possible way. He was a man whose whole objective in life was to attack and to sneer at virtue, and to undermine it in every way by every possible means, sexually and otherwise." Caught up in a wartime hysteria of prejudice and fear, Billing proved his case.

In 1921, Bosie instigated legal action against the *Evening News* after it published a scathing obituary, being mistakenly informed of his death. His most notorious case involved a pamphlet in which he claimed that Winston Churchill accepted a bribe from a German-born financier, Sir Ernest Cassels, to publish a misleading report of the battle of Jutland. Arrested in November 1923, and convicted of criminal libel, Bosie spent six months in Wormwood Scrubs. It had been his fondest wish to go to jail like Wilde. While there he wrote a poem, *In Excelsis,* his answer to *De Profundis.*

Reggie Turner returned to England and set about producing twelve novels in ten years, but without critical interest. From 1912 until his death in 1938, he lived mostly in Florence, where he was the life of the party. Somerset Maugham regarded him as the most amusing man he had ever met. Lionel Johnson, who had brought Wilde and Bosie together, died of alcoholism in 1902, as did Leonard Smithers five years later. John Gray, the putative model for Dorian, died a canon of the Diocese of St. Andrews and Edinburgh in 1934. More Adey died insane in 1945. Arthur Symons spent two years in mental hospitals, dying in 1945.

In 1936, Yeats gave the world his version of *The Ballad of Reading Gaol* in his anthology *The Oxford Book of Modern Verse.* By cutting seventy-one stanzas and removing some of Wilde's famous lines, such as those passages beginning with "Yet each man kills the thing he loves," Yeats eliminated what he regarded in the poem as "artificial, trivial, arbitrary," convinced that he had brought "into light a great, or almost great poem, as [Wilde] himself would have done had he lived." When Bosie realized that he was not included in the volume, he wrote a scathing letter to the editor of *The Daily Express.*

Willie Wilde's only child, Dolly, had a chaotic upbringing after her father died when she was four years old and her mother married Alexander Louis Teixeira de Mattos, a Dutch translator. She looked very much like Oscar and inherited the Wildean wit and fondness for alcohol. As a young woman in Paris, she was the lover of the American heiress Natalie Clifford Barney, a poet and notorious seducer of women who ruled over a salon on the rue Jacob, a street away from the hotel where Wilde had died. Despite encouragement from established authors, she refused to write. She died in 1941, three months before her forty-sixth birthday, the same age that her father and uncle had died.

Life changed slowly for homosexuals in England. The Wolfenden Report of 1957 recommended that a homosexual act committed in private between consenting adults should no longer be a criminal offense. A decade passed before the legislation was enacted. Wilde had predicted that the road would be long with monstrous martyrdoms.

STRIPPED OF REPUTATION and honor a century ago, Wilde has been regilded and brightly burnished, like the statue of "The Happy Prince," all transgressions forgiven, with a stained-glass window in Westminster Abbey and public statues in London and Dublin. His work has grown in popularity and importance; his plays are the gaiety of nations. His aesthetics still comfort the solitary artist who struggles against intolerance. His words demonstrate the value of graciousness, charm, and wit, which we all seek in relationships with people. Nowhere can these be taught so enjoyably as through the reading of Wilde. He stands for the right of art and language to shock, to undermine, and to unsettle, and for the right of a person never to apologize for love.

ACKNOWLEDGMENTS

❧

Many people contributed to this book, but two deserve special mention: my daughter, Deborah, who urged me to write it despite contradictory views that there was nothing more to say about Oscar Wilde, and Karl Beckson, whose encyclopedic knowledge of Wilde was a constant source of inspiration. Professor Beckson read a first draft and provided invaluable criticism, from which I have greatly profited. Another reader was Miles Merwin, who delighted in pouncing on anachronisms.

My research would have been impossible without the cooperation and intelligence of Merlin Holland, Wilde's grandson, executor of his estate, and a Wilde scholar. I appreciate his permission to quote from the letters of Lady Wilde and Constance Wilde. I am grateful to Sheila Colman, executor of Lord Alfred Douglas's estate, for permission to quote from his works.

I owe thanks to many people and institutions for their help and encouragement during the five years that it took to complete this biography. I am indebted to the William Andrews Clark Memorial Library in Los Angeles, the repository for most of Wilde's letters and manuscripts, where I was a research fellow. Special thanks to Suzanne Tatian and Stephen Tabor, who know so much about the Wilde collection there, and those who assisted them during my stay: Donal O'Sullivan, Renee Chin, and Nissa Perez. My research was facilitated by the wonderful staff at Columbia University's Butler Library, particularly the interlibrary loan department.

Beyond the Clark Library, I consulted material at the Henry W. and Albert A. Berg Collection at the New York Public Library; J. Pierpont Morgan Library, New York; Fales Rare Book Library, New York University; Harry Ransom Humanities Research Center, University of Texas at Austin; Rosenbach Museum and Library, Philadelphia; Library of Congress, Washington, D.C.; Princeton University Library; Trinity College Library, Dublin; National Library of Ireland, Dublin; Reading University Library; the Ross Collection at the Bodleian Library, Oxford; the British Library, and the Theatre Museum, London.

Other people have helped me in various ways, and I wish to acknowledge the kindness of Neil Bartlett, Professor Richard Blood, Maureen Borland, Bryan Cannon, Professor Masalino d'Amico, Philip Hoare, Mark Samuels Lasner, Joy Melville, and Mary Ellen Noonan. During my research and travel, I enjoyed much hospitality. I would like to thank Joan and Robert Cook, Jean and Sidney Engle, and Berthe and Alf Wallis. And a special salute to those animal companions—Maddie, Oscar, and Duse— without whom no writer can survive. Gratitude to my British editor at Bloomsbury, Rosemary Davidson, who contributed valuable suggestions and clarification. Words cannot express my appreciation to my agent, Geri Thoma, for her enthusiasm and support, and to my editor at Random House, Robert Loomis, whose courtly manners and unerring judgment are legendary.

Notes

⌦

The main repositories of material on Oscar Wilde's life and on the history of his plays are the William Andrews Clark Memorial Library at the University of California, Los Angeles; Henry W. and Albert A. Berg Collection at the New York Public Library; J. Pierpont Morgan Library, New York; Fales Rare Book Library, New York University; Harry Ransom Humanities Research Center, University of Texas at Austin; Rosenbach Museum and Library, Philadelphia; Trinity College Library, Dublin; National Library of Ireland, Dublin; and the Theatre Museum, London.

The following short titles are used frequently in the notes:

America: Lloyd Lewis and Henry Justin Smith, *Oscar Wilde Discovers America* (New York: Harcourt, Brace, 1936).

Clark: William Andrews Clark Memorial Library at the University of California, Los Angeles.

Critic: Oscar Wilde, *The Artist as Critic: Critical Writings of Oscar Wilde,* ed. Richard Ellmann (New York: Random House, 1969).

Dorian: Oscar Wilde, *The Picture of Dorian Gray,* ed. Peter Ackroyd (London: Penguin Classics, 1985).

Ellmann: Richard Ellmann, *Oscar Wilde* (New York: Knopf, 1988).

Fiction: Oscar Wilde, *Complete Shorter Fiction,* ed. Isobel Murray (New York: Oxford University Press, 1980).

Intentions: Oscar Wilde, *Intentions* (New York: Brentano's, 1907).

Letters: Oscar Wilde, *The Letters of Oscar Wilde,* ed. Rupert Hart-Davis (New York: Harcourt, Brace & World, 1962).

Mason: Stuart Mason, *Bibliography of Oscar Wilde* (London: Werner Laurie, 1914).

Mikhail: *Oscar Wilde: Interviews and Recollections,* ed. E. H. Mikhail, 2 vols. (London: Macmillan, 1979).

More Letters: Oscar Wilde, *More Letters of Oscar Wilde,* ed. Rupert Hart-Davis (New York: Vanguard, 1985).

NLI: National Library of Ireland.

Plays: Oscar Wilde, *The Importance of Being Earnest and Other Plays,* ed. Peter Raby (New York: Oxford University Press, 1995).

Poetry: Oscar Wilde, *Complete Poetry,* ed. Isobel Murray (Oxford: Oxford University Press, 1997).

Reading: University of Reading Library, Reading, England.

Trials: Famous Trials: Oscar Wilde, ed. H. Montgomery Hyde (1948; reprint, London: Penguin, 1962).

Writings: Oscar Wilde, *De Profundis and Other Writings,* introduction by Hesketh Pearson (London: Penguin Classics, 1986).

Yeats: W. B. Yeats, *Autobiographies* (London: Macmillan, 1955).

INTRODUCTION

xii   "one duty we owe." *Intentions,* "The Critic as Artist," pt. 1, p. 128.

CHAPTER ONE: LORD OF LIFE

1   "I made art." *Letters,* p. 466.

3   "There is nothing." *Plays, A Woman of No Importance,* p. 131.

3   "Everyone is good." Clark, unidentified newspaper clipping.

3   "The public is wonderfully tolerant." *Intentions,* "The Critic as Artist," pt. 1, p. 95.

3   "My name has two O's." Coulson Kernahan, *In Good Company: Some Personal Recollections* (London: John Lane, 1915), p. 208.

3   "He is to be called." Reading, Jane Elgee Wilde to unnamed correspondent, Nov. 22, 1854.

3   "Names are everything." *Dorian,* p. 231.

4   "I envy those men." Yeats, p. 87.

4   "The soul is born old." *Plays, A Woman of No Importance,* p. 111.

4   "How ridiculous of you." Kernahan, *In Good Company,* p. 208.

5   "the infamous St. Oscar." *Letters,* p. 720.

5   "Man is least himself." *Intentions,* "The Critic as Artist," pt. 2, p. 185.

5   "One should never trust." *Plays, A Woman of No Importance,* p. 110.

6   "was the first." R. G. F. Jenkins and G. O. Simms, *Pioneers and Partners: William Maturin and Henry Hogan* (Dublin: privately published, 1985), p. 80.

7   "the acknowledged voice." NLI, Lady Wilde to Lotten von Kraemer, Mar. 19, 1859.

7   "I, and I alone." C. J. Hamilton, *Notable Irishwomen* (Dublin: Sealy Bryers and Walker, 1909), p. 181.

7   "this German romance." Edmund Gosse, *Leaves and Fruit* (New York: Scribner's, 1927), p. 195.

8   "favourite romantic reading." *Fiction,* p. 3.

8   "a Baronet of £5,000." Reading, Jane Elgee to an unnamed correspondent, n.d.

8   "I don't care." Ibid.

8   "I am afraid." *Dorian,* p. 132.

9   "sense of morality." Joy Melville, *Mother of Oscar* (London: John Murray, 1994), p. 31.

9   "Do forgive me." Reading, Jane Elgee to an unnamed correspondent, 1850.

9   "I hate men." Ibid.

9   "Jane has some heart." Melville, *Mother of Oscar,* p. 51.

10   "To live in happiness." T. G. Wilson, *Victorian Doctor* (London: Methuen, 1942), p. 15.

10   "I do not think." William Wilde, *Narrative of a Voyage to Madeira, Teneriffe, and Along the Shores of the Mediterranean* (Dublin: William Curry, 1840), vol. 1, p. 389.

11   "I began to think." Ibid., p. 397.

12   "another of the many instances." Wilson, *Victorian Doctor,* p. 130.

12   "when he was only twenty-nine." *Letters,* p. 26.

13   "A family is a terrible encumbrance." Oscar Wilde, *The Plays of Oscar Wilde, Vera* (Boston: Luce, 1907), p. 52.

13   "They give people." *Plays, The Importance of Being Earnest,* p. 300.

13   "it is always the woman." *Dorian,* p. 105.

13   "For myself." Reading, Jane Elgee Wilde to an unnamed correspondent, n.d.

14   "If ever there was a nation." William Wilde, *Irish Popular Superstitions* (1852; reprint, Dublin: Irish Academic Press, 1979), p. 9.

14   "spoken Gaelic is hourly dying out." William Wilde, *Lough Corrib, Its Shores and Islands* (Dublin: McGlashon & Gill, 1867), p. 187.

14   "Saxon basis is the rough block." Jane Wilde, *Social Studies* (London: Ward and Downey, 1893), p. 124.

14   "With the coming." St. Paul [Minn.] *Globe,* June 18, 1882.

CHAPTER TWO: MERRION SQUARE

15   "Children begin by loving." *Plays, A Woman of No Importance,* p. 128.

15   *dreg due,* or blood fairy, see Davis Coakley, *Oscar Wilde: The Importance of Being Irish* (Dublin: Town House, 1994), p. 107.

16   "a great stout creature." Reading, Jane Elgee Wilde to an unnamed correspondent, n.d.

16   "At every single moment." *Letters,* p. 476.

16   the fashionable side. *Plays, The Importance of Being Earnest,* p. 266.

17   "You don't deserve." Robert Harborough Sherard, *The Real Oscar Wilde* (London: T. Werner Laurie, 1916), p. 89.

17   Oscar clapped his hands. Clark, Reginald Turner to A.J.A. Symons, Aug. 26, 1935.

17   "I don't care." *Dorian,* p. 31.

18   "Athá mé in." Vyvyan Holland, *Son of Oscar Wilde* (London: Hart-Davis, 1954), p. 54.; see also Richard Pine, *The Thief of Reason: Oscar Wilde and Modern Ireland* (Dublin: Gill & Macmillan, 1995), p. 120.

18   "as a Catholic child [does]." Coakley, *Oscar Wilde,* p. 40.

18   "Willie is my kingdom." Reading, Jane Elgee Wilde to unnamed correspondent, n.d.

18   "ready to spring forth." NLI, Jane Elgee Wilde to Lotten von Kraemer, May 6, 1875.

19   "opponents of common sense." *Letters,* p. 349.

19   "I look back." Reading, Jane Elgee Wilde to an unnamed correspondent, n.d.

19   "Alas! the Fates are cruel." Ibid.

19   "The best chance." Jane Wilde, *Social Studies,* p. 45.

20   "A Joan of Arc." Reading, Jane Elgee Wilde to an unnamed correspondent, n.d.

20   "Life has such infinite possibilities." Ibid.

20   "a very terrible thing." *Letters*, p. 783.

20   "the tragedy in one's soul." Ibid., p. 691.

20   "As for domesticity." *Fiction*, "The Remarkable Rocket," p. 135.

20   "a curious woman." *Dorian*, p. 70.

20   "Am I not fallen." Reading, Jane Elgee Wilde to an unnamed correspondent, n.d.

20   "strange" and "hypochondriacal." Ibid.

21   "richest white satin." *Irish Times*, Jan. 29, 1864.

21   "either a superb Juno." Jane Wilde, *Social Studies*, p. 111.

21   "In this world." *Plays, Lady Windermere's Fan*, p. 44.

21   "the truth is never pure." Ibid., *The Importance of Being Earnest*, p. 258.

22   "a decidedly animal and sinister expression." Terence de Vere White, *The Parents of Oscar Wilde* (London: Hodder & Stoughton, 1967), p. 172.

22   "consorts with low newspaper boys." Ibid., p. 190.

22   "When Miss Travers complained." Horace Wyndham, *Speranza* (London: Boardman, 1951), p. 92.

23   "mad" and "sneering." Melville, *Mother of Oscar*, p. 104.

23   "Genius has its penalties." Coakley, *Oscar Wilde*, p. 274.

23   "All trials are trials." *Letters*, p. 509.

24   "hear things that the ear." Ibid., p. 322.

24   "years younger than actual history records." Ibid., p. 25.

24   "half-civilized blood." Yeats, p. 138.

24   "I feel sure." *Plays, A Woman of No Importance*, p. 102.

24   "The English country gentleman." Ibid., p. 106.

24   "great melancholy carp." Holland, *Son of Oscar Wilde*, p. 54.

24   "Westward, ho!" William Wilde, *Lough Corrib*, p. 1.

25   "been accustomed, through my Father." Bodleian Library, Oxford University, Oscar Wilde to A. H. Sayce, May 28, 1879.

Chapter Three: Away from Home

26   "The only thing." *Fiction*, "The Remarkable Rocket," p. 130.

27   "romantic imagination." Clark, Louis Claude Purser, "Wilde at Portora."

27   "What is a Realist?" Clark, Louis Claude Purser to A. J. A. Symons, Jan. 28, 1932.

27   "I have forgotten." *Plays, An Ideal Husband,* p. 167.

27   "To the world." *Letters,* p. 253.

27   "clever, erratic." Purser to Symons, Jan. 28, 1932.

28   "terrible experiences." *Intentions,* "The Critic as Artist," pt. 1, p. 100.

28   "music was not articulate." *Dorian,* p. 42.

28   "I am *not* fond." W. S. Gilbert and Arthur Sullivan, *Patience; or Bunthorne's Bride!* (London: Chappell, 1911), p. 13.

28   "In examinations." *Critic,* p. 434.

29   "to go down." Purser to Symons, Jan. 28, 1932.

29   "sentimental friendships." Anthony Cronin, *Samuel Beckett: The Last Modernist* (New York: HarperCollins, 1997), p. 43.

29   "There was nothing." Alfred Douglas, *Oscar Wilde: A Summing-Up* (London: Duckworth, 1940), p. 113.

29   "When our eyes met." *Dorian,* p. 28.

30   "the talk in the dormitories." J. A. Symonds, *The Memoirs of John Addington Symonds,* ed. Phyllis Grosskurth (New York: Random House, 1984), p. 94.

30   "the voice of my own soul." Ibid., p. 99.

30   "with a rush." Michael Holroyd, *Lytton Strachey* (London: Book Club Associates, 1973), p. 101.

31   "Greek love for modern students." Symonds, *Memoirs,* p. 101.

31   "the unvintageable sea." David Hunter Blair, *In Victorian Days and Other Papers* (New York: Books for Libraries Press, 1969), p. 123; see also *Poetry,* "Vita Nuova," p. 25.

31   "Darling Mama." *Selected Letters of Oscar Wilde,* ed. Rupert Hart-Davis (London: Oxford University Press, 1979), p. 3.

32   "that little Isola." NLI, Speranza to Lotten von Kraemer, [1858].

32   "a mourner for life." Ibid., July 1867.

32   "never dreamed." Ibid.

33   "Daily work." Ibid.

33   "an affectionate, gentle, retiring, dreamy boy." Mason, p. 295.

33   "Tread lightly, she is near." *Poetry,* "Requiescat," p. 216.

33   "Strange, that my first." *Dorian,* p. 128.

34   "each man kills." *Writings, The Ballad of Reading Gaol,* p. 232.

34   "the world does not meet." Reading, Lady Wilde to unnamed correspondent, n.d.

34   "At Home, Saturday." Melville, *Mother of Oscar,* p. 115.

34   "The corner house." T. D. Sullivan, *A Guide to Dublin* (Dublin: Sullivan, 1876), p. 82.

35   "was a rallying place." Wyndham, *Speranza,* p. 68.

35   "treats her guests." *Lippincott's Monthly Magazine,* "The Picture of Dorian Gray," July 1890.

35   "Sir Humpty Dumpty." Ibid.

35   "Glad to meet you." Wyndham, *Speranza,* p. 70.

35   "By interesting them." Ibid., p. 76.

36   "By all means." Ibid.

36   "Welcome, my dear." Ibid., p. 71.

36   "Round what had once been." Ibid., p. 77.

36   "faded splendour." Anna de Brémont (Anna Dunphy), *Oscar Wilde and His Mother* (1911; reprint, New York: Haskell, 1972), p. 23.

36   "All women become like their mothers." *Plays, The Importance of Being Earnest,* p. 268.

CHAPTER FOUR: BUDDING AESTHETE

37   "There are moments." *Plays, Lady Windermere's Fan,* p. 29.

38   "did not astonish." L. C. Ingleby, *Oscar Wilde: Some Reminiscences* (London: T. Werner Laurie, 1912), p. 152.

39   "They were lovely." H. Montgomery Hyde, *Oscar Wilde: A Biography* (New York: Farrar, Straus and Giroux, 1975), p. 8.

40   "love art for its own sake." "The English Renaissance of Art" in *The Uncollected Oscar Wilde,* ed. John Wyse Jackson (London: Fourth Estate, 1991), p. 21.

40   "We spend our days." Ibid., p. 28.

40   "that book which has had." *Letters,* p. 471.

40   "Not the fruit." Walter Pater, *The Renaissance: Studies in Art and Poetry* ([1893]; reprint, Los Angeles: University of California Press, 1980), p. 188.

41   "Life imitates art." *Writings,* "The Decay of Lying," p. 74.

41   "something wonderful." Wyndham, *Speranza,* p. 73.

41   "just put in a butterfly." Hyde, *Oscar Wilde,* p. 11.

41   "In the morning." *The Epigrams of Oscar Wilde,* ed. Alvin Redman (London: Senate, 1996), p. 218.

41   "highest idea of humour." Hyde, *Oscar Wilde,* p. 13.

41 "coarse *amours.*" Ibid.

41 "Come home with me." Ibid., p. 12.

42 "first and best teacher." *Letters,* p. 338.

42 "There can be no doubt." J. P. Mahaffy, *The Principles of the Art of Conversation* (London: Macmillan, 1887), p. 1.

42 "Until you heard." Ulick O'Connor, *Oliver St. John Gogarty* (London: Granada, 1981), p. 31.

42 "One should absorb." *Dorian,* p. 131.

42 "Between me and life." Arthur Conan Doyle, *Memories and Adventures* (London: Hodder & Stoughton, 1924), p. 80.

42 "poets are born." W. B. Stanford and R. B. McDowell, *Mahaffy: A Biography of an Anglo-Irishman* (London: Routledge & Kegan Paul, 1971), p. 80.

42 "the scrupulously truthful man." *Pall Mall Gazette,* Dec. 16, 1887.

42 "telling of beautiful untrue things." *Writings,* "The Decay of Lying," p. 87.

43 "degrading the truth." *Saturday Review,* Nov. 17, 1894.

43 "national hero." *Writings,* "The Decay of Lying," p. 71.

43 "that strange and to us revolting." J. P. Mahaffy, *Social Life in Greece from Homer to Menander* (London: Macmillan, 1874), p. 118.

43 "We have in many cities." Ibid., p. 119.

44 "having made improvements." Ibid., p. viii.

44 "love that dare not." *Trials,* p. 201.

44 "It is beautiful." Ibid.

44 "Christ's place." *Letters,* p. 477.

44 "fascinated and dominated Art." Ibid., p. 481. See also Leo Steinberg, *The Sexuality of Christ in Renaissance Art and in Modern Oblivion* (New York: Pantheon, 1983).

45 "It is so easy." *Intentions,* "The Critic as Artist," p. 188.

46 "I don't care." L. C. Prideaux Fox, "People I Have Met," *Donahoe's Magazine* (Boston, Mass.), Apr. 1905, p. 397.

47 "to cheer dear old Oscar." Hyde, *Oscar Wilde,* p. 14.

47 "Run over to Oxford." Ibid., p. 15.

47 "two great turning-points." *Letters,* p. 469.

47 "the spendthrift." Ibid., p. 466.

47 "We never get back." *Dorian,* p. 46.

48 "It is a sad thing." Ibid., p. 34.

48 "I was the happiest." Hyde, *Oscar Wilde,* p. 17.

48 "distinguished name." *Letters,* p. 466.

48   "a young man." Ibid., p. 433.

48   "intellectually, with Elizabeth Barrett Browning." Ibid., p. 496.

48   "Is insincerity such a terrible thing?" *Dorian,* p. 174.

CHAPTER FIVE: MAGDALEN MANNERS

49   "I remember bright young faces." *Letters,* p. 181.

49   "I find it harder." Hesketh Pearson, *Oscar Wilde: His Life and Wit* (London: Harper, 1946), p. 45.

49   "These are the days." Blair, *In Victorian Days,* p. 120.

50   "a mezzo voice." Max Beerbohm's Notes on Wilde, Berg Collection, New York Public Library.

50   "one of the most alluring." Pearson, *Oscar Wilde,* p. 42.

50   "extra-ordinary conversational abilities." Blair, *In Victorian Days,* p. 117.

50   "my greatest chum." Ellmann, p. 44.

50   "His qualities were not ordinary." Holland, *Son of Oscar Wilde,* p. 250.

51   "brilliant and unreasonable." *More Letters,* p. 33.

51   "brimming bowls of gin-and-whisky punch." Blair, *In Victorian Days,* p. 118.

51   "boys will" about "everything." Ibid., p. 120.

51   "God knows?" Ibid., p. 122.

51   "been out every night." *Letters,* p. 12.

51   "with Swinburne." Ibid., p. 15.

52   "is extremely moral." Ibid., p. 23.

52   "who after an evening." Blair, *In Victorian Days,* p. 123.

52   "incurable impotency." Robert Secor, *John Ruskin and Alfred Hunt: New Letters and the Record of a Friendship* (Victoria, B.C.: University of Victoria English Literary Studies, 1982), p. 33.

52   "There is in you." *Letters,* p. 218.

53   "my golden book." Yeats, p. 130.

53   "I am sure." Blair, *In Victorian Days,* p. 126.

53   "Mothers, of course." Ruth Berggren, *The Definitive Four-Act Version of* The Importance of Being Earnest (New York: Vanguard, 1987), p. 25.

54   "The only God-anointed King." *Poetry,* "Rome Unvisited," p. 6.

54   "The intellect is." Jane Wilde, *Social Studies,* p. 70.

54   "Willie got introduced." Clark, Lady Wilde to Oscar Wilde, n.d.

55   "any real pleasure." *Letters,* p. 15.

55 "with everything filled." Ibid.

55 "I am sorry." Clark, Lady Wilde to Oscar Wilde, n.d.

55 "I am just going out." *Letters,* p. 24.

56 "too much *occupied.*" Ibid., p. 25.

56 "*real* Irish home." Clark, Willie Wilde to Margaret Campbell, Sept. 2, 1878.

56 "a pretty little bare-footed girl." Ibid.

56 "I look back." *Letters,* p. 31.

57 "This is an era." Ibid., p. 34.

57 "Seeing Greece." Ibid., p. 35.

57 "I was sent down." Ibid., p. 36 n.

57 "had become Hellenized." Blair, *In Victorian Days,* p. 136.

58 "One should either." *Critic,* p. 434.

58 "wretched stupidity." *Letters,* p. 36.

58 "more lovely than ever." Ibid.

58 "Well Done!" Peter Vernier, "A 'Mental Photograph' of Oscar Wilde," *The Wildean,* July 1998, p. 28. "Album for Confessions of Tastes, Habits and Convictions" was auctioned in 1997 by Christie's, London, for £23,000.

59 "I am little more than a boy." *Letters,* p. 37.

59 "little more than a stray sheet." Ibid., p. 43.

59 "I always say I." Ibid., p. 39.

59 "To say 'perhaps.' " Ibid., p. 47.

59 "my sonnet must be printed." Ibid., p. 40.

59 "You possess some beautiful." Ibid., p. 47.

59 "Why do you always write." Oscar Wilde, "Mr. Pater's Last Volume," *Speaker,* Mar. 22, 1890, p. 319.

59 "Was he ever alive?" Max Beerbohm's Notes on Wilde.

60 "to whom we were all." *Letters,* p. 42.

60 "It is a terrible disappointment." Ibid., p. 43.

60 "over so many miles." Ibid., p. 51.

60 "Oh Gloria, Gloria!" Clark, Lady Wilde to Oscar Wilde, n.d.

61 "I understand that some young man." Mrs. J. Comyns Carr, *Reminiscences* (London: Hutchinson, n.d.), p. 85.

61 "A year ago." *Poetry,* "Ravenna," p. 31.

61 "Worthless though the trinket be." *Letters,* p. 54.

62 "to eat of the fruit." *Letters,* p. 475.

62 "bird-haunted walks." Ibid.

62 "directly due to meningitis." Arthur Ransome, *Oscar Wilde: A Critical Study* (London: Martin Secker, 1912), p. 199.

63 "adopted mercury." Ellmann, p. 95.

63 "a shining row." *New York Tribune,* Jan. 3, 1882.

64 "conception of Wilde's character." Ellmann, p. 92n.

64 "interpretation of many things." Ibid.

CHAPTER SIX: ARTISTS AND BEAUTIES

65 "To drift with every passion." *Poetry,* "Hélas," p. 132.

67 "To get into the best society." *Plays, A Woman of No Importance,* p. 132.

67 "Individualism is." *Writings,* "The Soul of Man Under Socialism," p. 36.

67 "worth looking at." Oscar Wilde, "The Grosvenor Gallery," *Dublin University Magazine,* July 1873.

68 "seen and heard." John Ruskin, *Fors Clavigera,* July 2, 1877.

68 "The labor of two days." Horace Gregory, *The World of James McNeill Whistler* (New York: Nelson, 1959), p. 141.

69 "There was something." Ellen Terry, *Ellen Terry's Memoirs,* ed. Edith Craig and Christopher St. John (London: Gollancz, 1933), p. 231.

69 "I hate people." *Fiction,* "The Remarkable Rocket," p. 134.

69 "set the world." *Letters,* p. 61.

70 "You must come." *Dorian,* p. 70.

70 "Hip, hip, hurrah!" Arthur Gold and Robert Fizdale, *The Divine Sarah: A Life of Sarah Bernhardt* (New York: Knopf, 1991), p. 149.

70 "Yes, yes—you'll see." Ibid., p. 150.

70 "realised the sweetness." Oscar Wilde, "Literary and Other Notes," *Woman's World,* Jan. 1888.

70 "For thou wert weary." *Poetry,* "Phèdre," p. 98.

70 "Most men who are civil." Gold and Fizdale, *Divine Sarah,* p. 151.

71 "monstrous dresses." [Raymond] and Ricketts, *Oscar Wilde: Recollections* (London: Nonesuch Press, 1932), p. 16.

71 "the loveliest woman." Journal of J. E. Courtenay Bodley, Bodleian Library, Oxford University.

71 "great eager eyes." Lillie Langtry, *The Days I Knew* (London: Hutchinson, 1925), p. 60.

71 "so colourless." Ibid.

71   "She is more." *Plays, A Woman of No Importance,* p. 109.

71   "Lillie Langtry happens to be." Noel B. Gerson, *Lillie Langtry* (London: Hall, 1972), p. 9.

72   "striped awnings." Margot Asquith, *Remember and Be Glad* (London: James Barrie, 1952), p. 64.

72   "a soft black Greek Dress." James Brough, *The Prince and the Lily* (London: Hodder & Stoughton, 1975), p. 174.

72   "there is only one thing." *Dorian,* p. 24.

72   "The lotus-leaves." *Poetry,* "The New Helen," p. 91.

73   "You have only wasted." Ibid., "Roses and Rue," p. 101.

73   "What has he done." G. T. Atkinson, "Oscar Wilde at Oxford," *Cornhill Magazine,* May 1929, p. 562.

73   "How can you say." *Plays, An Ideal Husband,* p. 166.

74   "They are all so alike." Clark, Willie Wilde to Margaret Campbell, Sept. 2, 1878.

74   "a charming 'dull gold' dress." Clark, uncataloged newspaper clipping.

75   "Beauty is the grand characteristic." Reading, Lady Wilde to an unnamed correspondent, n.d.

76   "his own perfection." *Writings,* "The Soul of Man Under Socialism," p. 42.

76   "vivid personality." Ibid.

76   "limpid and utter." *America,* p. 15.

76   "Thou trumpet set." *Poetry,* "Fabien dei Franchi," dedicated "To My Friend Henry Irving," p. 127.

76   "childish love." Laurence Irving, *Henry Irving: The Actor and His World* (London: Faber & Faber, 1951), p. 579.

76   "Why should not degrees." Humphrey Carpenter, *OUDS: A Centenary History of Oxford University Dramatic Society* (New York: Oxford University Press, 1985), p. 39.

76   "As a rule." *Dorian,* p. 139.

77   "It is not good." Ibid., p. 113.

77   "How odd it is." *Letters,* p. 61.

77   "I cannot hold a Chair." John Dixon Hunt, *The Wider Sea: A Life of John Ruskin* (New York: Viking, 1982), p. 374.

77   "Do you know." Violet Hunt, "I Remember Oscar" and "My Oscar," Violet Hunt Collection, Olin Library, Cornell University.

77   "always talked less." Ibid.

77   "out of Botticelli." Ibid., Violet Hunt biographical notes.

77 "a little in love." Ibid., Violet Hunt diaries, Feb. 28, 1891.

78 "I really think." John Ruskin to Margaret Hunt, Feb. 24, 1875, Henry E. Huntington Library, San Marino, Calif.

78 "but infinitely delicate." Ibid., Jan. 26, 1872.

78 "the sweetest Violet." *Letters,* p. 64.

78 "wonderful radicalism." Ibid., p. 68.

78 "an enviable notoriety." Hunt, "My Oscar."

78 "as nearly as possible." Violet Hunt, *The Flurried Years* (London: Hurst & Blackett, 1926), p. 168.

78 "I believe that Oscar." Violet Hunt diaries, July 30, 1891.

79 "all the proposal." Hunt, "My Oscar."

79 "would never give." Violet Hunt, *Their Lives* (London: Stanley Paul, 1916), p. 98.

79 "Oscar's little water-colour." Florence Stoker to Philippa Knott, Mar. 14, 1923. Quoted with permission of Sir Rupert Hart-Davis.

CHAPTER SEVEN: AESTHETES AND DANDIES

80 "A man who can dominate." *Plays, A Woman of No Importance,* p. 132.

81 "Sardoodledom." George Bernard Shaw, *Our Theatres in the Nineties,* vol. 1 (London: Constable, 1932), p. 133.

82 "a stage carpenter." Frank Harris, *Oscar Wilde: His Life and Confessions* (1916; rev. ed., London: Constable, 1938), p. 257.

82 "Love ends in matrimony." Robert Hogan, *Dion Boucicault: His Life and Times* (New York: Twayne, 1969), p. 49.

82 "In the lone tent." *Poetry,* "Queen Henrietta Maria," p. 98.

83 "Will you accept one." *Letters,* p. 74.

83 "I have saved Russia." *Plays, Vera,* p. 75.

83 "that Titan cry." *Letters,* p. 148.

84 *"Mes premiers vers."* Mason, p. 285.

84 "only now, too late." *Letters,* p. 78.

85 "found out the force." Ellmann, p. 144.

85 "Swinburne and water." *Punch,* July 23, 1881.

85 "England is enriched." *Academy,* July 30, 1881.

85 "I live in terror." *Intentions,* "The Critic as Artist," pt. 1, p. 111.

85 "In an age like this." *Letters,* p. 79.

86 "We Irish are too poetical." Yeats, p. 135.

86 "coarse impertinence." *More Letters,* p. 37.

86 "It is only the unimaginative." "Olivia at the Lyceum," *Dramatic Review,* May 30, 1885.

86 "artistic creation is absolutely subjective." *Intentions,* "The Critic as Artist," pt. 2, p. 182.

86 "Art takes life." *Writings,* "The Decay of Lying," p. 68.

86 "Nobody else's work." "A Talk with Mr. Oscar Wilde," *Sketch,* Jan. 9, 1895.

86 "Good artists exist." *Dorian,* p. 81.

87 "The grand cool flanks." *Poetry,* "Charmides," p. 56.

87 "licentious and may do." Clark, Robert H. W. Miles to Oscar Wilde, Aug. 21, 1881.

88 "It is quite consummate." *Punch,* Oct. 30, 1880.

88 "The Lily had carried me." Ibid., Dec. 25, 1880.

88 "Why should he Be anything?" Ibid., Feb. 12, 1881.

89 "Aesthete of Aesthetes!" Ibid., June 25, 1881.

89 "Burne Jones suddenly hissed out." Hunt, "I Remember Oscar."

90 "To have done." *New York World,* Jan. 8, 1882.

90 "Though the Philistines." Gilbert and Sullivan, *Patience,* p. 13.

91 "to show the rich." George Woodcock, *The Paradox of Oscar Wilde* (New York: Macmillan, 1950), p. 111.

91 "a profound sensation." W. F. Morse to unnamed correspondent, Nov. 8, 1881, Pierpont Morgan Library, New York City.

CHAPTER EIGHT: A SECOND SELF

92 "Nothing should be able." *Writings,* "The Soul of Man Under Socialism," p. 25.

92 "knows me perfectly." *Letters,* p. 517.

92 "a clever and accomplished man." James Russell Lowell, *New Letters of James Russell Lowell,* ed. M. de Wolfe Howe (London: Harper Bros., 1932), p. 262.

93 "The gentleman who brings." *Letters,* p. 123 n.

93 "Their chilling touch." *Writings,* "The Decay of Lying," p. 71.

93 "I have nothing to declare." Frank Harris, *Oscar Wilde: His Life and Confessions* (London: Constable, 1938), p. 44.

93 "the Atlantic is a disappointment." *New York World,* Jan. 3, 1882.

94   "seem to get a hold." *Critic*, "The American Man," p. 61.

94   "On the whole." Ibid.

94   "When people are tied." Ibid., p. 62.

94   "Massa Wilde is too busy." *America*, p. 72.

94   "In a free country." *Letters*, p. 87.

94   "is rapidly becoming bald." Ibid.

94   "Did you hear." *Plays, The Importance of Being Earnest*, p. 253.

94   "first well-dressed philosopher." Ibid., *An Ideal Husband*, p. 212.

94   "Extraordinary thing." Ibid., p. 213.

95   "I now understand." *Letters*, p. 85.

96   "the lord of language." *Letters*, p. 458.

96   "Since you have heard." *America*, p. 58.

96   "sepulchral voice." *New York Times*, Jan. 10, 1882.

96   "a rhythmic chant." *New York World*, Jan. 3, 1882.

97   "It must be produced." Mikhail, p. 37.

97   "Nobody is sanguine." *America*, p. 28.

97   "utterly devoid of color." Ibid., p. 31.

97   "large and regular." *New York World*, Jan. 3, 1882.

97   "upper half of his person." *Washington Post*, Jan. 24, 1882.

97   "a short after-dinner jacket." *America*, p. 161.

97   "The essence of good dressing." *New York Daily Tribune*, Jan. 8, 1882.

98   "I have been quite amused." Mary Watson, *People I Have Met* (San Francisco: Francis, 1890), p. 48.

98   "If you survive." Richard Butler Glaenzer, *Decorative Art in America* (New York: Brentano's, 1906), p. 18.

98   "reading of a good vigorous attack." *America*, p. 205.

98   "I wished that I had one." Ibid.

98   "the poor man's friend." Ibid., p. 241.

98   "I know." *New York Tribune*, Feb. 12, 1882.

98   "Ah! Don't say." *Intentions*, "The Critic as Artist," pt. 2, p. 206.

98   "dreadful monstrosities." *America*, p. 251.

98   "hang them where time." Ibid.

98   "was noble and beautiful." Ibid., p. 178.

99   "I didn't expect." Ibid., p. 179.

99   "the basis for a new civilization." *Omaha Weekly Herald*, Mar. 24, 1882.

99   the term *homosexuality*. The *Oxford English Dictionary*'s first edition (1933)

notes that the term was first recorded in 1897; in the *OED*'s second edition (1989) the date given is 1892: the date for the English translation of Krafft-Ebing's *Psychopathia Sexualis.*

99   "I have come." *Philadelphia Press,* Jan. 18, 1882.

99   "I can only say." *America,* p. 75.

99   "Why, Oscar." Ibid., p. 76.

100   "Good-by, Oscar." Ibid., p. 77.

100   "I admire him." *Philadelphia Press,* Jan. 17, 1882.

100   "a great big, splendid boy." Horace Traubel, *With Walt Whitman in Camden,* vol. 2 (Boston: Small, Maynard, 1914), p. 145.

100   "of one of Ireland's noblest daughters." *America,* p. 224.

100   "I do not know." Michael J. O'Neill, "Irish Poets of the Nineteenth Century: Unpublished Lecture Notes of Oscar Wilde," *University Review,* Spring 1955.

100   "gift of natural eloquence." Jane Wilde, *Social Studies,* p. 134.

100   "one of the great tragedies." *Critic,* "Mr. Froude's Blue Book," p. 136.

101   "the easy victim." *Boston Transcript,* Jan. 28, 1882.

101   "I do wish." *Letters,* p. 92 n. 3.

101   "good and dramatic." Clark, Dion Boucicault to Oscar Wilde, [1882].

101   "As I look about me." *America,* p. 125.

102   "create an artistic movement." Ibid., p. 162.

102   "achieved a real triumph." Ibid., p. 128.

102   "I hate to fly." *Philadelphia Press,* June 17, 1882.

102   "galloped, racing." *Poetry,* "Ravenna," p. 31.

102   "with its grizzly bears." Oscar Wilde, *The Complete Works of Oscar Wilde,* vol. 7 (New York: Doubleday, 1923), "The American Invasion," p. 157.

102   "I was told." *Critic,* "Impressions of America," p. 9.

103   "The first course." *America,* p. 318.

103   "The amazement of the miners." *Letters,* p. 112.

103   "only rational method." *America,* p. 318.

103   "I was reproved." Ibid., p. 314.

104   "a man is." Bernard Thornton, "Oscar Wilde: A Reminiscence," *Theatre,* June 1918.

104   "It is very annoying." *Letters,* p. 121.

104   "No mention." Ibid.

104   "even the papers." Ibid., p. 110.

104   "lose heart." Clark, Joaquin Miller to Oscar Wilde, Feb. 9, 1882.

105 "Who are these scribes." Mason, p. 119.

105 "Perhaps after all." *Dorian,* p. 63.

105 "American women." *Plays, A Woman of No Importance,* p. 104.

105 "I come from a modern country." *Fiction,* "The Canterville Ghost," p. 59.

105 "an excellent example." Ibid., p. 60.

CHAPTER NINE: NEW SCENARIOS

106 "Experience is the name." *Plays, Lady Windermere's Fan,* p. 45.

106 "I thought you had sailed." Clark, Lady Wilde to Oscar Wilde, [1882].

106 "You are still the talk." Ibid.

106 "burst like a resplendent meteor." Clara Lanza, "Literary New York in the Eighties," *Bookman* (New York), Mar. 1920.

107 "Like many others." Elisabeth Marbury, "My Crystal Ball," *Saturday Evening Post,* Sept. 15, 1923.

108 "was gaudy and his shirtfront." *New York Times,* Oct. 24, 1882.

108 "I would rather have discovered." *America,* p. 404.

108 "As for the love-smitten." Ibid., p. 418.

108 "You have made me pretty." *Photography in Nineteenth-Century America,* ed. Martha A. Sandweiss (New York: Abrams, 1991), p. 67.

109 "the natural and infallible laws." Francis A. Durivage, "Delsarte," *Atlantic Monthly,* May 27, 1871.

110 "Do not yet despair." Percy MacKaye, *Epoch: The Life of Steele MacKaye,* vol. 1 (New York: Boni & Liveright, 1927), p. 444.

110 "with the great actresses." *Letters,* p. 125.

110 "The world is at our feet." MacKaye, *Epoch,* p. 446.

112 "a *chef d'oeuvre.*" *Letters,* p. 124.

112 "Shall we get hence?" James Rennell Rodd, *Rose Leaf and Apple Leaf* (Portland, Maine, 1906), p. 37.

112 "false friend." *Letters,* p. 144.

112 "Olympian attitude." James Rennell Rodd, *Social and Diplomatic Memoirs, 1884–1893* (London: Arnold, 1922), p. 25.

112 "I will certainly take care." *Fiction,* "The Devoted Friend," p. 124.

112 "should be left alone." Ibid., p. 117.

113 "I saw the wretched." *Dante Gabriel Rossetti and Jane Morris: Their Correspondence,* ed. John Bryson and Janet Camp Troxell (New York: Oxford University Press, 1976), p. 188.

113 "a subconscious influence." Yeats, p. 285.

113 "not nearly so nice." Hunt, "I Remember Oscar."

113 "Oh, Miss Violet." Hunt, *Flurried Years,* p. 13.

113 "full pouting pale lips." Hunt, *Their Lives,* p. 99.

114 "I like Wagner's music." *Dorian,* p. 70.

115 "Great Heaven!" Alvin Redman, ed., *The Epigrams of Oscar Wilde* (London: Senate, 1952), p. 163.

115 "I am glad." *Plays, The Importance of Being Earnest,* p. 265.

115 "are awfully expensive." *Plays, A Woman of No Importance,* p. 108.

115 "A cigarette is the perfect type." *Dorian,* p. 107.

115 "black upon white." Robert Harborough Sherard, *The Story of an Unhappy Friendship* (London: Hermes Press, 1902), p. 28.

115 "unfit for publication." *Letters,* p. 757.

116 "But you can read." *Poetry,* "The Sphinx," p. 143.

116 "The only thing." Ian Small, *Oscar Wilde Revalued: An Essay on New Materials and Methods of Research* (Greensboro, N.C.: ELT Press, 1993), p. 141.

116 "I don't want money." *Dorian,* p. 56.

117 "So nice and warm." Sherard, *Real Oscar Wilde,* p. 200.

117 "All *that* belonged." Ibid., p. 52.

117 "The only reflection." Clark, Robert Sherard to A. J. A. Symons, May 13, 1937.

118 "the look of someone." Walter Sickert, *A Free House! Or, the Artist as Craftsman,* ed. Osbert Sitwell (London: Macmillan, 1947), p. 44.

118 "the one Christian poet." *Letters,* p. 488.

118 "Verlaine is in the gutter." Ada Leverson, *Letters to the Sphinx from Oscar Wilde and Reminiscences of the Author* (London: Duckworth, 1930), p. 24.

118 *"au sexe douteux."* L'Écho de Paris, Dec. 17, 1891.

118 "Oscar Wilde's young man." Algernon Swinburne, *The Swinburne Letters,* ed. Cecil Y. Lang, vol. 4 (New Haven: Yale University Press, 1960), p. 312.

118 "English public." *Letters,* p. 303, trans. quoted in Ellmann, p. 352 n.

119 *"chef d'oeuvre."* Ibid., p. 136.

119 "Robert, this is very tedious." Sherard, *Real Oscar Wilde,* p. 238.

119 "The play in its present form." Mary Anderson to Oscar Wilde, n.d., private collection.

119 "is quite tragic." Vincent O'Sullivan, *Aspects of Wilde* (London: Constable, 1936), p. 120.

119 "Never be afraid." *Letters,* p. 143.

119 "It was not." de Brémont, *Oscar Wilde and His Mother,* p. 38.

120 "It comes as near failure." *New York Times,* Aug. 21, 1882.

120 "Kelly, Kelly." Clark, unpublished memoirs of James Edward Kelly, uncataloged.

120 "Dion Boucicault told me." Ibid.

120 "They say here." Mary Anderson to William Winter, Sept. 18, 1882 (partial letter), *Black Sun Books Catalogue* (New York).

CHAPTER TEN: MRS. OSCAR WILDE

123 "Our most fiery moments." *Letters,* p. 185.

125 "The real drawback." *Dorian,* p. 101.

125 "By the by." Ellmann, p. 234.

125 "I can't help." *Letters,* p. 152 n. 3.

126 "who relived their tragedies." Clark, Otho Lloyd to A. J. A. Symons, May 27, 1937.

126 "I can sympathize." *Dorian,* p. 64.

126 "Anybody can sympathize." *Writings,* "The Soul of Man Under Socialism," p. 50.

127 "a grave, slight violet-eyed." *Letters,* p. 154.

127 "I am so anxious." Ibid.

127 "I am with Oscar." Ibid., n. 3.

128 "No man has any real success." Redman, *Epigrams,* p. 42.

128 "a very good acting play." Hyde Collection, Mary Hyde (Viscountess Eccles), Constance Lloyd to Oscar Wilde, Nov. 11, 1883, quoted in Ellmann, p. 244.

128 "decidedly extra affected." *Letters,* p. 152.

128 "Well . . . may I propose." *Plays, The Importance of Being Earnest,* p. 263.

129 "Prepare yourself." *Letters,* p. 153.

129 "if Constance makes as good a wife." Ibid., p. 153 n. 2.

129 "I am so cold." Hyde, Constance Lloyd to Oscar Wilde, n.d. [1883].

129 "Do you not remember." Oscar Wilde, *The Duchess of Padua* (New York: Buckles, 1906), p. 66.

129 "We are, of course." *Letters,* p. 155.

129 "Do you believe." Hyde, Constance Lloyd to Oscar Wilde, [1883].

130 "I don't think." Ibid.

130 "She scarcely ever speaks." Ellmann, p. 255.

130 "It's a ridiculous attachment." *Fiction,* "The Happy Prince," p. 96.

130 "cold and practical." *Letters,* p. 153.

130 "I hear that Oscar's fiancée." Violet Hunt diaries, April 27, 1884.

130 "My Dear Little Sister." Clark, Willie Wilde to Constance Wilde [1884].

130 "My dear old Boy." Ibid., Willie Wilde to Oscar Wilde, Nov. 27, 1883.

130 "What will you do." Ibid., Lady Wilde to Oscar Wilde, Nov. 27, 1883.

131 "looked more like George IV." *Irish Times,* May 30, 1884.

131 "It's so wonderful." Clark, Robert Sherard to A. J. A. Symons, June 3, [1937].

131 "For my part." *Morning News* (Paris), June 10, 1884.

132 "a kind of pre-figuring type." *Dorian,* p. 158.

132 "Everything is sure." *Letters,* p. 157.

132 "Here am I." Ibid., p. 165.

133 "some deliberate artistic composition." Yeats, p. 132.

133 "absolutely delightful." *Letters,* p. 175.

133 "Modern wallpaper." Sherard, *Unhappy Friendship,* p. 74.

133 "fighting a duel." Hyde, *Oscar Wilde,* p. 226.

133 "Quill pens and notepaper." *Letters,* p. 183.

134 "perpetually performed a play." Yeats, p. 138.

134 "the most essentially womanlike." Locke Scrapbook, Billy Rose Theatre Collection, New York Public Library.

134 "What was a bud." *Letters,* p. 167.

135 "that curious love." *Intentions,* "Pen, Pencil and Poison," p. 66.

135 "For his sake." Pearson, *Oscar Wilde,* p. 103.

135 " 'My wife has a cold.' " *Letters,* p. 177.

135 "I love superstitions." Ibid., p. 349.

135 "The baby is wonderful." Ibid., p. 177.

135 "Every one has some secret reason." *More Letters,* p. 152.

136 "Desire is killed." Harris, *Oscar Wilde,* p. 285.

136 "A man with the toothache." Sherard, *Unhappy Friendship,* p. 57.

136 "chatters all day long." Clark, Constance Wilde to Emily Thursfield, Jan. 1, 1889.

136 "growing crooked." Ibid., June 25, Sept. 2, 1895.

136 "Irish gift of speaking well." Ibid., June 25, 1895.

136 "I have never learned." *Letters,* p. 181.

136 "a long and lovely suicide." Ibid., p. 185.

136 "Young Oxonians." Ibid., p. 186.

137 "I myself would sacrifice." Ibid., p. 185.

CHAPTER ELEVEN: CROSSING OVER

138   " 'Know thyself!' " *Writings*, "The Soul of Man Under Socialism," p. 27.

138   "I have always been." *Plays, The Importance of Being Earnest*, p. 265.

139   "a kiss may ruin." *Plays, A Woman of No Importance*, p. 153.

140   "there is no friendship possible." *Plays, Lady Windermere's Fan*, p. 28.

140   "The one charm." *Dorian*, p. 26.

140   "I hope you are enjoying." Clark, Oscar Wilde to Robert Ross, [1888].

140   "The children are enchanted." Ibid.

141   "must be ruthlessly set aside." Melville, *Mother of Oscar*, p. 148.

141   "to sum up a situation." Arthur Binstead, *The Works of Arthur M. Binstead*, vol. 1 (London: T. Werner Laurie, 1927), p. 231.

141   " 'Good morning.' " Ibid.

141   "peer round short-sightedly." James Edward Holroyd, "Brother to Oscar," *Blackwood's Magazine*, Mar. 1979, p. 231.

141   "personification of good nature." Ibid., p. 232.

142   "Quel monstre!" Ibid., p. 235.

142   "My Darling Boz." Clark, Willie Wilde to Oscar Wilde, [188?].

142   "Did you read Willie." Ellmann, p. 294.

142   "As for modern journalism." *Intentions*, "The Critic as Artist," pt. 1, p. 109.

142   "In the old days." *Writings*, "The Soul of Man Under Socialism," p. 40.

142   "To have a style." *Intentions*, "Pen, Pencil and Poison," p. 78.

142   "they limit the journalist." *Writings*, "The Soul of Man Under Socialism," p. 41.

143   "The light stole softly." *Fiction*, "Lord Arthur Savile's Crime," p. 32.

143   "talk itself." Oscar Wilde, "Should Geniuses Meet?" *Court and Society Review*, May 4, 1887.

144   "the Murray of matrimony." Oscar Wilde, *Pall Mall Gazette*, Nov. 18, 1885.

144   "healthy and harmless." "The Poets' Corner," Ibid., April 6, 1888.

144   "might have made his book." *Critic*, p. 80.

144   "any sense of limit." Ibid., p. 146.

144   "a mock-heroic poem." Ibid., p. 85.

145   "A man can live." Ibid., p. 21.

145   "by the silly vanity." Ibid., p. ix.

145   "too feminine." *Letters*, p. 194.

145   "aims at being the organ." Ibid., p. 203.

146   "snob to the marrow." *The Playwright and the Pirate: Bernard Shaw and Frank*

Harris, A Correspondence, ed. Stanley Weintraub (University Park: Pennsylvania State University Press, 1982), p. 35.

146   "Tomorrow I start." *Letters,* p. 196.

146   "to have been." Ibid., p. 205.

147   "Well, it's as good as true." Helena Maria Swanwick [Sickert], *I Have Been Young* (London: Gollancz, 1935), p. 65.

147   "I hope I will be able." Clark, Oscar Wilde to Helena Sickert, n.d. [1887].

147   "I am beginning." *Fiction,* "The Happy Prince," p. 100.

147   "I do not propose." Mason, p. 220.

147   "Really what will people." W. H. Auden, "An Improbable Life," *New Yorker,* Mar. 6, 1963, p. 159.

147   "I think the sonnet." *Letters,* p. 210.

147   "I have just been reading." Ibid., p. 205.

148   "Work never seems to me." Ibid., p. 352.

148   "You make up your mind." Sherard, *An Unhappy Friendship,* p. 55.

148   "Is it necessary." Hyde, *Oscar Wilde,* p. 125.

148   "I have known men." Yeats, p. 131.

149   "so indolent." Ibid.

149   "only two things." *Letters,* p. 276.

149   "a most reliable." *More Letters,* p. 86.

149   "platform ladies." *Pall Mall Gazette,* May 24, 1889.

149   "no false coils." *Rational Dress Society's Gazette,* Apr. 1889, p. 7.

150   "carve a Cerberus." Yeats, p. 361.

150   "No one will speak." Ellmann, p. 320.

151   "studies in prose." *Letters,* p. 219.

151   "being in turn." Holland, *Son of Oscar Wilde,* p. 52.

151   "really beautiful things." Ibid., p. 54.

151   "at its best." *Universal Review,* June 1888.

151   "some day to NICE people." *Fiction,* introduction, p. 9.

151   "what Life is." Ibid., "The Canterville Ghost," p. 87.

152   "lost much of their charm." Ibid., introduction, p. 2.

152   "amusing enough." *United Ireland,* Sept. 26, 1891.

152   "Could it be." *Fiction,* "Lord Arthur Savile's Crime," p. 27.

152   "wake the slumbering city." Ibid., p. 29.

152   "An odd feeling." Ibid., p. 30.

CHAPTER TWELVE: ENEMIES AND FRIENDS

153 "There are terrible temptations." *Plays, An Ideal Husband,* p. 193.

153 "his crimes seem." *Intentions,* "Pen, Pencil and Poison," p. 89.

154 "The fact of a man being." Ibid., p. 90.

154 "A Truth in art." Ibid., "The Truth of Masks," p. 263.

154 "What is termed Sin." Ibid., "The Critic as Artist," pt. 1, p. 129.

154 "the industrious prattle." Ibid.

154 "if the Greeks." Ibid., p. 119.

154 "the creative faculty." Ibid., p. 120.

154 "the record of one's own soul." Ibid.

154 "It is only by intensifying." Ibid., pt. 2, p. 156.

155 "We put each other out." Stanley Weintraub, ed., *The Playwright and the Pirate: Bernard Shaw and Frank Harris: A Correspondence* (University Park: Pennsylvania State University Press, 1982), p. 30.

155 "it was very witty." *Writings,* introduction, p. 15.

155 "It is through disobedience." Ibid., "The Soul of Man Under Socialism," pp. 22, 26, 46.

155 "Selfishness is not living." Ibid., p. 49.

155 "It was my sole experience." Weintraub, *Correspondence,* p. 31.

156 "Merrion Square Protestant pretentiousness." Ibid., p. 35.

156 "a citizen of all civilised capitals." Hyde, *Oscar Wilde,* p. 37.

156 "was incapable of friendship." Weintraub, *Correspondence,* p. 35.

156 "no enemies." Yeats, p. 133.

157 "half-civilized blood." Ibid., p. 138.

157 "Books of poetry." *Critic,* p. 150.

157 "the basis of literary friendship." Yeats, p. 131.

157 "overnight with labour." Ibid., p. 130.

157 "perplexed by my own shapelessness." Ibid., p. 136.

157 "at the happiest moment." Ibid.

157 "could not endure." Ibid., p. 138.

158 "is simply to charm." *Writings,* "The Decay of Lying," p. 72.

159 "citron green leather." *Dorian,* p. 198.

159 "Bending over their blocks." Robert Speaight, *William Rothenstein* (London: Eyre & Spottiswoode, 1962), p. 69.

159 "What a charming old house." Charles Ricketts, *Self-Portrait* (London: Peter Davies, 1939), pp. 12, 33.

159   "His face had grown full." Ibid., p. 28.

159   "a Hungarian bandmaster." Ibid., p. 29.

159   "the reasonable wife." Stephen Calloway, *Charles Ricketts: Subtle and Fantastic Decorator* (London: Thames and Hudson, 1979), p. 7.

159   "the most marvelous human relationship." Ibid., p. 10.

160   "the one house." Ricketts, *Self-Portrait*, p. 36.

160   "beauty out of a little coloured paper." Ibid., p. 39.

160   "Both you and Shannon." Ibid., p. 40.

160   "advantage and resentment." Ibid., p. 27.

160   "Ah, I suppose." Ibid., p. 17.

160   "everything to them." J. G. P. Delaney, *Charles Ricketts* (Oxford: Clarendon Press, 1990), p. 45.

160   "Why did you bring." Ricketts, *Self-Portrait,* p. 52.

161   "But you are." Ibid., p. 26.

161   "There were two personalities." [Raymond] and Ricketts, *Oscar Wilde*, p. 13.

161   "I like hearing myself." *Fiction,* "The Remarkable Rocket," p. 134.

161   "Flaubert had just told me." [Raymond] and Ricketts, *Oscar Wilde*, p. 37.

162   "I propose publishing." Ibid., p. 30.

162   "It is not a forgery." *Letters,* p. 250.

162   "half yours." Ibid., p. 247.

163   "Writing plays was liking copying." Locke Scrapbooks, ser. 3, vol. 480, Billy Rose Collection, p. 201.

163   "Men shake hands." Clyde Fitch, *Beau Brummell* (New York: John Lane, 1953), p. 26.

163   "Observe me, Mortimer." Ibid., p. 137.

164   "You precious maddening man." Clark, Clyde Fitch to Oscar Wilde, 1889.

164   "It is 3." Ibid., [1889].

164   "Oh! you adorable creature." Ibid., [1889].

164   "*Nobody* loves you." Ibid., [1890].

165   "To project one's soul." *Dorian,* p. 60.

165   "My real life." *Letters,* p. 426.

CHAPTER THIRTEEN: THE DORIAN PROPHECY

167   "Every impulse." *Dorian,* p. 41.

167   "sorrows never come." Masao Miyoshi, *The Divided Self* (New York: New

York University Press, 1969), p. 321.

168   "all the things." Ibid., p. 323.

168   "I am in love." Clark, Lionel Johnson to Arthur Galton, Feb. 18, 1890.

168   "fourteen times running." Ibid., Lord Alfred Douglas to A. J. A. Symons, July 8, 1930.

168   "the Overloved met." W. H. Auden, "An Improbable Life," *New Yorker,* Mar. 6, 1963, p. 162.

168   "I had seen." *Dorian,* p. 144.

168   "Laughter is not at all." Ibid., p. 30.

168   "his finely-curved scarlet lips." Ibid., p. 39.

170   "Every portrait that is painted." Ibid., pp. 27, 34.

170   "an artist should create." *The Mask, 1912–1913,* vol. 5 (Florence: Goldoni, n.d.), p. 19.

170   "To reveal art." *Dorian,* p. 21.

170   "All art is at once." Ibid., p. 22.

170   "each man lived." Ibid., p. 226.

170   "One pays for one's sins." *Plays, Lady Windermere's Fan,* p. 39.

171   "Yes; there is a terrible moral." *Letters,* p. 259.

171   "what I would like." Ibid., p. 352.

171   "played with the idea." *Dorian,* p. 66.

171   "nothing can cure." Ibid., p. 44.

171   "what I think I am." *Letters,* p. 352.

172   "with matters only fitted." *Scots Observer,* July 5, 1890.

172   "madly, extravagantly." *Lippincott's Monthly Magazine,* June 1890, p. 56.

172   "adored a young man madly." *Trials,* p. 112.

172   "You became to me." *Dorian,* p. 144.

172   "I love you." *Plays, Lady Windermere's Fan,* p. 28.

172   "personality." *Dorian,* p. 144.

172   "I went to look." Ibid., p. 71.

172   "Nowadays people know." Ibid.

172   "If you want." Ibid., p. 100.

172   "Whenever a man." Ibid.

173   "a man whom no pure-minded girl." Ibid., p. 183.

173   "is so fatal." Ibid.

173   "There is no such thing." Ibid., p. 21.

173   "Suddenly from a lumpy tussock." Ibid., p. 239.

173 "crouching by a little charcoal stove." Ibid., p. 223.

174 "I have a duty." André Gide, *Oscar Wilde,* trans. Bernard Frechtman (London: Kimber, 1951), p. 28.

174 "You have killed my love." *Dorian,* p. 115.

174 "There is always something ridiculous." Ibid., p. 117.

174 "If the British public." J. A. Symonds to Horatio Brown, July 22, 1890, in John Addington Symonds, *Letters and Papers of John Addington Symonds* (London: Murray, 1923), p. 240.

175 "effeminate frivolity." Karl Beckson, ed. *Oscar Wilde: The Critical Heritage* (New York: Barnes & Noble, 1970), p. 72.

175 "tedious and dull." Ibid., p. 260.

175 "All excess." *Letters,* p. 259.

175 "a dreadful book." [Raymond] and Ricketts, *Oscar Wilde,* p. 178.

175 "skill" and "subtlety." "A Novel by Mr. Oscar Wilde," *Bookman,* Nov. 1891.

175 "a wonderful book." *Letters,* p. 270.

175 "unmanly sickening." Beckson, *Oscar Wilde,* p. 77.

175 "It is the most wonderful piece." Clark, Lady Wilde to Oscar Wilde, [June 1890].

176 "extremely ugly." Belford, *Violet Hunt,* p. 65.

176 "a woman made." Ibid.

176 "heavy odours." Oscar Wilde, "A Bevy of Poets," *Pall Mall Gazette,* Mar. 27, 1885.

176 "came to London." O'Sullivan, *Aspects of Wilde,* p. 92.

176 "horrid old Jew." *Dorian,* pp. 77, 109.

176 "Oscar says he likes you." Alexander Michaelson, "Oscar Wilde," *Blackfriars,* Nov. 1927, p. 700.

176 "Never again did I speak." Ibid.

177 "an extremely recent." *Letters,* p. 311.

177 "You cannot be Oscar's friend." Michaelson, "Oscar Wilde," p. 701.

178 "the odious Silverpoints." Jerusha Hall McCormack, *John Gray: Poet, Dandy, and Priest* (Hanover, N.H.: University Press of New England, 1991), p. 144.

178 "sublime inversion." Marc-André Raffalovich, *Uranisme et unisexualité; Étude sur différentes manifestations de l'instinct sexuel bibliothèque de criminologie,* vol. 15 (Lyons: A. Storck, 1896), p. 78.

178 "The Rhine is of course tedious." *Letters,* p. 248.

179 "a huge success." Ibid., p. 282.

179 "a practiced writer." *New York Tribune,* Jan. 27, 1891.

179 "I am not satisfied." *Letters,* p. 282.

181 "the symbolic incarnation." J.-K. Huysmans, *À rebours* or *Against the Grain* (New York: Dover, 1969), p. 52.

181 "succeeded in rendering." Ibid.

181 "If the book." O'Sullivan, *Aspects of Wilde,* p. 32.

181 "le 'great event,' " H. P. Clive, *Pierre Louÿs* (Oxford: Clarendon Press, 1978), p. 71.

182 "I don't like your lips." Gide, *Oscar Wilde,* p. 33.

182 "nothing but harm." Ibid.

182 "what Thackeray calls the 'chief gift.' " Ibid., p. 15.

182 "I choose my friends." *Dorian,* p. 30.

183 "a large pasty face." Pierre Champion, *Marcel Schwob et son temps* (Paris: Grasset, 1927) p. 99.

183 "terrible absinthe drinker." Ibid.

183 "after the first glass." Leverson, *Letters to the Sphinx,* p. 39.

183 "a hallucinatory resurrector." Marcel Schwob, *The King in the Golden Mask and Other Stories,* trans. Iain White (New York: Carcanet, 1984), p. 4.

184 "gigantic, smooth-shaven." Ellmann, p. 351.

CHAPTER FOURTEEN: MORE THAN LAUGHTER

185 "Luxury—gold-tipped matches." David Cecil, *Max: A Biography* (London: Constable, 1964), p. 71.

187 "In the drama." *Writings,* "The Soul of Man Under Socialism," p. 44.

187 "Ladies and Gentlemen." A. E. W. Mason, *Sir George Alexander and the St. James's Theatre* (London: Macmillan, 1935), p. 224.

188 "she will be very nervous." *More Letters,* p. 114.

188 "You have had a brilliant success." Clark, Lady Wilde to Oscar Wilde, Feb. 24, 1892.

188 "It's perhaps not very proper." Ellmann, p. 366 n.

188 "Quite Too-Too." *Punch,* March 5, 1892.

188 "delightful and immortal." *Letters,* p. 312.

188 "unspeakable animal." Henry James, *Henry James Letters,* ed. Leon Edel (Cambridge, Mass.: Harvard University Press, 1980), p. 373.

189 "What does it mean?" W. Graham Robertson, *Life Was Worth Living: Reminiscences* (London: Harper, 1931), p. 125.

190 "I love fruit." Arthur Wing Pinero, *The Social Plays of Arthur Wing Pinero, The*

Second Mrs. Tanqueray (New York: Dutton, 1917), p. 82.

191   "How on earth." Plays, Lady Windermere's Fan, p. 54.

191   "one of those modern drawing room plays." Letters, p. 331.

191   "is, or should be." Ibid., p. 311.

191   "I do not think." Royal General Theatrical Fund, report of a speech Wilde gave on May 26, 1892, Berg Collection.

191   " 'This passion is too terrible.' " Letters, p. 331.

192   "The chief merit." Ibid., p. 309.

192   "I do not like it." Clark, Lady Wilde to Oscar Wilde, n.d. [1892].

192   "Your reward?" Plays, Lady Windermere's Fan, p. 35.

193   "With regard to the new speech." Letters, p. 308.

193   "Well, really I might be." Plays, Lady Windermere's Fan, p. 35.

193   "Every word of a comedy dialogue." More Letters, p. 112.

193   "It should run." Ibid., p. 113.

193   "Just like a large packing case." Plays, Lady Windermere's Fan, p. 22.

193   "It saves a great deal." More Letters, p. 111.

193   "The society that allows." Illustrated London News, Feb. 27, 1892.

194   "infantine . . . both in subject." Henry James Letters, p. 372.

194   "reconcile the things." Illustrated Sporting and Dramatic News, Apr. 9, 1892.

194   "I don't think." Plays, Lady Windermere's Fan, p. 44.

194   "only thorough playwright." Katharine Worth, Oscar Wilde (New York: Grove, 1983), p. 5.

194   "The adjective was unnecessary." Plays, Lady Windermere's Fan, p. 11.

195   "there are certain temperaments." Dorian, p. 101.

195   "Mr. Oscar Wilde." Daily Telegraph, Feb. 22, 1892.

196   "I hope you wrote." Clark, Lady Wilde to Oscar Wilde, n.d. [1891].

196   "A more scholarly and accomplished man." New York Herald, June 9, 1893.

196   "he was of no use." Madeleine Stern, Purple Passage: The Life of Mrs. Frank Leslie (Tulsa: University of Oklahoma Press, 1953), p. 160.

196   "I'm taking Willie over." Ibid., p. 164.

197   "rather exceptionally good-looking." Alfred Douglas, The Autobiography of Lord Alfred Douglas (London: Martin Secker, 1929), p. 23.

197   "That flowerlike sort." Bernard Shaw and Alfred Douglas: A Correspondence, ed. Mary Hyde (London: Murray, 1982), p. 4.

198   "I have no sympathy." Fiction, "The Remarkable Rocket," p. 135.

198   "It is awfully hard work." Plays, The Importance of Being Earnest, p. 270.

198   "To love oneself." Ibid., An Ideal Husband, p. 213.

198 "To love one's self." Clark, signed sheet of epigrams.

198 "A really well-made buttonhole." "Phrases and Philosophies for the Use of the Young," *Chameleon,* Dec. 1894, p. 1.

198 "A really exquisite buttonhole." Clark, epigrams.

CHAPTER FIFTEEN: TRANSLATING ECSTASY

200 "Ah! I have kissed." *Plays, Salome,* p. 91.

200 "green like a curious." [Raymond] and Ricketts, *Oscar Wilde,* p. 53.

200 "Yes, I never thought." Robertson, *Life Was Worth Living,* p. 125.

200 "the serpent of old Nile." *Letters,* p. 834.

201 "my own words." Kerry Powell, *Oscar Wilde and the Theatre of the 1890s* (Cambridge: Cambridge University Press, 1990), p. 42.

201 "The dress, the title." Ibid., p. 52.

201 "Thy mouth is like a band." *Plays, Salome,* p. 73.

201 "Woman lies at the base." Jane Wilde, *Social Studies,* p. 248.

201 "It is his eyes." *Plays, Salome,* p. 71.

202 "The mystery of Love." Ibid., p. 91.

202 "a walking compendium." *Letters,* p. 316, n. 5.

202 "I shall take out letters." *Pall Mall Budget,* June 30, 1892.

202 "Tyrian purple." *Letters,* p. 333.

202 "Parma violets." Cecil, *Max,* p. 91.

202 "fading" or "tired." *Letters,* p. 332–33.

202 "Only care must be taken." Lord Chamberlain's Records: 1909 and 1910, Manuscript Division, British Library.

202 "It is only the shudder." Edgar Saltus, *Oscar Wilde: An Idler's Impression* (New York: AMS Press, 1968), p. 20.

202 "an oriental Hedda Gabler." William Archer, "Mr. Oscar Wilde's New Play," *Black & White,* May 11, 1893.

203 "I felt pity." *Letters,* p. 293.

203 "an arrangement in blood." London *Times,* Feb. 23, 1893.

203 "Of course I plagiarise." Max Beerbohm, *Letters to Reggie Turner,* ed. Rupert Hart-Davis (London: Hart-Davis, 1964), p. 36.

203 "For the only artist." *Letters,* p. 348 n. 3.

203 "like a silver hatchet." Rothenstein, *Men and Memories,* p. 187.

203 "a vile constitution." Chris Snodgrass, *Aubrey Beardsley: Dandy of the Grotesque* (New York: Oxford University Press, 1995), p. 28.

204   "seeking everywhere for lovers." *Plays, Salome,* p. 75.

204   "Dear Aubrey is too Parisian." [Raymond] and Ricketts, *Oscar Wilde,* p. 51.

204   "When I have before me." *The Café Royal Story: A Living Legend,* ed. Leslie Frewin (London: Hutchinson Benham, 1963), p. 24.

204   "Don't sit." *New Criterion,* Jan. 1926.

205   "Yes, Yes, I look." quoted in "The Same Old Solotaire," *London Review of Books,* July 4, 1996, p. 22.

205   "schoolboy faults." *Letters,* p. 432.

205   "naughty scribbles." Matthew Sturgis, *Passionate Attitudes* (London: Macmillan, 1995), p. 153.

205   "whole thing must be a joke." Ibid.

205   "a polyphonic variation." *Oscar Wilde: A Collection of Critical Essays,* ed. Richard Ellmann (Englewood Cliffs, N.J.: Prentice-Hall 1969), p. 60.

206   "Drama, the most objective form." *Letters,* p. 589.

206   "but as the man." Kernahan, *In Good Company,* p. 316.

206   "Oh, I'm radiant." Max Beerbohm, *Herbert Beerbohm Tree: Some Memories of Him and His Art* (London: Hutchinson, 1920), p. 187.

207   "obviously mad." Beerbohm, *Letters to Reggie Turner,* p. 39.

207   "nothing escaped." Rothenstein, *Men and Memories,* p. 146.

207   "I am sorry to say." Beerbohm, *Letters to Reggie Turner,* p. 35.

207   "inborn and cannot ever be." *Anglo-American Times,* Mar. 25, 1893; also *Letters,* p. 290.

207   "silver dagger." S. N. Behrman, *Portrait of Max* (New York: Random House, 1960), p. 37.

207   "Giving lectures for him." Cecil, *Max,* p. 48.

207   "the gift of." Ibid., p. 68.

207   "Tell me." Leverson, *Letters to the Sphinx,* p. 42.

208   "I am so sorry." Clark, Constance Wilde to Oscar Wilde, Sept. 18, 1892.

208   "He has become mad." Clark, Constance Wilde to Mrs. Fitch, Sept. 14, 1892.

208   "As Herod in my *Salome.*" Hesketh Pearson, *Beerbohm Tree: His Life and Laughter* (London: Methuen, 1956), p. 65.

209   "My God! he must be supernatural." Ibid.

209   "wildest profligate who spills." Ibid., p. 69.

209   "Puritanism is not a theory." Ibid., p. 70.

209   "a woman's play." *Letters,* p. 335.

209   "Oh! no one." *Plays, A Woman of No Importance,* p. 157.

210   "foolish," "slippery." Pearson, *Beerbohm Tree,* p. 69.

210 "If I go." Mikhail, p. 239.

210 "too fluctuating—for *theatrical* purposes." Beerbohm Tree to Oscar Wilde, Dec. 12, 1891, Harry Ransom Humanities Research Center, University of Texas at Austin.

210 "Ladies and Gentlemen." Pearson, *Beerbohm Tree,* p. 71.

210 "People love a wicked aristocrat." Ibid., p. 67.

210 "Despite its qualities." *Bookman,* Mar. 1895.

210 "a clever, immature work." *Illustrated London News,* Aug. 5, 1893.

211 "My husband is a kind of promissory note." *Plays, A Woman of No Importance,* p. 114.

211 "The Book of Life." Ibid., p. 112.

211 "Women have a much better time." Ibid., p. 103.

211 "All the married men." Ibid., p. 114.

211 "As far as I can ascertain." quoted in *New York Herald Tribune,* July 21, 1946.

211 "dresses the part." *More Letters,* p. 119.

212 "I need not tell you." Ibid., p. 120.

212 "Your presence here." Clark, Elisabeth Marbury to Oscar Wilde, Nov. 10, 1893.

CHAPTER SIXTEEN: MOSTLY FAMOUS

213 "Desire, at the end." *Letters,* p. 466.

214 "This indeed is life!" *Café Royal Story,* p. 27.

214 "When I am in trouble." *Plays, The Importance of Being Earnest,* p. 293.

214 "What shall we do." Ibid., p. 270.

214 "sits as if blowing bubbles." Michael Field, *Works and Days,* ed. T. and D. C. Sturge Moore (London: Murray, 1933), p. 140.

214 "allowing the people." Ibid.

214 "a champagne dinner." *Letters,* p. 503.

215 "no more than the romantic expression." William Roughhead, *Bad Companions* (Edinburgh: Green, 1930), p. 178. See also Neil Bartlett, *Who Was That Man? A Present for Mr. Oscar Wilde* (London: Penguin, 1988), p. 141.

215 "had heard of rich men." *Dorian,* p. 154.

216 "a narcissus," *Letters,* p. 314.

216 "To the Gilt-mailed Boy." inscribed volume in Taylor Collection, Princeton University.

216 "These familiarities were rare." Douglas, *Autobiography,* p. 75.

216   "I blame myself." *Letters,* p. 429.

216   "revolting," "loathsome." Ibid.

216   "So far from his leading me." Douglas, *Autobiography,* p. 76.

217   "feasting with panthers." *Letters,* p. 492.

217   "closely bound up." *Writings,* "The Soul of Man Under Socialism," p. 32.

217   "Your defect was not." *Letters,* p. 425.

218   "I am one." Ibid., p. 468.

218   "I have never posed." Ibid., p. 479.

218   "The first duty." "Phrases and Philosophies for the Use of the Young," *Chameleon,* Dec. 1894, p. 1.

219   "If Bosie has really made." George Ives diaries, Nov. 15, 1894, Harry Ransom Humanities Research Center, University of Texas at Austin.

219   "After going among that set." Ibid., Jan. 1, 1895.

219   "Well, I shall find out." Ibid., Aug. 24, 1894.

219   "When the prurient." *Letters,* p. 375.

219   "sterile and uncreative." Ibid., p. 426.

220   "stayed smoking cigarettes." Ibid.

220   "Things are the wrong colour." Ibid., p. 327.

220   "the mere fact." Ibid., p. 644.

220   "Any boy found disobeying." Ibid., p. 334.

220   "lazy and luxurious." Ibid., p. 868.

220   "We do no logic." Ibid.

220   "I think him perfectly delightful." Ibid.

221   "exercised a sort of enchantment." Alfred Douglas, *Without Apology* (London: Martin Secker, 1938), p. 75.

221   "as simple and innocent." Rupert Croft-Cooke, *Bosie: Lord Alfred Douglas, His Friends and Enemies* (New York: Bobbs-Merrill, 1963), p. 93.

221   "kill me, they wreck." *Letters,* p. 336.

222   "I am true Love." *Aesthetes and Decadents of the 1890s,* ed. Karl Beckson (Chicago: Academy, 1981), p. 82.

222   "perhaps the thing." *Letters,* p. 437.

222   "I want everyone to say." Ibid.

223   "Love me, not with smiles." Pierre Louÿs, *Two Erotic Tales: The Songs of Bilitis,* trans. Mary Hanson Harrison (Evanston: Evanston Publishing, 1995), p. 275.

223   "chose at once." *Letters,* p. 410.

223   "Examinations are of no value." *Plays, A Woman of No Importance,* p. 131.

223 "I have done no work." *Letters,* p. 341.

223 "divided in interest." Ibid., p. 342.

224 "charming people should smoke." Ibid., p. 343.

224 "were spoiling each other's lives." Ibid., p. 431.

224 "a gentle and penitent child." Ibid., p. 435.

224 "aimless, unhappy and absurd." Ibid., p. 346.

225 "May Allah ease." Stanley Weintraub, *Reggie: A Portrait of Reginald Turner* (New York: George Braziller, 1965), p. 30.

225 TIME HEALS EVERY WOUND. *Letters,* p. 434.

225 "I am not going to try." Croft-Cooke, *Bosie,* p. 97.

226 WHAT A FUNNY LITTLE MAN. *Letters,* p. 446.

226 "his small hand." Ibid., p. 439.

226 "I think if you were dead." Ibid., p. 446.

226 "The prospect of a battle." Ibid.

226 "My Own Boy." Ibid., p. 326.

226 "the world is changed." *Dorian,* p. 260.

227 "I suppose you have come." *Trials,* p. 67.

227 "The letter is a prose poem." Ibid., p. 68.

228 "yellow satin could console one." *Dorian,* p. 140.

228 "A mixture of English rowdyism." London *Times,* Apr. 17, 1894.

228 "Have you seen *The Yellow Book?*" Leverson, *Letters to the Sphinx,* p. 53.

228 "It is dull." *Letters,* p. 354.

CHAPTER SEVENTEEN: A BROKEN LINE

230 "We can have in life." *Dorian,* p. 234.

230 "I little thought." Louis Hamon, *Cheiro's Memoirs: The Reminiscences of a Society Palmist* (London: Rider, 1912), p. 56.

231 "The mystery of the world." Ibid.

231 "It is only shallow people." *Dorian,* p. 45.

231 "Is the break still there?" Hamon, *Cheiro's Memoirs,* p. 56.

231 "I see a very brilliant life." *Letters,* p. 358 n.

231 "Death and Love." Ibid., p. 358.

231 "I am truly sorry." Clark, Lady Wilde to Oscar Wilde, Mar. 29, 1894.

231 "Now that I come." *Plays, The Importance of Being Earnest,* p. 287.

232 "the sheer passion of love." *Letters,* p. 361n.

232   "As a rule." *Plays, An Ideal Husband*, p. 169.

233   "The ten commandments." Ibid., p. 217.

233   "There is something entertaining." London Theatre Museum Library, unidentified newspaper clipping.

233   "One's past is what one is." *Plays, An Ideal Husband*, p. 185.

233   "strength and courage." Ibid., p. 193.

234   "working his way." *Pall Mall Gazette*, Jan. 4, 1893.

234   "I thank you." London Theatre Museum Library, unidentified newspaper clipping.

234   "so helpless, so crude." James, *Henry James Letters*, vol. 3, p. 514.

234   "Really? You care for *places*?" Leon Edel, *Henry James: The Middle Years, 1882–1895* (New York: Lippincott, 1962), p. 31.

234   "a fatuous fool." Ibid.

234   "How *can* my piece." James, *Henry James Letters*, vol. 3, p. 514.

235   "I have come." Ibid., p. 521.

235   "hideously, atrociously dramatic." Ibid., vol. 4, p. 9.

235   "from nearly twenty years." Ibid., p. 10.

236   "ugly Swiss governess." *Letters*, p. 360.

236   "I have been doing nothing." Ibid., p. 362.

236   "first act is ingenious." Ibid.

236   "He led a happy, idle life." *Trials*, p. 121.

236   "being with those who are young." Ibid., p. 127.

236   "ploughed through the waves." Holland, *Son of Oscar Wilde*, p. 199.

236   "long rambling castles." Ibid., p. 54.

237   "I invented that magnificent flower." *Letters*, p. 373.

237   "I love drinking Bovril." *Athenaeum*, Sept. 29, 1894.

237   "Bovril Company informs us." Ibid., Oct. 13, 1894.

237   "a morbid and middle-class affair." Berggren, *The Definitive Four-Act Version of* The Importance of Being Earnest, p. 26n.

237   "Of all sweet passions." Croft-Cooke, *Bosie,* p. 353.

238   "The home seems." *Plays, The Importance of Being Earnest*, p. 286.

238   "When you are not." *Letters*, p. 439.

238   "the first noble sorrow." Ibid., p. 375.

238   "I am sorry." Ibid., p. 384.

239   "are equally good." Ibid., p. 369.

239   "I think it would be." Clark, Elisabeth Marbury to Oscar Wilde, Mar. 15, 1895.

239   "This scene that you feel." Hesketh Pearson, *The Last Actor-Managers* (London: Methuen, 1950), p. 28.

239   "I'll send you a box." Ibid., p. 78.

239   "I fly to Algiers." *More Letters,* p. 67.

240   "One felt less softness." Gide, *Oscar Wilde,* p. 27.

240   "Prudence!" Ibid., p. 30.

240   "Would you like to know." Ibid., p. 29.

240   "as beautiful as bronze statues." Jonathan Fryer, *André and Oscar: Gide, Wilde and the Gay Art of Living* (London: Constable, 1997), p. 112.

240   "I hope to have quite." Gide, *Oscar Wilde,* p. 28.

240   "quite exquisite." *More Letters,* p. 128.

240   "the beggars here." Ibid.

240   "I hope you're like me." Fryer, *André and Oscar,* p. 112.

240   "It's impossible to gauge." Ibid., p. 113.

241   "great pleasure of the debauched." Ibid., p. 119.

241   "there is no such thing." *Letters,* p. 671.

242   "so bad, so disappointing." Ibid., p. 378.

243   "stepped past the limits." Constance Wilde to Arthur Humphreys, June 1, 1894, quoted in Sotheby's catalog of July 23, 1985.

243   "not far short." Ibid.

243   "I am the most truthful person." Ibid.

243   "how much I love you." Ibid., Aug. 11, 1894.

243   "must not talk." Clark, Constance Wilde to Arthur Humphreys, Oct. 22, 1894.

CHAPTER EIGHTEEN: THE LAST FIRST NIGHT

245   "Some kill their love." *Poetry, The Ballad of Reading Gaol,* p. 153.

247   "A man who marries." *Plays, The Importance of Being Earnest,* p. 259.

247   "The play *is* a success." Mason, *Sir George Alexander,* p. 78.

248   "Mabel a daisy." Leverson, *Letters to the Sphinx,* p. 34.

248   "No" "it must be." *New Criterion,* Jan. 1926.

248   "On the contrary." *Plays, The Importance of Being Earnest,* p. 307.

248   "Well, wasn't I right?" Mason, *Sir George Alexander,* p. 79.

248   "left a grotesque bouquet." *Letters,* p. 383.

249   "stood uttering every foul word." Ibid., p. 438.

249   "I don't see anything." Ibid., p. 384.

250 "into motion the forces." Ibid., p. 491.

250 "serious lies to a bald man." Ibid., p. 493.

251 "No doubt he will perform." *Trials,* p. 8.

251 "It is not friendly." Guy Deghy and Keith Waterhouse, *Café Royal: Ninety Years of Bohemia* (London: Hutchinson, 1956), p. 83.

251 "to be dogged." *Letters,* p. 360.

252 "You stated that your age." *Trials,* p. 105.

253 "Ah no, Mr. Carson." Ibid., p. 116.

253 "a man of great taste." Ibid., p. 125.

253 "Did you ever kiss him?" Ibid., p. 133.

255 "If the country." Ibid., p. 149.

255 "I hope Oscar." Ibid., p. 152.

255 "Yellow Book under his arm." London Theatre Museum Library, various newspaper accounts.

256 "Don't you keep Christmas." O'Sullivan, *Aspects of Wilde,* p. 106.

257 "fashionable and well-aired." Berggren, *The Definitive Four-Act Version of* The Importance of Being Earnest, p. 123.

257 "dirty, dingy." *Illustrated Police Budget,* May 4, 1885.

257 "A slim thing." *Letters,* p. 389.

257 "Everyone tried to outdo." *Trials,* p. 164.

258 "I know and admire." *Letters,* p. 376.

258 "What is to become." Ibid., p. 389n.

258 "Misfortunes one can endure." *Plays, Lady Windermere's Fan,* p. 18.

259 "face looked almost bloodless." *Illustrated Police News,* Apr. 20, 1895.

259 "committed the act." *Trials,* p. 175.

260 "degraded." Ibid., p. 235.

260 "the love that dare not." Ibid., p. 200.

260 "repeatedly exists between an elder." Ibid., p. 201.

260 "simply wonderful." Beerbohm, *Letters to Reggie Turner,* p. 102.

260 "though they may have erred." George Ives Diary, May 26, 1895, Harry Ransom Humanities Research Center, University of Texas at Austin.

261 "came tapping with his beak." Yeats, p. 288.

261 "If you stay." Ibid., p. 289.

261 "made the right decision." Ibid.

261 "At least my vices." Ibid., p. 291.

261 "one must have a heart." Leverson, *Letters to the Sphinx,* p. 42.

262   "This trial seems to be." *Trials,* p. 253.

262   "stableman's gait and dress." *Letters,* p. 492.

263   "People who can do." *Trials,* p. 272.

263   "And I?" Ibid., p. 273.

CHAPTER NINETEEN: TOUCHING SORROW

264   "Clergymen, and people." *Letters,* p. 473.

264   "I should hate." Ibid., p. 115.

264   "even in prison." *Writings,* "The Soul of Man Under Socialism," p. 29.

265   "For sleep, like all wholesome things." *Daily Chronicle,* Mar. 24, 1897.

265   "I had to keep everything." *Trials,* p. 278.

265   "step back and view them." Robert Harborough Sherard, *The Life of Oscar Wilde* (London: T. Werner Laurie, 1906), p. 389.

265   "The terror of a child." *Daily Chronicle,* May 28, 1897.

266   "third-rate, badly-written religious books." Ibid., Mar. 24, 1897.

266   "too critical, too intellectually subtle." *Intentions,* "The Critic as Artist," pt. 2, p. 170.

266   "the diary that we all carry." *Plays, The Importance of Being Earnest,* p. 273.

266   "To have altered my life." *Letters,* p. 705.

266   "It even smelt bad." *Trials,* p. 284.

267   "The prisoner is either locked up." *Daily Chronicle,* Mar. 24, 1897.

267   "One of the tragedies." Ibid.

268   "Must it be cut?" "The Story of Oscar Wilde's Life in Reading Jail," *Bruno's Weekly* (New York), Jan. 22, 1916.

268   "He had the eyes." Ellmann, p. 497.

268   "Oscar Wilde, I pity you." Sherard, *Real Oscar Wilde,* p. 137.

269   "I like hearing myself talk." *Fiction,* "The Remarkable Rocket," p. 134.

269   "the sign of the widow's son." Sherard, *Real Oscar Wilde,* p. 140.

269   "very repentant." Clark, Constance Wilde to Emily Thursfield, Oct. 12, 1895.

270   "first heard a nightingale's song." Ibid., Jan. 5, 1895.

270   "May the prison help him!" Ellmann, p. 498.

270   "such a terrible thing." Clark, Constance Wilde to Lily Wilde, [Feb. 5, 1896].

271   "For many reasons." Clark, Willie Wilde to More Adey, Feb. 4, 1896.

272   "revolting and grotesque." *Letters,* p. 400.

272   "have nothing to do." Ibid., p. 401.

272   "If Oscar asks me." Ellmann, p. 500.

272   "Tell him I know." Croft-Cooke, *Bosie*, p. 138; Alfred Douglas, *Oscar Wilde and Myself* (London: John Long, 1914), p. 177.

272   "altered every man's life." *Letters*, p. 488.

272   "that little tent." *Poetry, The Ballad of Reading Gaol*, p. 155.

272   "no other Irishman." *Neue Freie Presse*, Apr. 23, 1905.

273   "It was the triumph." *Letters*, p. 429.

273   "There is a luxury." *Dorian*, p. 125.

273   "much perilous stuff." *Letters*, p. 514.

273   "No!" Wilde exclaimed. Charles Ricketts, *Self-Portrait* (London: Peter Davies, 1939), p. 47.

274   "one last glimpse." *Trials*, p. 297.

275   "No prisoner has ever." *Letters*, p. 461.

275   "with the dignity." Ibid., p. 563.

275   "Sphinx, how marvellous." Ibid.

275   "I look on all." Ibid.

276   "he broke down." Ibid., p. 564.

CHAPTER TWENTY: MISBEGOTTEN YESTERDAYS

277   "It is only shallow people." *Dorian*, p. 45.

279   "had grown to feel." Rothenstein, *Men and Memories*, p. 362.

280   "He is sure." John Rothenstein, *The Life and Death of Conder* (London: Dent, 1938), p. 165.

280   "Laughter is the primeval attitude." *Dorian*, p. 30.

280   "Pitiful family." Edmond and Jules de Goncourt, *Journal: Mémoires de la vie littéraire, 1891–1896*, vol. 4 (Paris: Flammarion, 1956), p. 797.

281   "I'm writing an essay." Mikhail, p. 350.

281   "I have come to loathe." Barnaby Conrad III, *Absinthe: History in a Bottle* (San Francisco: Chronicle, 1988), p. 16n.

281   "Alcohol, taken in sufficient quantities." Redman, *Epigrams*, p. 165.

281   "beginning at the end." *Letters*, p. 575.

282   "I begin to realise." Ibid., p. 577.

282   "I have made Aubrey buy." *More Letters*, p. 151.

282   "I adore this place." *Letters*, p. 585.

282   "pilgrimage to the sinner." Ibid., p. 596.

282   "I want to have a poet." Ibid., pp. 597, 619.

283 "Why are you." Ibid., p. 612.

283 "such lovely little fellows." Ibid., p. 582.

283 "I have now." Ibid., p. 607.

283 "I feel him." Ibid., p. 577.

283 "You are made." Ibid.

283 "is the knowledge." Ibid., p. 595.

283 "I am so glad." Ibid., p. 600.

283 "no longer the lyrical madman." Gide, *Oscar Wilde*, p. 47.

284 "One should never go back." Ibid.

284 "little *gamins*." *Letters*, p. 617.

284 "no heart to write." Ibid., p. 639.

284 "I am not in the mood." Ibid.

285 "I will publish." O'Sullivan, *Aspects of Wilde*, p. 102.

285 "the most learned erotomaniac." *Letters*, p. 630.

285 "personally charming." Ibid., p. 656.

285 "I am greatly hurt." Ibid., p. 635.

285 "Poor Oscar cried." Croft-Cooke, *Bosie*, p. 158.

285 "I feel that my only hope." *Letters*, p. 637.

285 "Do remake my ruined life." Ibid.

285 "Yes: I saw Bosie." Ibid., p. 638.

286 "The Triad of the Moon." Ibid., p. 649.

286 "He laboured over it." Douglas, *Oscar Wilde and Myself*, p. 122.

287 "more than he loves." *Letters*, p. 648.

287 "I cannot live." Ibid., p. 644.

287 "I must remake my maimed life." Ibid., p. 647.

287 "A wonderful personality." Ibid., p. 661.

287 "I am engaged." Ibid., p. 775.

287 "a face chiselled." Ibid., p. 787.

287 "like a young St. John." Ibid., p. 776.

288 "How can she really imagine." Ibid., p. 653.

288 "lost that supreme desire." Croft-Cooke, *Bosie*, p. 168.

288 "I loved you." *Dorian*, p. 117.

288 "He has been sweet." Croft-Cooke, *Bosie*, p. 168.

289 "Russian Elder." *Letters*, p. 698.

290 "the *maladie*." Ibid., p. 696.

290 "Nobody here seems to feel." Clark, Elisabeth Marbury to Leonard Smithers, Jan. 25, 1898.

290   "a moving piece." *Daily Telegraph,* Feb. 27, 1898.

290   "It is frightfully tragic." Hyde, *Oscar Wilde,* p. 387.

290   AM IN GREAT GRIEF, *Letters,* p. 729.

290   "did not feel it." Ibid.

290   "My way back." Ellmann, p. 566.

291   "If we had only met." *Letters,* p. 730.

291   "When I read it." Ibid., p. 721.

CHAPTER TWENTY-ONE: STEALING HAPPINESS

292   "O we are wearied." *Poetry,* "Panthea," p. 94.

292   "I'm so alone." Gide, *Oscar Wilde,* p. 47.

292   "I have lost." *Letters,* p. 708.

293   "a curious and bitter lesson." Ibid., p. 791.

293   "A patriot put in prison." Ibid., p. 705.

293   "I saw at once." Rothenstein, *Men and Memories,* p. 362.

294   "I live a very ordinary life." *Letters,* p. 743.

294   "the public liked to hear." Ibid., p. 780.

294   "one can get nothing." Ibid., p. 717.

294   "one can't get railway-tickets." Ibid., p. 812.

294   "I have been *seven* times." *More Letters,* p. 171.

295   "Nothing fattens so much." *Letters,* p. 763.

295   "I can't afford." Ibid., p. 828.

295   "Of course I cannot bear." Ibid., p. 740.

295   "the harvest-moon." Ibid., p. 767.

295   "quite an imp." Ibid., p. 768.

295   "rather like a handsome bamboo walking-stick." Ibid., p. 834.

295   "by the lack of intellect." Ibid., p. 774.

296   "like a rose-leaf." Ibid., p. 739.

296   "Maurice has won." Ibid., p. 710.

296   "So you love Maurice?" Ibid., p. 732.

296   "How is my golden Maurice?" Ibid., p. 739.

296   "rests his hope." Ibid., p. 756.

297   "was rather like a public meeting." Ibid., p. 749.

297   "A delightful evening." Ibid., p. 748.

297   "sodomist outcasts." Clark, Vincent O'Sullivan to Arthur Symons, [192?].

297   "Frank insists." *Letters,* p. 770.

298 "the exquisite taste." Ibid., p. 776.

298 "My dear Frank." Ibid., p. 781.

298 "I hope to be happy." Ibid., p. 782.

298 "It was very tragic." Ibid., p. 783.

298 "There is something." Ibid., p. 719.

299 "wide chasms." Ibid., p. 785.

299 "One has always sad memories." Clark, Lily Wilde to Oscar Wilde, May 7, [1899].

299 "Swiss people are carved." *Letters,* p. 784.

299 "Mellor carries out the traditions." *More Letters,* p. 180.

299 "The chastity of Switzerland." *Letters,* p. 792.

299 "Whatever I do." Ibid., p. 791.

299 "Life is rather dust." Ibid., p. 795.

300 "I have had a very bad time." Ibid., p. 737.

300 "it is always a bore." Ibid., p. 804.

300 "Don't have with *me.*" Ibid., p. 815.

300 "I have no doubt." Ibid., p. 721.

301 "Oscar *meant* well." George Ives Diary, Feb. 23, 1905, Harry Ransom Humanities Research Center, University of Texas at Austin.

301 "It is a poor little Bohemian hotel." *Letters,* p. 767.

301 "literary resort." Ibid., p. 768.

302 "God saved the genius." Laurence Housman, *Echo de Paris: A Study from Life* (London: Cape, 1923), p. 30.

302 "very pleasant Christmas." *Letters,* p. 813.

302 "Our present-day literature." Ted Morgan, *Maugham: A Biography* (New York: Simon & Schuster, 1980), p. 76.

302 "My throat is a lime kiln." *Letters,* p. 817.

302 "Poisoning by mussels." Ibid.

302 "a sort of blood poisoning." Ibid., p. 818.

302 "when one is cooped up." Ibid., p. 727.

303 "a sweet singer." Ibid., p. 816.

303 "It will be delightful." Ibid.

303 "the only city." Ibid., p. 826.

303 "I do nothing." Ibid., p. 825.

303 "I really must become a Catholic." Ibid., p. 819.

303 "built again his own palace." Mikhail, p. 480.

304 TERRIBLY WEAK. *Letters,* p. 837.

304 "Ah! Robbie." [Raymond] and Ricketts, *Oscar Wilde,* p. 59.

304 "And what have I." *Letters,* p. 848.

304 "I will never outlive." Ibid., p. 849.

304 "You are qualifying." Ibid., p. 848.

305 "I have had a dreadful dream." Ibid., p. 849.

305 "He has not once hinted." Clark, Reggie Turner to Robbie Ross, Nov. 27, [1900].

305 "You dear little Jew." *Letters,* p. 852.

305 "The diagnosis." Ellmann, p. 582.

305 ALMOST HOPELESS. *Letters,* p. 853

305 "the cherub with the flaming sword." Ibid., p. 859.

305 "when roused Wilde gave signs." Ibid., p. 857.

306 "Oscar's end was as quiet." Clark, typescript for a new preface to *The Life and Confessions of Oscar Wilde* by Frank Harris and Lord Alfred Douglas (London: Fortune Press, 1925), p. 15.

307 "if a man needs an elaborate tombstone." *Letters,* p. 169.

EPILOGUE

310 "I think [Wilde]." Hoare, *Wilde's Last Stand,* p. 152.

311 "artificial, trivial." Beckson, *Encyclopedia,* p. 425.

SELECTED BIBLIOGRAPHY

⁂

Amor, Anne Clark. *Mrs. Oscar Wilde: A Woman of Some Importance.* London: Sidgwick & Jackson, 1983.

Bartlett, Neil. *Who Was That Man? A Present for Mr. Oscar Wilde.* London: Penguin, 1993.

Beckson, Karl. *London in the 1890s.* New York: Norton, 1992.

———. *The Oscar Wilde Encyclopedia.* New York: AMS Press, 1998.

———, ed. *I Can Resist Everything Except Temptation and Other Quotations from Oscar Wilde.* New York: Columbia University Press, 1996.

Beerbohm, Max. *Around Theatres.* London: Hart-Davis, 1953.

———. *Letters to Reggie Turner.* London: Hart-Davis, 1964.

———. *A Peep into the Past.* Brattleboro, Vt.: Stephen Greene, 1972.

Belford, Barbara. *Bram Stoker: A Biography of the Author of* Dracula. New York: Knopf, 1996.

———. *Violet: The Story of the Irrepressible Violet Hunt and Her Circle of Lovers and Friends—Ford Madox Ford, H. G. Wells, Somerset Maugham, and Henry James.* New York: Simon & Schuster, 1990.

Bell, Archie. *The Clyde Fitch I Knew.* New York: Broadway, 1909.

Birnbaum, Martin. *Oscar Wilde: Fragments and Memories.* London: Elkin Mathews, 1920.

Blair, David Hunter. *In Victorian Days and Other Papers.* 1939; reprint, New York: Books for Libraries Press, 1969.

Borland, Maureen. *Wilde's Devoted Friend: A Life of Robert Ross.* Oxford: Lennard, 1990.

Bray, Alan. *Homosexuality in Renaissance England.* New York: Columbia University Press, 1995.

Bristow, Joseph. *Effeminate England: Homoerotic Writing after 1885.* New York: Columbia University Press, 1995.

Brough, James. *The Prince and the Lily.* London: Hodder & Stoughton, 1975.

Cahill, Thomas. *How the Irish Saved Civilization.* New York: Doubleday, 1995.

Calloway, Stephen. *Aubrey Beardsley: A Biography.* London: HarperCollins, 1998.

Cecil, David. *Max: A Biography.* London: Constable, 1964.

Clive, H. P. *Pierre Louÿs: A Biography.* Oxford: Clarendon Press, 1978.

Coakley, Davis. *Oscar Wilde: The Importance of Being Irish.* Dublin: Town House, 1994.

Cohen, Ed. *Talk on the Wilde Side: Toward a Genealogy of a Discourse on Male Sexuality.* London: Routledge, 1993.

Croft-Cooke, Rupert. *Bosie: Lord Alfred Douglas, His Friends and Enemies.* New York: Bobbs-Merrill, 1963.

Curry, Wade Chester. "Steele MacKaye: Producer and Director." Ph.D. diss., University of Illinois, Urbana, 1958.

d'Arch Smith, Timothy. *Love in Earnest: Some Notes on the Lives and Writings of English "Uranian" Poets from 1889 to 1930.* London: Routledge & Kegan Paul, 1970.

de Jongh, Nicholas. *Not in Front of the Audience: Homosexuality on Stage.* London: Routledge, 1992.

Dollimore, Jonathan. *Sexual Dissidence: Augustine to Wilde, Freud to Foucault.* Oxford: Clarendon Press, 1991.

Donoghue, Denis. *Walter Pater: Lover of Strange Souls.* New York: Knopf, 1995.

Douglas, Alfred. *The Autobiography of Lord Alfred Douglas.* London: Martin Secker, 1929.

Dowling, Linda. *Hellenism and Homosexuality in Victorian Oxford.* Ithaca: Cornell University Press, 1994.

Duncan, Barry. *The St. James's Theatre: Its Strange and Complete History.* London: Barrie and Rockliff, 1964.

Fawkes, Richard. *Dion Boucicault: A Biography.* London: Quartet Books, 1979.

Fryer, Jonathan. *André and Oscar: Gide, Wilde and the Gay Art of Living.* London: Constable, 1997.

Gagnier, Regenia A. *Idylls of the Marketplace: Oscar Wilde and the Victorian Public.* Aldershot: Scholar Press, 1987.

Gide, André. *Oscar Wilde.* Bernard Frechtman, trans. London: William Kimber, 1951.

Harris, Frank. *Oscar Wilde: His Life and Confessions.* 1916; rev. ed., London: Constable, 1938.

Hoare, Philip. *Wilde's Last Stand: Decadence, Conspiracy and the First World War.* London: Duckworth, 1997.

Holland, Merlin. *The Wilde Album.* New York: Henry Holt, 1998.

Holland, Vyvyan. *Son of Oscar Wilde.* London: Hart-Davis, 1954.

Hyde, H. Montgomery. *Oscar Wilde: A Biography.* New York: Farrar, Straus and Giroux, 1975.

Kohl, Norbert. *Oscar Wilde: The Works of a Conformist Rebel.* New York: Cambridge University Press, 1980.

Lawler, Donald L. *An Inquiry into Oscar Wilde's Revisions of* The Picture of Dorian Gray. New York: Garland, 1988.

Leverson, Ada. *Letters to the Sphinx from Oscar Wilde and Reminiscences of the Author.* London: Duckworth, 1930.

Lucie-Smith, Edward. *Symbolist Art.* London: Thames & Hudson, 1985.

Mason, A. E. W. *Sir George Alexander and the St. James's Theatre.* London: Macmillan, 1935.

McCormack, Jerusha Hall. *John Gray: Poet, Dandy and Priest.* Hanover, N.H.: University Press of New England, 1991.

Melville, Joy. *Mother of Oscar.* London: Murray, 1994.

Munthe, Gustaf, and Uexküll Munthe. *The Story of Axel Munthe.* New York: Dutton, 1953.

O'Sullivan, Vincent. *Aspects of Wilde.* London: Constable, 1936.

Pearson, Hesketh. *Oscar Wilde: His Life and Wit.* London: Harper, 1946.

Pine, Richard. *The Thief of Reason: Oscar Wilde and Modern Ireland.* Dublin: Gill & Macmillan, 1995.

Powell, Kerry. *Oscar Wilde and the Theatre of the 1890s.* Cambridge: Cambridge University Press, 1990.

Price, R. G. G. *A History of* Punch. London: Collins, 1957.

Raby, Peter, ed. *The Cambridge Companion to Oscar Wilde.* Cambridge: Cambridge University Press, 1997.

Redman, Alvin, ed. *The Epigrams of Oscar Wilde.* London: Senate, 1952.

[Raymond, Jean Paul], and Charles Ricketts. *Oscar Wilde: Recollections.* London: Nonesuch, 1932.

Mrs. Robinson. *The Graven Palm: A Manual of the Science of Palmistry.* London: Arnold, 1911.

Ross, Margery, ed. *Robert Ross: Friend of Friends.* London: Cape, 1952.

Rothenstein, William. *Men and Memories.* New York: Coward-McCann, 1931.

Sandulescu, George, ed. *Rediscovering Oscar Wilde.* Princess Grace Irish Library, vol. 8. Gerrards Cross: Colin Smythe, 1994.

Sedgwick, Eve Kosofsky. *Between Men: English Literature and Male Homosocial Desire.* New York: Columbia University Press, 1986.

Shaw, George Bernard. *Our Theatres in the Nineties.* London: Constable, 1932.

Shaw, George Bernard, and Alfred Douglas. *A Correspondence,* ed. Mary Hyde. London: Murray, 1982.

Sherard, Robert Harborough. *The Real Oscar Wilde.* London: T. Werner Laurie, 1916.

———. *The Story of an Unhappy Friendship.* London: Hermes, 1902.

Sinfield, Alan. *The Wilde Century: Effeminacy, Oscar Wilde and the Queer Moment.* London: Caswell, 1994.

Small, Ian. *Oscar Wilde Revalued: An Essay on New Materials and Methods of Research.* Greensboro, N.C.: ELT Press, 1993.

Snodgrass, Chris. *Aubrey Beardsley: Dandy of the Grotesque.* New York: Oxford University Press, 1995.

Stokes, John. *In the Nineties.* New York: Simon & Schuster, 1989.

———. *Oscar Wilde: Myths, Miracles, and Imitations.* Cambridge: Cambridge University Press, 1996.

Sturgis, Matthew. *Aubrey Beardsley: A Biography.* Woodstock, N.Y.: Overlook, 1998.

Weintraub, Stanley. *Reggie: A Portrait of Reginald Turner.* New York: Braziller, 1965.

Worth, Katharine. *Oscar Wilde.* New York: Grove, 1983.

INDEX

PHOTOGRAPHIC AND ILLUSTRATION CREDITS

❧

SIR WILLIAM WILDE: William Andrews Clark Memorial Library, University of California, Los Angeles.

LADY WILDE: William Andrews Clark Memorial Library, University of California, Los Angeles.

OSCAR AS A CHILD: William Andrews Clark Memorial Library, University of California, Los Angeles.

MOYTURA HOUSE: Author photo.

WILDE IN 1876: William Andrews Clark Memorial Library, University of California, Los Angeles.

WILDE IN 1878: Courtesy of Merlin Holland.

WILDE WITH COLLEGE FRIENDS: William Andrews Clark Memorial Library, University of California, Los Angeles.

WILDE'S SKETCH OF FLORENCE BALCOMBE: Harry Ransom Humanities Research Center Art Collection, the University of Texas at Austin.

FLORENCE BALCOMBE: Courtesy of Ann Dobbs.

VIOLET HUNT: Wallis Collection.

LILLIE LANGTRY: Library of Congress.

SARAH BERNHARDT: Library of Congress.

WILDE IN 1881: William Andrews Clark Memorial Library, University of California, Los Angeles.

PROGRAM FOR *PATIENCE:* Private collection.

CARTOON BY GEORGE DU MAURIER: *Punch,* Feb. 12, 1881.

CARTOON BY GEORGE DU MAURIER: *Punch,* Oct. 30, 1880.

WILDE IN FUR COAT: Photograph by Napoleon Sarony, Library of Congress.

WILDE IN HAT AND CAPE: Photograph by Napoleon Sarony, Library of Congress.

WILDE IN 1884: Courtesy of Christie's, London.

WILDE IN 1889: William Andrews Clark Memorial Library, University of California, Los Angeles.

ROBBIE ROSS: Courtesy of Robert Baldwin Robertson.

JOHN GRAY: From *In the Dorian Mode: A Life of John Gray,* by Brocard Sewell (Padstow, Cornwall: Tabb House, 1983).

THE WOMAN'S WORLD: August 1888.

CONSTANCE WILDE AND CYRIL: Courtesy of Merlin Holland.

WILDE AND BOSIE: William Andrews Clark Memorial Library, University of California, Los Angeles.

HAYMARKET THEATRE PROGRAM: Private collection.

BABBACOMBE CLIFF: Author photo.

ST. JAMES'S THEATRE: From *The St. James's Theatre: Its Strange and Complete History,* by Barry Duncan (London: Barrie and Rockliff, 1964).

CARICATURE BY ALFRED BRYAN: *The Entr'acte,* Sept. 1, 1883.

CARICATURE BY BERNARD PARTRIDGE: *Punch,* March 5, 1892.

WILDE IN 1892: William Andrews Clark Memorial Library, University of California, Los Angeles.

FRONTISPIECE: From *Salome* by Oscar Wilde (London: The Bodley Head, 1894).

BOSIE IN 1893: From *The Autobiography of Lord Alfred Douglas* (London: Martin Secker, 1929); courtesy of Sheila Colman.

REGGIE TURNER: From *Letters to Reggie Turner,* ed. Rupert Hart-Davis (London: Rupert Hart-Davis, 1964).

FRONT PAGE: *The Illustrated Police News,* May 4, 1895.

CAFÉ DES TRIBUNAUX: Courtesy of the Oscar Wilde Society.

ERNEST DOWSON: From *Ernest Dowson* by Mark Longaker (Philadelphia: University of Pennsylvania Press, 1945).

AUBREY BEARDSLEY: Frederick H. Evans photograph, reproduced with permission, from *Beardsley: A Biography,* by Stanley Weintraub (New York: Braziller, 1967).

WILDE AND BOSIE IN 1897: William Andrews Clark Memorial Library, University of California, Los Angeles.

WILDE IN 1900: William Andrews Clark Memorial Library, University of California, Los Angeles.

HÔTEL D'ALSACE: Courtesy of Merlin Holland.

WILDE ON DEATHBED: Photograph by Maurice Gilbert, William Andrews Clark Memorial Library, University of California, Los Angeles.

WILDE'S GRAVE AT BAGNEUX: Courtesy of Merlin Holland.

JACOB EPSTEIN'S MONUMENT: Author photo.